A SHORT TREATISE
ON
THE VIRGIN MARY

A SHORT TREATISE ON THE VIRGIN MARY
6th edition

René Laurentin

Translated by Charles Neumann, SM

Foreword by Robert L. Fastiggi

Postscript translated by Annie Hounsokou

The Catholic University of America Press
Washington, D.C

Foreword, acknowledgments,
and translation of postscript copyright © 2022
The Catholic University of America Press

Translation of remainder of text © 1991,
The Blue Army of Our Lady of Fatima, USA Inc.

Originally published as
Court Traité sur la Vierge Marie, 6ème éd.
Paris: F.-X. de Guibert © 2009

All rights reserved

Library of Congress Catalogue No. 91072217

(1991 edition)

ISBN 978-0-8132-3506-6

eISBN 978-0-8132-3507-3

ACKNOWLEDGMENTS

The Catholic University of America Press would like to thank the following individuals and institutions for their help in bringing forth the definitive English edition of this work of Fr. Laurentin, based on his final (6th) edition of the French text.

First and foremost, the Press thanks Nathan Lefler of the University of Scranton for bringing the work to the Press's attention and taking on thankless editorial tasks in the absence of a living author or editor, including consultation on the translation of the postscript. The Press also thanks Robert L. Fastiggi, not only for the foreword, but also for his help and counsel throughout the process. The Press also thanks several anonymous reviewers who provided helpful input.

The English-language rights for the entire 6th French edition belong to *GROUPE ELIDIA*, who granted permission for this publication. The main body of the book (including the abbreviations, general introduction, two parts, appendices, and indices) was translated by Charles Neumann, SM, and previously published. It is used with permission of the copyright holder; the Press wishes to thank Barb Ernster and her colleagues of the World Apostolate of Fatima, USA, for their help and attention in arranging for these rights. The postscript was newly composed by Laurentin for the 6th French edition and has been translated by Annie Hounsokou.

Special thanks to Sam Sheng of CompuDesign for typesetting the new portions of this text and to Olivia Schmitz for the cover design.

Finally, the Press thanks the faithful scholars who serve on its faculty Editorial Committee, without whose careful scrutiny of potential publications, this university press could not function.

Veni Sancte Spiritus, veni per Mariam.

TABLE OF CONTENTS

Acknowledgments for the CUA Press Edition. v
Abbreviations xiii
General Introduction. xvii
Foreword to the CUA Press Edition by Robert L. Fastiggi. xxi

FIRST PART:
DOCTRINAL DEVELOPMENT 1

    INTRODUCTION TO THE FIRST PART 3
        Preliminary Stage: Presence and Silence. 4
        The Old Testament. 6

    FIRST PERIOD: MARY IN SCRIPTURE. 8
        Galatians 4:5 8
        Mark. 10
        Matthew. 12
        Luke. 15
        John 33
        Conclusion. 46

    SECOND PERIOD: FROM THE GOSPEL OF JOHN
    TO THE COUNCIL OF EPHESUS (90–431) 50
       1. Silent Growth: The Eve-Mary Antithesis
          Explored (2nd Century). 52
       2. Divine Maternity, Virginity, Holiness:
          A Time of Hesitation (End of the 2nd Century
          to Last Quarter of the 4th Century) 57
       3. Advancing Solutions (373–431) 61
       4. Two New Problems 67
          The Problem of the Assumption (377). 67
          The Problem of the Immaculate Conception (430). 68
       5. Mary's Entry into Christian Worship. 71

THIRD PERIOD: FROM THE COUNCIL OF EPHESUS
TO THE GREGORIAN REFORM (431–1050)......... 76
  1. The East.. 76
      Assumption 83
      Immaculate Conception...................... 86
      Intercession, Mediation, Spiritual Maternity........ 88
  2. The West 93
      Assumption, Conception, Salvific Cooperatio 95
  3. The Tenth Century............................. 99

FOURTH PERIOD: FROM THE 11TH CENTURY
TO THE COUNCIL OF TRENT (1050–1563)........ 103
  Immaculate Conception, Assumption, Mediation....... 106
  A New Perspective............................... 109
  Impact of This Change........................... 115
  Decadence (13th to 15th Centuries) 117

FIFTH PERIOD: THE POST-TRIDENTINE
MARIAN MOVEMENT (1563–1958)............... 126
  The Marian Movement of the 17th and 18th Centuries.... 127
  The 19th Century................................ 135
  From 1900 to 1958 137

SIXTH PERIOD: THE NEW ERA OF VATICAN II
AND ITS PREPARATION 142
  The Ebb of the Marian Movement 144
  Repercussions of the Movements of Aggiornamento 145

EPILOGUE... 153
  1. A Glance Backward........................... 153
  2. A Glance Forward 155
      The Message of the Council 155
      Faith and Myth................................ 156
      The Anthropological Approach 158
      The Pneumatological Approach.................. 159

SECOND PART:
DEVELOPMENT IN THE DESTINY OF MARY 163

INTRODUCTION TO THE SECOND PART 165
  Excellence and Shortcomings of the Deductive Method... 165
    A. Difficulties in the Choice of Principle............. 166
      1. Principle of Analogy as Starting Point.......... 167

2. Relationship as Starting Point	170
B. Difficulties in Developing onsequences from the First Principle Chosen	172
The Method to Be Chosen	177
The Virgin and Time	178

FIRST STAGE: BEFORE THE ANNUNCIATION— MARY, CHOICE FRUIT OF ISRAEL 182

1. The Immaculate Conception: Mary's Original Purity...................... 184
2. Israel's Climax in the Advance toward Salvation: Mary's Faith............................... 190
3. Mary's Position in the Human Family........... 190

SECOND STAGE: MARY, MOTHER OF THE SAVIOR GOD................................. 193

A. Mary's Motherhood.......................... 194
   1. Conscious and Free Motherhood............. 194
   2. Holy Motherhood......................... 196
   3. Divine Motherhood 201
B. The Relationship Involved in Mary's Motherhood.... 209
   1. Unique Relationship 209
   2. Transforming Relationship 209
   3. Analysis of the Divine Motherhood as Relationship............................ 211
      a. Implications of the Mother of God Relationship 212
         (1) Real Foundation................... 212
         (2) Permanent and Special Foundation...... 213
            (a) Similarities between Divine Motherhood and Sacramental Character..................... 215
            (b) Differences between Divine Motherhood and Sacramental Character..................... 216
      b. Qualities Befitting a other Whose Son is God........................... 221
   4. The Gift of Divine Motherhood: Summary...... 227
      a. The Gift in the Order of Structure.......... 227
      b. The Gift in the Order of Life............. 227
C. Elements Appropriate to the Divine Motherhood..... 230

    1. Virginal Motherhood 230
    2. Social Motherhood...................... 232
    3. Motherhood Involved in the Work of Salvation 233

THIRD STAGE: MARY AT THE REDEMPTIVE
SACRIFICE..................................... 235
Mary Associated in the Redemption by Her Consent 236
    1. Associated in the Redemption in the Name
       of the Redeemed 237
    2. Associated in the Redemption in Virtue
       of Her Holiness 239
    3. Associated in the Redemption in Her Role
       as Mother.............................. 240

FOURTH STAGE: FROM CHRIST'S DEATH TO THE
END OF THE EARTHLY DESTINY OF MARY...... 244

FIFTH STAGE: MARY'S ASSUMPTION—THE VIRGIN,
ESCHATOLOGICAL IMAGE OF THE CHURCH 248
The Assumption................................ 248
Mary at the End of Pilgrimage 251
"With the Lord Forever" (1 Thes. 4:17) 251
Maternal Knowledge 251
Maternal Activity............................... 252
"Mediation".................................... 256
Queenship 258
Eschatological Image within the Risen Church........ 259

SIXTH STAGE: THE PAROUSIA.................... 260

CONCLUSION..................................... 263

Appendix # 1: The Virgin Mary in the Old Testament 267
    1. Moral Preparation 269
    2. Typological Preparation...................... 269
    3. Prophetic Preparation........................ 270
       a. Eschatological Texts Applying Both to
          Mary and to the Church................... 271
       b. Texts Relative to the Mother of the Messiah...... 272
          (1) Genesis 3:15—The Posterity of the
              Woman, Enemy of the Serpent........... 272
          (2) Isaiah 7:14—The Maiden, Mother
              of Emmanuel 275
          (3) Micah 5:1–4—"She Who Is to Give Birth"... 277

	4. The Background of These Three Prophecies....... 278	
	5. A Note on Mary and Wisdom 282	
Appendix # 2:	Mary's Decision of Virginity............... 284	
Appendix # 3:	Parallels of the Magnificat with the Old Testament 287	
Appendix # 4:	The Origins of the Title *Theotokos*.......... 290	
Appendix # 5:	Mary in the Infancy Apocryphals 294	
	1. Antiquity of the *Protevangelium of James* 294	
	2. Implications of the *Protoevangelium*............. 295	
	3. Weight of the Apochryphals 296	
Appendix # 6:	The Weight of the Assumptionist Apocryphals........................... 299	
Appendix # 7:	John 19:25–27 and the Spiritual Motherhood among Eastern Writers 302	
Appendix # 8:	The First Marian Feast in the West 305	
	1. Last Sunday of Advent: Northern Italy, mid-5th Century............................ 306	
	2. January 18: Gaul, 6th Century.................. 306	
	3. January 1 (Octave of Christmas): Rome, between 550 and 595 307	
	4. Wednesday and Friday of the Tenth Month Fast (later, Advent Ember Days): Rome, Beginning of the 7th Century 307	
	5. December 18 (Octave before Christmas): Spain, 656 308	
Appendix # 9:	The Philosophic Principle that Motherhood Relates to a Person 310	
Appendix # 10:	The *Katharsis* of Mary at the Annunciation..... 313	
Appendix # 11:	The Three Dogmatic Aspects of Mary's Virginity 316	
	1. Virginity before Birth (ante partum) 316	
	2. Virginity after Birth (post partum)............... 318	
	a. Is Mary's Virginity after Birth (post partum) Not the Fruit of a Tradition Properly Called Historical? 319	

        b. Do Certain Texts of Scripture Not Attest that
Mary Had Other Children than Jesus?......... 320
    3. Virginity in Childbirth (in partu)................ 324
        Contemporary Difficultie 325
        Renewed Interest in the Question (1952–1960) 325
        The Decree of the Holy Offi e................. 328
        The Doctrine of Vatican II.................... 329
        Meaning of this Doctrine..................... 331

Appendix # 12: Why Did Pius XII Not Define
        Mary's Death?.......................... 335
    1. Does Tradition Teach the Death of Mary as
       It Teaches Her Assumption? 335
    2. Is Mary's Death Implied in the Dogmatic
       Affirmation of the Assumption? 337

Bibliography.. 344

Name and Subject Index 365

Index to Scripture References 381

POSTSCRIPT to 6TH EDITION........................ 393
    1. The Immaculate Conception 396
    2. Virginity................................... 397
    3. Mother of God.............................. 404
    4. Participation in the Redemption 410
    5. The Assumption............................. 411

ABBREVIATIONS

Alma Socia Christi	*Alma Socia Christi* (Acts of International Mariological Congress, Rome 1950), Rome, Academia Mariana, 1951–1958, 13 vols.
CSEL	*Corpus scriptorum ecclesiasticorum latinorum,* Vienna.
DACL	*Dictionnaire d'archéologie chrétienne et de liturgie,* Paris, 1924–1953, 13 vols.
Denz., Denz.-Schön	H. Denzinger, *Enchiridion Symbolorum et Definitionum,* 33rd ed., Barcelona, Herder, 1967. (The first number given refers to editions prior to the 32nd; the second, in parentheses, to editions after the 32nd. Where only the latter editions contain the desired reference, the work is abbreviated Denz.-Schön.)
DTC	*Dictionnaire de théologie catholique,* Paris, 1903–1965, 16 vols.
EM	*Etudes mariales* (Proceedings of the Société Française d'Etudes Mariales), Paris, Lethielleux, 1935–.
EphM	*Ephemerides mariologicae.*
EstM	*Estudios marianos* (Proceedings of the Sociedad Mariológica Española), Madrid, 1941–.
ETL	*Ephemerides theologicae louvanienses.*
GCS	*Griechische christliche Schriftsteller,* Berlin.
JTS	*Journal of Theological Studies.*
Jurgens	W. Jurgens (ed.), *The Faith of the Early Fathers,* Collegeville, Liturgical Press, 1970.

Laurentin, Court traité	R. Laurentin, *Court traité de théologie mariale*, 1st ed., Paris, Lethielleux, 1953.
Laurentin, Jésus au Temple	R. Laurentin, *Jésus au Temple. Mystère de Pâques et foi de Marie en Luc 2, 48–50*, Paris, Gabalda, 1966.
Laurentin, La question	R. Laurentin, *La question mariale*, Paris, Seuil, 1963 (ET: *The Question of Mary*, New York, Holt-Rinehart-Winston, 1965).
Laurentin, La Vierge	R. Laurentin, *La Vierge au concile*, Paris, Lethielleux, 1965.
Laurentin, Luc 1–2	R. Laurentin, *Structure et théologie de Luc 1–2*, Paris, Gabalda, 1957.
Laurentin, Marie, l'Eglise	R. Laurentin, *Marie, l'Eglise et le sacerdoce*, Paris, Lethielleux, 1952, 2 vols.
Laurentin, Present Crisis	R. Laurentin, *The Present Crisis in Mariology. Rise or Fall of Mariology* (Mimeographed lecture notes) Dayton, University of Dayton, 1968.
Maria et Ecclesia	*Maria et Ecclesia* (Acts of International Mariological Congress, Lourdes 1958), Rome, Academia Mariana, 1959–1960, 16 vols.
Maria in Sacra Scriptura	*Maria in Sacra Scriptura* (Acts of International Mariological Congress, Santo Domingo 1965), Rome, Academia Mariana, 1967, 6 vols.
Maria	H. du Manoir, *Maria*, Paris, Beauchesne, 1949–1964, 7 vols.
MGH	*Monumenta Germaniae historica*, Berlin.
MS	*Marian Studies* (Proceedings of the Mariological Society of America), Paterson-Washington, 1950–.
NRT	*Nouvelle revue théologique.*
NTS	*New Testament Studies.*
PG	J. Migne, *Patrologia graeca*, Paris.
PL	J. Migne, *Patrologia latina*, Paris.
PO	R. Graffin, F. Nau, *Patrologia orientalis*, Paris.
RB	*Revue biblique.*
Rev. Bén.	*Revue bénédictine.*
RSPT	*Revue des sciences philosophiques et théologiques.*
RSR	*Recherches de science religieuse.*
TS	*Theological Studies.*
TUU	*Texte und Untersuchungen*, Berlin.

Abbreviations

Virgo Immaculata	*Virgo Immaculata* (Acts of International Mariological Congress, Rome 1954), Rome, Academia Mariana, 1955–1958, 18 vols.
Willis	J. Willis (ed.), *The Teachings of the Church Fathers*, New York, Herder and Herder 1966.
ZKT	*Zeitschrift für katholische Theologie.*

GENERAL INTRODUCTION

The Marian celebrations of the pontificate of Pius XII — the definition of the Assumption (1950), the Marian Year (1954), the centenary of Lourdes (1958) — together with the kind of ebb that followed and the difficulties that arose at Vatican II (1963-1964) have gradually led to what is today called "the Marian question." Countless questions, in fact, have arisen among the Christian people. Since faith has God for its object and since no saint has ever been the object of a definition of faith, why the place given Mary in dogma? In the light of the "silence of Scripture" about her, how has she come to take such an important place? To what degree does the extraordinary development of Marian doctrine have its source in revelation, to what degree does it rise from the depths that psychoanalysis brings to light? In the impulse that carries Christians toward Mary, how much is due to sentiment and how much to faith? Does anything substantial actually remain once one has discarded the pietistic dross characteristic of a certain kind of devotional literature? Finally, does not the "ecumenical era" which we have now entered suggest putting the Virgin Mary in the shade? Is this the direction present changes are taking? Is it something normal or something improper? In a word, what is the future of Marian doctrine and devotion in the postconciliar age?

These and many other questions, it is felt, do not admit

of individual and separate replies, for they all hang together closely. What Christians are looking for today is an overall view in which all such problems find their place and the light of their solution. *A Short Treatise on the Virgin Mary* is offered as a concise and objective essay answering this demand.

A word of explanation is in order concerning the change of title from that given the preceding edition, *A Short Treatise of Marian Theology.* Three reasons have suggested the modification of the last part of this title. In the new title the object of the essay, the Virgin Mary, Mother of God, is presented more clearly and without needless complication. Moreover, there is less risk of enshrouding under the wraps of pseudo-science and pointless abstraction the existential reality of Mary's role in the history of salvation and in the communion of saints. Finally, there is properly speaking no genuine "Marian theology" — that is, no knowledge of God that would be Marian — but rather a Christian theology where the Virgin Mary occupies the special place to be explored in these pages. Obviously we are accustomed to the looser manner of speaking implied by "Marian theology," and to many other such approximations. The spirit of Vatican II, however, invites us not to remain prisoners of a backward vocabulary that would tend to make of "Mariology" a jealously guarded specialty and of "Marian devotion" a sector apart in Christian cult. However strong the force of habit, it is worth our effort to build our knowledge of Mary on the foundation of a terminology that is beyond dispute. The chances will thus be much greater of dissipating the many prejudices kept alive today by questionable manners of expression. Too often the "Mariology" of recent centuries took its point of departure from a defective terminology. It is time to seek a point of departure rather in the reality attested by the sources and to express this reality in a terminology made to order and properly nuanced in every respect.

Mary and Time

If the word "treatise" were understood as an abstract elaboration, a rigid formulation, it would convey a wrong idea of the present study. In fact, the mystery of Mary does not at all exhibit the logic of a theorem, but rather that of a free destiny open to the sometimes disconcerting impulses of the Spirit. The most characteristic if not the deepest trait of this destiny and of the doctrine that attempts to give an account of it seems to be the element of *time* — the law of duration and of progress. Any treatise that would telescope this significant element by an excess of logic would thereby be missing the essential message or at least something essential to it.

Our Plan

Duration, progress — this is the law according to which Mary came to be known little by little within the Church. Almost absent from the primitive message, absent also from the preaching that took place while she was yet present on earth in the midst of the Church, she was in the most obvious sense of the word "discovered" from this initial presence onward.

Duration, progress — this is also, indeed primarily, the law according to which Mary lived. Her life is a constant progress: from the obscurity of faith to the light of the beatific vision; from the pure gratuitousness of the original gift to the summit of merit that God's grace brought to fruition in her in the course of her life; from her initial receptivity to the ultimate unfolding of her maternal mission; from the radical and inwardly secret fullness of grace at her first instant of life to the manifest and outwardly social fullness that she radiates today in the communion of saints.

This is the double progression that we shall be studying.

In the first part of our essay we shall see how the Church in history gradually becomes conscious of the mystery of Mary. In the second part we shall enter the heart of the mystery itself to see how Mary's destiny developed from the Immaculate Conception to the Assumption and the Parousia.

FOREWORD TO THE CUA PRESS EDITION

On April 7, 1958, Cardinal Angelo Roncalli, the Patriarch of Venice—during a conference held in Padua on the 100th anniversary of the apparitions of Lourdes—recommended a book by "a young and illustrious French theologian, René Laurentin." The book recommended by the future Pope St. John XXIII was entitled *Sens de Lourdes* (The Meaning of Lourdes), and he referred to this work as a theological and historical "Summa" on Lourdes, which displayed profound doctrinal research that was "most felicitous, serious, and exhaustive." In the same address, Cardinal Roncalli spoke of his admiration for "the most precious volume" of Fr. Laurentin entitled, *Court traité de théologie Mariale* (*A Short Treatise on Marian Theology*), which was first published in 1953

I am very happy that The Catholic University of America Press is publishing an English version of the sixth edition of *A Short Treatise*, which was renamed *Court traité sur la Vierge Marie* (*A Short Treatise on the Virgin Mary*) in 1967 after Vatican II.[1] This sixth edition, published in 2009, contains an

---

1. Jacques Perrier, "Sous le manteaux de la Vierge" in *Études Mariales: Actes de la 73ᵉ session de la Société Française d'Études Mariales, Strasbourg, 3–6 septembre 2018: Mariologie et Anthropologie en Dialogue, Hommage à René Laurentin,* textes réunis et présentés par Brigette Waché (Abberville: F Paillart, 2019), 168.

important postscript (*postface*) in which Fr. Laurentin looks back on developments in Marian theology since Vatican II.

Laurentin's *Short Treatise* has received praise not only from Cardinal Roncalli but from many Mariologists as well. It offers a concise but comprehensive overview of Mary in Scripture, Church history, and doctrine, and it provides multiple appendices that examine important issues such as Mary in the Apocrypha, Marian feasts, and the "three dogmatic aspects of Mary's virginity"—before, during, and perpetually after giving birth. In his well-respected *Introduction to Mariology* (CUA Press, 2021), Fr. Manfred Hauke makes multiple references to *A Short Treatise* as well as to over a dozen other writings of Laurentin. Fr. Michael O'Carroll, CSSp, has stated that Fr. Laurentin "must be ranked among the very great Marian theologians" of the 20th century.[2]

René Laurentin was born in Tours, France, on October 19, 1917, and he died at the age of 99 in Évry, a suburb of Paris, on September 10, 2017. In 1934 he enrolled in the Carmelite Seminary at the Catholic University of Paris. In 1938 he obtained a license in philosophy with a concentration in the thought of St. Thomas Aquinas. In the same year, he also obtained a license of letters in philosophy from the Sorbonne. During World War II, he served in the military. In May of 1940—while in Belgium—he was taken as a prisoner of war. He remained in detention for five years in Germany. After the war, he returned to France, and he was ordained a priest on December 8, 1946. He went on to study for a double doctorate: one in letters from the Sorbonne in 1952 and the other in theology in 1953 from the Institut Catholique of Paris. His doctoral thesis in letters focused on Marian iconography. His doctorate in theology was on the priesthood of Mary, which was published in 1953 as *Marie, l'Église et le sacerdoce: L'Étude historique, l'Étude théologique*. Laurentin was not interested in the question of

---

2. Michael O'Carroll, CSSp, *Theotokos: A Theological Encyclopedia of the Blessed Virgin Mary* (Eugene, OR: Wipf and Stock, 2000), 215.

women priests but in Mary's priesthood of mediation.³ He was aware that Pope Pius X, on May 9, 1906, had approved a prayer with the invocation "*Maria Virgo Sacerdos, ora pro nobis*" (Mary, Virgin Priest, pray for us).⁴ But he was also aware that the Holy Office, on March 29, 1916, had issued a decree forbidding any paintings or images of the Blessed Virgin Mary dressed in priestly vestments.⁵ Laurentin's exploration of the priesthood of Mary, however, showed his willingness to pursue interesting and controversial topics using a historical approach.

Fr. Laurentin's approach to Mariology is historical and cultural as well as theological. His more than 150 books and numerous articles show a broad range of interests ranging from Scripture, the charismatic movement, apparitions, saints, and mystics. He began his teaching career at the Catholic University of Angers, but he also taught on theological faculties in Florence, Milan, Rome, and North America. From the 1970s until the early 2000s, he taught summer courses at the International Marian Research Institute in Dayton, Ohio. The Marian Library in Dayton contains a collection of his notes and outlines for lectures and courses. This collection shows his interest in subjects such as "the Marian Question in an Ecumenical Age," "Mary and the Second Vatican Council," "Mary and the Holy Spirit," "the Holiness of Mary," "Marian Apparitions," "Mary and African Theology," "Mary and Anthropology," "Mary and Liberation," "Marian Pilgrimages," "Mary in the History of Salvation," "Mary as Educator," and "Mary the Charismatic."⁶

Fr. Laurentin served as an expert or *peritus* at Vatican II, and he played a role in the drafting of chapter eight of Vatican

---

3. Perrier, 167.
4. *Acta Sanctae Sedis* 40 (1907), p. 110.
5. Denzinger-Hünermann, 43rd ed. (2012), no. 3632.
6. I would like to thank Kayla Harris of the Marian Library at the University of Dayton for providing access to the Fr. René Laurentin Collection. I would also like to thank Fr. Johann Roten, SM, and Dr. Gloria Falcão Dodd, of the International Marian Research Institute at Dayton, for their kindness in providing added insights and materials on Fr. Laurentin.

II's Dogmatic Constitution on the Church, *Lumen Gentium*, which focused on The Blessed Virgin Mary, Mother of God, in the Mystery of Christ and the Church. He was a longtime member of the Pontifical Marian Academy International, and he was asked by the Holy See to investigate the life of Mother Aimée de Malestroit (Yvonne Beauvais), a French Augustinian mystic, whose cause for beatification was being considered. Fr. Laurentin always tried to be faithful to the Church's Magisterium. Although he manifested support for the apparitions of Vassula Rydén and Medjugorje—which have never been approved by the Church as supernatural—Fr. Laurentin always recognized that the final judgment on apparitions belongs to the Church's Magisterium and not to private theologians like himself.[7] He received numerous awards for his work in Mariology, and in 2009, he was named a Monsignor as a Prelate of his Holiness, Pope Benedict XVI.

In 1979 the US Catholic journal, *The Wanderer*, published an article questioning Fr. Laurentin's orthodoxy because of his alleged link to the "phenomenological school" of interpretation. He responded in a letter noting that he has "never diminished Catholic dogma in any way." On the contrary, he has always come to the defense of Catholic dogma "not without suffering blows and difficulties at a time when some of these dogmas are effectively being disputed or neglected by Catholics."[8] He stated that he has "always shown the greatest independence of spirit, not wanting to have any sources other than the Scriptures and the Tradition of the Church."

Fr. Laurentin's many writings can be grouped into several distinct genres. First, there are his writings on Marian theology

---

7. Indeed, his lack of attachment to these contemporary phenomena is evident in the postscript to this sixth edition (pg. 417), where he writes, "in spite of the considerable work I have dedicated to the apparitions of the Virgin, I do not think that spiritual renewal will come from that avenue."
8. A copy of Fr. Laurentin's 1979 letter to *The Wanderer* is in the Laurentin Collection at the Marian Library in Dayton.

—a term he preferred to Mariology. *A Short Treatise on the Virgin Mary* would be included in this genre. Then there are his Scriptural and theological writings. In this category are books on such topics as the Gospel of Luke, the Eucharist, the Gospels, the life of Jesus, and the reality of the devil. Another category includes his writings on the Second Vatican Council and the life of the Church. His book on Catholic Pentecostalism could be placed in this genre, as well as his book on evangelization. Books on apparitions constitute another category in his *oeuvre*. He published eight books on Lourdes and six on Medjugorje. He also published books on the apparitions at Pontmain and La Salette as well as books on lesser-known apparitions such as those from San Nicolas in Argentina. He published a book by himself on Marian apparitions in general, and in 2007, he co-authored with Patrick Sbalchiero the *Dictionnaire des "Apparitions" de la Vierge Marie*, which is over 1300 pages in length. Laurentin's writings on saints and mystics form another genre of publications. He was a great storyteller, and his publications include biographies of St. Bernadette Soubirous of Lourdes, St. Thérèse of Lisieux, St. Catherine Labouré, St. Louis Grignion de Montfort, Alphonse de Ratisbonne, and Mère Yvonee-Aimée de Malestroit.

Fr. Laurentin's writings on apparitions, saints, and mystics, reveal a certain consistency. The same is true of his writings on Scripture. His writings on Marian theology, however, show certain developments during and after Vatican II. For example, in 1951, Fr. Laurentin published a historical study on the Marian title of co-redemptrix.[9] In this study, he traces the use of the Marian title co-redemptrix, by saints, theologians, and spiritual writers. He mentions those who opposed the title, but he provides examples of papal approval and uses of the title in the 20th century. In light of these papal uses of co-redemptrix, he writes that "it would at least be gravely temerarious to attack

---

9. René Laurentin, *Le Titre de Coréredmptrice: Étude historique* (Rome: Editions "Marianum; Paris: Nouvelles Editions Latines, 1951).

its legitimacy."[10] He also notes that "it is certain that the use of *co-redemptrix* is now *legitimate*."[11]

In his 2009 postscript to *A Short Treatise on the Virgin Mary* (as appears translated at the end of this book), he takes a different position. He characterizes the title, "co-redemptrix" as a reduction of "Theo-centrism to Mario-centrism." The titles and privileges of Christ are transposed to Mary. As he writes: "He [Christ] was a mediator, she was a mediatrix; He was a redeemer, so she was a co-redemptrix, and so on." Fr. Laurentin believes that these titles are given to Mary "without sufficient emphasis on the differences or the relationship of dependence." "They wanted," he claims, "to make Mary another Christ (as with the pope, *alter Christus*, when he is in truth his vicar, his visible delegate as successor of Peter)."

Defenders of the Marian titles of co-redemptrix and mediatrix could respond by noting that they never make Mary another Christ or ignore her relationship of dependence. Moreover, they could cite the papal uses of these titles, as Fr. Laurentin himself noted in his 1951 study. It's clear that, after Vatican II, Fr. Laurentin moved away from his position of 1951. Along these lines, it's curious that Fr. Laurentin in his 2009 postscript makes only one brief mention of John Paul II. He does not mention that the Polish pope referred to Mary as the co-redemptrix at least six times during his pontificate, and he likewise referred to her as the Mediatrix of all graces at least nine times.[12] Surely, St. John Paul II was not trying to

---

10. Laurentin, 28: "*Il serait gravement téméraire, pour le moins, de s'attaquer à sa légitimité.*"
11. Laurentin, 36: "*Ce qu'il y a de certain, c'est que l'emploi de corredemptrix est dès maintenant légitime.*"
12. On John Paul II's uses of co-redemptrix, see Mark Miravalle, "*With Jesus: The Story of Mary Co-redemptrix* (Goleta, CA: Queenship Publishing, 2003), 189–212. On John Paul II's references to Mary as Mediatrix of all graces, see the citations noted by Msgr. Arthur B. Calkins at: https://www.motherofallpeoples.com/post/mary-mediatrix-of-all-graces-in-the-papal-magisterium-of-pope-john-paul-ii (accessed December 1, 2021)

make Mary "another Christ." It's important, though, to note that Fr. Laurentin—while describing the title, co-redemptrix, as ambiguous—nevertheless affirms "Mary's active participation in Christ's redemption," and he regrets that some have tried to devalue this participation since Vatican II.

One area in which Fr. Laurentin comes across as more traditional is his defense in the postscript of Mary's virginity in giving birth and her absence of labor pains. He states that it is "regrettable that critical theologians and the filmmaker Delannoy should portray Christmas through dramatic shrieks of Mary." This affirmation of her complete virginity includes a warning against excessive and invasive speculation about the physical details of Mary's body and the reduction of God's Fatherhood to a human fatherhood, while fundamentally seeking to integrate this teaching with a refl ction on the nature of motherhood in general and the supreme privilege of Mary's divine motherhood; it is a discussion worth reading in its entirety.

The publication of this final sixth edition of *A Short Treatise on the Virgin Mary* will provide readers with a clear, concise, and comprehensive overview of Marian theology from one of the 20th century's most esteemed Mariologists. Even those who might disagree with Fr. Laurentin on certain points will still appreciate his masterful treatment of Mary in Scripture as well as his clear exposition of the Catholic dogmas of Mary's divine maternity; her threefold virginity; her Immaculate Conception, and her glorious Assumption. Fr. Laurentin lived almost a century on this earth, and he made a remarkable contribution. *A Short Treatise on the Virgin Mary* will likely remain a classic for many years to come.

Robert L. Fastiggi
Bishop Kevin M. Britt Chair of Dogmatic Theology
 and Christology
Sacred Heart Major Seminary, Detroit, Michigan
Member of the Pontifical Marian Academy
 International
Former president (2014–2016) of the Mariological
 Society of America

FIRST PART

DOCTRINAL DEVELOPMENT

INTRODUCTION TO THE FIRST PART

Knowledge about the Blessed Virgin develops in the Church according to a characteristic curve, with a growth that is not continuous but rhythmic. To describe it the movement of a rising tide comes to mind. Just as each wave surges up, crests, breaks and then flows back until the following wave carries it further, so each period of history first has a kind of presentiment of some hidden feature of Mary's character, then discovers it with a fervor that sometimes runs to excess and often is not without struggle. Thereafter everything calms down again: the new acquisitions of knowledge flow on gently in silence.

Dogmatic development finds yet a better analogy in living reality, if one thinks of the growth of a tree with spring succeeding winter again and again, and bringing blossoms that in turn give way to silent ripening. This kind of growth in Marian doctrine is observable throughout the twenty centuries about to be surveyed. It appears especially in three series of facts: the quantity of writings, their quality, and the appearance of new concepts and formulations.

Thus the development about to be followed naturally falls into six stages:

1. The period of the revelation committed to Sacred Scripture.
2. The patristic age up to the Council of Ephesus (431).
3. From Ephesus to the Gregorian Reform (c 1050).
4. From the end of the 11th century to the end of the Council of Trent (1563).
5. The post-Tridentine period.
6. The era of Vatican II.

At the threshold of this development a preliminary stage is to be noted, one during which the *silent presence* of the Virgin Mary has not yet become the object of any *teaching.*

Preliminary Stage: Presence and Silence

Pentecost can be taken as the starting-point. On that day the Church manifests herself visibly. Apostolic preaching begins. The first Christian catechesis takes shape under the impulse of the Holy Spirit. Peter speaks, and Mary is there (Acts 1:14).

She is there with the apostles, a few women, and the relatives of Jesus (Acts 1:14), amid the group of some "one hundred and twenty persons" gathered together in the Cenacle. She is there, not among the twelve official witnesses (Acts 1:22; cf. 1:13), ministers of the word (Lk. 1:2) who occupy the foreground of attention (Acts 1:21–22, 2:14; cf. 2:32), but among the hundred others. Peter speaks (2:17), but he does not speak of her.

This silence is due neither to forgetfulness nor simple chance. It is part of the program of that Christian catechesis whose boundaries were clearly fixed by the apostle even before Pentecost: "Jesus . . . from the time when John was baptising until the day when he was taken up from us" (Acts 1:22). Peter will remain faithful to this program throughout his entire preaching, as is evident from his addresses reported in the Acts of the Apostles (2:17–36, 10:36–43) and from the Gospel according to Mark which, no doubt in developing it slightly, sets down the last stage of the oral catechesis. Now it is precisely during the period whose limits are thus set up — the time of Jesus' public life — that Mary was separated from him, apart from some rare instances.

Shortly after the middle of the first century the birth and infancy account, where Mary has such a prominent place, was added as a kind of prologue to the Christian catechesis (Mt. 1-2, Lk. 1-2). Toward the end of that century in the Gospel according to John (2:1-12; 19:25-27) the two episodes of the public life where Mary plays a positive role take their place in gospel story. No doubt these first bits of information on the *Mother of Jesus* were introduced into the primitive catechesis in the face of heresies of Docetist stamp that tended to make of Christ a kind of phantom who suddenly appeared or descended from heaven in an adult state like a new Adam. To recall that he had been born, that he had a mother, was therefore to affirm that he truly belonged to the human race.

However that may be, for a time whose precise duration escapes us the Mother of Jesus is alive and lives in the Church without there being any explicit mention of her. Her prayer and intercession remain hidden. Mary herself does not seem to be conscious of the extent of her influence nor is it known by those around her. She is a living organ of the body of Christ, but she is not the object of any teaching. Like certain sacraments, she is a reality in the life of the Church, and more precisely in the communion of saints, before becoming the object of dogma. Little by little this reality obscurely experienced in the communion of saints will find its explicit formulation. As the mystery of Christ is more fully explored, the role of Mary therein is discovered. The first expressions of this role appear as the gospels take shape. They will be the object of our investigation shortly.

The Old Testament

But before this "initial silence" that is a prelude to the first writings of the New Testament God had already spoken. Some would expect an historical sketch of the Virgin Mary to begin with a presentation of the "prophecies" of the Old Testament. However these anticipations do not belong formally to history. If they are examined according to the historical method, from the viewpoint of the inspired author and his contemporaries, they leave us in a dense fog. Those prophecies in which some announcement of the Virgin Mother of the Messiah can be discerned are actually fleeting indications that deliver their full meaning only after the event. They are not an anticipated description of the future, but a door half ajar on a future that is still enigmatic. Before Christ's coming it was not possible to go beyond the question, "Who is this" (Song 3:6, 6:10), not even possible to give [any firm identity] to the being there referred to in the singular number. To what degree did the woman whose place in the messianic kingdom was sketched stand for the entire collectivity, the Church? To what degree was she a woman without equal, the mother of the Messiah? Or again, did she stand for several women? To reply to these questions, even to formulate them, before the Virgin Mary appeared would have been indeed difficult. But in the aftermath it would become possible to answer, "It was she." Retrospectively, therefore, with the evangelists we discover a sketch of the Virgin in Gn. 3:15, Is. 7:14, and Mi. 5:2.[1]

To take this position is not to deny that God predestined the Virgin Mary from of old, that he prepared her, that he even sketched some traits of her character in the Old Testament. But the position does affirm that all this must be considered in the light without which these data do not unlock their meaning. Thanks to this position, a number of

---

1. Vatican II simply confirmed this view. Cf. *Lumen Gentium* 55.

problems that would clutter up our study can be treated in an appendix.² What is involved is, after all, only a recognition of how hidden in the Old Testament was the message that became manifest in the New.

---

2. Appendix #1, *infra.*

FIRST PERIOD

MARY IN SCRIPTURE[1]

The first indications of the role of Mary, the fundamental data to which nothing substantially new will be added, are contained in the New Testament which was in the process of composition for about fifty years up to its completion toward the end of the first century with the Gospel according to Saint John. In the New Testament the Mother of Jesus occupies a place that, materially speaking, is of little importance though full of meaning. These basic data, which are of God's own word, deserve particular attention at the very beginning of our study. The course of their development will now be taken up, a development discernible within Revelation itself, from Gal. 4:5 (about 50 A.D.) to the Gospel of John (about 90 A.D.).

Galatians 4:5

In an incidental way the Virgin appears in the Letter to the Galatians. This is perhaps the oldest witness that has been preserved.[2] In very involved terms it represents the first level of the message of the New Testament:

---

1. Bibliography on Mary in Scripture, *infra,* pp. 347–350.
2. It was composed either in 48–49 during Paul's sojourn at Antioch, or between 53 and 58 during his sojourn at Ephesus. Cf. E. Osty, *Les Epîtres de saint Paul,* Paris, Siloé, 1945, p. 11. S. Lyonnet, *Les Epîtres aux Romains et aux Galates,* Paris, Cerf, 1953, holds the second hypothesis more probable.

"When the appointed time came, God sent his Son, born of a woman, born a subject of the Law, to redeem the subjects of the Law and to enable us to be adopted as sons" (Gal. 4:4–5; cf. Rom. 1:3).

The structure of this sentence is to be noted. Four ideas are paired off two by two in a balanced scheme:

| born of a *woman* | to enable us to be adopted as *sons* |
| subject of the *Law* | to redeem the subjects of the *Law* |

It is tempting to prolong one or the other of the axes of this double alignment of concepts. Protestants stop at the vertical axis: the association of *woman* with *law* is no title of glory for Mary (Gal. 3:15–4:7; cf. Rom. 2:21–4:25; 7). Catholic mariologists fix on the horizontal axis: "born of a woman . . . to enable us to be adopted as sons"; and if they glimpse there however dim an allusion to the woman of Gn. 3:20, Eve, "mother of all those who live," they orient their commentaries in the direction of Mary's spiritual maternity. Both associations — woman and law, human birth of the Son of God and adoptive filiation of Christians — are indeed founded in the text. The first corresponds to the Pauline theme of the abasement of the Son of God, his "kenosis," and describes the "condition of a slave" (Phil. 2:7) that Christ took on for us. The second affirms that this abasement is the point of departure and the means of a salvation that culminates in divine adoption.

All that being said, the comparison between the *woman* and the *law* should not be pushed too far: the objective realities in question — on the one hand this person who becomes Mother of the Savior and on the other this abstract code — are too different. Neither should the second comparison be pushed too far: nothing authorizes us to suppose that Saint Paul attributes a personal role to Mary in the adoptive filiation. What he tells us amounts to this: a woman assured the insertion of Christ into the human race "when the appointed time came." Who is that woman? What is her name? Is she a simple material instrument or an instrument of choice? From the outside it is possible to pile up references and arguments to "make this text speak." But the text guards its laconic silence. So silent is it that, in the opinion of a recent Catholic article, Saint Paul would have been ignorant of the virginal birth.[3]

Mark

Mark's only two texts on "the Mother of Jesus" (3:31–35, 6:1–6) both have the same incidental character. They exhibit moreover a negative, or at least a restrictive, tone that is so striking that mariologists themselves have of recent date given them the name "antimariological verses."

In the first text, common to the synoptic gospels, Jesus brushes aside the intrusion of relatives of his come to take him away from a ministry they judge fraught with the irrational. He replies that his "true family" consists of his disciples:

> "His mother and brothers now arrived and, standing outside, sent in a message asking for him. A crowd was sitting around him at the time the message was passed to him, 'Your mother and brothers and sisters are outside asking for you.' He replied, 'Who are my mother and my brothers?' And looking round at those sitting

---

3. A. Legault, "Saint-Paul a-t-il parlé de la maternité virginale?" *Sciences Ecclésiastiques* 16 (1964), 481–495. E. de Roover, "La maternité virginale de Marie dans l'interprétation de Galates 4:4," *Studiorum Paulinorum Congressus internationalis catholicus 1961,* Rome, 1963, vol. 2, pp. 17–43, gives the history of the interpretation of this verse, which has been largely Marian and virginal since Tertullian, *De Carne Christi* 20, PL 2:786a.

in a circle about him, he said, 'Here are my mother and my brothers. Anyone who does the will of God, that person is my brother and sister and mother' " (Mk. 3:31–35; Mt. 12:46–50; Lk. 8:19–21).

In the other text (Mk. 6:1–6)[4] his fellow-countrymen refuse to believe in him precisely because he is only "the carpenter, the son of Mary." Knowledge of Jesus *according to the flesh* obscures knowledge of him *according to the Spirit.*

For a long time these texts were neglected. Absent from the series of Marian encyclicals that the popes have multiplied over the past century, they have finally been taken up by Vatican II. They close off what would be a dangerous blind alley for mariology, the attribution to Mary of a greatness based solely on a flesh and blood relationship. They forbid any exaltation of Mary's maternity independently of the correlative gifts of grace that the remainder of the New Testament will lead us to discover.

* * *

The other two synoptic evangelists do not stop there. *Matthew* (shortly before 70 A.D.) and *Luke* (shortly thereafter) have gathered still older traditions and speak to us of Mary's role in the origin of Christ. This first formal treatment of her role does not seem foreign to the living presence of Mary in Christ's life and in the primitive Church. *Luke* seems to have received from Mary herself, though indirectly, what he knows about the Infancy Gospel: twice he refers to the "words," that is, in biblical parlance, to the events on whose meaning she meditated in her heart (Lk. 2:19, 51). He refers to her surprise (2:33, 48) and momentary incomprehension

---

4. It has been asked whether "son of Mary" in place of the more normal expression "son of Joseph," which is moreover employed in the parallel texts (Lk. 4:22 and Jn. 6:42), is not an allusion to the virginal birth of which Mark does not explicitly speak.

(1:29, 34, and especially 2:50), states of mind on which the light of further revelations or meditations was retrospectively cast. Similarly, it was from living with Mary as her son that John, to whom the dying Lord entrusted his mother (19:27), learned what he tells us somewhat later (about 90 A.D.) of the mystery of Mary, ideal personification of the Church.

The texts about to be analyzed are short and it would be a simple matter to copy them down. But on investigation they prove to be laden with meaning. Their place in the structure of Revelation, their references to the Old Testament, their links with one another give them a value that does not appear at first sight. Their meaning does not come across as a sum of data that can be added up but rather as a series of mutually confirming insights that throw a new light one on the other. They are like the counterpoint melodies in a Bach cantata, taking on their full value only in association with one another. In this respect the harmony between *Luke* and *John* is particularly remarkable.

Matthew

The first evangelist gives us the key to the prophecy of Is. 7:14:

"The maiden *(ha 'almah)* is with child and will soon give birth to a son whom she will call Emmanuel."

Mystery and ambiguity enshroud the text of Isaiah. Too often short cuts are taken in the task of discovering the virginal conception in it. The text does not have the Hebrew word *b^etulah* which properly means "virgin," but *'almah* which means "a maiden of marriageable age," not necessarily a virgin (Gn. 24:43; Ex. 2:8; Ps. 68:26; Song 1:3, 6, 8, and especially Prov. 30:19). Some would say that the Greek translation of the Septuagint before Christ's time took a great step forward in this regard when it translated the Hebrew word by *parthenos,* the Greek word for "virgin." But one can hardly insist on any progress in terminology therein implied, since in the same Septuagint translation Dinah, who was raped, is nevertheless called by the same name "virgin" *(parthenos* here also) in Gn. 34:3. If the prophecy of Isaiah is read in the framework of the time when it was written it is not clear that he wished to affirm a virginal conception. What the term "maiden" or "virgin" does signify in this text, surely, is that the child spoke of is her first-born.

At times much is made of the fact that apparently this maiden receives the task of giving a name to her son and thus exercises a right that normally belongs to the father; no father therefore seems to have been involved in this birth. But the mother of Ishmael (Gn. 16:11) and the mother of Samson (Jg. 13:24) also fulfill this name-giving role, even though the fathers in both cases are quite active, as appears from each of the narratives.

Moreover, if the Septuagint translation is said to show some "progress" toward a recognition of virginity here *(parthenos* for *'almah),* mention should also be made of the fact that this same translation exhibits a regression on the other point of the name-giving, since according to the Septuagint translation the king Achaz is to give a name to the child in Is. 7:14: *"You* will give him the name Emmanuel," the prophet says to the king.

On the other hand, Isaiah's oracle cannot be tossed off lightly. It presents evident intimations of a messianic character such as the eschatological coloring of the immediate context and the transcendental qualities of Emmanuel in passages that follow (Is. 9:1–6; 11:1–9).

Even if, as is most probable, for the immediate future the oracle envisages the birth of Hezekiah, it envisages the Messiah and his Mother on a further and distant level. The Septuagint has brought this eschatological level into relief. The mysterious prophetic present of the Hebrew participle is there made into a future verb: "The maiden is with child" becomes more specific in "The virgin will conceive."

In citing this Septuagint reading Matthew recognizes Mary, the mysterious Virgin, sketched in dim outline. It is she who conceived virginally, by the Holy Spirit (Mt. 1:18, 21; cf. Is. 11:2), to the exclusion of all carnal intervention (Mt. 1:18, 25). Certainly it was not Is. 7:14 that gave him the idea *a priori* of a virginal birth. Rather, in order to discover the meaning of this disconcerting fact about Jesus' origin, known from traditions emanating from Jesus' own family, he had recourse to Isaiah's oracle.

With the above considerations in mind it is possible to read his entire text with profit:

> "This is how Jesus Christ came to be born. His mother Mary was betrothed to Joseph; but before they came to live together she was found to be with child through the Holy Spirit. Her husband Joseph, being a man of honour and wanting to spare her publicity, decided to divorce her informally. He had made up his mind to do this when the angel of the Lord appeared to him in a dream and said, 'Joseph, son of David, do not be afraid to take Mary home as your wife, because she has conceived what is in her by the Holy Spirit. She will give birth to a son and you must name him Jesus, because he is the one who is to save his people from their sins.' Now all this took place to fulfill the words spoken by the Lord through the prophet: 'The virgin will conceive and give birth to a son and they will call him Emmanuel,' a name which means 'God-is-with-us' " (Mt. 1:18–23).

"God-is-with-us": In Isaiah's context these words had only an indeterminate sense and could be understood to mean a simple divine assistance (Is. 8:8, 10). With Matthew they begin to disclose the sense that the Church recognizes in them today, the divinity of the Messiah. In this fullness of meaning is to be found the conjunction of two great series of texts that run through the whole Old Testament, one of them elevating the Messiah even to divine attributes, the other describing the descent of a divine hypostasis (the Word, Wisdom) among men.[5]

Luke

In passing from Matthew to Luke one is struck first by the differences. To begin with, the choice of episodes is different. In his first two chapters Matthew makes mention of the visit of the Magi, the slaughter of the innocent children, the flight into Egypt. Luke gives attention in his first two chapters to the annunciation, the visitation, the presentation and the finding of the child in the Temple. Matthew's first two chap-

---

5. The ascending movement which tends toward a divinization of the Messiah proceeds from 2 Sam 7:12-17 and Is. 9:5-6. Cf. Ps. 2:2; 45 (44):7; 72 (71): 5-12; 110 (109):1-5. The movement suggesting the descent of a divine hypostasis appears in Pr. 8; Sirach 24 (cf. 1:1-10); Wisd. 7:15-30; in these texts Wisdom, coming from the mouth of God, is pleased to dwell among men. Dan. 7:13-14 is in this same direction.

The two movements are seen to merge particularly as one follows the evolution of the idea of kingship in the Old Testament. At the beginning, in Samuel's day, there was opposition and contradiction between the kingship of Yahweh, on whom the theocratic regime was founded, and kingship conferred on a man (1 Sam. 8:6-19). But little by little Yahweh King of Israel (Num. 23:21; Dt. 33:5; Is. 6:1-12; Mich. 2:13; Zeph. 3:15) and the Messiah Son of David (2 Sam. 7:12-17) tend to coalesce. The trend can be followed in Is. 9:6 and Ps. 2, 44, and 109 cited at the beginning of this note; cf. also Ps. 72 (71). The point of convergence most remarkable on the level of the Old Testament is undoubtedly Dan. 7:13-14, where the "Son of Man" appears on the clouds of heaven and seems to exercise the royal functions of Wisdom (Pr. 8:15-16; Wisd. 8:1).

The two lines merge again in the gospel of the Annunciation, where the Son promised to Mary realizes, to a degree superior to all the Old Testament texts, the traits of both the Davidic descendant and Yahweh, the transcendental king.

ters have universalist overtones: visitors from the Orient, Jesus' flight to a foreign country. Luke's first two chapters, on the contrary, are centered on Christ's relationship with Israel, Jerusalem, the Law, and the Temple. His accounts have evidently been drawn up to nourish the spirituality of a Judaeo-Christian environment.

There are differences also in the two genealogies, in line with the freedom of interpretation characteristic of the epoch. One point only should be remembered: in his version of the genealogy of Christ Matthew took care to mention the foreign women who open up a perspective beyond Israel; Luke for his part looked for this universalist opening at the origin of the genealogy, by tracing Christ's ancestors back beyond Abraham to the first man and the God who created him (Lk. 3:38). Luke ends his genealogy with the words, "Son of Adam, son of God." Traced back in this way to the creation of the man who was prototype of all, the mystery of the virginal birth reveals its deeper meaning and scope: it is the beginning of the new creation announced by the prophets.

Underneath these differences which appear at first glance the two infancy gospels exhibit the same essential narratives: the birth at Bethlehem, the childhood at Nazareth, the name Jesus given by the angel (Mt. 1:21; Lk. 1:31), the virginal conception by the Holy Spirit. Joseph did not play any part therein (Mt. 1:18, 25; Lk. 1:34–35), but he remains the genealogical link that unites Jesus to David (Mt. 1:16; Lk. 3:23). For the ancients, in fact, descent is less a biological than a juridical and moral affair. Moreover, it is there that the divergences between the two genealogies find their explanation. This agreement of the two evangelists who are the echo of two traditions so different and who are unaware of each other's work gives great historical weight to their concordant witness concerning the essential events.

Finally, each of them refers to the great dynastic prophecies: 2 Sam. 7:14 (the heir promised to David), Is. 7:14 (the Virgin who conceives), and Mi. 5:2 (the "one who is to give birth" in the city of David; cf. Mt. 2:5–7 and Lk. 2:14).

What is of interest to us is that Luke introduces new material concerning the Mother of Jesus. Here the key difference is the following: *Matthew* presents the infancy story from the viewpoint of Joseph, head of the Holy Family and witness of the mystery of the virginal birth. Joseph is the one we see acting, reflecting, struggling with God and men. Mary is in the background. Was her commitment in this mystery conscious and personal? The first Gospel leaves us in ignorance on this point. *Luke,* on the contrary, writes from Mary's point of view. She is the center of his narrative, she who "kept" her memoirs "in her heart" (2:19, 51).

Thus it is that we learn the first origin of the mystery, the message brought by the angel Gabriel. Thus it is that Mary's reactions (1:29, 34), her conduct (1:39–56), her prayer (1:38, 46, 54; cf. 2:19, 51), her attitude towards God are described. Luke insists on her faith, similar to our own in its obscure condition (1:29; 2:50), yet unfailing and thus in sharp contrast with that of Zechariah, as appears from the comparison of these two parallel texts:

The Angel to Zechariah Lk. 1:20	*Elizabeth to Mary* Lk. 1:45; cf. 38
You will be silenced since you have not believed my words, which will come true.	Blessed are you who have believed, because what has been promised to you by the Lord will be fulfilled.

We discover, finally, that Mary's virginity was the object of a definite decision. To the angel who announces a happy motherhood she objects, "But how can this come about, since I am a virgin?" (Lk. 1:34) — a strange reply on the part of an engaged person, in an epoch when engagement already comprised all the rights of marriage.[6] Unless violence is to be done to the text, the following meaning must be recognized in it: inspired by God, Mary had decided not to know man in the biblical sense of this expression (cf. Gn. 4:1; 17:25; 19:5, 6; 38:26, etc.).[7]

---

6. Perhaps more should be said. At the beginning of the Annunciation account Luke presents the Virgin as a *parthenos emnēsteumenē*, usually translated "betrothed virgin." Now, in Lk. 2:5 the same expression *emnēsteumenē* certainly means "married." It would be logical to harmonize the two translations, as the Vulgate does in employing in both cases the word *desponsata* (betrothed). The translators are hard put: most follow Osty in translating "fiancée" for the first text and "spouse" for the second. Lagrange translates "fiancée" for both (which is somewhat surprising in 2:5 at Jesus' birth). H. Diepen (*Ons Geloof* 28 (1946), 146–167) translates "married" in both cases. D. Frangipane, C. Lattey, and F. Ceuppens (cf. Laurentin, *Luc 1–2*, p. 105, n. 3) have readopted this solution, which seems the most probable. In this case the first verse of the Annunciation narrative would strikingly announce the disconcerting phenomenon that dominates the entire account, the mystery of the *married virgin*. (Since St. Bernard's day it had been debated whether this first verse said something commonplace, as would apparently fit the situation of a bride-to-be in any Galilean village, or something solemn, as the tone and position of the verse seemed to imply.) It would seem, in the *married virgin* hypothesis, that the mystery is presented in reference to Is. 7:14, which may have several points of contact with Lk. 1:26 and 31:

Lk. 1:26 and 31	Is. 7:14
The angel . . . was sent to a *virgin*.	Behold the *virgin*
. . . "You are to *conceive and bear a son* and *you must name him Jesus*."	shall *conceive and bear a son* and shall *call his name* Emmanuel.

Luke 1:34 "How can this come about, since I am a virgin?" would bring us to the heart of the mystery — the decision of virginity formulated by Mary and undoubtedly recognized and accepted by her spouse. Cf. Laurentin, *Luc 1–2*, pp. 175–189.

7. On Mary's decision of virginity, cf. Appendix #2, *infra*.

The spiritual portrait of Mary is summed up in the contrast of her humble human situation with her grandeur in the order of grace. She is the poor woman on whom God's favors have been heaped (1:28) — a contrast that is in reality a harmony, such as was already manifested, in opposition to judgments of purely human wisdom, in the revealed message of the Old Testament. In the Magnificat Mary reveals her lucid consciousness of this condition of hers. She puts herself in the ranks of "the poor," among "the humble" whom Scripture calls the chosen portion of Israel. The Lord has looked upon her in her poverty — even, it seems, because of this very poverty of hers (1:48). She is the type of the poor whom the Lord delights in exalting (1:52).[8]

---

8. The Greek words *tapeinōsis* (Lk. 1:48) and *tapeinos* (1:52) almost defy translation and usually are rendered in words suggesting lowliness, abasement, poverty, humility, etc. The Semitic substratum is clear: '*ānaw* = poor, '*ānawah* or '*ānî* = poverty. Both these words have a whole history.

Originally they simply signified material indigence (Lev. 19:10; 23:22; Dt. 15:11; 24:12; Is. 10:2; Jer. 22:16, etc.) and its exploitation by the rich, on whom the Law imposed restraint (Ex. 22:20–24; Dt. 24:12–17; Lev. 19:20; 23:22). Gradually the word "poor" took on a very deep religious meaning, especially in the Psalms (probably because God was pleased to reveal himself to poor people, to the humble, the oppressed, rather than to the rich and powerful). It is among the class of the "poor" that Israel's religious ascent develops, along with its piety and prayer, its hope and expectation.

According to Luke's gospel, Mary is among this group. In her is to be found the spiritual triumph of the humble along with the fulfilment of their hopes. Jesus is in the same group. He proposes himself as the model of humility of heart (Mt. 11:29) and proclaims that those who understand it are blessed (Lk. 6:20). The depth of the discovery of this evangelical secret by St. Therese of the Child Jesus is well known: "Yes, I have come to understand humility of heart" (*Novissima Verba*, September 30, Lisieux, 1926, p. 193).

In the first edition of this *Short Treatise* it was suggested that a study of "the progress of this notion of poverty throughout the Old Testament, its climax in the Virgin of the Magnificat and in Christ, and its value for our life" would be rich in interest. This project was on its way to realization at the time with A. Gelin, *Les pauvres de Yahvé*, Paris, Cerf, 1953

This exaltation of Mary by God's gratuitous choice is one of the salient themes of the first chapter of Luke's Gospel. The angel Gabriel greets her with the name *kecharitōmenē* (1:28). The word defies translation in most languages. Recourse must be had to a circumlocution such as "one who has won God's favor," or "object of God's favor." The word is a perfect participle and in Greek the perfect tense indicates permanence or stability. A favor that is stable and definitive is therefore implied. Furthermore, this name is given her from on high; it is Mary's true name in the eyes of God, her name of grace. Indeed, the name *kecharitōmenē* is formed from the word *charis,* meaning "grace," as its root. Mary is the "object of favor" in a preeminent way.[9] She is "the-one-who-has-found-grace" *(charin),* in the words of the Angel Gabriel in Lk. 1:30.

This initial greeting of praise is prolonged throughout the accounts of the annunciation and the visitation. The Lord is with her (1:28), the Holy Spirit comes down upon her (1:35), great things are accomplished in her (1:49) thanks to her faith (1:45), and "that is why" (as she herself recognizes) "all

---

(ET: *The Poor of Yahweh,* Collegeville, Liturgical Press, 1964), where Chapter 6 is consecrated to Mary.

9. It is out of a concern for exactness that the expression is not translated simply "full of grace." If Luke had meant "full of grace," he would have said *plērēs charitos.* But this expression is used only for Christ in Jn. 1:14. This is not without significance, for the Word made flesh has the fulness of grace from within by his very divinity. In Mary grace is purely and simply the fruit of gratuitous love and kindness. Probably it is not by chance that the inspired text, in speaking of Mary's grace, does not refer to it as a thing possessed by the Virgin, but as a gift of God. The text thus considers grace not from the angle of created effects but from the angle of the cause of grace, God's creative kindness. In verse 30 Gabriel comments, "You have won God's favor." No doubt the love of God for her whom he names preeminently "the object of his favor" (one could even say "the beloved") realizes a fulness in her; thus the translation of the Vulgate here represents a valid dogmatic interpretation, but it is a transposition rather than a translation.

generations will call [her] blessed" (1:48). No other biblical personage has been given such strong praise, and without anything said to the contrary.

Were it not the inspired text, one would be tempted almost to wonder whether the Christocentrism of the gospels were here in default. In Lk. 1:35 the angel tells Mary, "The Holy Spirit will come upon *you* and the power of the Most High will cover *you* with its shadow." In the light of Is. 11:2 would it not have been more normal to say that the Holy Spirit was coming on the Emmanuel rather than on his Mother? In Lk. 1:42 Elizabeth proclaims Mary's blessing before that of her Son and adds, "Why should I be honoured with a visit from the *Mother of my Lord?*" even though the honour that falls to her is actually the visit of the *Lord* rather than of the Mother. She adds, "For the moment *your greeting* reached my ears, the child in my womb leapt for joy," even though in reality the benefit of the visitation is to be attributed to the action of Mary's Child rather than to Mary's voice.

That Mary should thus be placed in the forefront is most astonishing and gives food for reflection to those who fear that they do Christ some offense in exalting his Mother. On the other hand, there is no justification for making short shrift of the Christocentrism of the gospels. For quite evidently Christ remains throughout all these scenes the center of concern. He is "the glory of the people of Israel" (1:32) and, in the first place, of his Mother in Israel, she who is the place of his repose and the sign in which he begins to manifest himself (1:39–45; 2:12, 16, 27, 35).

Nor does the rest of the third Gospel tone down this initial praise. One day while Jesus was speaking,

"a woman in the crowd raised her voice and said, 'Happy the womb that bore you and the breasts you sucked.' But he replied, 'Still happier those who hear the word of God and keep it' " (11:27–28, a passage proper to Luke).

Some interpreters would have it that Jesus' words contradict those of the woman, and that he should be understood as saying, "Happy are those who have faith *and not* the one who gave birth to me." Luke, for his part, does not understand the words in this sense, for twice he witnesses that Mary is "happy" (1:45), and "forever" (1:48), *precisely* because of her faith: "Happy *(makaria)* is she who has believed," Elizabeth says (1:45), and Mary replies, "All generations will call me happy *(makariousin)*" (1:48). In addition, he presents Mary as the first to hear the word of God (1:28–38) and to keep it in her heart (2:19, 51). The conclusion is inescapable that Jesus does not let himself become his Mother's detractor.[10] Lk. 11:28, like Mk. 3:31–35, averts any purely material conception of the glory that is Mary's and brings to light the twofold religious foundation of that glory: the Virgin's faith and, still more deeply, God's plan of putting all his delight in her (1:28, 30) and accomplishing great things in her (1:49).

In a word, the first two chapters of Luke lead us back to our point of departure. They form a marvelous commentary on the vaguer expressions of Saint Paul, "Born of a woman, subject of the Law."

Born of a woman — such is the theme of the annunciation and birth narratives (Lk 1:28–2:20). *Subject of the Law* — the theme of the circumcision (2:21), the purification (2:22–39), the trip to Jerusalem "according to the custom" for the feast of the Passover (Lk. 2:40–51). And if this subjection to the Law is an abasement for the transcending God, it is not humiliation, but glory for whomever he visits and wherever he stays. "Light" (Lk. 2:32) shines on the Temple servants

---

10. Compare Lk. 11:29 with Lk. 18:18. To the young man who calls him "Good Master" Jesus replies, "Why do you call me good? No one is good but God alone." In these words he neither denies that he is God nor that he is good, but he wishes to raise the young man's concern to a level higher than that of flesh and blood and the purely external. He acts in the same way with the woman who declares Mary "blessed for having borne him."

when Jesus obeys the Law. Grace touches anyone he approaches, from the time of his conception (Lk. 1:41-45; 2:8-20, 25-38, 47). He submits to the Law (Lk. 2:22-24, 27, 39; cf. 42), though he is its master; it is not to be abolished, but to be fulfilled (cf. Mt. 5:17). Still more has he come to confirm and fulfill in grace the woman whom he has chosen as his Mother. This is what Luke's Gospel tells us. This is the light the companion of Paul gives us for understanding retrospectively how the schematic text of Gal. 4:4 is to be interpreted: the woman of whom Jesus is born is a chosen woman. She is the first to whom it was given to benefit from all the grace and joy that stems from the abasement of God's Son.

The message of Luke's first two chapters on the Virgin Mary invites a verse by verse commentary. Their density is the equal of the Johannine texts. Besides, these two chapters show Luke's talent, however much he was helped by his source or by some special light from on high; his work here bears even the mark of genius. And as with every text so marked, commentaries will never unfold all the richness of meaning. We shall limit ourselves, therefore, to the gospel of the annunciation (1:26-38) and, since even this text goes beyond our present scope, we shall further restrict ourselves to giving its biblical background.

The remarkable thing about this text is that it is literally a web of scriptural allusions. For example, the angel's words concerning the miraculous conception, "Nothing is impossible with God" (1:37), are a literal repetition of the angel's words in Gn. 18:14 to Sarah concerning her conception, likewise miraculous. The reason for this weaving together of scriptural passages begins to appear as the Magnificat is examined. In this canticle almost every phrase is the echo of some passage of the Bible, as appears from the table in Appendix #3. Mary there appears so penetrated with the word of God that she becomes its faithful echo. Thus it should cause no astonishment if God speaks to her in the same tone: to the Virgin nourished by the Scriptures the divine messenger speaks the language of the Scriptures. For anyone ignorant of this language the message will remain closed. It is worth the effort, therefore, to look in scriptural language for the key elements of the angel's message.

The annunciation gospel is composed of three parts. The breaking in of the good news (Lk. 1:28-29) is followed by two series of precisions, one concerning the human origin of the Messiah (30-33), the other in more veiled terms concerning his divine origin (34-36).

1. The first part begins with a proclamation of Messianic joy: "Rejoice!" In fact, the first word of the angel, *chaire,* does not correspond to the ordinary Hebrew greeting of peace, *shalom,* the equivalent of our "Good day!" or "Hello!" It is rather the echo of the greetings of Messianic joy addressed by the prophets to the Daughter of Zion in Zech. 9:9, Joel 2:21-27, and especially Zeph. 3:14-17. Once this motif of eschatological joy has been proclaimed, it is the Lord who is to come into the midst of Israel, or, translating in its etymological sense the expression *bequirbēk* employed here, "in the womb" of Israel. The message of the angel echoes that of Zephanaiah but this time with respect to an immediate realization.

The pedagogy of this first revelation of the Incarnation leaves one amazed. It is something accomplished without elaborated conceptual material, simply by the virtual application of the Old Testament scriptures to the new event. Illuminated by Scripture, the event discloses its divine dimensions; actualized by the event, Scripture attains a marvelous and unforeseen fulfillment.

An examination of the parallel developments of these two symmetric texts step by step will throw light on our subject. The joy announced by the angel is messianic joy, the eschatological joy expressed by Zephanaiah (first line above). Mary, who receives the angel's message, is the "Daughter of Zion": she stands for Israel at this decisive hour (second line). The presence of the Lord in Israel's midst, this new and mysteri-

Prophet's Message to Israel	*Angel's Message to Mary*
Zeph. 3:14–17	Lk. 1:28–33
Rejoice (chaire)	*Rejoice (chaire)*
Daughter of Zion . . .	so highly favored.
The *King* of Israel, Yahweh,	The *Lord*[11]
is *IN* you *(bequirbēk)*	is *WITH* you
Do not be afraid, Zion,	*Do not be afraid*, Mary . . .
Yahweh your God	Listen,
is *in your womb (bequirbēk)*	you are to conceive *in your womb*
	and bear a son
as a strong *Savior (yôšî'a)*	and you must name him "*Yahweh Savior.*"[12]
	He will *reign*. . . .

ous presence announced for the last days, becomes a conception and a childbearing for her (lines 3–7). Finally, Ze-

---

[11]. "The Lord Adonai" *('adōnāi)* was the word used by the Israelites to replace the name "Yahweh" so often written in the Bible, beginning with the time when it became the rule no longer to pronounce the sacred name. (Hence the practice of the Massoretes, who vocalized the name "Yahweh" with the vowels of "Adonai".) In Lk. 1:29 "the Lord" therefore is the strict equivalent of "Yahweh," which is the reading in the parallel passage of Zeph. 1:14.

[12]. The names of many of the biblical personages have a meaning (cf. Gen. 4:1, 25; 21:6; Is. 7:14; Hos. 1:4, 7, etc.). This is especially the case in announcements of a birth, when God prescribes the name that will characterize the child and his mission (Gen. 16:16; 17:5, 15; 2 Sam. 12:25; Is. 7:14, etc.). Just as the name of John the Baptist means "Yahweh is gracious," because the mission of the precursor is the signal for God's supreme work of gracious mercy, so the name of Jesus signifies "Savior," as Mt. 1:21 clearly says: "You must name him Jesus *(yēšû'a* = Yahweh Savior), because he is the one who is to save *(yošia')* his people from their sins." R. Laurentin, "Traces d'allusions étymologiques en Luc 1–2," *Biblica* 37 (1956), 435–456; 38 (1957), 1–23, shows that the Hebrew source

phanaiah designates the one whom she is to bear under the name "Yahweh Savior." According to the Hebrew, this is the very meaning of the name "Jesus," designated by the angel, and this name thereby takes on the fullness of its etymological meaning. Thus in Luke as in Matthew, and even more clearly, two apparently divergent promises find their realization: the reign of the Son of David and the theocratic reign of Yahweh himself, both announced by prophets, are one and the same reign.

Mary was disturbed by this message (Lk. 1:29). Understandably so. Her emotion does not stem from the fainthearted fear to which it is attributed sometimes. It comes from the shock of one of those encounters with God that shake the strongest spirits. It comes from a messianic joy that bursts in along with an astoundingly unbelievable affirmation that the angel makes in veiled terms and that in clear language would mean "Salvation has arrived! You are going to be the Mother of a transcendent Messiah who is identified with the Lord himself! You are the new Israel where God is coming to dwell."

The angel will go on to clear up this double affirmation of messiahship and divinity.

2. He first specifies the ascendancy of the Messiah as man, taking up the terms of the fundamental prophecy, that of Nathan to David.

3. The last pericope consists of the angel's reply to Mary clarifying the divine origin of the Messiah, as the second had done for his human origin:

> "The Holy Spirit will come upon you and the power of the Most High will cover you with its shadow. And so the child will be holy and will be called Son of God" (Lk. 1:35).

---

apparently used by Luke contained intentional and evident allusions to the names of the principal personages in the account, not only John and Jesus, but Elizabeth and Zachary also, and perhaps even Mary.

Nathan to David 2 Sam. 7:12–16	Gabriel to Mary Lk. 1:32–33
(The order of verses is changed to pair off parallel elements.)	
12. I will *preserve* the offspring of your body after you, and make his sovereignty secure. I will be a father to him and *he a son to me.*	He will be *great* (root *gdl*) and will be called *Son of the Most High.* The *Lord God* will give him
16b. Your *throne* will be established forever.	the *throne* of his ancestor David;
16a. Your house and your *sovereignty* will *always* stand secure before me	he will *rule forever* over the house of Jacob,
Cf. 13 I will make his *royal throne* secure *forever.*	and his *reign* will *have no end.*

The scope of this title, Son of God, emerges retrospectively from a comparison with the other passages where it is solemnly applied to Jesus: the manifestation of the Father at the baptism of Jesus (Lk. 3:22) and at his transfiguration (9:35), the confession at Caesarea (Mt. 16:16), and the decisive testimony for which Christ was to pay with his life (Lk. 22:70). In the light of the Old Testament Mary would be able to penetrate the meaning of the title. The divine overshadowing, designated by the characteristic word *episkiasei,* evoked

ing, designated by the characteristic word *episkiasei,* evoked the cloud which was the sign of Yahweh's presence. This cloud was seen for the first time when the Mosaic worship was established. With its *shadow* it *covered* the Ark of the Covenant, while the glory of God — that is, God himself — filled it from within. In her turn Mary is going to be the object of this double manifestation: a presence from above that signifies transcendence, and a presence of the Lord from within. That is what is implied in the comparison of two texts:

Ex. 40:34	*Lk. 1:35*
The *cloud*	The *power of the Most High*
covered the Tent of Meeting	will *cover* you with its shadow
and the *glory of Yahweh* filled the tabernacle	And so the child will be holy and will be called *Son of God.*

The same idea seems to be taken up in the episode of the visitation, a story told in reference to the account of the transfer of the Ark in 2 Sam. 6:1, 14. We shall not insist on the more subtle comparison that can be made between these two narratives.[13]

---

13. The episode of the Visitation is drawn up in close parallelism with 2 Sam. 6:1–14, the story of the transportation of the Ark of the Covenant, narrated just before the messianic prophecy (7:1–17) to which Lk. 1:32–33 alludes. The events, the atmosphere, the terms used to describe them correspond closely: the ascent of the Ark (2 Sam. 6:5) and the ascent of Mary (Lk. 1:39); the joyous outcry of the people and Elizabeth's cry of greeting; the exultation of David and of John the Baptist. At times the expressions are in striking correspondence with each other:

The theme is taken up a final time at the end of the infancy gospel. As Jesus enters the Temple Simeon greets him as "the glory of Israel" (Lk. 2:32). This is a divine title. The glory of Yahweh that had deserted the Temple once it was bereft of the Ark of the Covenant now reenters the Temple as Mary comes there carrying Jesus. Thus it is that Simeon can die

2 Sam. 6	Lk. 1
9. "However can the *Ark of Yahweh* (= *My Lord*) *come to me?*"	43. "Why should I be honored with a *visit from the mother of My Lord?*"
11. The Ark of Yahweh *remained* for *three months* in the house. . . .	56. Mary *remained* about *three months* in the home of Elizabeth.

In short, in the marvelously artful account of the Visitation the image of the Ark of the Covenant is worked into the person of Mary, and here and there in a typological approach it is possible to see that the "Lord" whose mother she is is no other than the "Lord" who resided in the Ark.

The identification of Jesus with the Lord God seems hinted at also by Elizabeth's words (Lk. 1:42) which take up the praise given Judith:

Judith 13:18f (Vulgate 23f)	Lk. 1:42
May *you* be *blessed beyond all women* on earth and *blessed* be the *Lord God.*	*Blessed* are *you the most of all women,* and *blessed* is the *fruit of your womb.*

The eulogy here is identical, but the last line hints at an equivalence between "the Lord God" and "the fruit of your womb." Of course, one may hesitate over this or that correspondence of terms, but the overall convergence is striking. For a more detailed study within the framework of the literary type in which such parallelisms are expected, cf. Laurentin, *Luc 1–2*, pp. 43–116.

happy (Lk. 2:26, 29): he now can "see death" since he has "seen the glory of the Lord." The time has been fulfilled. Here Mary, eschatological Daughter of Zion and new Ark of the Covenant, accomplishes her mission in a way in bringing to the Temple the one whose place it properly is. This is what Jesus himself will affirm in the very last episode of the infancy gospel, that of his being found in the Temple: "I must be in my Father's house" (Lk. 2:49).

It has often been debated whether Mary perceived the divinity of Christ at the time of the annunciation. Theologians generally used to answer affirmatively, on the basis of "arguments of fittingness." But the exegetes would object that the infancy gospel did not agree with these "arguments." The biblical allusions strung up and down the text of Luke's first two chapters lead us beyond this objection.[14] They imply two things, in fact: the message of the annunciation mysteriously identifies Jesus with Yahweh himself; and Mary, versed in the Scriptures since she herself also speaks the language of the Scriptures, was capable of grasping these intimations. Thus the arguments of the exegetes and those of the theologians actually converge instead of meeting each other head on. (What was on each side a contrived element is thus surmounted, namely, the exclusively historicist interpretation of exegetes entrenched in positions taken up in the antimodernist quarrel, and the artificial constructions imposed by theologians on Scripture.) The benefit of recent exegetical research is that it has at last led us to understand

---

14. No attempt will be made here to give the distinctions that specialists would want to find. To what extent were these hints of Christ's divinity given Mary *on the day of the Annunciation?* To what extent are they the work of the evangelist writing long afterwards? Such questions are beyond the scope of a treatise as brief as this. They can be treated only in dependence on problems from which the reader has been spared, problems such as the *literary type* of the infancy gospel and its redactional mode. The reader desirous of a further treatment of the question is referred to Laurentin, *Luc 1–2,* pp. 165–175 (Annexe 1, "Quand Marie eut-elle connaissance de la divinité de son Fils?").

something about the approach with which Mary, this Jewish woman of the Old Testament, received the revelation of the mystery of the Incarnation. It would not be right to think that she was ignorant of everything and that God accomplished this mystery by surprise. Nor should it be imagined that by infused knowledge she received "the whole tract on the Incarnation," as a pious author once wrote. She did not have at hand the conceptual framework evoked by the term "Incarnation," nor even the abstract formulas by which the first councils made the existential language of Scripture more explicit. No, Mary remained poor in the conceptual and scientific order. Her knowledge of Jesus remained obscure, wrapped and enshrouded in difficulties. One episode stands as an example. When Mary found Jesus again in the Temple after three days, she cried out:

> " 'My child, why have you done this to us? See how worried your father and I have been, looking for you.' 'Why were you looking for me?' he replied. 'Did you not know that I must be in my Father's house?' But *they did not understand* what he meant" (Lk. 2:48–50).

Thus the knowledge that Mary had received was not such as to permit her to understand *everything* immediately, especially in the context of this disturbing *trial*. Not only was she disturbed by the long search for her Son; Jesus here uses for the first time a teaching method of his that in the long term is rich in result but at first hearing always causes puzzlement. In his reply he takes up the term used in the question addressed to him, but in an entirely different sense, a spiritual sense. "Your father," Mary had said in speaking of Joseph, the foster father. "My Father," Jesus replied without any hint of transition — but he was speaking of his heavenly Father.

Lastly, it is above all worthy of note that Jesus seems to contradict himself when he affirms that he must remain in his Father's house, that is, in the Temple, and nevertheless immediately returns to Nazareth, to the home of his foster father

(2:51). Like the gospel of the annunciation, that of the finding in the Temple is incomprehensible as long as it is read only on the level of a factual anecdote. It expresses a mystery, the Paschal mystery, to be exact, and that is what Luke intends to bring home to us. The child Jesus acts out a prophetic gesture whose meaning is his return to his Father. The meaning of that gesture in the city of Jerusalem (Lk. 2:41, 43, 45), at the time of the passover feast (Lk. 2:41, 42), that is, at the place and time of the event of twenty years later, is explained by Jesus himself when he says "I must be in my Father's house" (Lk. 2:49).[15] This first word of Christ has the same meaning as his last, the one that according to Saint Luke will immediately precede his death: "Father, into your hands I commit my spirit" (Lk. 23:46). Luke mentions the "three days" of separation during which Mary was looking for Jesus (Lk. 2:46) because they prefigure the three days of his death during which he will likewise be sought by the holy women. And the words the child Jesus addresses to Mary, his Mother, "Why were you looking for me?" are quite similar to those that the risen Jesus will address to Mary Magdalen, "Why look among the dead for someone who is alive?" (Lk. 24:6).

To express Mary's anguish Luke uses a very strong word (2:48) by which he elsewhere designates the sufferings of Hades (Lk. 16:24–25; cf. Acts 20:38). He probably sees here the first realization of Simeon's prophecy about "the sword" that will pierce Mary's life. This realization is itself prophetic. The anguish described in Lk. 2:35 and 48, over and above the event of Christ's childhood, refers to the mortal anguish surrounding his Passion and, more deeply, his return to his Father, in whose presence he must hereafter be sought.

---

15. "About the affairs of my Father" is a misinterpretation. In the Septuagint, in the New Testament, in the Fathers, and in classical Greek, as well as in the papyri, the complete expression *einai en tois tou* ("to be in the . . . of . . .") always has a local sense, *never an active sense*. Cf. Laurentin, *Jésus et le Temple*, pp. 47–72.

In an extended study on this subject[16] an effort has been made to show that what Mary "did not understand" according to the evangelist, what she meditated on in her heart (2:51) and came to understand only in the aftermath, is the Paschal mystery, the culmination of the annunciation promises. From Jesus' infancy on Mary had the first and very obscure inkling of that mystery, a prefiguration of it already marked quite evidently with the sign of sorrow. There above all is to be found the root of Mary's inability to understand, and not in the fact that Jesus refers to himself as "Son of God." For of the latter mark about him Mary had already long ago learned, according to Luke himself (1:32 and especially 1:35).

In a word, the light and shadow of Mary's faith must be described as Scripture itself gives information about it. The Mother of Jesus did not yet know the future; she had only some imperfect notion that Jesus was to return to his Father by ways full of mystery and sorrow for her. She knew that Jesus was the Son of God, but this knowledge, more profound than ours, was also less explicit; it was more real, less conceptual. She would not have known how to put it in terms of "nature" and "person," but the Gospel does give us an idea of how in her way of knowing she penetrated to the essential, and much more intensely and vibrantly than we.

Luke makes no further mention of Mary in the account of the Passion. He has the habit of rounding out each stage of his account by accumulating in one passage whatever concerns the personage he is then treating, even at the cost of anticipating later events, as is done with John the Baptist in 3:19-20. In Lk. 2:35-52 the anticipation is prophetic.

John[17]

By contrast, the Gospel according to John directly treats the relationship of Mary with the Savior's Passion. And this

---
16. Cf. Laurentin, *Jésus et le Temple.*
17. On Mary in the gospel of John cf. bibliography, *infra,* pp. 349-350.

is one among many other links by which Luke and John are connected. The second complements the first as if they represented two stages of a continuous effort of reflection, the later effort taking place around the disciple that Jesus loved and to whom the Mother of the Saviour had been entrusted.

No attention will be given here to the prologue where John refers to the virginal birth and to the symbol of the Ark of the Covenant.[18] If in fact these passages are a prolongation

---

18. The word *eskēnōsen* is ordinarily translated "dwelt" but it means something more. Its root implies an allusion to the *skēnē,* that is, the tent or tabernacle where God resided since the making of the Covenant (Ex. 40:34–35; cf. 25:8; 26, etc.). John explicitly brings out this nuance in Apoc. 21:3, "Behold the tent *(skēnē)* of God with men; he will tent *(skēnōsei)* with them." It will be noted that in this text (and apparently in Apoc. 11:19 and 12:1, two closely linked verses) the "tent" is also a "woman": "I saw the holy city, the new Jerusalem, coming down from God out of heaven, *as beautiful as a bride all dressed for her husband,* and then I heard a loud voice call out from the throne, 'Behold the *tent* of God with men. . . .' " (21:2–3). "Then the sanctuary of God in heaven opened, and the *Ark of the Covenant* could be seen inside it. . . . Now a great sign appeared in heaven: a *woman,* adorned with the sun. . . . She was pregnant" (11:19–12:1).

It should be added that the Prologue of St. John's gospel seems closely related to the infancy gospel, with both the same themes and the same expressions:

John 1	Luke 1–2

The Precursor: John the Baptist

6.	A man came, sent by God.	1:5–25 and 57–58
	His name was John.	1:13 "You will call him John"
7.	He came as a witness, as a witness to speak for the light	Cf. 1:44 and 76–80
		Cf. 1:76–78; 2:32
	so that everyone might believe. . . .	Cf. 1:17, 76–77

of Luke's first two chapters, the Virgin Mary does not appear explicitly therein, but only by simple allusion.

Jesus Finds No Place Among His Own

9.	The true light . . . that enlightens all men . . .	2:32 "a light to enlighten the nations"
11.	came to his own domain	2:3–4 "in *his own* city . . . Bethlehem"
	and his own people did not accept him.	2:7 "There was no place for them. . . ."

Virginal Birth

13.	Not born of blood or of the desire of the flesh or of the desire of man,	1:34–35
		1:34 "I do not know man"
	but of God.	1:35 "The power of the Most High will cover you. . . ."
14.	And the Word was made flesh and pitched his tent among us . . .	1:35; cf. 1:39–46 explained *supra*, n. 13, in reference to 2 Sam. 6.

Divine Filiation and Grace in Jesus

and we saw his glory . . .	2:30 and 32: "My eyes have seen . . . the glory"
only Son of the Father,	1:32 and 35 "Son of God"; cf. 2:49
full of grace and truth.	2:40 "The grace of God rested on him." Cf. 2:52.

She comes out in relief, on the contrary in an original way in chapters 2 and 19 of John's Gospel, the wedding feast at Cana and the Calvary scene. These two texts take on all their importance if attention is paid to their *points of contact* and to the *place* they occupy in John's Gospel.

1. *Their points of contact.* Each of the texts concerns Mary's role at Jesus' hour, that "hour" which throughout the gospel refers in the final analysis to the glorious and saving cross. In each of the two passages the evangelist calls the Virgin "the Mother of Jesus," but Jesus himself addresses her as "Woman." These two titles twice placed in such proximity are no trivial matter, for according to Semitic usage the second of them is unaccustomed. A son would properly use the term "Mother." The clue discernible here appears also in other parallelisms that cannot be studied now; it leads back to Gn. 3:15, the promise made to Eve after the Fall in Yahweh's words to the serpent:

"I will make you enemies of each other: you and the *woman,* your offspring and her offspring. It will crush your head and you will strike its heel."

By a skein of converging hints John leads us to see in Mary the one who in the new creation begun at the coming of the Word has a role analogous to that of Eve.[19] Mary is the *woman* par excellence, associated with the New Adam, *"Mother of all who live"* (Gn. 3:20 and Jn. 19:27).

2. *The place of these passages in John's Gospel.* The place John gives the episodes of Cana and Calvary in his Gospel is no less remarkable. These two scenes frame in the ministry of Jesus. One is the occasion of his first miracle, the miracle inaugurating his public life and providing a foundation for the faith of his disciples (2:11); the other is the "hour" when

---

19. A. M. Dubarle, "Les fondements bibliques du titre mariale de Nouvelle Eve," RSR 39 (1951), 49–64 (= *Mélanges Jules Lebreton,* t. I).

"all is consummated." (19:22 and 30). This is the Semitic procedure of inclusion[20] whose use here is evidence of the importance John gives to "the Mother of Jesus."

The structural design of these two texts now begins to emerge: as two supporting columns (Jn. 2 and 19:26-27) they rest on the same biblical foundation of Gn. 3:15 and 20. Grasping their mysterious meaning is another matter.

The Cana episode can cause puzzlement:[21]

---

20. There would even be here a strengthened inclusion, if the Prologue alludes to the virginal birth, as would seem to be the case. John's whole gospel, and not just his presentation of the public life of Jesus, would be framed in by texts mentioning Mary's role.

21. The exegesis of the Cana narrative (Jn. 2:1-12) is difficult. The heart of the problem is the following. Since the expression "What is it to me and to you?" is always used in the Bible to *turn away* or *refuse* (Jgs. 11:12; 2 Sam. 16:10; 19:23; 1 Kgs. 17:18; 2 Kgs. 3:13; 9:18; 25:21; Hos. 14:1; Jer. 2:18; Mk. 1:24; 5:7; Lk. 4:34; 8:28), how is it that Jesus, after having made this kind of reply, nevertheless heeds Mary's request? Why does he say that his hour has not yet come, since within the very hour he is going to show his glory (Jn. 2:11)? These difficulties and a few others are all interrelated. They have been the object of a series of remarkable works that have little by little thrown new light on the whole question, first among them F. M. Braun, *La mère des fidèles,* Paris-Tournai, Casterman, 1953 (ET: *Mother of God's People,* Staten Island, Alba, 1967) and M. E. Boismard, *Du baptême à Cana,* Paris, Cerf, 1956. The first work seems to overstress the separation intended by Jesus: account must be taken of Jn. 2:12 (which Braun does not cite). As to the second, one hesitates in face of the ingenious solution — perhaps too ingenious? — of proposing an interrogative translation, "Has not my hour already come?" The best studies on the subject, profiting from these earlier ones, are by Charlier, Michaud, and Feuillet, cited in the bibliography, *infra,* p. 350.

The treatment given here stops short of debated interpretations and attempts to hold to five strong points: 1) Jesus accomplished the miracle at Mary's request. 2) Mary understood that he was going to heed her request, and thus spoke as she did to the servants. 3) This miracle is of great importance: it is Jesus' first manifestation of himself (Jn. 2:11; cf. 1:14) and founds the faith of his disciples. (It is always in connection with the disciples that John presents Mary. Cf. Jn. 19:25-27 and Apoc. 12:17 "Those who bear witness for Jesus.") 4) There is a relationship of inclusion

"When they ran out of wine, since the wine provided for the wedding was all finished, the mother of Jesus said to him, 'They have no wine.' Jesus said, 'Woman, why turn to me? My hour has not come yet' " (Jn. 2:3–4).

Jesus' words here are reminiscent of the ones he addressed to his Mother when she found him in the Temple after a brief anticipation of his ministry: "Why were you looking for me? Did you not know that I must be in my Father's house?" (Lk. 2:49). And another analogy between John and Luke is suggested here. Jesus' words in both cases betoken a separation of the Son and his Mother during the Savior's ministry. A separation, however, that is not absolute, since Mary will accompany her Son to Capernaum with the disciples (Jn. 2:12). A separation only provisional, since she will be at his side again in the mystery of suffering when his hour will have come (Jn. 19:25–27). A separation, finally, that is rich in benefit, of which Jesus gives his Mother a pledge: at her request he accomplishes the miracle that inaugurates his messianic career. And Mary seems to understand that her wish has been heeded, in spite of the negative reply, since she immediately invites the servants to be attentive, "Do whatever he tells you" (Jn. 2:5; cf. Gn. 41:55).

Notice must be taken of the framework in which this inauguration of Jesus' mission takes place. John saw in the feast and marriage of Cana a symbol not only of the Eucharistic feast but of the eschatological marriage of God and humanity signified and prepared by the Eucharist.[22] It will be recalled that in Jesus' parables the banquet is symbolically

---

between Jn. 2:1–13 and 19:25–27. 5) For John the wedding has an eschatological meaning.

22. O. Cullmann, *Les sacrements dans l'Evangile johannique,* Paris, Presses Universitaires, 1951, pp. 36–41. On the link between the Eucharist and the eschatological wedding, cf. Lk. 22:16.

presented as the type of the eschatological banquet (Mt. 22:1–14; 25:1–13; Lk. 12:37; 22:2, 9). Marriage, such as at Cana when Jesus began his mission, is presented as the figure and pledge of the heavenly nuptials which will be the consummation of this ministry. In the framework of this symbolism the efficacious intercession of the Mother of Jesus at Cana is the sign and prelude of her intercession in heaven.

Separated from her Son during his public life, Mary will be at his side again at Calvary and the dying Jesus will more explicitly entrust her with her mission:

> "Near the cross of Jesus stood his mother and his mother's sister, Mary the wife of Clopas, and Mary of Magdala. Seeing his mother and the disciple he loved standing near her, Jesus said to his mother, 'Woman, this is your son.' Then to the disciple he said, 'This is your mother.' And from that moment the disciple made a place for her in his home" (Jn. 19:25–27).

The scope of a text given such an important place by the evangelist must not be minimized. Many have seen there only a personal and private act: Jesus confided his Mother to Saint John, they say, so that she not be abandoned to lonesomeness.[23] Perhaps this basic meaning of the passage is not totally to be discarded: here as often in John's Gospel the

---

23. This interpretation was favored by the preoccupations of controversy. From Jn. 19:26–27 an argument against those who denied Mary's virginity *post partum* was drawn from this passage: If Jesus had to confide Mary to St. John, it is because she had no other children to take her in.

The spiritual interpretation of Jn. 19:25 had only two representatives before the 12th century: Origen (d. 254; cf. *infra*, p. 73, n. 31) and George of Nicomedia (end of 9th century; cf. *infra*, Appendix # 7). The other eastern authors cited in Appendix #7 do not use Jn. 19:25–27. It is in the West with Anselm of Lucca (d. 1086) and Rupert of Deutz (d. 1129) that the spiritual interpretation belatedly runs its course (cf. *infra*, p. 112, n. 20).

deeper sense comes to light through a concrete reality, as Christ the source of life appears through the multiplication of loaves, or Christ the light of the world through the cure of the man born blind, etc. But the text summons us not to remain fixed in this simply material sense. As the words unfold, "This is your son" precedes "This is your mother." It is John who is first confided to Mary — and this is all the more surprising in that John's own mother seems to be present there at the foot of the cross.[24]

In this solemn account where every fact seems to have been selected in terms of the realization of a prophecy, verses 25–27 do not form some kind of insert where, losing sight of the perspective of salvation, John would be letting us in on some family affair. Like all the others, the fact in question here is bound up with the Redemption and refers to the accomplishment of the Scriptures. In the background surely is Gn. 3, perhaps Gn. 3:15 where the woman and her offspring are so intricately involved in the struggle wherein salvation is at stake, or more precisely Gn. 3:20 where Adam gives "the woman" her name and function of "Mother of all who live." Christ assigns Mary an analogous role in the new creation. He makes it known at this "hour," which is the hour of renewal, in this "garden" (19:41), reminiscent of the garden of the Fall (Gn. 3:24) and chosen as the site for the beginning of a new world. She becomes the mother of all the disciples of the Savior in the person of the well beloved disciple. This new motherhood that she contracts, a motherhood taking the form of an exchange, at the very hour when her Son dies, is strikingly clarified by Eve's words in Gn. 4:25:

> "God has granted me other offspring *in place of* Abel, since Cain has killed him."

---

24. Mt. 27:56 "The mother of the sons of Zebedee." John designates her perhaps in Jn. 19:25 in the words "the sister of his mother." P. Benoit, *Passion et Résurrection,* Paris, Cerf, 1966, p. 216.

It can be asked whether Christ's words "Behold your mother" have an efficacious and creative value as do sacramental words, or whether they simply declare what has been wrought, namely, the painful bringing to birth of a new people announced for the Daughter of Zion by the prophet (Is. 26:17; 66:8-9; Jn. 16:21), a birth realized on Calvary. The second of these solutions seems to be the more probable, since in John's Gospel the words "Behold" or "This is" followed by the mention of the personage whose role in the mystery is being disclosed are words that *reveal* rather than words that *effect* something (Jn. 1:29, 36, 47).[25] On Calvary Jesus brings to light in the person of Mary what is going to be accomplished in the Church: the new birth of Christians.[26]

The Johannine Gospel casts light back on *Apocalypse 12*, a mysterious text that is a meeting place for all the biblical avenues leading to the Virgin Mary. The text reads as follows:

"Now a great sign appeared in heaven: a woman, adorned with the sun, standing on the moon, and with the twelve stars on her head for a crown. She was pregnant, and in labour, crying aloud in the pangs of

---

25. A. Feuillet, "Les adieux du Christ à sa mère et la maternité spirituelle de Marie (Jn. 19:25-27)," NRT 86 (1964), 469-489. The author took up this theme anew in his paper at the International Mariological Congress at Santo Domingo, "De muliere parturiente et de maternitate spirituali Mariae secundum evangelium sancti Johannis (16:21; 19:25-27)," *Maria in Sacra Scriptura*, Rome, Academia Mariana, 1967, vol. 5, pp. 111-122, and in *Biblica* 47 (1966), 169-184; 361-380; 557-573.

The pattern of Jesus' words — "Behold" with the designation of John and of Mary — is found also in Jn. 1:29, 36, 47. All these cases are "words of revelation" and not "words of power." They do not accomplish any transformation as do the sacramental words, but announce a mystery — here the mystery of the spiritual maternity of Mary and of the Church. Cf. M. de Goedt, "Un schème de révélation dans le quatrième Evangile," NTS 8 (1961-1962), 142-150.

26. Cf. the bibliography, *infra.*, p. 350.

childbirth. Then a second sign appeared in the sky, a huge red dragon which had seven heads and ten horns..., and the dragon stopped in front of the woman as she was having the child, so that he could eat it as soon as it was born from its mother. The woman brought a male child into the world, the son who was 'to rule the nations with an iron sceptre' (Ps. 2:9), and the child was taken straight up to God and to his throne, while the woman escaped into the desert, where God had made a place of safety ready, for her to be looked after in the twelve hundred and sixty days" (Apoc. 12:1–6).

Then Michael and his angels throw out of heaven the "great dragon," the ancient serpent, the one called the devil or Satan. Cast down onto earth with his angels he continues the fight:

"As soon as the devil found himself thrown down to earth, he sprang in pursuit of the woman, the mother of the male child, but she was given 'a huge pair of eagle's wings' (Dt. 32:11) to fly away from the serpent into the desert, to the place where she was to be looked after for 'a year and twice a year and half a year' (Dan. 7:25). So the serpent vomited water from his mouth, like a river, after the woman, to sweep her away in the current, but the earth came to her rescue; it opened its mouth and swallowed the river thrown up by the dragon's jaws. Then the dragon was enraged with the woman and went away to make war on the rest of her children, that is, all who obey God's commandments and bear witness for Jesus" (Apoc. 12:13–17).

It will readily be recognized that this text is obscure. Prophecy is mingled with events and with ways of viewing them. The account follows an order that is geared not to chronology but to typology.

The Marian interpretation of the passage is debated.

Rather rare with the Fathers, this interpretation was at first excluded by the scientific exegetes of an earlier generation. Beginning in 1953, however, a change of direction set in. In the mind of quite a number of renowned exegetes — Braun, Cerfaux, Dubarle, LeFrois, Feuillet, Lyonnet, cited at the end of this study in the bibliography, 9d4 — Apocalypse 12 refers to Mary and to the People of God at the same time, as do Jn. 19:25–27 and Lk. 1:28–55 and 2:35. But whereas these latter texts put the person of Mary in the foreground, Apoc. 12 refers in the first place to the community. Nonetheless the terms also fit Mary, who is preeminently the eschatological culmination of Israel, the Daughter of Zion giving birth to the Savior.

This manner of designating two realities at one and the same time is disconcerting for the western mind of today. It occurs frequently however in the Bible and corresponds to a deep understanding of God's plan. In John 6, for example, the bread of life designates the manna, faith, and the Eucharist, all at the same time, because these three realities correspond to the same divine plan. Likewise in Lk. 1–2, Jn. 19:25–27, and Apoc. 12 Israel, Mary, and the Church are all three referred to together as historical stages of one and the same eternal plan on which the whole attention of the inspired author is fixed.

The beginning of the passage echoes the prophecy of Is. 7:14 taken up by Mi. 5:1–2. As the *'almah* of Isaiah, the woman of the Apocalypse is a sign *(sēmeion)*. But here she appears in her triumph; the moon "under her feet" seems to indicate that she is raised above the vicissitudes of which this constantly changing planet is the symbol. As with Mary in Jn. 19:25–27, this heavenly personage is repeatedly designated by the word "woman" (Apoc. 12:1, 4, 12, 13–17). As with Mary, she is taken to be the Mother of Christ,[27] and

---

27. Apoc. 12:4–6, 12–13. The citation of Ps. 2:9 (perhaps the most clearly messianic of all the Psalms) in Apoc. 12:5 gives assurance that the "male child" here is Christ and not *only* the new people of God.

mother of the disciples of Christ, who are called "the rest of her children" (Apoc. 12:17). This last term is an echo of Gn. 3:14–15, where also the serpent (Apoc. 12:9 and 14) is at war against "the woman" and "her descendants":

Gen. 3: 14–15	Apoc. 12: 9, 13 and 17
God said to the *serpent*. . . .	The great dragon, the *primeval serpent* known as the devil or Satan. . . .
'I will make you enemies of each other: you and the *woman,*	sprang in pursuit of the *woman* . . . , but she was given a huge pair of eagle's wings to fly away from the serpent into the desert.
your offspring and *her offspring.*	Then the dragon was enraged with the woman and went away to make war on the *rest of her children,* that is, all who obey God's commandments and bear witness for Jesus.

To these points of contact between Genesis 3 and Apocalypse 12 could be added another, the *pains of childbearing* mentioned in Gn. 3:16 and Apoc. 12:2. For many centuries this was the detail that militated against the Marian interpretation of this passage: pain ill befitted a virgin birth. But comparison with another passage clears up the difficulty. In Apoc. 5:6 Christ appears in heaven as "a Lamb that seemed to have been sacrificed" (Cf. Jn. 19:36). The pains of the woman who in Apoc. 12:2 appears in the heavens are a counterpart of the immolation of the heavenly Lamb.[28]

Thus we are led back not to the birth at Bethlehem but to Christ's word from on the cross: "Son, this is your mother" (Jn. 19:25). There is question of Mary's spiritual motherhood and of the compassion by which the Mother of Jesus shared the sufferings of the immolated Lamb. John 19 and Apocalypse 12 closely correspond to each other. In both texts Mary's motherhood with respect to the disciples is envisaged in a context of pain (Jn. 10:25; Apoc. 12:17). In the Gospel the scene takes place on earth; in the Apocalypse, in heaven. Christ's immolation is prolonged there, as is Mary's pain: John, who sees glory in the Passion, continues to see the Passion in glory.[29]

---

28. L. Cerfaux, "'La vision de la femme et du dragon de l'Apocalypse en relation avec le Protévangile," ETL 31 (1955), 31, envisages another explanation: "An ancient author speaking in biblical and poetic language of a birth (virginal or not . . .) will use normal expressions. A woman in labor, about to give birth, means simply a woman who gives birth to a child." While proposing this explanation, Cerfaux does not exclude Braun's, which moreover is taken up also by Feuillet and is the one proposed above in the text. Somewhat weak from the exegetical point of view, this latter explanation has support in tradition, in that the moral interpretation of Apoc. 12 developed only after the time when authors envisaged a moral explanation of the pains of labor.

29. It should be added that serious exegetes have tried to see a hint of the Immaculate Conception in Apoc. 12. Cerfaux, *op. cit.,* pp. 32–33, is of the opinion that in Apoc. 12 Mary appears as "predestined to be the very beginning of the Church, and by the very fact possessing holiness . . . and the immaculate perfection of a world being born . . . , to a degree higher than all the saints." A. M. Dubarle, "La femme couronnée d'étoiles," *Mélanges bibliques . . . A. Robert,* Paris, Bloud, 1957, p. 518, reaches a similar conclusion: "Even before the attacks of the dragon, the woman appears surrounded with resplendent glory. As the new Jerusalem, she is a heavenly being, though still subject to the trials of earthly life. Here one can see the predestination of the Virgin in a brilliantly vivid description of its beginning. However this royal dignity does not prevent suffering and

Should the text be taken for an explicit revelation of the bodily glorification of Mary? The liturgy of the Assumption uses this text, welcoming an ancient tradition that dates back to Epiphanius (shortly before 377) though it does not crop up too frequently after him. The text does effectively supply expressions suggestive of the mystery: this mother who appears in the heavens above the recurring vicissitudes of time (12:1), this woman raised up on the wings of the great eagle (12:14), finally, the "place prepared" by God (12:6). In this last detail Braun sees heaven designated under the same terms as in Jn. 14:2.[30] All these expressions are capable of suggesting the mystery of the Assumption. The liturgy does not expect more of them, but simply recognizes in Apoc. 12 the biblical icon of the Assumption.

But on the level of strict exegesis nothing is more difficult than to weigh the value of these suggestions. Here there is question no longer of *contemplating* the dogma of the Assumption but of *establishing* it rigorously on its foundations. On this score prudence suggests imitating the caution shown by Pius XII: though he uses this text in the new Mass of the Assumption, though he mentions it in the Apostolic Bull *Munificentissimus* among the figures dear to the Scholastics, he does not make of it the biblical foundation of his dogmatic definition.

Conclusion

In the sixteenth century Protestants and Catholics too easily fell into agreement in speaking about the silence of Scripture on the Virgin Mary. This silence became a pretext for the former to renounce all mariology, and for the latter

---

contradiction. . . ." These hints, nevertheless, are very vague and distant, and to speak of them in terms of the Immaculate *Conception* is to go beyond the perspectives of exegesis alone.

30. Braun, *op. cit.,* pp. 161–168 (ET: pp. 158–163).

to develop a parascriptural mariology not without its dangers. The long-lived and ill-starred slogan about such silence should be laid to rest. Fortunately it is losing ground today, since Protestants are being led by the Scriptures to find Mary again, while Catholics are finding her again in the Scriptures.[31] Certainly, the Virgin's place in the Bible is a very discreet one. She appears there in connection with Christ, and not for her own interest. But her importance consists precisely in the intimacy of her bonds with Christ, bonds that appear to us in so many converging details.

In drawing up a list of the data supplied by Scripture on the Virgin Mary two classes of details must be distinguished: first, a nucleus of firm and precise information, and then a halo of suggestions.

1. Mary is a holy person, Virgin, and Mother of the Savior. Alone of all the saints she is present at all the basic moments of the history of salvation: not only at the beginning (Lk. 1–2) and the end (Jn. 19:27) of Christ's life in the mysteries of the Incarnation and the redemptive death, but also at the

---

31. The exploration of the theological riches of chapters one and two of Luke's gospel has been realized by both Catholic and Protestant exegetes. S. Lyonnet opened the way in *Biblica* 20 (1939), 131–141; H. Sahlin (Lutheran) took up the matter and was followed by the Anglican A. G. Herbert. The inquiry advanced more deeply on the Catholic side with Lyonnet again in *Ami du Clergé* 66 (1956), 33–48 and R. Laurentin, *Structure et théologie de Luc 1–2*, Paris, Gabalda, 1957. M. Thurian (Protestant) took up the essential conclusions of this study again in his book *Marie, figure de l'Eglise*, Taizé, 1962 (ET: *Mary, Mother of All Christians*, New York, Herder and Herder, 1964).

In a similar way concerning St. John, Braun profited from the insights of R. Bultmann, *Das Evangelium des Johannes*, Göttingen, 1941, p. 521. Bultmann interprets the text in the sense of a spiritual motherhood, with Mary here being the symbol of the Church. The Protestant F. Quievreux, "La maternité spirituelle de la Mère de Jésus dans saint Jean," *Supplément de la Vie Spirituelle* 5 (1952), # 20, 101–134, arrives at the spiritual motherhood also, but by the contestable paths of numerical symbolism. Cf. E. Hoskyns, in the following note.

inauguration of his ministry (Jn. 2) and at the birth of the Church (Acts 1:4). It is a discreet presence, silent most of the time, animated by the impulse of a pure faith and a love prompt to seize and follow the plans of God and the aspirations of men (Lk. 1:38, 39, 46–56; 2:22; Jn. 2:3).

2. This presence receives its full meaning when the living contact these texts have with one another and with the rest of the Bible is recognized, or better yet, when the texts are put back into the broad currents of biblical theology from which they stem. Mary appears at the culmination of the chosen people's history with a role like that of Abraham: by faith she takes possession of the promise he had received in faith. She is the summit where the chosen people give birth to their God and become the Church. If, according to the hints given by John and Luke, the perspective of Israel's history is enlarged into cosmic history and if Christ is seen inaugurating a new creation, Mary appears at this origin of salvation in a place corresponding to that of Eve:[32] she receives the word of life next to the new tree of life, where the

---

32. On the theme of the new creation in Luke, see the suggestions of A. Feuillet, "Marie et la nouvelle création," *Vie Spirituelle* 81 (1949), 467–478, and J. Schmitt, article in RSR 24 (1950), 371. Luke traces Christ's genealogy back to Adam, thinking perhaps of the Pauline theory of the New Adam. It is not improbable that in presenting the dialogue between Mary and the angel Gabriel he had in mind that between Eve and the serpent. But if, following the example of the Fathers, theologians have the right to develop objectively valid suggestions, the exegete must remain prudent in the matter.

On the contacts of John with Genesis 1–3, cf. E. Hoskyns, "Genesis 1–3 and St. John's Gospel," JTS 31 (1920), 210–218. The author shows how the fourth evangelist readily brought the first creation into contact with the coming of Christ, the new creation where the Holy Spirit again plays his role (Gen. 1:1 and Jn. 19:30). Hoskyns sees this rapprochement throughout, from the expression "In the beginning" (Jn. 1:1 and Gen. 1:1) to the final scenes in the "garden" (Jn. 19:41) which seem to imply an allusion to the garden of the original fall, including also the contact presented in the text above between Gen. 3:15, 19 and Jn. 2:1–2; 19:25–27.

first woman had welcomed the word of death, and thus becomes the new "mother of all who live." Here is a whole anthropology of woman, and one that opens out on God.

The sketch is indeed rich, but imprecise. The Holy Spirit did not define all the details of it, but this is in keeping with art which never materially reproduces all the details of a countenance. With time the Church will come to understand more fully the meaning of this sketch given so far only in outline.

SECOND PERIOD

FROM THE GOSPEL OF JOHN TO THE COUNCIL OF EPHESUS (90–431 A.D.)

The age of the Scriptures is followed by a complex period to which the year 431 can be assigned as limit, the year of the Council of Ephesus in the East and the year following the death of St. Augustine in the West.

This time division calls for two observations:

1. The period whose boundaries are thus set up cannot be put on the same level of importance as the one just studied. During the preceding period God was speaking. The message he delivered in words and actions was enclosed in Scriptures that are beyond compare, having in all truth (and not in pious metaphor) the Holy Spirit as their principal author. At the end of this first period revelation is closed, according to classical doctrine. Nothing more can be added to it from without. The Church is hereafter in possession of her treasure (Mt. 13:52); she cannot invent further but only keep taking her inventory, bringing truths into light, making them bear fruit. This is an unending task, rich in discovery and sometimes in surprise. In every man's life history it is only relatively late, often in the "evening of life," that the subsoil of infancy reveals what unsuspected riches were hidden in it.

Recollected experience lives a silent life in the memory of individuals and of peoples, and there with time it unfolds its genuine value. The memory that Irenaeus had kept of the teaching of Polycarp comes to mind as an example. Still more apropos is the word of Jesus himself, "The Holy Spirit . . . will remind you of all I have said to you." (Jn. 14:25; cf. 14:20). In the Church's memory revelation ripens and is transformed, and in a particularly surprising way the same thing happens inside that revelation to the countenance of Mary, the Mother of Jesus.

2. The Council of Ephesus does not bear any mark of abrupt innovation. It does not of a sudden set in motion a wave of piety toward the Virgin. Rather than a point of departure, it is the terminus of a long process that for some time was unrecognized, a process under way for about a century on the level both of doctrine and of culture. In the aftermath the "Marian" character of this Council was very much overstressed. The issue at stake and the object of debate at Ephesus was the unity of Christ and the "communication of idioms," as the term has it — in other words, the attribution to the second Person of the Trinity of whatever happened to him as a result of his Incarnation in our humanity: *God* was born, *God* suffered, *God* died on the cross. Though the patriarch Nestorius' challenge of the title *Theotokos* (Mother of God) was the determining occasion of the Council, it is not exact to say that this title was "defined" at Ephesus. Moreover the torchlight procession with which the people celebrated Nestorius' deposition, according to the testimony of St. Cyril, was gratuitously transformed by much later historians into a procession in honor of the Virgin Mary.

As a date, then, 431 does not exhibit to scientific history the "Marian" relief it was to take on in later history. It does, however, remain important for the object of this study, inasmuch as the official confirmation given the title *Theotokos* and the way this succinct expression came into relief after

431 dominate further developments. Thus it is that the Marian piety of the East, already in full bloom at the time of the Council, definitively found its doctrinal center and Christocentric focus.

During the period between the death of John the evangelist and the Council of Ephesus, light began to play more brightly on Mary's divine maternity, on her integral virginity, and on her holiness. This illumination took place in three phases:

1. A time of discretion and silence (90–190 A.D.)
2. A time of laborious hesitations (190–373 A.D.)
3. Finally, a time of harmonious solutions (373–431 A.D.).

At the end of this period two new problems are raised, problems that will take on considerable dogmatic importance in the nineteenth and twentieth centuries. During this period also the Virgin Mary enters definitively into the Christian cult and life of prayer. A fourth and fifth subsection in this part will treat these last two points.

1. Silent Growth:
The Eve-Mary Antithesis Explored
(2nd Century)

After the period of the Scriptures there follows what could be described as a stretch of fog and mist. In the Christian literature of the second century, inasmuch as it is known to us, the Virgin Mary occupies only a tiny place. Texts about her are rare and do little more than repeat in lustreless terms what Matthew and Luke had with much more relish: Mary is the Mother of Jesus, she is a virgin in her conceiving. The scriptural information is reduced almost to its simplest expression and a part of its wealth remains hidden. Mary's features concealed in the shadow, almost as in a fog.

Nevertheless toward the end of this quiet century a development builds up on one point. The parallel between Mary and Eve suggested by John and Luke is explicitly treated by two authors: Saint Justin (d. c.165) raises the question in passing,[1] and Saint Irenaeus (d. c.202) gives it theological status.[2]

This theme has a twofold importance, for doctrinal development on the one hand, and still more for the integration of Mary into the history of salvation. During this period the theme does not become the object of discussion, as will other themes later to be studied, but rather offers the substance of an eminently positive meditation. The thought of the Fathers of the Church is intuitive more than deductive, symbolic more than logical; it does not advance in the form of syllo-

---

1. *Dialogue with Trypho* 100, 4–6, ed. G. Archambault, *Justin, Dialogue avec Tryphon,* Paris, 1909, vol. 2, pp. 122–124, PG 6:709c; ET of excerpt: Jurgens, # 141: "He became man by the Virgin so that the course which was taken by disobedience in the beginning through the agency of the serpent, might be also the very course by which it would be put down. For Eve, a virgin and undefiled, conceived the word of the serpent, and bore disobedience and death. But the Virgin Mary received faith and joy when the 'angel Gabriel' announced to her the glad tidings *(euaggelizomenou)* that the 'Spirit' of the Lord would 'come upon' her and 'the power of the Most High' would 'overshadow' her, for which reason 'the Holy One' being 'born of her' is the 'Son of God' (Lk. 1:35). And she replied, 'Be it done unto me according to thy word' (Lk. 1:38)."
2. Among the many studies of the Marian theology of St. Irenaeus, cf. especially the following: G. Jouassard, "Le 'premier né de la Vierge' chez saint Irénée et saint Hippolyte," RSR 12 (1932), 509–532 and 13 (1933), 25–27, along with the article cited *infra,* p. 71, n. 26; J. Garçon, *La mariologie de Saint Irénée,* Lyon, Paquet, 1932, with a bibliography of earlier studies, p. 3; B. Przbylski, *De Mariologia Sancti Irenaei Lugdunensis,* Rome, 1937; N. F. Moholy, "Saint Irenaeus, the Father of Mariology," *Studia Mariana . . . VII, First Franciscan National Marian Congress . . . 1950,* Burlington (Wis.), Franciscan National Marian Council, 1952, pp. 129–187; G. Jouassard, "La théologie mariale de saint Irénée," *Les Actes du VIIe Congrès marial national: L'Immaculée Conception,* Lyon, 1954, pp. 265–274.

gisms but by the confrontation of theses and symbols rich in truth. Between Eve and Mary the Fathers discern a parallel and a contrast. The situation of each is parallel, since in both cases a woman, a virgin, is author of a moral act on which hinges the salvation of all humanity. But their personal commitment sets up a contrast, since Eve defies God and disobeys, whereas Mary believes and is obedient. The result is, on the one hand, sin and death, and on the other, salvation and life.

Irenaeus gives bold relief to a theme only outlined by Justin. With Irenaeus the Eve-Mary parallel is not simply a literary effect nor a gratuitous improvisation, but an integral part of his theology of salvation. One idea is the key to this theology: God's saving plan is not a mending or a "patch-up job" done on his first product; it is a resumption of the work from the beginning, a regeneration from head downwards, a *recapitulation* in Christ. In this radical restoration each one of the elements marred by the fall is renewed in its very root. In terms of the symbol developed by Irenaeus, the knot badly tied at the beginning is unknotted, untied in reverse *(recirculatio)*: Christ takes up anew the role of Adam, the cross that of the tree of life. In this ensemble Mary, who corresponds to Eve, holds a place of first importance. According to Irenaeus her role is necessary to the logic of the divine plan. After having announced the broad outlines of the divine program, he links up Mary's role with it by the adverb *consequenter,* an expression so bold and disconcerting that it is shorn of its force by most translators:

> "*Consequently,* . . . there is Mary, the obedient virgin. . . . Eve, still a virgin, was disobedient and became for herself and for the whole human race a cause of death. Mary, a virgin and obedient, became for herself and for the whole human race a cause of salvation. . . . From Mary to Eve there is a taking up again of the same path

(recirculatio). . . . For what is tied together could not otherwise be untied than by untangling the knot from which the tie-up had arisen. . . . That is why in beginning his genealogy with the Savior Luke went backwards to Adam,[3] showing thereby that [the true movement of generation] does not run from these ancestors toward the Savior but from him toward them, according to regeneration in the gospel of life. And thus it is that Eve's disobedience was untied by Mary's obedience: for what the virgin Eve tied up by her disbelief, the virgin Mary untied by her faith" (*Adversus Haereses*, 3, 22).[4]

---

3. While Mt. 1:1–16 enumerates the generations descending from Abraham to Christ, Lk. 3:23–28 moves back from Christ to "Adam who was of God." This suggested to Irenaeus that Adam depends on Christ, according to the genealogy of grace.

4. *Adversus Haereses* 3, 22, ed. Massuet in PG 7:958–960; ed. Sagnard in *Sources chrétiennes* 34, Lyon-Paris, 1952, pp. 378–382 (where the *consequenter* is inadequately translated "en connexion étroite"); ET of excerpt in Jurgens, # 224. [The translation in the text above is based on the author's French rendering.] In this first of Irenaeus' texts his thought is accessible in its source, where it springs from his theology of the *recapitulatio* and *recirculatio*. Later texts of Irenaeus express the same idea: a) *Haereses* 5, 19, 1, PG 7: 1175a–1176a, ed. Harvey II, pp. 375–376: "Quemadmodum adstrictum est morti genus humanum per virginem, salvatur per virginem . . . — Just as the human race was bound over to death by a virgin, so it is saved by a virgin. . . ." b) *Epideixis* 33, PO 12 (1919), p. 685 (Armenian text and English translation) and pp. 772–773 (French translation). A revised French translation was proposed by M. M. L. Froidevaux, RSR 39 (1951), 372 (= *Mélanges Jules Lebreton,* vol. 1): "It was by means of a disobedient virgin that man was stricken, fell, and died; similarly, it was by a Virgin who obeyed God's word that man . . . again recovered life. . . . It was just and necessary for Adam to be restored in Christ, so that mortality might be absorbed and swallowed up in immortality, and for Eve to be restored in Mary, so that a Virgin who had become the advocate of a virgin might efface and abolish a virgin's disobedience by her own virginal obedience." These texts were studied by G. Jouassard, "La Nouvelle Eve chez les Pères Anténicéens," EM 12 (1954), 37–40. The

Understandably this parallel is not a simple collation of the account of the Annunciation with the account of the Fall. A middle term, the divine plan, unites the two elements. Eve was a preliminary sketch; Mary is the restoration and completion of the project which the first woman had caused to miscarry, and so too is the Church. The two contrasts, Eve-Mary and Eve-Church, will run their course through the writings of the Fathers. They will climax in a comparison rich in positive points of agreement between Mary and the Church, as suggested in the following diagram:[5]

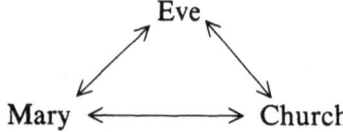

At the beginning the two divergent branches of this parallel are markedly differentiated: in welcoming salvation Mary takes on the role Eve had *at the time of* the Fall, whereas the Church, drawn from the side of the new Adam (Gn. 2:21 parallel to Jn. 19:34) takes on Eve's role *before and after* the Fall as Adam's spouse and helper and by him "mother of all who live" (Gn. 3:20). But slowly and progressively all the features of Eve's role will be recognized in Mary. As early as 377 Epiphanius sees in her the "mother of all who live," according to the expression Gn. 3:20. The last detail of the parallel, however, will not be drawn out until during the second half of the thirteenth century when Mary is spoken of as "a helpmate fit" for the new Adam, according to the words of Gn. 2:18 (cf. *infra,* "FOURTH PERIOD," especially note 30).

---

texts on Gen. 3:15 represent an independent strain of thought coming from another set of ideas studied by R. Laurentin, "L'interprétation de Genèse 3:15 . . ." EM 12 (1954), 93–97.

5. On the Eve-Mary and Mary-Church parallels, cf. bibliography, p. 359.

Leaving aside these anticipations and returning to the second century it can be said in conclusion that Justin and especially Irenaeus single out an element of doctrinal development. They bring to light the meaning of Mary in the plan of salvation. Mary plays an inaugural role analogous to that of Eve. This implies a whole theology of woman, as she appears not passive and secondary but in many respects active and directive. With Irenaeus this line of thought attains a force of expression that has never been surpassed. Later writers will broaden the bases of the comparison but to our day no one has expressed it in a way more compact or more profound.

2. Divine Maternity, Virginity, Holiness: A Time of Hesitations (End of the 2nd Century to Last Quarter of the 4th Century)

Following this stretch of half-silence broken at its end by the great voice of Irenaeus comes the clamor of an initial struggle brought on by thoughtless invective. Instead of advance there is painful hesitation. Four points are the object of this first theological reflection: the title of Mother of God *(Theotokos)*, Mary's virginity *after* childbirth — and in the birth itself of Jesus *(virginitas post partum* and *virginitas in partu)* — and finally, the holiness of Mary.[6]

1. The first notion becomes clear smoothly and by degrees. The origins of the title *Theotokos* are unknown.[7] Witnesses

---

[6]. What follows is dependent on the study of G. Jouassard, "Marie à travers la patristique. Maternité divine, virginité, sainteté," *Maria* 1 (1949), pp. 59–157. Cf. also Jouassard, "Deux chefs de file en théologie mariale . . . Epiphane et Ambroise," *Gregorianum* 42 (1961), 6–12 and 27–29.

[7]. On the origins of the title *Theotokos* cf. Appendix # 4.

prior to 325 are doubtful and apocryphal. But beginning with that date evidence of the title is multiplied. The expression is spread abroad universally, even in the Church of Antioch at the time when Nestorius is bringing it into question; he himself seems to have employed it in his earlier preaching. A century of calm possession therefore preceded the controversy that arose in 430.

The other three points, on the contrary, disentangle themselves only in an atmosphere of contradiction.

2. The perpetual virginity of Mary *(virginitas post partum)* was denied by Tertullian and other authors following his lead, the first of them Bonosus, condemned around 392.[8]

3. The thesis of the virginal integrity of Mary in childbirth *(virginitas in partu)* encountered similar difficulty and left Saint Jerome hesitant at least, stout defender as he otherwise was of Mary's perpetual virginity.[9]

4. The holiness of Mary comes to light in still more labored a manner. Several Fathers see nothing awry in the thought that there would be some lack of faith or some other sin in the Mother of Jesus; the Greeks are particularly so minded: Origen, Basil, Gregory of Nazianz, John Chrysostom (with special stress), and Cyril of Alexandria himself.[10]

In the West Ambrose and Augustine give the doctrine its definitive foundation. More slowly and not without debate the East soon reaches the same conviction. After the Council of Ephesus the last patches of error and indecision dissipate rapidly.

These difficulties and the attendant opposition can occa-

---

8. Jouassard, "Marie à travers . . ." pp. 100, 105–108.

9. *Ibid.,* pp. 108–113.

10. G. Jouassard, "Sainteté de Marie chez les Pères," EM 5 (1947), pp. 11–33, and "L'Interprétation par saint Cyrille d'Alexandrie de la scène de Marie au pied de la Croix," *Virgo Immaculata,* Rome, Academia Mariana, 1955, vol. 4, pp. 28–47. Cf. *idem,* "Marie à travers . . ." pp. 91–100 and 114–122. G. M. Ellero, "Maternità e virtù di Maria in S. Giovanni Crisostomo," *Marianum* 25 (1963), 420–446.

sion surprise. At first hearing they may even scandalize certain readers. There is no point in hiding them, since truth cannot be served by painting a false picture, and its integrity demands loyal acceptance of all the facts. There remains the task of understanding their meaning. Why did this groping and these misunderstandings occur? Two reasons may be given:

In the first place, it was proper that the Virgin should remain veiled for a while during an epoch when the mother-goddesses of paganism still held sway over the minds of men. The danger here was not unreal. In 377, at a time when Mary was beginning to find her place in Christian cult, Saint Epiphanius had to use energetic language in reproving the "Collyridians," women who had improvised a liturgy patterned on pagan usage and involving priestesses who offered sacrifice to Mary in the form of loaves called *collyrida*.[11] In the sixth and seventh centuries traces could still be found of an opinion defending the eternal preexistence of Mary;[12] a Coptic papyrus of the seventh century condemns it.[13]

In the second place, God seems to have willed here as elsewhere to leave it to the effort of the human intelligence

---

11. *Panarion* 79, PG 42:740c–756a; GCS 37 (Epiphanius 3), pp. 475–484.

12. Pseudo-Caesarius of Nazianzus (c.518–530), *Dialogus* 1, PG 38:905. Question 40 begins "What do you think of the Virgin Mary? Is she created or uncreated?" But no response is given to the first part of the question. Theodosius of Alexandria (d. 565) seems to allude to the same opinion in his *Homily on the Dormition,* ed. Chaine, *Revue de l'Orient chrétien,* p. 308, where Christ says to Mary, "I did not want to let you know death. . . . But if that happened to you, wicked men would take you to be a heavenly power that had descended on earth and would deem . . . the Incarnation . . . to be an illusion."

13. F. Robinson, *Coptic Apocryphal Gospels, Texts and Studies,* IV, 2, Cambridge, 1896, pp. 2 and 5: "Let whoever says Mary is a *dynamis* be anathema. . . . Let whoever says that the Virgin was not born as we are be anathema." P. Duprey, *Proche Orient chrétien* 4 (1954), 299 and 5 (1955), 306, has assembled texts leading him to the conjecture that these are opinions in the extreme wing of the Julianists.

to discover certain aspects of the truth, having given sufficient ground for them. Perhaps it was his way of assuring that man would not react toward revelation with that ennui and disaffection that seizes him before a truth offered ready-made; perhaps he thereby enabled man to enjoy the rich taste proper to truths that have had to be dearly won; perhaps here again he was raising man to the role of fellow worker (1 Cor. 3:9), a role not without purpose. At any rate, bound up with such play given to human initiative was the risk of groping search and reversal that is inescapably the other side of created freedom. This is assuredly one of the keys to the history of salvation.

A comparison can serve to illustrate the course of these shortcomings. In an ancient monument sometimes a fresco will be discovered hidden under some more recent coat of plaster. The first blows of the chisel on this outer coat are at times going to mar the underlying image. Absorbed as he is in his scraping away, the workman may not immediately be aware that he is destroying a precious piece of art. Something like this happened in the third and fourth centuries. Preoccupied with some other object than the Virgin Mary, preachers in search of striking examples and controversialists carried away by the heat of their arguments used her to make some point or other. This maneuver led them, without their noticing it, to trample under foot the mystery of holiness or virginity of which she is the outstanding witness; certain aspects of the dogma still badly explained were thus distorted. Fortunately errors such as these, to the contrary of the damage suffered by a fresco, can be repaired, for they belong to the order of vital and spiritual reality: revealed truth bears within itself the principle of its own regeneration.

In the presence of the premature formulations coming from these preachers and polemicists the Christian conscience reacts. A controversy breaks out. There is hesitation, reflection, impassioned argument. But more or less rapidly the partial answers give way to the whole answer, the true answer. Once found, this answer satisfies the legitimate demands of the two parties to the controversy and harmoniously fits into the ensemble of Christian doctrine.

The problem of the development of dogma emerges here in all its complexity and, at the same time, with a warning against certain over-simplifications. Scrupulous examination of the facts forbids prematurely classifying as "truth" or "error" opinions expressed before the Christian conscience had become fully aware of a problem. Still less justifiably can their proponents be divided into "friends" and "enemies" of the Virgin. Saint Cyril is certainly a better theologian than Nestorius; but nothing proves that he was more "fervent" toward the Virgin Mary, to whom he did not hesitate to ascribe certain weaknesses and sins. The truth attained at the end of each phase of dogmatic development appears less as the counterpart of an error than the happy medium between two errors or (more exactly and in order to eliminate the idea of compromise suggested by the expression "happy medium") as the crest where two inclines of revelation meet. Dogma in its integrity ordinarily presents itself as the summit meeting of two partial and complementary aspects of the word of God.

It is thus that the conflicts raised in the fourth and fifth centuries along with their harmonious resolution can be understood.

3. Advancing Solutions
(373–431 A.D.)

1. Mary's perpetual virginity *(virginitas post partum)* found its apt and proper expression between two misapprehensions. It would have been a serious error to propose this doctrine as a corollary of Manichaean theses on the intrinsic

perversity of marriage.[14] Helvidius was an adversary of the Manichaeans and suspected that their ideas had made inroads among the promoters of asceticism. Carried away by his enthusiasm he wanted to deprive his opponents of every pretext of this kind. Taking whatever is at hand, as is done in the heat of polemic, he hurriedly seized upon the gospel passages where there is question of the brothers of the Lord[15] (in reality, according to Palestinian usage, his cousins) and presented Mary as the model for mothers of large families. But neither the Manichaeans nor their impulsive adversaries were correct. Any tie that would bind the fact of Mary's virginity to an erroneous motive had to be broken. With Jerome, Ambrose, and Augustine,[16] the Christian conscience rapidly perceived that Mary's exclusive consecration to God was not reconcilable with the exclusive body gift implied by marriage, however noble it is.

2. The question of Mary's virginity at the time of the birth of Christ *(virginitas in partu)* was in still more delicate a situation. Those most inclined to propose this doctrine were Docetists, for whom Christ's body was only an appearance. The apocryphal gospels had dangerously set out along this way.[17]

---

14. On this intrusion of Manichaeism into the question of virginity, see Jouassard, "Marie à travers . . ." p. 106, n. 24; p. 108, etc.

15. On this question see the article "Frères du Seigneur" in *Dictionnaire apologétique de la foi catholique* II, col. 131–148, and especially "Brüder . . . Jesu" in *Lexicon der Marienkunde* and "Brethren of Jesus" in *Sacramentum Verbi* I, pp. 86–88. The interpretation given in these articles is more and more admitted by Protestants; cf. for example G. Schmied, "Ma croyance en Marie," *Dialogue sur la Vierge,* Lyon, Vitte, 1951, pp. 20–24.

16. Jouassard, "Marie à travers . . ." pp. 108–111, and "Deux chefs . . ." p. 28.

17. Jouassard, "Marie à travers . . ." pp. 82, 109–112. J. C. Plumpe, "Some Little-known Early Witnesses to Mary's 'Virginitas in partu'", TS 9 (1948), 567–577, conscientiously studied the witness of several apocryphal writings which he judged to date from the end of the first century to the

In the violence of their struggle against Docetism Tertullian and Saint Jerome (in the first part of his career) resorted to an extremist kind of realism in insisting on the normal character of Christ's coming to birth. They even had recourse to descriptions in bad taste. It was not an easy matter to reconcile the two demands of the faith — integral physical and corporal maternity, and integral physical and corporal virginity. Here again it was necessary to disengage them from the false principles with which certain authors had compromised them, and this was the task of Ambrose.[18] He saw two things clearly: Christ's birth was not a phantom birth but a real one, and it was not ordinary but miraculous. The bishop of Milan carefully traces the dividing line between what is natural and what is supernatural in this childbearing.[19] In

---

middle of the second. But what is to be thought of the primitive text of these moving accounts of which we possess only late versions? On evaluating such witnesses see what is said *infra,* Appendix #5, on the infancy apocryphals, and Appendix #6, on the apocryphals of the Assumption.

18. Cf. the excellent studies of C. Neumann, *The Virgin Mary in the Works of Saint Ambrose,* Fribourg, University Press, 1962, pp. 105–180; J. Huhn, *Das Geheimnis des Jungfrau-Mutter Maria nach dem Kirchenvater Ambrosius,* Würzburg, Echter-Verlag, 1954, pp. 110–116; G. Jouassard, "Deux chefs . . ." pp. 20–26.

19. *De Incarnationis dominicae sacramento* 54, PL 16:832ab: "Multa . . . in Eodem (sc. Christo) et *secundum naturam* invenies et *ultra naturam.* Secundum conditionem etenim corporis, in utero fuit, natus est, lactatus est, in praesepio est collocatus, sed supra conditionem Virgo concepit, Virgo generavit, ut crederes quia Deus erat qui novabat naturam et homo qui secundum naturam nascebatur ex homine — Many things . . . you will find in Him both according to nature and above nature. According to the human condition he was in the womb, was born, was nursed, was placed in a manger, but beyond the human condition the Virgin conceived, the Virgin begot Him, so that you might believe that it was God who was renewing nature and a man who according to nature was being born of man."

A precision of vocabulary should be added: the expression *virginitas post partum* (virginity after birth) today signifies that Mary kept her virginity *after the birth of Christ.* But with the ancients it sometimes

becoming incarnate, God did not abolish the flesh but brought it a pledge of its eschatological renewal. Thus Mary found herself freed of the servitude expressed in Gn. 3:16, "You shall give birth to your children in pain," and her virginity remained intact. This discovery is much indebted to the biblical doctrine of the "new creation" promised by the prophets and of the "new birth" by which it is inaugurated. For Christ's birth is the replica and the manifestation of his eternal birth, and the exemplar and pledge of baptismal birth; his human birth participates in the condition of these other two births of which it is the cosmic sign. It is also an anticipation of the eschatological birth.

3. Opposition concerning Mary's holiness was more complex and less clear-cut and admitted of resolution without great controversy. Events can be schematically presented as follows. On the one hand there was a progressive discovery of the Virgin's holiness (closely tied in with the discovery of her virginity); on the other hand there was a tendency, in face of the pharisaical self-sufficiency of certain ascetics, to underline that Christ is "alone the Holy One," and that all men are sinners. Preachers were strongly tempted to find in the Mother of the Savior herself an example of this universal penchant for evil of which they so wished to convince their audiences. Using the Scriptures with that levity sometimes found among preachers and moralists, they thought they found vainglory, doubt, or presumption in her conduct.[20]

---

designated what today we call *virginitas in partu* (virginity at birth). Thus the antiphon, "*Post partum* Virgo inviolata permansisti — After childbirth you remained a pure virgin," has in view Mary's virginal integrity in function of the mystery of Christmas, not her perpetual virginity. Its intended meaning is the permanence of her virginal integrity during Christ's birth.

20. The principal text invoked was Lk. 2:35. The sword foretold by Simeon was taken as the announcement of a doubt in Mary's soul at the time of the Passion. Cf. the bibliography, *supra,* p. 58, n. 10. On St. Augustine's elimination of these doubts, prepared for by St. Ambrose, cf. *infra,* p. 69, n. 23.

Such an example was capable of catching attention, but it also shocked Christian faith. The intention of these preachers was good and their principles in the main were excellent: Christ is "alone holy" in himself, alone metaphysically incapable of sin, alone never in need of redemption. But they went astray in confusing Mary with the common lot of humanity here. Little by little the light of revelation dissipated these errors. The holiness without taint that is Mary's was dogmatically recognized without further contest.

4. The title *Theotokos* (Mother of God) was the object of the most marked theological opposition. After more than a century of calm acceptance of this formula, the need was felt of reflecting on it to find exactly where the correct interpretation of it lay between two opposed errors. One error, against which Nestorius had taken up arms, would have made the Virgin the Mother of Christ in his divinity, and this was all the more menacing an error since mythology still nourished imaginations with the figure of the "mother-goddess." The other error, that of the Nestorians themselves, outlawed the title and refused to recognize the truth it contained: it failed to see that to deny that the *Mother of Christ* is *Mother of God* is to deny that Christ is God. The happy medium consisted in holding that the Virgin is Mother of God for having borne, in his humanity, a Son who is personally God. This is what the Council of Ephesus made perfectly clear.[21]

The sharpness of these debates can be easily understood, though their complicated course is perhaps over-simplified here. Apart from the fact that a healthy reaction against the pagan cults was creating a climate unfavorable to the appreciation of Mary's role, the people most inclined to emphasize her privileges were those least aware of the dogmatic counterpart these privileges had. The Manichaeans, who held

---

21. On the details of the controversy cf. G. Jouassard, "Marie à travers..." pp. 122–136; Nilus a Sancto Brocardo, *De Maternitate divina ... Nestorii Constantinopolitani et Cyrilli Alexandrini sententia*, Rome, 1944; T. Camelot, *Ephèse*, Paris, Orante, 1962, pp. 1–75.

marriage in contempt, were more disposed than others to defend Mary's virginity after childbirth; the Docetists, who denied the reality of Christ's body, were most disposed to defend her virginity in giving birth *(in partu)*; the Pelagians, who abusively championed man's natural will-power, were staunch defenders of her perfect holiness; and minds still seduced by pagan cults showed high esteem for the title *Theotokos*. It cannot be claimed that these heretics were the promoters of Mary's privileges. They served rather as scarecrows frightening the faithful away from her, because their principles (or their explicit affirmations) shed a false light on Mary's attributes. It was not easy to distinguish these caricatures from the first authentic affirmations of Mary's privileges. Those who were combating error in all its forms were tempted to consider these first formulations of dogma en bloc as branches of an evil tree which should be uprooted.

However little the atmosphere of these controversies, which today are a matter of history, can be reconstructed, it is understandable how these obsessions and suspicions hampered the explicitation of Marian doctrine. The true servants of the Church were not always those who attributed new titles of glory to the Virgin — "new jewels to her crown," as is sometimes said — but rather those who set such titles in their true light. Far from being narrow, they were great minds capable of viewing things in perspective and of taking into consideration all the aspects of a truth, and thus of associating each Marian "privilege" with its counterpart, without which it would have taken the form of a heresy. Thus her perpetual virginity *(post partum)* was viewed in association with the grandeur of marriage; her virginity in childbearing *(in partu)* with the reality of the Incarnation; her holiness with her quality of being a redeemed person; the divine fruit of her maternity with the human humility of its foundation, namely, a bodily generation similar to that of other men, except that it was virginal. Developed independently of these complementary truths, the dogmas that became explicit in the fourth and fifth centuries would have risked taking the shape of a gnosis foreign to the body of Christian doctrine.

4. Two New Problems

Other examples of this process can be found toward the end of the period now being studied. Two new questions crop up at that time: the Assumption shortly before 377, and the Immaculate Conception in 430.

a. *The Problem of the Assumption (377)*

Saint Epiphanius, the bishop of Salamis, raised this first question concerning the end of Mary's earthly career. He did so in an altogether incidental way in his famous letter to the Christians of Arabia, inserted in his *Panarion* in 377. He had never heard, he said, of any tomb of Mary at Jerusalem nor of her death there. He does not even know whether she died or not. He understands only that her end was something worthy of her and in it he surmises there probably was some prodigy involved. But in the absence of any information thereon, he prefers to imitate the silence that the sacred writings keep. In them, in fact, there is not a word about

> "the death of Mary, nor about whether she died, nor about whether she was buried or was not buried. . . . Scripture has kept complete silence because of the greatness of the prodigy, in order not to strike the mind of man with excessive astonishment. For my own part, I do not dare speak of the matter. I shall keep my mind on it to myself and remain silent" (*Panarion,* 78, 10–11).[22]

---

22. *Panarion* 78, 10–11; PG 42:716ad; GCS 37 (Epiphanius 3), pp. 461–462. Cf. Joussard, "Deux chefs . . ." pp. 12–14.

After having shown that Lk. 2:35 can be taken to suggest that Mary died as a martyr and that, to the contrary, Apoc. 12:14 seems to imply she was taken alive into heaven, he resumes his thought:

> "It is possible that that came about in Mary's case. I do not affirm it, however, in any absolute way, and I do not say that she remained immortal. But neither do I affirm that she is mortal. Scripture, in fact, has risen above the human mind and left this element unknown out of reverence for this incomparable Virgin, in order to cut short any base or ignoble thought in her regard. Did she die? We simply do not know" *(Ibid.).*

With the question thus raised, a double reply will soon begin to take shape: the reply of the liturgy that will celebrate the *dies natalis* of the Virgin, and the reply of the apocryphals that will recount, in one yarn strung along to another however contradictory, Mary's last moments, her funeral, the exceptional condition of her body and soul in the region beyond the tomb and in the heavenly realm, etc. The outcome of all this will be taken up later.

As far as the present period under study is concerned, it will be sufficient to single out the lesson, which again is the same: the true servants of the faith were not the authors of these apocryphals, improvising tales borrowed from mythical lore as if to describe every detail of Mary's death, but rather the sober Epiphanius, formulating the question with a sharp sense of mystery, and later on the theologians who made the legendary accounts of the Dormition pass through the crucible of dogmatic criteria.

b. *The Problem of the Immaculate Conception (430)*

The same lesson, in still more striking a manner, emerges in another field of inquiry toward the end of the period being studied. In the course of the gigantic conflict that pitted St. Augustine against the Pelagians, two skirmishes raised the problem of Mary's holiness with sharpening intensity.

1. It is not possible to give an extended treatment of Pelagianism here. This heresy was a reaction against Manichean pessimism and took the form of an excessive optimism concerning the capabilities of human nature, to the detriment of the necessary role of grace. During the first phase of his controversy Pelagius argumentatively presented Augustine with the case of the Virgin "whom it is *necessary to recognize as sinless.*" Until then no one had expressed Mary's holiness in such a clear-cut formula. In such heated argumentation there could have easily arisen the temptation to dismiss the heretic's thesis. Saint Augustine resolved the difficulty from the beginning with a genial touch. He granted his opponent's statement, but gave it a wholly different meaning: this sanctity of hers was an *exception, having God's grace as its principle,* and not free will alone.[23]

2. Julian of Eclanum carried the conflict onto more delicate terrain in discussing the absence not of actual sin but of the sin of the human race. This Pelagian author was thus the

---

23. An exposition of Pelagius' objection on the Virgin ("quam dicit 'sine peccato confiteri necesse esse pietati' — whom he says 'piety demands that we believe to be without sin' ") and Augustine's answer (". . . Maria de qua propter honorem Domini, nullam prorsus, cum de peccatis agitur, haberi volo quaestionem — . . . Mary, concerning whom I wish to raise no objection when it touches the subject of sins, out of honor to the Lord") will be found in *De natura et gratia* 42; CSEL 60, pp. 263–264; PL 44:267; ET of excerpt, Willis #584. Cf. Jouassard, "Marie à travers . . ." p. 115, and "Deux chefs . . ." pp. 15–19.

A Pelagianizing conception of Mary's holiness will be found in certain Byzantine authors of the 14th century, notably Nicholas Cabasilas (d. c.1388) and Demetrius Chrysoloras (d. c.1400), who goes so far as to say that she "acquired" a "greater beauty" than that of the first man, "not by grace but by her own work." (Unedited text, Escorial 164, fol. 76v, cited by A. Wenger, "La nouvelle Eve dans la théologie byzantine," EM 13 (1955), p. 56.)

first to deny explicity that the Virgin Mary had ever been subject to the sway of original sin. To Augustine he objected, "By the original condition [that you attribute to her] you give Mary herself over to the devil." Augustine himself cites the famous objection as it must have been made to him.[24]

Here the bishop of Hippo did not in reply show as masterly a touch as in the preceding controversy. He sought a way out with an ambiguous text. Looking back on his text, of course, it is possible to discern the two requirements of tradition, namely, the universal need of redemption and Mary's exceptional mode of redemption in being preserved from all sin. But subsequent authors for centuries to come were to see in Augustine's text a denial of the privilege of her Immaculate Conception.[25]

Here again the apparent defender of the Virgin, Julian of Eclanum, was a heretic. He presented a true attribute in a false light: for him the Immaculate Conception was not a unique privilege nor even a particular effect of divine grace, but simply the common lot of all Christians. In reply Augustine was correct in emphasizing the universal sway of original sin and the necessity of grace for overcoming sin. The eventual dogmatic definition of the Immaculate Conception will be incomparably closer to Augustine than to his adversary, when it affirms the *unique* character of Mary's privilege and the element of *preservation by the Redeemer's grace* which is its very essence.

---

24. Cited by St. Augustine, *Opus imperfectum adversus Julianum* 4, 122; PL 45: 1417 "Tu ipsam Mariam diabolo, nascendi conditione transcribis — You write Mary herself off to the devil by the circumstances of her birth."

25. *Ibid.,* PL 45:1419 "Non transcribimus diabolo Mariam conditione nascendi, sed ideo: quia ipsa conditio solvitur gratia renascendi — We do not write Mary off to the devil by the circumstances of her birth, but for this reason: these very circumstances are taken care of by the grace of rebirth." Jouassard, "Marie à travers . . ." pp. 116–121 gives a commentary on this text.

However, for having been prematurely presented in a distorted form by the heretics and for having thereby encountered the opposition of Saint Augustine, the idea of the untainted conception of Mary will for centuries remain suspect in the West. Thus it is that the Latins, hitherto considerably ahead in this matter, will now fall behind the Greeks, while among the latter the appreciation of Mary's original holiness will continue to grow on into the eighth and ninth centuries.

5. Mary's Entry Into Christian Worship

Did the Christians of the time consider themselves in living relationship with Mary in the communion of saints?

Toward the end of this period certain authors express the conviction that the motherhood of the *Theotokos* overflows beyond the person of Jesus and has a universal value in the order of salvation. About 377 Epiphanius calls Mary "Mother of all who live" by analogy and contrast with Eve.[26] Severian of Gabala (d. after 408) calls her "Mother of salvation."[27] Shortly after this period Theodotus of Ancyra (d. before 448)[28] will call her "Mother of the economy," referring to the "economy of salvation" familiar to Greek terminology. Proclus of Constantinople (d. 446) will bring the underlying idea out into the open in saying that Mary "engendered the Mystery."[29]

The perspective here is not that of Saint Paul who in some way opposes the condition of Christ in his birth with his

---

26. Epiphanius, *Panarion* 78, 18; PG 42:728c; GCS 37 (Epiphanius 3), p. 468. Cf. Jouassard, "Deux chefs . . ." pp. 15–19. There is already a glimmering of the idea in St. Irenaeus, according to Jouassard, in an article in *Nouvelle Revue Mariale* 1955, #7, 217–232.
27. *Oratio 6, De mundi creatione* 10, PG 56:498.
28. *Homily 4*, PG 77:1393c; cf. 1351–1352.
29. *tiktousa mustērion*, in *Sermon 13*, 19, PG 65:729b.

condition as the risen one, his abasement in the flesh with his new life in the spirit. The perspective is rather that of Luke 1–2 and John 1, where the Incarnation is presented as already the radiant origin of the mystery of salvation. The texts that have just been cited do not consider Mary's role in the economy as issuing from the Resurrection, nor do they yet attribute to her any activity or motherly sentiment with regard to Christians. Retrospectively they consider the Incarnation in the light of the Resurrection of which it was the guarantee, and in that light they grasp the universal scope both of the consent given by Mary at the origin of salvation and of the motherhood that flowed from her consent. In such texts this origin of salvation is not a thing of the past; it has about it an enduring quality. The mystery of the Annunciation is for them salvation come into this world, the germ of the mystery around which the entire life of the Church gravitates. The same must be said of texts of this period that are found in the West.[30]

Is there perhaps more in the earlier text of Origen (d. 253/4) that refers not to the mystery of the Incarnation but to the last will and testament of Jesus, "Son, here is your mother?" Origen expresses himself as follows:

---

30. For the Latin writers Augustine opens the way with the famous text of *De Virginitate* V, 5 and VI, 6, CSEL 41, pp. 239–240: ". . . *mother in spirit*, not of our Head, the Savior, of whom rather she is born spiritually . . . , but clearly mother of the members that we are, for she cooperated out of love so that there might be born in the Church the faithful, who are members of Christ their Head." The love referred to is Mary's love in the mystery of the Annunciation. This text is cited by Vatican II, *Lumen Gentium,* explicitly in art. 53 and implicitly in art. 63. Cf. R. Laurentin's commentary in *La Vierge au concile,* Paris, Lethielleux, 1966, pp. 153–159.

For St. Peter Chrysologus (d. 450) likewise, Mary is "mother of the living" inasmuch as she engendered Christ who is life: *Sermo 140 De Annuntiatione,* PL 52:576b; cf. his *Sermons* 64 (*loc. cit.* 380a), 74 (409ab), and 99 (479a).

"The first-fruits of all the Scriptures are the gospels, and the first-fruit of the gospels is the gospel that John haṣ given us. No one can understand the meaning of this gospel unless he has rested upon the breast of Jesus and from Jesus has received Mary as his mother" (*In Johannis Evangelium,* praef. #6).[31]

Today this text would be read as saying that Mary exercises a maternal activity thanks to which Christians understand and live the gospel. As a matter of fact, Origen puts things the other way round: those who understand and live the gospel are identified with Christ, and this identification permits them to be called "sons of Mary" according to Jn. 19:25. In a word, to hold to an interpretation in the perspective of the text, it is not Mary who acts as mother but Christians who with the help of grace act in such a way that she becomes their mother. Nilus the Ascetic (d. 430) echoes Origen in calling Mary "mother of those who live according to the gospel."[32]

Prayer addressed to Mary is another development that emerges in this period. A papyrus uncovered about 1938 exemplifies this kind of prayer:

"Under the cover of your mercy we fly to you, *Theotokos* (Mother of God). Do not reject the petitions [that we address you] in our need, but save us from danger, [you] who alone are chaste and blessed."[33]

---

31. *In Johannis Evangelium,* praef. 6; PG 14:34ab; ed. Preuschen GCS 10 (Origen 4), pp. 8–9. On the limits of this text cf. H. Holstein, "Marie et l'Eglise chez les Pères Anté-nicéens," EM 9 (1951), pp. 21–22.

32. *Epistolae* I, 266, PG 77:179d. There is no other text on this subject for the present period.

33. Papyrus 479 of the John Rylands Library, Manchester. Dom Mercenier, "L'antienne la plus ancienne," *Muséon* 52 (1939), 229–233, was the first to give a commentary on this find. He dated the work from the

The prayer known as the *Sub tuum* is easily recognizable here. Thought for quite some time to be a medieval composition, this prayer is heard of "prior to the Council of Ephesus."[34] Whatever the hypothesis, Gregory of Nazianz[35] in 379 testifies to a prayer that a virgin named Justina likewise addressed to Mary when in danger of losing her virginity. These witnesses would lead to the conclusion that the cult which Epiphanius stigmatized as an abuse in 377[36] is actually a deviation of popular devotion, which elsewhere was finding its authentic form in the Church.

Other information that is less striking but more certain, more essential, and more significant reveals the Virgin Mary beginning to find her place in the liturgy. As the mystery of the Incarnation becomes the object of celebration, the infancy gospels of Luke 1–2 and Matthew 1–2 take their place

---

third century. Subsequent literature, in great abundance, is more reserved about the date and suggests probably the fourth century. Cf. bibliography in E. Cecchetti, "Sub tuum praesidium," *Enciclopedia Cattolica* 11:1468–1472; G. Besutti, "Bibliografia mariana 1952–1957," *Marianum* 20 (1958), # 2985–2990, published separately, Rome, Marianum, 1959. The best reconstruction of the prayer — certain words are lost on the frayed papyrus — is that of O. Stegmüller, "Sub tuum praesidium," ZKT 74 (1952), 76–82. It is adopted by G. Jouassard, "Maternité spirituelle: Première tradition," EM 16 (1959), pp. 59–60, and by T. Koehler, "Maternité spirituelle, Maternité mystique," *Maria* 6 (1961), pp. 571–574. On the influence of the *Sub tuum* in the West, cf. G. Meerssemann, *Der Hymnos Akathistos im Abendland,* Freiburg/Schweiz, Universitätsverlag, 1958, vol. 1, p. 15, vol. 2, pp. 258–259, and H. Barré, *Prières anciennes de l'Occident à la Mère du Sauveur,* Paris, Lethielleux, 1963, p. 20.

34. Mercenier had first dated the text from the 3rd century. Stegmüller deepened the investigation and situated the papyrus between 325 and 450. The prayer is "prior to the Council of Ephesus" in the opinion of M. Jourjon, "Aux origines de la prière d'intercession de Marie," EM 23 (1966), p. 46.

35. Gregory of Nazianzus, *Oratio* 24, PG 35:1180d–1181a. The text is studied in Jourjon, *op. cit.,* pp. 43–44.

36. Epiphanius, *Panarion* 78, PG 42:737b, stresses that "Mary is not God and does not have a heavenly body."

therein and from then on inspire prayer, reflection, and commentary. As early as the middle of the fourth century, before Saint Basil, the East is making mention of the Virgin in the canon of the Mass. The expression *communicantes* with which this prayer begins is a reference to Rom. 12:13 where certain manuscripts have the word *mneiais* (*memoriis* — memory) in place of *chreiais* (*necessitatibus* — needs).[37]

The humble origins of prayer to Mary in the course of the fourth century so closely condition the blossoming of Marian devotion in the following period, and the transition is so imperceptible, that it will be better to present the whole of this development within the framework of this next period.

---

37. This point was established definitively by Dom Frenaud at the International Mariological Congress at Lisbon in August 1967. The Prior of Solesmes died a few days afterward on the Lisbon-Fatima highway, victim of an automobile accident. His paper can be rightly considered the most important communication read at the Congress.

Ramon Roca Puig, *Himne à la Verge Maria "Psalmus responsorius." Papir llati del segle IV,* Barcelona, 1965, studies an unedited hymn of the fourth century. A very interesting composition, it sums up the apocryphal gospels of the infancy of Mary and the birth of Christ. Its last stanza evokes the marriage feast at Cana, showing thereby that the Virgin Mary is indeed the theme giving unity to the composition. But to entitle it "Hymn to the Virgin" is a misnomer, for nowhere does it address the Virgin; it praises her rather in the third person. Thus the conclusion to which Barré's masterful research led him remains unchanged: no prayer is known that is addressed to the Virgin Mary in the Latin world before the middle of the fifth century.

THIRD PERIOD

FROM THE COUNCIL OF EPHESUS TO THE GREGORIAN REFORM (431–1050)

The key event of the third period in the development of Marian doctrine now to be taken up is the extension of the place given Mary in Christian cult and particularly the appearance of feasts celebrated in her honor. These feasts occasion a theological reflection of which Mary is the object. Their celebration gives rise to a flowering of prayers, poems, and homilies that go on increasing in number. Thus new features of Mary's character receive attention.

This liturgical development takes place quietly, imperceptibly, and without any event that can be attached to a precise date. The Church's life in general and her liturgical life in particular grew from within at this time without being structured by authoritative decision.

1. The East

The process begins in the East, where two very different developments are to be distinguished.

The first has origins going back earlier than Ephesus, and it will be necessary to backtrack a moment to observe them. The Virgin Mary became a part of the liturgy when the mystery of the Incarnation, root of the Paschal mystery, began to be celebrated. This celebration appeared in two forms. The first was the feast of Epiphany, known in the East as early as the second century. But this feast, centered on Christ's manifestation at his baptism, did not concern Mary.[1] However, at Jerusalem about the time of the pilgrimage of Etheria (late fourth to fifth centuries) Epiphany is centered on the birth of Christ with a nocturnal celebration at Bethlehem. And here the mother of Jesus is naturally in the picture.[2] The second celebration was that of Christmas, probably originating at Rome toward the end of the third century and centered on Christ's birth as a historic event. In Cappadocia it is celebrated as early as 375. One of Saint Basil's homilies mentions that the prophecy from the seventh chapter of Isaiah on the virgin who is to conceive was read then, as well as the gospel passages from Mt. 1:18–25 and 2:1–12 on the conception and virginal birth.[3] This gospel, however, as has been seen, gives Mary only an unobtrusive place secondary to Joseph. In this feast her place hardly went beyond the terms of the creed, "Conceived by the Holy Spirit, born of the Virgin Mary."

The feast called in Greek *Hypapante* — that is, the feast of the "meeting" of Christ with Simeon (Lk. 2:22–35) — is known from the end of the fourth century[4] and like the

---

1. The first evidence of the feast is found among the Gnostics, for whom the sudden appearance of Christ at his baptism ruled out any notion of his preceding terrestrial existence, along with the virginal conception and birth. Cf. D. Montagna, "La liturgia mariana primitiva," *Marianum* 24 (1962), 89.
2. *Ibid.*, 91–92. Etheria's pilgrimage dates from the end of the fourth century or the second decade of the fifth.
3. PG 31:1457–1476. Cf. Montagna, *op. cit.*, 88–93.
4. From the fourth century on, the feast of *Hypapante* was celebrated at

preceding was celebrated as a feast of Christ. It sums up the whole mystery of the Incarnation, declares Hesychius of Jerusalem (d. after 451).[5] Now, Mary has a place in this mystery, since it is she who according to the gospel of the feast (Lk. 2:22–38) presents Jesus in the Temple and receives the message that "a sword will pierce [her] own soul." Little by little these elements are going to be brought to light in preaching, not always to advantage: according to an opinion expressed by Origen, for example, the "sword" announced by Simeon signified a doubt on Mary's part and the scandal that she would take at Christ's Passion.

The Virgin Mary comes into bolder relief in another celebration[6] mentioned from the fourth century on in Cappadocia and before 431 at Constantinople. It was a commemoration of which she was the object and it was made during Advent, probably on the Sunday before Christmas. For that occasion the reading was taken not from the announcement made to Joseph according to Matthew's gospel, but from the annunciation to Mary according to Lk. 1:26–35. Preachers were thus led to comment on the angel's greeting in which is found the prototype of prayer addressed to Mary: "Rejoice, so highly favoured! The Lord is with you" (Lk. 1:28). The earliest homily composed for this occasion, according to

---

Jerusalem on February 14, forty days after Epiphany. Thence it passed into Capadocia and elsewhere (Montagna, *op. cit.,* 93–97). An unedited homily attributed to St. John Chrysostom seemed to bear witness to the existence of this feast at Antioch from the end of the fourth century. But G.M. Ellero, "Maternità e virtù di Maria in S. Giovanni Crisostomo," *Marianum* 26 (1964), 64–65, proved the inauthenticity of this homily (which pleaded for the transfer of the feast from February 14 to February 2). At Antioch, therefore, the celebration of the feast is not sure before the sixth century. At Constantinople in 602 it was still being celebrated on February 14 (H. Higgins, "Note on the Purification," *Archiv für Liturgienwissenschaft* 2 (1952), 81–83).

5. *In S. Deiparam* 2, PG 93:1468b.
6. Montagna, *op. cit.,* 98–105.

the present state of research, was pronounced at Caesarea in Cappadocia between 370 and 378. Manuscript tradition is probably correct in attributing it to Gregory of Nyssa. In it is found this commentary:

> "Let us say aloud, in the words of the angel: 'Rejoice, object of God's favor! The Lord is with you (...).' From you has come the one who is perfect in dignity and in whom rests the fulness of divinity. 'Rejoice, object of God's favor! The Lord is with you,' the king with the servant (Lk. 1:38); he who sanctifies the universe, with the immaculate one; the most beautiful among the children of men, with the beautiful one — in order to save man made in his image."[7]

Another homily that is also attributed to Gregory of Nyssa and meant for the same celebration extends the commentary to the words, "Of all women you are the most blessed" — words of Elizabeth (Lk. 1:42) which some manuscripts attribute also to the angel of the Annunciation (Lk. 1:28). The homily calls Mary "blessed,"

> "because among all virgins you have been chosen,
> because you have been judged worthy of sheltering
>   such a Lord,
> because you welcomed the one who fills everything . . . ,
> because you became the treasure of the spiritual
>   pearl."[8]

---

7. Homily edited by G. La Piana in *Rivista storica critica delle scienze teologiche* 5 (1909), 548–563; revised version in D. Montagna, *La lode alla Theotokos,* Rome, Marianum, 1963, p. 98. The manuscript attributes the work to Gregory of Nyssa. A grafitto at Nazareth, *Chaire Maria,* seems earlier (2nd–3rd century), according to P. E. Testa.

8. PG 62:766, a homily falsely attributed to John Chrysostom. Cf. the table of rectifications in *Court Traité,* 1st edition (1953), p. 163, and D. Montagna in *Marianum* 24 (1962), 120.

In the homily of Proclus of Constantinople, shortly before Ephesus, the Virgin stands out strikingly:

> "Today the feast of the Virgin *(parthenikē panēguris)* invites us to praise. It is the holy *Theotokos,* the Virgin Mary, who has summoned us here."[9]

At Antioch between 411 and 548[10] and in Egypt[11] there is evidence of similar celebrations, though in January (for Egypt on January 16). In a word, Mary is taking her place in the Christmas cycle. She is entering the liturgy as a mysterious satellite within the Incarnation.

At Jerusalem from about the fifth century there is a celebration of another type called "The Day of Mary *Theotokos*" and fixed on August 15. The feast has an origin different from those just treated. Beginning with the second century the anniversary day of martyrs was being celebrated as the day of their birth in heaven *(dies natalis).*[12] Later these commemorations were extended to some of the great ascetics, and then to Mary on the occasion of the controversy of Ephesus. The feast instituted at Jerusalem around the year 431 celebrated Mary as *"Theotokos."* Toward the beginning of the sixth century, and in part under the influence of the apocryphals that narrated Mary's last days on earth, the feast acquired both a different object and different name. It became the "Dormition," the "Passing" (transitus), the "Assumption," and thus took on the character of a *dies natalis.*[13] Toward 600 the Emperor Maurice extended this solemnity

---

9. PG 65:679.
10. B. Capelle, "Le témoignage de la liturgie," EM 7 (1949), 45–46.
11. *Ibid.,* 47–48.
12. On the origin of Marian feasts cf., for example, M. Righetti, *Manuale di storia liturgica,* Milan, Ancora, 1946, t. 2, c. 9, # 172–174, pp. 268–272. At Smyrna, beginning with the second century, the anniversary of the death of Polycarp (155) was celebrated with a Eucharistic gathering.
13. Montagna, *Marianum* 24 (1962), 110–114. On the name of this feast, an object of hesitation, cf. *infra,* p. 84, n. 22.

to the entire empire and it became the principal Marian feast.[14]

Thereupon the feasts of the Virgin began to multiply. The Nativity of Mary, fixed on September 8, is known from the middle of the sixth century.[15] The feast of her conception, modeled on the feast of John the Baptist's conception, was located nine months earlier on the calendar, on December 9. It appears toward the end of the seventh century and the beginning of the eighth.[16] Around the same time there arises the feast of the presentation of Mary.[17] The inspiration for these three feasts came from the *Protoevangelium of James*. Dating from the end of the second century, this apocryphal gives an account of Mary's birth patterned on that of Christ, according to Mt. 1-2 and Lk. 1-2. An angel brings Joachim word of the birth of his daughter Mary. Anne conceives miraculously at that very moment. Welcomed with great joy

---

14. PG 147:292. Another Marian feast existed at Constantinople before the middle of the sixth century, the deposition of the Virgin's robe at the Church of the Blachernae. The celebration surrounding this relic is not without relation to the object of the feast of the Assumption: reverence was paid the robe in default of a body, which the earth had not been worthy to keep, as is witnessed in the Euthemiac history, which may date from the mid-sixth century. A. Wenger, *L'Assomption de la Très Sainte Vierge dans la tradition byzantine du VIe au Xe siècle. Etudes et documents,* Paris, Institut d'études byzantines, 1955, has entirely renewed the study of this question.

15. L. M. Peretto, "Recenti richerche sul Protevangelo di Giacomo," *Marianum* 24 (1962), 131-132.

16. M. Jugie, *L'Immaculée Conception dans l'Ecriture et dans la tradition orientale,* Rome, Academia Mariana, 1952, pp. 135-145. Cf. C. A. Bouman's article in E. D. O'Connor (ed.), *The Dogma of the Immaculate Conception,* South Bend, Notre Dame University Press, 1958, pp. 116-161.

17. This feast is found later in the West. It was adopted in 1372 by Gregory XI on the suggestion of an ambassador of the king of Cyprus to the court of Avignon (H. Leclercq in DACL 14:1729-1731). But it is found already in England in the 11th century.

at birth, the child is presented in the Temple at the age of three.[18] The apocryphals were widely used in preaching and are a primary source of iconographic subject-matter.[19]

As to the feast of the Annunciation (March 25), it is like the *Hypapante* an essentially Christological feast, but the Virgin Mary becomes more prominent in it.[20] The gospel of the Annunciation, in fact, offered the occasion for embellishing the greeting "Rejoice" and for tirelessly developing prayers and praises addressed to the Mother of God. The East began turning them out in increasing fervor and abundance from the sixth and seventh centuries on.

Hence two types of celebrations can be distinguished in this period. The first come from the deeper movement of the liturgy and are biblical and Christological. The others grow out of popular devotion and are nourished by less untarnished sources such as the apocryphals of the infancy and the assumption, and these celebrations will later be extensively refined. In them the mystery of Mary as a person is brought into much bolder relief.

The feasts of the first type originated before Ephesus, whereas the others bear the mark of this council and its aftermath. In this development the dynamic element is the angelic salutation. The dogmatic root is Mary's role in the Incarnation and the title *Theotokos* which in its every aspect is the object of untiring meditation and celebration.

The importance of the liturgical factor can scarcely be exaggerated in a study of this development. Obviously the liturgy is not the objective source of revelation, as Pius XII

---

18. Cf. *infra,* Appendix # 5, on the apocryphals, as well as the article cited *supra,* p. 77 n. 1.

19. J. de Mahuet, "L'Orient et l'iconographie mariale de l'Occident," EM 19 (1962), pp. 162–174. J. Lafontaine Dosogne, *Iconographie de l'enfance de la Vierge dans l'empire byzantin et en Occident,* Brussels, 1964.

20. Montagna, *Marianum* 24 (1962), 114–118: the essential contribution of this article is in distinguishing the homilies and lyrical compositions stemming from the Advent liturgy (the Acathistos Hymn is of this number) and the feast of the Annunciation on March 25, a later feast.

was to underline. But it is the privileged place where the sources of revelation are assimilated in life and brought to light. Each year feasts provide an occasion of preaching, and preaching crosses the boundary from evoking the presence of the person celebrated to praying to her. Preaching prepared the way for the liturgical prayers that begin to multiply in the sixth century. Thus theological reflection on the Virgin Mary found favorable atmosphere. In this liturgical atmosphere both faith and understanding went to work, not in an effort of abstraction divorced from life but in community prayer. This liturgical factor stimulated new developments, some negative, some positive. The readiness with which certain doctors of the preceding period had attributed to the *Theotokos* the failings common to sinful mankind now becomes unthinkable. Like a morning fog the last patches of error vanish in the warm light of liturgical celebration. The last privileges of Mary — the Assumption, her original holiness, her intercession or, if preferred, her mediation — come into view.

Assumption

The background of development on the Assumption should be recalled from the previous period. Shortly before 377 Epiphanius had raised the question, "How did Mary's earthly life end?" Raised in passing, the question had no immediate echo, at least not to our knowledge, but it takes on importance when a Marian feast begins to be celebrated. Then interest is deeply stirred, and quite understandably so. The feastday of a saint was normally the day of his death, his *dies natalis.* Thus the feastday of the *Theotokos* was spontaneously considered to be a commemoration of the day when she left this world.[21] The curiosity of the faithful can

---

21. Palestine here played a pilot role in three domains: the *liturgical* (the Marian celebration of August 15 has its oldest witnesses there), the *theological* (the oldest doctrinal documents are found there: homilies of Theoteknos and perhaps of Modestos of Jerusalem), and the *archaeological* (the Virgin's tomb).

easily be surmised: How did Mary leave this earth? So can the plight of the preacher at a loss for an answer.

With the growing attention given this question an answer shaped up in two very different directions, in fable and in theological reasoning.

1. As was to be expected from the fact that it is the human faculty quickest to act and hardest to control, imagination got a head start. By the end of the fifth century pious stories destined to satisfy popular curiosity had begun circulating. Each one of them had its contribution to make.[22] A picture was drawn first of Mary's funeral. Then the story followed her beyond death. Here the scenario took a double shape. Some, like the Pseudo-John, tell of an assumption of the body *without the soul being reunited:* Mary's mortal remains lie incorrupt beneath the tree of life until the day of judgment. Others show a more genuine intuition, despite the unfounded and bizarre details: a wave of excitement sweeps through the Church as Mary's end approaches. She has been informed of her end from on high. Miraculously summoned together, the apostles outdo one another in their eulogies. Christ comes to take the soul of his Mother (which Byzantine iconography will represent under the form of a beautifully dressed baby). Finally the body of the *Theotokos,* gloriously revived, rejoins her soul in heaven.[23]

---

22. Traces of this hesitation are found in the different names assigned to this feast: Assumption *(analēpsis)* with Theoteknos (probably second half of the 6th century), Passing *(metastasis, transitus)* with others, Dormition *(koimēsis)* which will prevail in the East by the eighth century. Cf. Wenger, *op. cit.,* pp. 100–103.

The same hesitation appears in the tales found in the apocryphals. They emphasize the death but are brief or silent on the bodily Assumption. Thus, for example, John of Thessalonica (d. shortly before 649) has no word of any bodily resurrection of Mary, though his source makes much of it. On this source, cf. the following note.

23. Wenger, *op. cit.,* pp. 15–96 and 209–262, has entirely renewed the question of the apocryphals. He discovered and edited (pp. 209–242) the hitherto unknown source of John of Thessalonica that dates from the end of the fifth century or the beginning of the sixth. He thus was able to

Reactions to all this varied widely. Without further reflection the more credulous let themselves be carried away by the glittering details of the story. Others had only disdain for these moving accounts that were often mutually contradictory and lacked all authority.

2. A better way was taken by still others. They eliminated or rejected whatever in the background of these accounts was found to be disquieting or purely fictitious. They established on a theological foundation whatever there could be of value in the pious stories of the apocryphals.[24] Theoteknos of Livias, for example, gave the opinion:

"It was fitting . . . that the body that carried God, that was God's repository, divinized, incorruptible, illuminated by the divine light, should be raised in glory with the soul pleasing to God."[25]

The theological effort thus begun in the sixth century[26] reached a golden age in the eighth century with Germanus

---

reconstitute the filiation of innumerable apocryphals, in the East as well as in the West. These discoveries confirmed the positions taken by G. Jouassard, "L'Assomption corporelle de la Sainte Vierge et la Patristique," EM 6 (1948), pp. 103–104. M. Haibach-Reinisch, *Ein neuer Transitus Mariae des Pseudo-Melito,* Rome, Academia Mariana, 1962, has independently clarified the inextricable case of another apocryphal, the Pseudo-Melito, thanks to the discovery of a new Latin version. This version bears evidence of a more archaic state and eliminates the objections that seemed to forbid dating it earlier than the sixth century. Cf. the constructive review by D. Montagna, *Marianum* 27 (1965), 175–195.

24. On the worth of the Assumptionist apocryphals, cf. *infra,* Appendix # 6.

25. Theoteknos of Livias, *Homily on the Assumption (analēpsis) of the Holy Theotokos* 9, edited by Wenger, *op. cit.,* p. 277.

26. The homily of Theoteknos dates from between 550 and 650, more probably before 600. It is no doubt the oldest theological composition extant on the Assumption. Even supposing the authenticity — and this is a problem — of the *Encomium in Dormitione* attributed to Modestos of Jerusalem (d. 634; PG 86b: 3277–3312), this work would have little chance of being earlier. Cf. Wenger, *op. cit.,* pp. 103–104.

of Constantinople (d. c.733),[27] Andrew of Crete (d. 740),[28] Cosmas Vestitor (d. c.740),[29] and especially Saint John Damascene (d. before 753).[30] It ran on calmly and smoothly, without suffering either from debate or from pedantry, in the liturgical atmosphere of the feast of August 15, as the Holy Spirit guided the faith of the Church in its search for further explicitness.

Immaculate Conception

The formulation of the dogma of the original holiness of Mary proceeded more harmoniously and in its advance did

---

27. Germanus of Constantinople: Three homilies of this author *On the Dormition* are given in PG 98:340–372. A monograph, somewhat superficial, was devoted to him by E. Perniola, *La Mariologia di san Germano*, Roma, Monti, 1954. An unpublished work has since been edited by V. Grumel in *Revue d'études byzantines* 16 (1958), 183–205.
28. Andrew of Crete: Three homilies of this author *On the Dormition* appear in PG 97:1045–1109. Cf. the bibliography on him in Laurentin, *Marie, l'Eglise*... vol. 1, pp. 24–25, n. 24; also E. Follieri, "Un canone inedito di S. Andrea di Creta per l'Annunciazione," in *Collectanea Vaticana in honorem cardinalis Albaredo*, Vatican, 1962, pp. 337–357.
29. Cosmas Vestitor: a Latin version of his four homilies (made at Reichenau in the 10th century) is all that remains. An edition and study of it are found in Wenger, *op. cit.*, pp. 140–184 and 313–362.
30. John Damascene: The three homilies of this author *On the Dormition* are found in PG 96:700–761 (partial French translation, G. Hesbert, *L'Assomption*, Paris, Plon, 1952, pp. 55–78). Principal monographs on his Mariology: V. A. Mitchel, *The Mariology of St. John Damascene*, Turnhout, 1930; C. Chevalier, *La mariologie de saint Jean Damascène*, Rome, Pont. Inst. Orient., 1936; V. Grumpel, "La mariologie de saint Jean Damascène," *Echos d'Orient* 40 (1937), 318–346. On the questions of authenticity, cf. *Court Traité*, 1st edition, pp. 170–171. On the date suggested for his death, cf. J. M. Hoeck, article in *Orientalis Christiana Periodica* 17 (1951), 5, n. 1, and G. Garitte, article in *Muséon* 67 (1954), 73–75, both of whom show that the date established by S. Vailhé, *Echos d'Orient* 9 (1906), 28–30, rests on a confusion.

not at this point attract as much attention. As with the Assumption, the discovery here also is made thanks to a liturgical celebration. The feast of the Conception appears toward the end of the seventh century. Its origins are unassuming indeed. In his gospel Luke recounts the annunciation of the birth of John the Baptist (1:5–25) and that of Jesus' birth (1:26–38). Each of these two mysteries was the object of a feast. In a similar pattern a feast tended to take shape around a third annunciation, that of Mary, such as it was recounted by the apocryphals. Here again these tales furnished not the doctrinal substance but the spark which set off doctrinal reflection. What name could be given to this new feast? Preference at first wavered back and forth among three titles: Annunciation *(euaggelismon)* of the Holy *Theotokos* (or of Joachim and Anne), Conception of Anne (a title that risked suggesting awkwardly that the *active* conceiving by Saint Anne was the object of the feast), and *Conception of Mary*. This last title won out.[31] In liturgy and in preaching, then, the conception of Mary, "all holy" and "all pure," came to be celebrated. To express this double notion the Greek language had on hand a marvelous collection of epithets. These panegyrics are the first sketch of the dogma of the Immaculate Conception, a sketch still quite imprecise. On the one hand, Mary's initial purity had not yet been collated with the universality of Christ's redemption. On the other hand, the poetic language of the Byzantine homilists is so enthusiastic that oratorical overstatement is difficult to distinguish from dogmatic affirmation. In waxing eloquent over John the Baptist's conception some preachers, carried away by the impulse of their devotion or of their fluency, go as far as to call his conception "holy, divine, and glorious."[31a] Language of this kind in such a context devalues the first affirmations of the "immaculate conception" of Mary and

---

31. Jugie, *L'Immaculée Conception* . . . pp. 137–140.
31a. *Ibid.*, p. 139.

suggests that they not be too quickly given probative value. With more perspective, however, it can be seen that the Byzantines did not put the conception of the *Theotokos* on the same level as that of John the Baptist. And the difference between the two will go on being confirmed. If the first stages of this development are viewed in the light of the dogmatic explicitness reached in our day, it becomes possible to recognize that the early lyricism, stirred up by the impulse of the Spirit, was actually focused and directed toward a truth still hidden in what its sources implied.

Intercession, Mediation, Spiritual Motherhood

As to Mary's intercession or mediation, no particular liturgical feast is involved here. The development of this doctrine coincides with the development of Marian cult. Already Irenaeus had glimpsed in Mary the one who pleads for Eve, the advocate of Eve, though his meaning is still the object of discussion.[32] In the fourth century Gregory of Nazianz and the Greek papyrus that has preserved the *Sub tuum* supply evidence that she was invoked in peril. The Council of Ephesus exalts the universality of Mary's role with regard to mankind. One of the speeches given at the close of the council invokes her, not as a particular saint but as the universal saint whose prerogatives sum up those of the Church at large:

> "We greet you, Mary, Mother of God,
> venerable treasure of the whole world,
> light that has never gone out . . . ,
> never destroyed temple containing the one who cannot be contained,
> Mother and Virgin . . . ,

---

32. On Mary, Eve's advocate according to St. Irenaeus, cf. M. Jourjon, "Aux origines de la prière d'intercession de Marie," EM 23 (1966), pp. 38–42.

By you the Trinity is blessed,
by you the Cross is venerated throughout the whole world,
by you heaven is thrown into joy,
by you the angels and archangels are delighted,
by you the demons are put to flight,
by you the devil tempter is thrown from heaven,
by you the fallen creature is raised to heaven,
by you the whole world in the grip of idolatry has reached the knowledge of truth,
by you holy Baptism comes to those who believe,
by you the oil of gladness,
by you churches are founded throughout the world,
by you peoples are led to conversion."[33]

Whatever its scope, this "by you," is already in the framework of mediation. The idea is that through Mary, the *Theotokos,* God has come into the world, and through him everything there is. Certain authors situate this role of intermediary at the Annunciation. Thus Andrew of Crete says:

"She is mediation *(mesiteuei)* between God's sublimity and the lowliness of the flesh, and she becomes mother of the Creator."[33a]

According to Andrew of Crete again, the angel Gabriel, God's ambassador, exercises a role of "mediator" from the

---

33. *Hom. 4 Ephesi in Nestorium habita quando septem ad sanctam Mariam descenderunt* 4, PG 77:992bc. This homily was pronounced by an unknown author in November 431 after Cyril's departure (E. Schwartz, *Acta Conciliorum oecumenicorum,* t. 1, vol. 1, fasc. 8, p. 104). The homily gives the key to this surprising assimilation of Mary's person to the universal Church: "Let us glorify Mary, ever a Virgin, *that is to say, the whole Church."* A text attributed to Ephrem (ed. Lamy, 1, pp. 531–533) says in similar vein: "We call the Church also by the name of Mary." R. Caro in *Marianum* 29 (1967), 21–31, attempted to restore the homily to St. Cyril, but this thesis has met with reserve.

33a. *Sermon 1, On the Nativity,* PG 97:808c.

standpoint of heaven analogous to that of Mary from the standpoint of earth.[34]

But another avenue opens up leading to the *present* intercession or mediation of Mary in favor of mankind. From the fourth century on recourse had been had to the martyrs as exercising an intercession or mediation,[35] not alongside that of Christ but inside the mystery of Christ. In that class Mary begins to be seen occupying the first place. In a sermon on the Assumption Germanus of Constantinople (d. c.733) expresses in the most exact terms this second theme of Mary's present mediation:

"When you take leave of us for God we gain in you a mediatrix *(mesītin).*"[35a]

The most ancient use of the noun "mediatrix" *(mesītis)* of which evidence is certain and undisputed is found in a curious context in a work of Romanus Melodos (d. mid-6th century). Eve, aroused from the sleep of death by the birth of the Savior, goes to prostrate herself along with Adam at the feet of Mary who is caressing her newborn infant. Mary directs words of consolation to them:

"Hold back your tears. Receive me as your mediatrix *(mesītin)* with the one who has been born of me."[35b]

---

34. On Gabriel's mediation and the two aspects of Mary's mediation (in the original mystery of the Annunciation and in her daily action toward men) numerous texts will be found in Laurentin, *Marie, l'Eglise . . .* , vol. 1, pp. 52–54.

35. Thus, for example, Gregory of Nazianzus speaks of the "divinization of which the martyrs are mediators *(mesiteuousi)*" in *Oratio XI ad Gregorium Nyssen.* 5, PG 35:837c; cf. Nicetas' commentary there, PG 35:838 n. 12.

35a. Sermon on the Assumption, PG 98:365c.

35b. *Hymn on the Nativity,* Stanza 11, ed. *Sources chrétiennes,* t. 110, p. 103.

And immediately she pleads for the two guilty ones. This is formally the description of an intercession, but in imaginary circumstances. Basically the theme is the one put into circulation by Irenaeus in the second century: "Mary, advocate of Eve." But Romanos painted the scene poetically and transposed it, for Irenaeus had been thinking less of Christ's birth than of the Annunciation when Mary's consent took up anew and radically destroyed the consent given by Eve to the serpent.

The "mediation" of Mary therefore has a history that is more complex and uneven than is commonly thought. The appeal to her intercession, a phenomenon that broadens out considerably during this period, gives rise to a host of other terms: help,[36] protection, patronage,[37] etc. "Mediation" is one formula among many others.

Toward the end of this third period authors here and there begin to discover that Mary is animated with motherly feelings toward men,[38] and George of Nicomedia (late 9th cen-

---

36. *Boethēia* and the title *boēthos:* Eustratiades, *The Theotokos in Hymnology* (in Greek), Paris, Champion, 1930, a collection of iconographic titles of Mary, contains a column for these two terms.

37. *Prostasia* and the title *prostatis* (patroness, protectress): Eustratiades, *op. cit.*, pp. 65–66, two columns for these terms.
  Presbeia and the title *presbus* (ambassadress): Eustratiades, *op. cit.*, p. 64, a quarter-column only for these two terms.

38. In the East, Germanus of Constantinople (d. 733) is perhaps the first to conceive of Mary's motherhood as the exercise of a role implying maternal sentiments. The texts known up to now surely do not advance that far. The *teknopenthō* of *Serm. in Dormitione,* PG 98:348c, should probably be translated "afflicted for your *child,*" because of the sufferings of the Passion, rather than "afflicted for your *children.*" As to the text of *Epistle 2,* PG 98:162a, where Mary intercedes as a mother *(mētrikōs),* the context *(mētera autou kuriōs huparchousa)* and parallel texts (e.g., *Homilia* 9, 9, PG 98:381a) prove that the meaning intended is "Mother *of the Savior,*" as in the *"Monstra te esse matrem,"* whose sense is "Show that you are the Mother *of Jesus,* powerful over his heart." In the *Homily on the Deliverance of Constantinople,* edited by V. Grumel in *Revue d'études byzantines* 16 (1958), 198 and 205, Germanus advances a step further in saying, "His mother is filled with maternal solicitude for us and

tury) perceives that she exercises a maternal function with regard to the disciples, in virtue of Christ's word, "Son, this is your mother" (Jn. 19:26).[39]

To sum up, Mary's quality of *Theotokos* (Mother of God) was something clearly recognized at the beginning of this important period. Attention now is brought to bear on the implications of this mystery, that is, on what the beginning and the end of Mary's destiny were, on what her relations are with Christians in the communion of saints. More and more clearly the position of the *Theotokos* appears higher than that of the saints, and also more universal.[40]

---

accords us her kindness and protection in our perils." However G. Jouassard, "Maternité spirituelle de la Vierge, premières amorces dans la tradition," EM 16 (1959), p. 80, n. 111, hesitates over the translation: would *mētrōa* not here refer to Christ, as in PG 98:352? Nonetheless he very clearly leans toward the translation proposed by Grumel, cited immediately above.

The thought of John the Geometer (2nd half of 10th century) is more firm. For him Mary is *"not only the mother of God,* but the mother of us all . . . for she has for *all* men an *affection* and a *tenderness* . . . , Mother of all . . . taking them into her arms" (*Discourse on the Assumption* 59, ed. Wenger, *op. cit.,* p. 406); "mother of all and of each, *loving us* more than could be said" (*Ibid.,* 67, p. 411); he addresses this appeal to her intercession: "You are our mother, obtain pardon for us" (*Ibid.,* 70, p. 414). Intercession and spiritual motherhood, two themes hitherto independent of each other, are joined in these texts.

The preceding note mentioned the hesitations occasioned by the text of Germanus of Constantinople. As to the Pseudo-Ephrem, *Precatio 8* in *Opera, graece,* ed. Assemani, III, 543c, "As a mother *(hōsper mētēr)* you do not cease to be favorable toward us," nothing proves that it is prior to John the Geometer.

39. On the interpretation of Jn. 19:25–27 in the sense of spiritual motherhood, cf. *infra,* Appendix #7.

40. Beginning with the 5th–6th centuries Mary is declared "higher than the angels, and even than the cherubim" (Laurentin, *Marie, l'Eglise* . . . vol. 1, p. 90). "She surpasses *(huperanechei)* all the saints that we honor," says a homily attributed to Basil of Seleucia (d. shortly after 458) and, at any rate, hardly later than the beginning of the sixth century (*Homily 39,* 6, PG 85: 448b).

2. The West

With the Latin writers development moves along more slowly in this period, as if in the wake of the East, notably in what concerns the liturgy.

Here again the seed of development is the feast of Christmas, established at Rome by the end of the third century as has already been said, for this feast offers the occasion of highlighting the gospel of Christ's birth.

In the Christmas cycle a more explicit celebration of the Virgin Mary appears between the end of the fifth and the middle of the seventh century, depending on the place. Its form, name, and date of celebration vary: the last Sunday of Advent, the Wednesday and Friday of the tenth month (December) fast later known as the Christmas Ember Days, December 18 (octave before Christmas), January 1 (octave after Christmas), even January 18. These dates are significant. Whatever be the form, the earliest celebrations of the Virgin are closely tied to the feast of Christ's birth. They make the role of the Virgin Mother in this mystery stand out.[41]

Little by little four feasts brought over from the East are introduced at Rome:[42] First the *Hypapante* (February 2);

---

41. Cf. *infra,* Appendix #8.

42. The question of the introduction of these four feasts at Rome has been entirely renewed by A. Chevasse, *Le Sacremantaire gélasien,* Paris, Desclée, 1958, pp. 375–402. Earlier it was thought that the four feasts had been introduced at the same time. Some even thought this was by the sudden authority of a pontifical decree. The important text of Pope Sergius (687–701) supposed to be a decree of this sort only *extends* to the other three feasts the procession already customary for the feast of February 2. This basic text, preserved in the *Liber pontificalis* (I, 376) is as follows: "Constituit autem ut diebus Adnuntiationis Domini, Dormitionis et Nativitatis sanctae Dei Genitricis semperque Virginis Mariae ac sancti Simeonis, quod Ypapanti Graeci appellant, letania exeat a sancto Hadriano, et ad Sanctam Mariam populus occurrat — He decreed that on the days of the Lord's Annunciation, of the Dormition and the Nativity of the holy Mother of God and ever Virgin Mary, and of holy Simeon — a feast

then, toward 650, the Dormition or Assumption (August 15); somewhat later, the Annunciation (March 25); and finally, shortly before the end of the seventh century, the Nativity of Mary (September 8). The first and third of these feasts were formally feasts of the Lord; now their Marian orientation receives more stress. The "Annunciation of the Lord" becomes the "Annunciation of Mary"; the *Hypapante* becomes the feast of "Mary's Purification." Both the other feasts were formally feasts of the Virgin. The basic one is the Dormition, which has the character of a *dies natalis.* Very early it comes to comprise an orientation toward her bodily Assumption: the prayer entitled *Veneranda* intimates that the Mother of God "cannot be held back by the bonds of death."[43]

As in the East these feasts occasion liturgical compositions,[44] as well as a fund of preaching that until today has attracted little scholarly interest.[45] Ildefonsus of Toledo (d.

---

which the Greeks call *Hypapante* — the procession should start at St. Hadrian and the people should meet at St. Mary."

43. "Veneranda nobis Domine hujus est diei festivitas in qua sancta Dei Genetrix mortem subiit temporalem, nec tamen mortis nexibus deprimi potuit, quae Filium tuum Dominum nostrum de se genuit incarnatum — Venerable to us, O Lord, is the feast of this day on which the holy Mother of God underwent temporal death and yet could not be held by the bonds of death, she who of herself brought forth incarnate your Son, our Lord." Cf. the studies of B. Capelle, "Témoignage de la liturgie," EM 7 (1949), pp. 48–51, and "Mort et Assomption de la Vierge dans l'Oraison Veneranda," *Ephemerides Liturgicae* 66 (1952), 241–251. Cf. *Marianum* 15 (1953), 256–259.

44. H. Barré, "Antiennes et répons de la Vierge," *Marianum* 29 (1967), 153–254. This article bears out the interest of the antiphons of the feast of Christmas, prior to St. Gregory the Great. The antiphons of the Marian feasts that appear in the seventh century show less originality and are especially centos and adaptations. Cf. also H. Barré, *Prières anciennes de l'Occident à la Mère du Sauveur,* Paris, Lethielleux, 1962, pp. 19–58.

45. Barré's works have brought to light this period, unscrambling the filiation and dating of a dozen pseudo-Augustinian compositions scattered

667) is the author of a special treatise on virginity.⁴⁶ This author singles out the theme, "To serve God and Mary,"⁴⁷ and puts it in sharp relief. Possibly of African origin, the theme will play an important role in medieval spirituality.⁴⁸

Assumption, Conception, Cooperation in Salvation

In this atmosphere which is less brilliant and more subdued than that of the Orient the three points whose development among the Byzantines has just been studied — the bodily Assumption, the Immaculate Conception, and Mary's present role with regard to mankind — apparently remain stationary.

Toward the beginning of the ninth century Autpert⁴⁹ is

---

from the fifth to the eighth century; cf. his "Sermon pseudo-augustinien, appendice 121," *Revue des études augustiniennes* 9 (1963), 111–137, and *Prières anciennes*... pp. 27–30.

46. On this author, cf. J. M. Cascante, *Doctrina mariana de S. Ildefonso de Toledo,* Barcelona, Casulleras, 1958, and the review by H. Barré, *Marianum* 21 (1959), 406–407, as well as idem, *Prières anciennes*... pp. 30–34. Two other Spaniards of the mid-sixth century should be mentioned: St. Leander of Seville, a precursor for the theme of the spiritual motherhood (cf. *infra,* p. 97, n. 54), and his successor, St. Isidore of Seville, who seems to have influenced St. Ildefonsus.

47. "Servire Deo et Mariae." Cf. Barré, *Prières anciennes*... pp. 31–32.

48. Controversies stimulate reflection on particular points: the adoptionist quarrel, the controversy over images. Cf. H. Barré, "L'apport marial de l'Orient à l'Occident de saint Ambroise à saint Anselme," EM 19 (1962), pp. 61–64.

49. Ambrose Autpert, *Sermo in Assumptione,* PL 89:1275c–1276d: "Homo mendaciter non fingat apertum quod Deus manere voluit occultum. Vera autem de ejus Assumptione sententia haec esse probatur ut secundum Apostolum, sive in corpore, sive extra corpus ignorantes, assumptam super coelos credamus — Let man not deceitfully imagine open what God willed to remain hidden. The correct opinion on her Assumption is that, not knowing (in the words of the Apostle) whether in the body or outside the body, we believe that she was assumed into heaven."

joined by Radbertus, whose work long will be taken as that of Saint Jerome,[50] in rejecting the bodily Assumption which the apocryphals proposed in their incredible tales. For Radbertus, as for Autpert, the feast of August 15 has as object the glorification of Mary's soul, and there is no way of knowing what happened to her body. Such writing has about it a note of quality. In many respects it marked a positive stage of development. Used in the liturgy and enjoying as it did the authority of Saint Jerome, it blocked the progress of belief in the Assumption until the beginning of the next period. At that time the authority of another pseudonymous writing,

---

50. Letter *Cogitis me* (= *Ep. 9 ad Paulam et Eustochium de Assumptione*, appearing among the works of St. Jerome, PL 30:122c–142d). Serious reasons have suggested the attribution of this work to Paschasius Radbertus (d. 865).

In the last few years three authors, independently of each other, have questioned this attribution:

1. J. R. Geiselmann, "Die betende Kirche und das Dogma von der leiblichen Aufnahme Mariens," *Geist und Leben* 24 (1951), 366–367, developed arguments of internal criticism.

2. A. Wenger had raised difficulties of external criticism: the comparison of MS Lyon 628, which seemed to date from the first years of the ninth century, with MS Paris 14 302 gave reason to believe the composition was prior to the beginning of Radbertus' career.

3. Dom C. Charlier, who for years had been exploring the same approach, reached similar conclusions: "Alcuin, Florus et l'apocryphe hiéronymien 'Cogitis me' . . ." *Studia patristica 1,* TUU 63 (1957), pp. 70–81.

H. Barré, "La lettre du Pseudo-Jérôme est-elle antérieure à Paschase Radbert?" *Revue Bénédictine* 68 (1958), 203–226, took the entire question up again with new information. He concluded (p. 224), "Far from having to be put into question and from being compromised, the attribution to Paschasius Radbertus is not at all shaken. It continues to rest on solid foundations against which no valid objection has yet been raised." The attribution was confirmed by the critical edition of A. Ripberger, *Der Pseudo-Hieronymus — Brief IX "Cogitis me". Ein erster marianischer Traktat des Mittelalters von Paschasius Radbert,* Freiburg/Schweiz, Universitätsverlag, 1962.

attributed this time to Saint Augustine,⁵¹ would prevail over the Pseudo-Jerome's work, as will be seen later.

Concerning the Immaculate Conception, the text of Saint Augustine which was studied earlier⁵² and the inexact ideas of the time on the mode of transmission of original sin served to block any unfolding of belief. No liturgical feast existed yet to bring attention to this mystery.

As for Mary's mediation,⁵³ her spiritual maternity,⁵⁴ and

---

51. *De Assumptione,* PL 40:1141–1148. Unknown author belonging to Anselm's milieu, late 11th to early 12th century. Cf. *Court Traité,* 1st edition, p. 130.

52. Cf. *supra,* pp. 68–71.

53. *Note on the origins of the title "Mediatrix" among Latin authors:* This title appears for the first time in the sixth century in an isolated case and without any echo: the Pseudo-Origen (Latin author) studied by Dom G. Morin, *Revue Bénédictine* 54 (1942), 3–11. He calls Mary *"Vitae mediatrix,"* evidently because of her role at the very origin of salvation: *Homilia in Mt. 12:38* in *Florilegium casinense,* t. 2, p. 154b.

In the mid-ninth century the title "mediatrix" in the formal sense of intercession passed from the East to the West, thanks to Paul the Deacon, who translated from Greek into Latin a *Life of Theophilus* in which this title is found (ed. J. Bollandus, *Acta Sanctorum,* Venice, Colet, 1725, at February 4, in t. 1, Februarii, p. 486). The critical edition with references to the original Greek was brought out by G. G. Meersseman, "Kritische Glossen op de Griekse Theophilus-Legende (7e eeuw) en Haar Latijinse Vertaling (9e eeuw)" in *Mededelingen van de Koninklijke Vlaamse Academie voor Wetenschappen, Letteren en schone Kunsten van Belgie, Klasse der Letteren* 25 (1963), # 4, also published apart in 36 pages. This appears to be the only use of the term in the ninth century.

A single case also in the tenth, three in the eleventh, and suddenly more than five in the twelfth century are known. The author has in preparation a *Histoire du titre de médiatrice* and suggests consulting in the meantime his *Marie, l'Eglise*... vol. 1, pp. 52–55 (on the origins of the title in the East) and vol. 2, pp. 76–77, n. 54 (on the origins in the West).

54. *Note on the spiritual motherhood:* Mary's motherhood with regard to mankind was sporadically expressed beginning with the fifth century, but in a root sense and without development, not yet implying any daily psychological relation of Christians with Mary. For St. Augustine (d. 431) Mary is mother of the members *(mater membrorum)* inasmuch as she is

even her cooperation on Calvary,[55] there are surprising an-

---

mother of the Head *(capitis mater)* whom she engendered in charity. For St. Peter Chrysologus (d. 450) she is "mother of the living" *(mater viventium)* inasmuch as she engendered Christ who is the Life *(Sermo 140 de Annunciatione,* PL 52:576b; cf. *Sermo 64,* 380a; *74,* 409ab; *99,* 479a). The collection entitled *Orationale visigothicum* compiled in Spain in the seventh century expresses a new idea, Mary's motherly sentiments and attitudes toward her children: "Receive into the open bosom of your mercy *(pietatis)* the people who hasten to you . . . May we ever live in your service *(in tua servitudine)*. . . . Protect us here below by your abounding affection *(multiplici* affectu tuearis)" J. Vivès (ed.), *Oracional Visigótico,* Barcelona, Vivès, 1946, p. 76. Cf. Barré, *Prières anciennes . . .* p. 33. This expression of Mary's motherly sentiments remains isolated for about three centuries. For the Carolingian epoch it is found again only (and independently moreover) with Ambrose Autpert; for him also Mary "considers as her sons" those who are incorporated into Christ *(filios deputat quos gratia consociat).* She embraces them in the maternal affection she has for Christ and intercedes with him for them *(cum suis intercessionibus . . . et materno affectu . . . id facit), Sermo in Purificationem* 7, PL 89:1297bc. In the context Autpert calls Mary "Mother of the elect" because she "engendered their brother," that is to say, Christ. He also calls her "Mother of the nations" *(mater gentium), Sermo de Assumptione 5* (= Ps. = Augustine *Sermo 208*), PL 39:2131, implicitly referring to Gen. 17:4 where Abraham is called "Father of nations" *(pater gentium).* This expression he took from an earlier author, Pseudo-Ildefonsus of the late seventh or early eighth century, *Sermo "Scientes fratres",* PL 96:271a (= Ps.-Jerome, PL 30:144, and Ps.-Maximos, PL 57: 866c). In the thirteenth century the expression passed into the Marian litanies of Venice, G. G. Meersseman, *Freiburger Zeitschrift für Philosophie und Theologie* 1 (1954), 153.

A beautiful text of St. Leander of Seville (d. 600/601), *De Institutione Virginum,* PL 72:878c, should be noted, where Mary is called "Mother of virgins" *(mater et dux virginum),* because she "engendered them by her example" *(exemplo suo genuit, loc. cit.,* 877d).

55. Without any boldness of expression, Milo of St. Amand (d. 871) opens a more promising avenue. He begins to glimpse the scope of Mary's role on Calvary *(De sobrietate,* II, vv. 12–18, MGH, *Poetae medii aevi* III, p. 645):

> Tu portas paradiso aperis quas clauserat Eva
> Letiferum vetita dum carpit ab arbore malum
> Sed crucis in ramis pomo pendente salubri

ticipations on all three points. But the anticipations remain altogether isolated and do not as yet give rise to development at this time.

If then the period from the sixth to the ninth century has little remarkable about it, this is due to two facts which must not too hastily be judged negatively. First, the literature of the West is less lyrical than that of the East, but also more reflective. It does not yet move along the pathways which will be so frequented from the eleventh century to the thirteenth. By this standard it may appear timid and somewhat archaic. But that is only the reverse of its profound quality of reflection. And secondly, the reflection of this time remains centered on the mysteries of the earthly life of Christ, notably on the Annunciation and the infancy mysteries. Mary continues to be considered in function of Christ and of the mystery of salvation.

3. The Tenth Century

It is not without reason that the tenth century has a bad reputation. On the stage of general history the Carolingian renaissance had all too short a day, without living up to its promises.[56] Charlemagne's work rapidly tumbled in ruins.

> Progenito de carne tua, tu planctibus instans,
> Gaudia quis (= quibus) mundo veniunt iam clave recepta
> Dulcis adoptivos ad caeli culmina natos.

The gist of this text, envisaging the scope of Mary's compassion, may be rendered thus: You open the gates of Paradise. Eve had closed them in picking the deadly fruit from the forbidden tree. But as for you, while on the branches of the cross there hung the fruit of salvation and the child of your flesh, assisting him as you did with your tears by which joy comes into the world, you lead your adoptive children to the heights of heaven whose key you have found again.

56. Is the Carolingian epoch a period of Marian renaissance or Marian decadence? In an article with new and remarkable documentation, E.

Further invasions ravaged Christendom. Authors dwindled in number. Nevertheless in the light of the more accurate scholarship recently devoted to this period one would do well to refine the previously unilateral judgments pronounced on this "century of iron and darkness," particularly in what concerns the Virgin Mary.

In reality, life went on even during this difficult epoch.

In the East John the Geometer proves himself quite an original thinker.[57]

In the West the heritage of preceding centuries is devotedly guarded. Sporadically the seeds of renewal seem on the point of sprouting. At the end of the century at the abbey of Reichenau a monk translates a collection of Byzantine homi-

---

Sabbe, "Le culte marial et la genèse de la sculpture médiévale," *Revue belge d'archéologie et d'histoire de l'art* 20 (1951), 101–125, has clearly answered decadence. The facts brought up by the author must be duly noted. But his judgment calls for refinement. The Carolingian period is not characterized by any outburst of sensibility (Barré, *Prières anciennes* ... p. 59–124). Doctrine is well represented by Paul the Deacon (d. after 785, PL 95:1565d–1574a), Alcuin (d. 804) who is at the origin of the votive Mass of the Virgin on Saturday, Walafrid Strabo (d. 849), Paschasius Radbertus (d. c855), author of the famous letter *Cogitis me,* Ratramnus (became a monk c825), Rabanus Maurus (d. 856), Hincmar (d. 882), Milo of St. Amand (d. 871; cf. preceding note), and the School of Auxerre, whose patrimony Barré has gathered together again from where it was scattered under different names in the Latin Patrology (PL 95:1200b–1204b; 96:272–277; 118:765–770. Cf. H. Barré, *Les Homéliaires carolingiens de l'Ecole d'Auxerre,* Vatican, 1962). Undoubtedly none of these authors attains the originality of Autpert (d. 784 at the threshold of the Carolingian period), who himself owes something to little known authors of the seventh century (cf. *Court Traité,* 1st edition, pp. 125, 129). At least the Carolingian authors give evidence of serious, balanced, and sometimes original reflection. Their devotion toward the Virgin, neither affective, tender, nor exalted, is sober, solid, and traditional. These conclusions are confirmed by L. Scheffczyk, *Das Mariengeheimnis im Frömmigkeit und Lehre der Karolingerzeit (Erfurter theologische Studien 5),* Erfurt, St. Benno Verlag, 1959.

57. Cf. *supra,* p. 92, n. 38.

lies[58] and thereby opens up the way for the advance of belief in the Assumption. The title "Mother of mercy"[59] and also that of *Redemptrix*[60] appear for the first time in isolated

---

58. *Codex Augiensis LXXX*, studied by Wenger, *op. cit.*, p. 148–172. The MS contains nine Greek homilies on the Dormition: two of Andrew of Crete (PG 97: 1045–1072 and 1089–1109), four of Cosmas Vestitor (ed. Wenger, *op. cit.*, pp. 337–362), one of Germanus of Constantinople (PG 98:340–353) and two of John Damascene (PG 96:700–753).

59. John of Salerno, *Vita Sancti Odonis* 2, 20, PL 133:724ab. Written about 945, the work recounts that the Virgin appeared to Odo of Cluny (d. 942) and told him, "Ego sum mater misericordiae." Toward 1025 the monk Syrus reported that St. Maïeul obtained a cure in praying to Mary as "Mother of mercy" (*Vita Sancti Maioli* 2, 12, PL 137:760c). This title figures in *Sermo 4* (PL 141:323c) of St. Fulbert of Chartres (d. 1029). One hesitates about the scope these authors gave the title: "Mother merciful toward her children" or "Mother of Christ who is mercy"? The context where there is question of a direct action of Mary would favor the second sense. However St. Peter Damian (d. 1072), who insists still more on Mary's intercession, adds an *"ipsius"* in his text of *Sermo 46 in Nativitatem B.V.* (PL 144:761b), showing clearly that "mercy" here designates the person of Christ whose Mother is Mary: "Rogamus te clementissima, *ipsius pietatis et misericordiae (sc. Christi) mater*, ut . . . tuae intercessionis auxilium habere mereamur in coelis — We beg you, most loving Mother of *him who is mercy and kindness itself*, that . . . we may be worthy to have the help of your intercession in heaven." Nevertheless, cf. *Sermo 44* (PL 144:740ad) of the same author, where Mary is merciful and is the depositary of the "treasure of God's mercies." In short, the authors of the 10th–11th century dwell on the idea that Mary gave us "Him who is mercy," and imperceptibly discover along this approach Mary's motherly mercy toward her other children.

60. "Sancta Redemptrix mundi, ora pro nobis": Litany of the Saints, handed down in a psalter of French origin preserved at the Cathedral of Salisbury, MS 180, fol. 171 vb, edited by F. E. Warren, "Un monument inédit de la liturgie celtique," *Revue celtique* 9 (1888), 88–96. There is one other use of the title in the eleventh century, another in the fourteenth.

In the fifteenth and sixteenth centuries the title spreads further. Its boldness begins to cause concern, all the more since what is more and more envisaged is Mary's *immediate* cooperation in the Redemption. The need is felt therefore to underline that Mary is only associated and dependent in her role, and to this end a prefix is added: *redemptrix* becomes *con-*

instances. The unknown writer who coined the latter title must not have measured the boldness involved in it; in line with a customary figure of speech he intended the title as a short way of saying "Mother of the Redeemer." The title will be abused later on and theology will rectify it; at the time it served as a pointer to further reflection. Finally, to a very notable degree prayer to Mary becomes more fervent, more filial, and more profound in these troubled times.[61]

In short, once again the alternating rhythm of advances and halts is discernible here, the rhythm of spring and winter that has characterized this doctrinal development. But for all that it is important not to overdo the contrast. The quiet reserve of the tenth century is not the silence of death. It is the still and hidden life of things in winter, when strength is gathering for the rebirth.

---

redemptrix or *co-redemptrix*. Christ is not spoken of as *co*redeemer but Redeemer; Mary is not called Redemptrix but co-redemptrix. This latter title will thus gradually replace the older one. However the extreme reserve of the papal magisterium in this regard should be noted. Only Pius X and Pius XI used the term *coredemptrix*, and in altogether minor contexts which did not commit their magisterium. On the whole history cf. R. Laurentin, *Le titre de Corédemptrice. Etude historique,* Paris, Lethielleux, and Rome, Marianum, 1951.

G. Meersseman, the most knowledgeable expert on the origin of litanies (cf. *infra,* p. 104, n. 1) gave the author the following explanation of the first uses of the title *Redemptrix:* it represents the Marian transposition of a series of Christological invocations occurring at the beginning of litanies.

61. Barré, *Prières anciennes* . . . pp. 100–127.

FOURTH PERIOD

FROM THE ELEVENTH CENTURY TO THE COUNCIL OF TRENT (1050–1563)

During the preceding period the East played the leading role in the development of Marian theology while the West followed in several areas, notably in the liturgy. In others it remained stationary, as in the question of the Immaculate Conception and especially the Assumption. This situation will now be reversed. To be sure, the Eastern writers of the thirteenth and fourteenth centuries outline some original syntheses; sometimes they even apply to their tradition the conceptual framework offered by western Scholasticism. But the fall of Byzantium (1453) soon puts an end to this development. During the present period and those to follow, devotion and reflection concerning the Virgin Mary remain alive in the East but tend to become closed in. This will reach a point even where the Easterners will be discomfited when tardily and in their own manner the Latins give expression to the Immaculate Conception, the original idea of which they owed to the Byzantines. From the viewpoint of development adopted in this study, there will be little further to say about the East. Before the chapters in which they were in the forefront are concluded, justice should be rendered them: the

Latins of the beginning of this period still owe them the decisive part of their own inspiration.[1] What is more, the separation culminating in 1054 will henceforth be for the western world a factor of impoverishment, particularism, and imbalance.

---

1. Cf. H. Barré, "L'apport marial de l'Occident à l'Occident, de saint Ambroise à saint Anselme," EM 19 (1962), pp. 27–89. The main Eastern contributions to Western thought in Marian doctrine, as covered in Barré's article, would be the following:

    a. The apocryphals of the infancy and the Assumption are brought to the West at a very early date (pp. 44–46). They play a considerable role in the liturgy and especially in art. Latin iconography reflects the eastern models directly, and these latter are entirely dependent on the apocryphals (Mahuet, *op. cit.*, pp. 145–183).

    b. At the end of the seventh century four Marian feasts are imported to Rome (cf. *supra,* p. 93).

    c. At a date difficult to determine (9th century or shortly thereafter) three Marian homilies — two of Proclus (d. 446) and one of Antipater of Bostra (d. after 451) — are substituted for Latin readings in which Mary's corporal glorification was not yet envisaged (Wenger, *op. cit.,* pp. 141–144).

    d. In the Carolingian era Paul the Deacon's translation of the *Life of Theophilus* transmits to the West the theme of the merciful Virgin and the title "mediatrix" (cf. *supra,* p. 97, n. 53).

    e. Toward 800 the Akathistos hymn is translated into Latin (G. Meersseman, *Der Hymnos Akathistos* . . .) as also the *Sub tuum* (PL 78:799d 8).

    f. At the end of the tenth century a group of homilies on the Assumption is translated at the abbey of Reichenau (cf. *supra,* p. 101, n. 58). Cf. Barré, *loc. cit.,* pp. 78–88.

    g. At the end of the eleventh century (toward 1060) the feast of the Conception, instituted in the East toward the end of the seventh century, passes over to Ireland, whence it spreads onto the continent beginning with the second half of the twelfth century (cf. *infra,* p. 107, n. 8).

    h. In the twelfth century the MS Heiligenkreuz 12 attempts to fill in the silence of the "illustrious ones" of the East on the Assumption by citing eastern witnesses: Pseudo-Dionysius (PG 3:681), Germanus of Constantinople (PG 98:357ab), the Euthymiac history (PG 96:747–752), and Cosmas Vestitor (Wenger, op. cit., p. 176, where the Latin version of Cosmas' homilies is found; cf. H. Barré, "Dossier complementaire," EM 8 (1950), pp. 67–68).

What date can be assigned to the beginning of the new stage in the West? Nothing is more difficult than to discern the first appearances of a living reality. Distant and isolated anticipations have been noted in the period preceding. Somewhat more precise beginnings emerge in Fulbert of Chartres (d. 1031),[2] and Odilo of Cluny (d. 1049).[3] The movement picks up speed with St. Peter Damian (d. 1072),[4] Anselm of Lucca (d. 1086), and Gottschalk of Limburg (d. 1095).[5] But, apart from this preamble, if the actual blossoming of the new phase is sought, there can be little hesitation: its key author is Saint Anselm of Canterbury (1033-1109). His thought touches on Mary's compassion, her intercession, her maternal role with regard to mankind, her perfect holiness, her exaltation, and a boundless confidence to be placed in her. All this wealth is centered on a fundamental intuition: "the admirable reality that Mary has given birth to God" *(Mira res . . . Maria Deum genuit).* It is around Anselm that the first writings in favor of the Immaculate Conception will spring up, as well as the work of the Pseudo-Augustine which in a decisive way sets the devel-

---

2. The Marian works of Fulbert of Chartres were compiled critically by the simultaneous efforts of J. M. Canal and H. Barré between 1962 and 1964. R. Laurentin, "Bulletin mariale," RSPT 50 (1966), 544-545, drew up a list of the works and bibliography on them.

Fulbert inaugurated a new interpretation of Gen. 3:15: *Ipsa conteret caput tuum* was taken to signify the victory of Mary over concupiscence (PL 141:320d-321a). Cf. R. Laurentin, "L'interprétation de Gen. 3:15 dans la Tradition," EM 12 (1954), pp. 102-104 and 125, n. 74.

3. *Sermons* 1, 3, 4, 12, PL 142:991-1088. (*Sermons* 13 and 14 are borrowed from earlier authors: *Court Traité,* 1st edition, p. 144).

4. *Sermons,* PL 144:505-924. (Several sermons of Nicholas of Clairvaux — 11, 23, 40, 43, and 60 concern Mary — are mixed with this collection; cf. *Court Traité,* 1st edition, pp. 144-145). *Hymns* 44-61, PL 144:933c-939c and 940-941a. (The other hymns are inauthentic; cf. *Court Traité,* loc. cit.).

5. Ed. G. Dreves, *Godescalcus Lintpurgensis . . . ,* Leipzig, Reiland, 1897.

opment of the dogma of the Assumption on its way again.[6] St. Bernard is only a witness of this current of thought, a witness with more marks of contrast than ordinarily thought. Certain acquisitions he solidified in striking formulas that passed on to posterity, but on other points his influence served rather to brake the movement, as will be seen shortly.[7]

The main lines of doctrinal development strikingly evident in this period are now to be examined.

Immaculate Conception, Assumption, Mediation

The feast of the "Conception" established by the Greeks toward the end of the seventh century remained unknown to

---

6. PL 158–159. Cf. J. Bruder, *The Mariology of Saint Anselm of Canterbury,* Dayton, 1939 — a more detailed bibliography in *Court Traité,* 1st edition, pp. 146–148 — and especially H. Barré, *Prières anciennes...* pp. 287–307, where an important chapter (the last) is consecrated to St. Anselm of Canterbury, showing his importance on the level of prayer as well as of theology.

7. The critical edition of St. Bernard's works has been undertaken by Dom J. Leclercq. The *In laudibus Virginis matris* is found in *S. Bernardi opera omnia,* Rome, 1966, t. 4. The ensemble of texts on Mary contained in PL 182–184 has been conveniently collected and translated by P. Aubron, *L'Oeuvre mariale de saint Bernard,* Paris, Cerf, 1935, with indications of Migne's numbering, and by P. Bernard, *Saint Bernard et Notre-Dame,* Paris, Desclée, 1953. For bibliography and treatment of questions of authenticity cf. *Court Traité,* 1st edition, pp. 152–154. (Leclercq's subsequent work indicates that PL 184:1013–1022, seemingly authentic, was put together by a secretary). The essential study is H. Barré, "Saint Bernard docteur marial," *Analecta sacri ordinis cisterciensis* 9 (1953), 92–113. St. Bernard's Marian theology is sober, profound, traditional, and spiritual. But it must be said clearly that it occupies a limited place in the ensemble of his work. He was able, for example, to preach on the feast of the Assumption without saying a word on Mary (PL 184:1001c–1010a). He contributes no new theme of any importance. He was so mistrustful of innovations that he opposed the Immaculate Conception (*Ep. 174,* PL 182:333–336; cf. *Sermo 2 in* Assumptione 8, PL 183:420d) and kept silence about any bodily Assumption. Often he gave the acquisitions of the 11th–12th centuries the stamp of approval that assured their triumph in the West.

the Latins for a long time. Brought over by some unknown monk returning from the East, it appeared in England toward 1060 but with the Norman conquest (1066) disappeared almost as soon, without leaving any other trace than a memory, though a memory tinged with regret at its passing. Thus it was that the feast was enthusiastically reinstituted about 1127–1128 on more solid foundations, passing soon into Normandy and thence to the rest of Europe,[8] despite the opposition of St. Bernard. Somewhat undetermined at the beginning, the object of the feast is clarified little by little, not without struggle.[9]

---

8. X. Le Bachelet, "L'Immaculée Conception," DTC 7:978–989, thought he had found the origins of the feast of the Conception in Ireland around 900. But this affirmation did not hold up against critical research. The fundamental studies on the origins of the feast are: A. W. Burridge, "L'Immaculée Conception dans la théologie mariale de l'Angleterre du Moyen-Age," *Revue d'histoire ecclésiastique* 32 (1936), 570–597; P. Grosjean, "La prétendue fête de la Conception dans les Eglises celtiques," *Analecta Bollandiana* 61 (1943), 91–95; A. M. Cecchin, "L'Immacolata nella liturgia occidentale al secolo XIII," *Marianum* 5 (1943), 58–114.

9. The theological problem of the Immaculate Conception was raised by the introduction of the feast of the Conception. The twelfth century situation remains quite complex. There were adversaries of the feast, in the front rank St. Bernard (*Ep. 174,* PL 182:332–336) and Peter of Celle (*Ep. 171* and *173,* PL 202:613–632). The feast had also its defenders — they were the immense majority — but they did not for all that support the Immaculate Conception; their positions were diverse and perplexed.

Some celebrated only the promise of the future Mother of God (as did, for example, the two anonymous authors published by H. Barré in *Sciences ecclésiastiques* 10 (1958), 353–359). The anonymous Parisian author of the late 13the century (Bibliothèque Nationale MS Lat. 5347, fol. 200 v., *ibid.,* 352) included in the word "conception" only the "sanctification" of Mary in her mother's womb.

Others held to the original holiness of Mary, but in very different senses. Some understood her holiness to begin at the moment of her conception; others with her spiritual conception, that is, with the infusion of the soul marking the beginning of Mary's personal existence.

Still other explanations presented themselves, and some were ridiculous. The Pseudo-Comestor and the anonymous author at Heiligenkreuz

Ever since the Carolingian epoch the Assumption had been in a critical phase, as has been seen (p. 55). Writing under the pseudonym of St. Jerome, Radbertus had launched a harsh attack on the *bodily* Assumption: Scripture did not inform us in the least about what happened to Mary's body, he observed, and on this matter the tales of the apocryphals are no safe guide. For almost three centuries this argument held fast. Nevertheless, certain documents coming from the East had made their way into tenth century Europe, and thus a reversal of opinion began to take shape, reaching expression by the twelfth century. Toward the end of the eleventh, in fact, an anonymous author using the name of St. Augustine[10] wrote a treatise in favor of the bodily Assumption. This Pseudo-Augustine quickly outshone the Pseudo-Jerome. And doctrinal merit rather than a false passport were mainly responsible. The Pseudo-Augustine fully recognized the

---

had recourse to the strange hypothesis of a *"vena pura,"* a particle of the body of Adam, that had remained apart from sin and been transmitted from generation to generation until from it Mary was born.

They all were wrestling with a problematic falsified by the Augustinian idea that the cause of the transmission of original sin was the impurity of the *libido* involved in every human generation. Some tried to explain that the act of Mary's parents was free of *libido,* others that the effect of this *libido* had been neutralized by God, either in his preventing the effect from taking place (Eadmer), or in his destroying the effect immediately (Osbert of Clare), or in his destroying it the moment the fetus was animated. As a matter of fact, the problem was poorly set up. The generative act is not tainted with sin nor is it this act that sullies human nature; yet the human nature that is transmitted is sullied. It is not surprising that time would be needed to emerge from this maze and many another.

What is moving is to follow the efforts of the faith as it seeks to express itself in such a new area, amid notions still poorly unraveled and tied in yet with all kinds of confusion (original sin, its transmission, conception, animation, etc.). Still more remarkable is the way Eadmer succeeds, amid so many difficulties, in approaching substantially the idea that Mary was preserved from sin by a special grace of God.

10. Numerous hypotheses have been proposed on the date of the author (*Court* Traité, 1st edition, p. 130). The certain and very limited conclusions of H. Barré have been adopted here.

criticisms directed against the apocryphals and instead founded the Assumption on a serious theological basis, treating the problem raised by doctrinal development here, and doing so with a precision remarkable for the age.[11]

It should be noted also that beginning with the eleventh century, and especially with the early twelfth, the title "Mediatrix,"[12] hitherto exceptional in the West, is found spread abroad widely.

A New Perspective[13]

A study as brief as this should focus its attention not so much on the detail of the ideas and new institutions[14] that crop up everywhere at this time, as on the key intuition that gives rise to them.

One basic appraisal can be made: at the end of the eleventh

---

11. In particular the celebrated methodological reflection should be recalled: "Fecunda est . . . veritatis auctoritas, et *dum diligenter discutitur, de se gignere quod ipsa est cognoscitur* — The authority of truth . . . bears fruit, and *when it is diligently debated, it is known to beget of itself what it is*" (PL 40:1143). "Sunt etiam quaedam quae quamvis ex toto omissa sint, vera tamen ratione creduntur, ad quod ipsa convenientia rei quemadmodum dux et praevia creditur — Certain things even there are which, although totally omitted (i.e., passed over in silence by Scripture), are rightly believed; the very fittingness of things is trusted as a guide and leader in this regard" (*Ibid.*, 1144).

12. Cf. *supra*, p. 97, n. 53.

13. This shift in perspective has been excellently described by H. Coathalem, *Le parallélisme entre la Sainte Vierge et l'Eglise dans la tradition latine jusqu'à la fin du XIIe siècle (Analecta Gregoriana 74)*, Rome, Gregorianum, 1954, the delayed printing of a thesis defended in 1939.

14. The listing of the Marian discoveries and innovations of the twelfth century has not yet been completed. H. Barré, "Une prière d'Eckbert de Schönau au saint coeur de Marie," EphM 2 (1952), 409–423, has shown how, for example, the first prayer to the heart of Mary appears at that time. (Eckbert was abbot of Schönau from 1166 to 1184.) G. G. Meersseman, "Etudes sur les anciennes confréries dominicaines," *Archivum Fratrum Praedicatorum* 22 (1952), 5–176, has drawn attention to the appearance and rapid multiplication of Marian confraternities, etc.

century Marian theology widens its horizon. Prior to this Mary had been considered for the most part in the mystery of Christ's infancy. Her role on *Calvary* and in the *present life of the Church* remained in the shadow.[15] Crossed here and there before, this boundary will henceforth be left behind everywhere.

1. In the first place, the attention hitherto centered on Mary's role in the Incarnation, root and pledge of salvation, is extended to her role in the sacrifice of Calvary. Obviously it did not take until the eleventh century for Mary to be recognized as having played a role in the salvation of the world. But apart from two or three imprecise intimations, this role had not been considered beyond Christ's infancy. At the dawn of the twelfth century Mary's presence on Golgotha captures the attention of authors and reveals riches unsuspected until then. They discover her compassion,[16] her

---

15. As always, whenever anything new appears it is possible to find distant harbingers of it in more or less isolated predecessors. Thus St. Ambrose commented on the presence of Mary on Calvary in almost the same terms in three texts (*In Lc.* 10, PL 15:1837–1838; *De Inst. Virg.*, 5, PL 16:318; *Ep. 63 ad Vercell.* 109–110, PL 16:1218bc), though his presentation is very reserved and concerned above all about the Redeemer's transcendence. On the role that Mary exercises from heaven in the present life of the Church the texts earlier than the 11th–13th centuries are more numerous.

Obviously the 11th–13th centuries do not constitute a revolution or a complete turnabout, which would be a heresy. But various points which had been envisaged only hesitantly, inchoatively, or sporadically now became the object of firm, distinct, and systematic consideration and moved into the foreground. Elements which had appeared disjointed or even scattered in previous periods now join together and assume recognizable form.

16. St. Peter Damian (d. 1072) is the first known witness of the theme of Mary's compassion on Calvary. But he did not express its theological importance. Commenting on the brief sentence of Lk. 2:35, "A sword shall pierce your soul," he limits himself thus: "Ac si diceret dum Filius tuus senserit *passionem* in corpore, te etiam transfiget gladius *compassionis* in mente — As if he were saying that when your Son would feel the *passion*

active union with the offering of her Son,[17] the ecclesial dimension of her faith during the three days of his death *(triduum mortis).* [18] They finally grasp the implications of the

---

in his body, the sword of *compassion* would transfix you also in spirit" *(Sermo 46 in Nativitatem B.V.,* PL 144:748a). This theme has been studied by H. Barré, "Le Planctus Mariae," *Revue ascétique et mystique* 28 (1952), 244-246. The earlier text on the theme from Milo of St. Amand was cited supra, p. 98, n. 55.

17. Concerning the offering made by Mary on Calvary, Arnold of Bonneval opens the way in his *De Laudibus Virginis,* PL 189:1727a: "Unum holocaustum ambo (sc. Christus et Maria) pariter offerebant — Both (Christ and Mary) together offered a single holocaust." On Arnold's texts cf. Laurentin, *Marie, L'Eglise* . . . vol. 1, pp. 145-153. Haunted by a restrictive text of St. Ambrose (PL 16:1218bc) whose terms he takes up anew, Arnold broadens these limits by developing suggestions of St. Bernard *(Sermon on the Twelve Stars,* PL 183:429d and 437c-438a; *Sermon on the Nativity, ibid.,* 441cd) and the resulting views are both rich and balanced.

Concerning the offering made by Mary at the time of the presentation of Jesus in the Temple, the lead probably falls to St. Bernard (Laurentin, *Marie, L'Eglise* . . . vol. 1, pp. 132-182). This may well be the most original innovation of the abbot of Clairvaux who, in using Autpert, goes beyond him without hesitation *(Loc. cit.,* pp. 140-143). Two other texts, not at hand at the time of Laurentin's study, may be earlier than St. Bernard, although that is not certain: Geoffrey of Vendôme (d. 1132), *Sermo 7 de Purificatione,* PL 157:262d, and Abelard, *Hymnus 38 in Purificationem* . . . PL 178:1793a (composed at St. Gildas, thus between 1125 and 1136). The terms are in part identical with those of St. Bernard.

18. The theme that the faith of Mary alone remained alive during the death of Christ (as the last candle of the office of Tenebrae) is met with for the first time in Odo of Ourscamp (d. 1171), *Quaestiones* II, 56, ed. J. Pitra, *Analecta novissima spicilegii Solesmensis,* t. 2, Rome, Tusculanis, 1878, p. 53: "Maria Magdalena . . . passione turbata hanc fidem amisit, etiam cum discipulis; *cujus infidelitatis matrem Domini solam immunem credimus —* Mary Magdalen . . . overcome by the passion lost this faith (sc. in Christ's divinity), as did his disciples; *only the Mother of the Lord, we believe, remained immune to this loss of faith."* (The work was written about 1160.) On the considerable expansion this theme will undergo during the Middle Ages and its variations in the Renaissance, cf. Y. Congar, "Incidence ecclésiologique d'un thème de dévotion mariale," *Mélanges de*

dying Christ's words, "This is your mother."[19] Until then, thanks in part to arguments stemming from controversy, Christ's words had been understood as a gesture of filial piety: he was confiding his mother to Saint John in her abandonment. Hereafter the spiritual sense of Jesus' words will be seen: Mary was given to be mother of men.[20] Little by little the idea dawns that in her own way she cooperated in the sacrifice of Calvary.[21]

2. Meanwhile the perspective is being broadened in a second direction. Prior to this period Mary had been considered as part of the mysteries of Christ's infancy in the perpetually enduring quality these mysteries have. If attention had begun to focus, for example with Autpert, on her present and active role today, this kind of consideration was only a passing matter and it remained rooted primarily in the perpetuity of the infancy mysteries. When, for instance, it was said that

---

sciences religieuses 7 (1950), 277–291. A complete listing is given by H. Barré, "Marie et l'Eglise, du Vénérable Bède à Saint Albert le Grand," EM 9 (1951), pp. 83–84, and Laurentin, *Marie, l'Eglise* . . . vol. 1, pp. 138–139.

19. Jn. 19:26.

20. In the East, Origen and George of Nicomedia (cf. *supra,* p. 92, n. 39) are the only witnesses of the spiritual sense for the first ten centuries, and their views moreover are still restrained.

In the West there is nothing earlier than Anselm of Lucca (d. 1086) in his *Oratio I,* ed. A. Wilmart, *Revue ascétique et mystique* 19 (1938), p. 53, lines 98–104. Jesus said, " 'Ecce mater tua,' ut tanto pietatis affectu pro omnibus recte credentibus mater gloriosa intercederet . . . et adoptatos in filios . . . custodiret — 'Behold your mother,' so that this glorious mother might intercede with so great tenderly affection for all who rightly believe . . . and might keep them as adopted children." The same theme is found in Rupert of Deutz (d.1135), *Com. in Joannem* 13, PL 169:789c–790c. Cf. G. Duclos, *La Vierge Marie dans l'histoire du salut selon Rupert de Deutz,* Typewritten thesis, Rome, Gregorian, 1953, pp. 91–102.

21. All the elements of the problem are already found with Arnold of Bonneval (cf. *supra,* n. 17). A similar density of expression will not be met with for quite some time.

Mary "destroyed all heresies," the reference was less to any present intervention exercised from on high than to her act of faith at the Annunciation, an act victorious once for all time.[22] Mary's present role was explained by saying that we continue to benefit from what the Virgin did at the beginning of Christ's life, and that we do this in entering into communion with the fundamental mysteries of the history of salvation. Henceforth it will be said rather that Mary does all this today from heaven, because she is our mother, our queen, our mediatrix, and ultimately because she is the Mother of God, powerful in her influence on his love. From the mystery-filled perspective where everything gravitated around the plenitude realized once and for all in Christ, authors have shifted to an analytical perspective where attention is focused on what Mary daily accomplishes here below, in virtue of the titles and privileges that are hers. The new element is not that the Virgin's daily role has been "discovered": it was already spoken of after a fashion by Autpert, Alcuin, and Radbertus.[23] What is new is that this role is considered systematically as a present action performed from on high by Mary, who was taken body and soul to heaven,[24] an action per-

---

22. A. Emmen, "Cunctas haereses sola interemisti. Usus et sensus hujus encomii B.M. Virginis in liturgia, theologia et documentis pontificiis," *Maria et Ecclesia* 9 (1961), pp. 93–159, suggests that the antiphon in question is of Greek origin and earlier than 650–700. However, H. Barré, "Antiennes et répons . . ." *Marianum* 29 (1967), 196, #67, inclines toward the Roman origin mentioned in the legend.

23. Autpert, *supra*, p. 97, n. 54. Alcuin (*Inscriptio 86*, PL 101:749b and MGH *Poetae* I, 305) addresses Mary in these terms: "Dies nostros precibus rege semper et ubique — Rule over our days always and everywhere by your prayers." Radbertus, *Letter "Cogitis me"* 3, PL 30:124c. Rabanus Maurus, *In natali S. Mariae,* PL 110:55a. Paul the Deacon, *Sermo I in Assumptione,* PL 95:1569c.

24. An example: a text of Ambrose Autpert was cited *supra*, p. 97, n. 54, in which Mary's spiritual motherhood takes the concrete form of "intercession" and of "motherly affection." But Autpert understands all this not so much in terms of an action performed from heaven during the era of

formed today in virtue both of prerogatives acquired during her life on earth and of the intermediary position she occupies between Christ, who is above her, and the world below.[25] Very typical in this respect is the new image found with Hermann of Tournai (d. 1137): Mary is "the neck of the Church" *(Collum Ecclesiae).*[26] She is "between Christ and the Church," St. Bernard will say even more clearly.[27]

---

the Church, but rather as the ever living presence of an action exercised by Mary on the day of the Purification, when she "offered" Jesus to Simeon: *"Non desinit . . . offerre* quem genuit, Redemptorem electis uniri facit — *She does not cease to offer* the one she begot, she brings the Redeemer into union with the elect." Of course, this is a simple nuance, for Autpert, of all the ancient authors, is the one who most clearly sketched in advance the discoveries that were to be made in the twelfth century. But this important nuance has its historical interest.

It is at the end of the eleventh century and especially during the twelfth, that Mary's spiritual motherhood with regard to men progressively takes on its concrete shape and its localization in heaven. Representatives are St. Peter Damian and especially St. Anselm (*Oratio 52,* PL 158:956ab–957a) along with his disciples Eadmer, Hermann of Tournai, and William of Malmesbury. In the thirteenth century this theme becomes the subject of a special chapter and the object of an *ex professo* study with Richard of St. Lawrence, *De laudibus* IV, 1, # 11–12, in *Alberti Magni . . . opera,* ed. Borgnet, t. 36, p. 327, and with Pseudo-Albert, *Mariale,* q. 145 *Utrum ei conveniat esse matrem omnium, ibid.,* t. 37, pp. 204–206. Cf. H. Barré, "Marie et l'Eglise . . ." EM 9 (1951), pp. 77–80. For anticipations of the theme cf. *supra,* pp. 85–88, n. 26–32 and p. 91, n. 38, and *infra,* Appendix #7.

25. On these themes cf. Barré, "Marie et l'Eglise . . ." EM 9 (1951), pp. 94–99.

26. *De Incarnatione* 8, PL 180:29d–30a.

27. "Vellus est medium *inter* rorem et aream (Jgs. 6:37–40), mulier inter solem et lunam (Apoc. 12:1), Maria inter Christum et Ecclesiam constituta — The fleece is in the middle *between* the dew and the ground, the woman between the sun and the moon, Mary between Christ and the Church." St. Bernard, *In Dom. infra Assumpt.* 5, PL 183:432a.

The image of the aqueduct that channels grace is found for the first time in St. Bernard, *Sermo de Aqueductu,* PL 183:437–438.

The title "Mater Ecclesiae" appears for the first time in the twelfth

Impact of This Change

What is the significance of this change? It corresponds first of all to a new religious consciousness of duration. In meditating on the life of Christ the Fathers did not have the feeling that it was distant in time. They were taken up with the perpetuity of these mysteries. They had the feeling of perpetually gravitating around a mystery that escaped time-limits: the liturgical cycle remains the striking impression of their state of mind. Progressively, and with the thirteenth century marking a definite stage, more attention will be given to the stability proper to the cosmos and to time, a stability such that one is deeply rooted in them both. Thus the mystical life will be considered less as a return to the source and more as a laying hold of the source, less as an entry into a mystery that does not pass away and more as a daily descent of mystery into the moving duration of this world which has to be fashioned to God's image. Hereafter contact with Christ will be sought less by way of commemoration and more by raising one's gaze toward heaven. Hence the presentation of heaven in medieval art takes on growing importance, later to yield to that abusive portrayal of the heaven-struck gaze by then become the commonplace of pietistic religiosity.

This change of spatial and temporal perspective in the

---

century with Berengaudus (c. 1125), *In Apoc.* 12, PL 17:876cd: "Possumus per mulierem (Apoc. 12:1) . . . et beatam Mariam intelligere eo quod ipsa mater sit Ecclesiae; quia eum peperit qui est caput Ecclesiae; et filia sit Ecclesiae quia maximum membrum est Ecclesiae — In the 'woman' of Apoc. 12:1 . . . we can understand Mary, inasmuch as she is herself mother of the Church, because she brought forth him who is head of the Church; and inasmuch as she is daughter of the Church, because she is the Church's most important member." The title "mother" is balanced by those of "daughter" and "member" of the Church. Earlier witnesses of the title "Mother of the Church" are at least doubtful (Laurentin, *La Vierge* . . . pp. 174–175). The title remains quite exceptional up to recent years.

religious world is accompanied by another, less noticed but in need of little more than being recalled here: the subjective point of view begins to overshadow the objective, persons become more important than mystery.

This double shifting of perspective extends very far beyond the case of Mary. It corresponds to a turning-point in civilization and culture. An analogous evolution takes place at this time in the sacramental order: the personal presence of Christ, till then enwrapped in the whole of the Eucharistic mystery, now comes to the forefront. Likewise the person of Mary, hitherto enveloped in some way within the objective mystery of the Church, is brought into clearer light. In the Eucharist what had earlier been seen was the return to the redemptive sacrifice by way of sign. Henceforth the Eucharist is seen more readily as the effective presence of Christ on earth, and the "reproduction" or "reiteration" of his sacrifice.

As will be surmised, these changes of perspective open unexplored horizons and renew theological reflection. But they also have their danger. No doubt they make it possible to grasp authentic aspects of the realities of the faith, but risk sets in when these newer insights, which had unfolded within the ancient and fundamental perspective, tend to supplant or even to eliminate the latter. The twelfth century and in great measure the thirteenth still keep things in balance, in part thanks to a living contact maintained with the Fathers of the Church. But later on, this fruitful tension gives way to enthusiasm over the new perspective alone. The viewpoint of former times tends to become the patrimony of archeologists. To be sure, the objects of faith remain the same, but they tend to be considered from a narrower angle. The perennial quality of the mysteries is lost sight of, in favor of becoming engrossed in the movement of time; the point of view of the religious object is forgotten, in favor of becoming wrapped up in an increasingly barren attention to the subject — and this inflexible turn will take on dramatic proportions with the

Renaissance. Marian theology shifts in the direction of a personal exaltation of the queen of heaven, setting aside her place in the Church. The unfurling of her activity toward her clients, the succession of her miracles — these now win attention more than does her exemplary role at the starting-point of the history of salvation. The stages of this decadence must now rapidly be surveyed.

Decadence (13th to 15th Centuries)

Armed as it was with the most lucid and powerful of philosophical instruments, the thirteenth century succeeded in putting order in many a domain that had felt the impact of the excited discoveries of the twelfth century. But Mariology was among the less fortunate of these domains. The Marian synthesis that was most conspicuous at the time and that exercised most influence was the famous *Mariale super missus est,*[28] attributed till recently (1954) to St. Albert the Great. This work exhibits the first symptoms of the decadence. It is the first effort made to tie in the whole of Mariology systematically with a unique guiding principle, but in this very effort it tends to make Mariology a closed system. The principle of synthesis chosen is narrow. It is the all-containing quality of the grace that is Mary's, a "plenitude" that includes the diverse gifts distributed among all other creatures. Thus it is that the author finds in Mary the universality of human knowledge, the properties of the angels, and the grace of the seven sacraments, including penance, which she is held actually to have received, and holy orders, whose dignity, grace, and powers she is held to have possessed eminently.[29] The work does, in fairness, have its merits. For

---

28. The work appears in *B. Alberti Magni . . . Opera,* ed. Borgnet, Paris, Vivès, 1898, t. 37, pp. 1–362, and ed. Jammy, Lyons, 1651, t. 20, pp. 1–156.
29. Laurentin, *Marie, l'Eglise . . .* vol. 1, pp. 183–194. At the time of

the most part a sharp sense of Christ's transcendence counterbalances the excessive inventory of Marian privileges. Mary's association with the Savior is pointed up in new and striking formulations: she is the associate of Christ *(Socia Christi)*, and in an expression taken from Gn. 2:21 "a helpmate like to him" *(adjutorium simile sibi);* here the Eve-Mary parallel is enriched with a last trait, neglected until then.[30] In all these respects the *Mariale* is remarkable. Today

---

writing (1953) the author still believed, as did everyone else, that St. Albert was the author of the *Mariale* and he was concerned about the severity with which he felt obliged to comment on what was taken to be the work of a doctor of the Church.

In a certain sense a fundamental principle was already discernible in St. Anselm, the outstanding figure of the preceding period in the history of Marian theology: "Maria Deum genuit . . . mira res." Barré, *Prières anciennes...* pp. 294-299, had already demonstrated this. But the principle had not yet given rise to any systematic undertaking, and, what is especially notable, it was Christocentric and not Mariocentric. Thus the innovations of the Pseudo-Albert bear an early responsibility in setting Marian theology on the way to decadence.

30. Hermann of Tournai, or of Laon (d. 1137) had applied to Mary the *"adjutorium simile sibi —* helpmate like himself" of Gen. 2:18 (*De Incarnatione* 2, PL 80:36b), but he seems to have thought of her as "helpmate to the Father" rather than "helpmate of Christ" (H. Barré, "La nouvelle Eve dans la pensée médiévale d'Ambroise Autpert au pseudo-Albert," EM 14 (1956), p. 12). The Pseudo-Albert seems therefore to be the herald of this new theme. Why did this element of the Eve-Mary parallel end up being the last to be exploited?

a. This title, "helpmate like himself," was linked to the episode of Eve's being drawn from Adam's side (*ex latere Adam,* Gen. 2:18-20), and thus was considered a specific attribute of the Church, which was born on Calvary from Christ's side.

b. St. Ambrose had set up an impressive barrier against the Marian interpretation of the title, in three texts where he raised the problem of Mary's role at the foot of the cross: *"Jesus non egebat adjutore* ad redemptionem omnium — Jesus *did not need a helper* for the redemption of all" (*Ep. 63,* 110, PL 16:1218c and *In Lc.* X, 132, PL 15:1837c), and "Sed Christi Passio *adjutorio non eguit —* But Christ's Passion *needed no helper"* (*De Inst. Virg.* VII, 49, PL 16:350bc). Among Greek authors no

it is possible to pronounce a sober judgment on both the greatness and the weakness of this work which in its time was praised to the skies and ordinarily preserved from criticism by its attribution to Albert the Great. But it is not his work, as two scholars demonstrated almost simultaneously in 1954.[31] The genuine author, who is placed in the second half of the thirteenth century, remains unknown. Mariological circles were stirred deeply by the discovery of this false attribution, as deeply, for example, as literary circles would be if the thesis denying to Shakespeare his dramas were scientifically justified.

More than the Pseudo-Albert with his principle of all-containing grace, St. Thomas Aquinas advanced Marian doctrine by his contributions to a knowledge of the mystery

---

application of Gen. 2:18 to Mary has been found before Cabasilas (d. after 1396). Even with him the Theotokos is presented not as the helpmate of *Christ* but of *God:* "Eve was a helpmate *(boēthos,* Gen. 2:18) for Adam. Only Mary helped *(eboēthēsen)* God in the manifestation of his goodness" *(Hom. in Nativ.,* PO 19:482, lines 35–38).

31. A. Fries, *Die unter dem Namen des Albertus Schriften (Beitrage 37, 4),* Münster, Aschendorff, 1954, situates the *Mariale* toward the end of the thirteenth century. B. Korošak, *Mariologia sancti Alberti Magni eiusque coaequalium (Bibliotheca mariana medii aevi 8),* Rome, Academia Mariana, 1954, situates it before St. Bonaventure. F. Pelster, "Zwei Untersuchungen," *Scholastik* 30 (1955), 388–401, who expertly treats the divergences of detail between the two previous works, supports Korošak's mid-13th century dating. A listing of these studies is found in R. Laurentin, "Que reste-t-il de l'oeuvre mariale d'Albert le Grand?" *Supplement à la Vie Spirituelle* 38 (1955), 348–360.

A. Kolping, "Zur Frage des Textgeschichte Herkunft und Entstehungzeit des anonymus 'Laus Virginis'," *Recherches de théologie ancienne et médiévale* 25 (1958), 285–288, suggests attributing the famous *Mariale* to Engelbert of Admont, but this is only a conjecture.

The numerous monographs consecrated to Albert the Great's Mariology (a bibliography in J. B. Carol, *De Corredemptione,* Rome, 1951, p. 164, n. 2) have thus become out of date. Hereafter one should consult A. Fries, *Die Gedanken des Heiligen Albertus Magnus über die Gottesmutter (Thomistische Studien 7),* Freiburg/Schweiz, Paulus, 1959.

of Mary, Mother of God, and of the *relationship* involved in this mystery.³² Mariologists have sometimes expressed the regret that he did not carry through from this notion of relationship to a complete Marian synthesis. But there is hardly any regrettable inferiority implied in the fact that for him the Virgin Mary was not the object of a science apart, or that he spoke of her only "in context," that is, in function of Christ, as did the other doctors of his age. Moreover, had he attempted a synthesis, it would have been marred by the difficulties relative to the Immaculate Conception that he inherited and was not able to overcome.

Without accomplishing a synthesis either, Duns Scotus opens a breach in these last-mentioned difficulties.³³ When he

---

32. G. Roschini, *La mariologia di San Tommaso,* Rome, Belardetti, 1950, pp. 24–33, gives a good bibliography of works consecrated to the Mariology of the Angelic Doctor. R. Laurentin adds some in an article in *Bulletin Thomiste* 8 (1947–1953), 1091, n. 1. Since 1854 very many authors have made St. Thomas into an unacclaimed immaculist. Concerning the most important of these attempts, J. A. Robilliard in an article in RSPT 39 (1955), 464–465, has explained why the cause is a hopeless one. It remains no less true that principles are found in St. Thomas' works which serve to establish and profoundly explain the Immaculate Conception.

33. C. Balic, *Joannis Duns Scotti, Doctoris mariani, theologiae Marianae elementa (Bibliotheca mariana medii aevi 2),* Sibenik, Kacic, 1933, and *Joannes Duns Scotus, Doctor Immaculatae Conceptionis,* Rome, Academia Mariana, 1954.

G. Roschini, *Duns Scoto e l'Immacolata,* Rome, Marianum, 1955 in very scholarly manner presented all the arguments capable of minimizing the historical importance of Scotus. A widespread controversy followed, the chronicle of which is given by R. Laurentin in an article in *Supplement à la Vie Spirituelle* 35 (1955), 467–470 and *Vie Spirituelle* 101 (1959), # 456, 545–548. Cf. also G. Bessutti, *Bibliografia mariana 1952–1957,* Rome, Marianum, 1959, pp. 67–69, # 1286–1322.

Scotus' importance remains considerable. His principle merit is in having *taken up* and *turned back* the main objection currently given, that a sinless conception compromised the universal Redemption. On the contrary, Scotus replied, the Redeemer's perfection requires that he have *preserved* (and not simply *purified*) the holiest of creatures from sin.

began teaching at Paris in the last years of the thirteenth century, the Immaculate Conception was universally disowned by theologians.[34] Therefore out of fear of censure he was able to propose it only as an opinion. But his line of argument modified the whole approach to the question to the point of reversing this situation. Later authors did little more than recognize or refine the value of the arguments he drew up. The change of mind occurred rapidly. In 1439 the theologians gathered at Basel for the council were in agreement for defining the Immaculate Conception as a dogma of faith.[35] The definition, duly drawn up in correct form, remained without effect because the council had ceased to be in communion with Rome. But the consensus that lay behind its promulgation (and that was no longer to be found at Trent) is significant.

The diffusion of this belief in the Immaculate Conception ought not to lead to an exaggeration of the accomplishments of this period. What is represented is rather the strong impact of Scotus' ideas than any broad theological progress properly so called. Once the fifteenth century has been reached, there is no longer anything worthy of note, except for the important decisions of Sixtus IV in officially adopting the feast of the Conception at Rome and in protecting the immaculist thesis against the violent attacts of Bandelli.[36] By

---

34. On the lack of recognition generally suffered by the idea in the thirteenth century and the spread of the immaculist thesis beginning with Scotus and Ware, see F. de Guimaraens, "La doctrine des théologiens sur l'Immaculée Conception de 1250 à 1350," *Etudes Franciscaines* 3 (1952), 181–204; 4 (1954), 23–52, 167–188. On the spread of the idea in Spain, see A. Braña Arrese, *De Immaculata Conceptione B. V. Mariae secundum theologos hispanos saeculi* XIV, Rome, Academia Mariana, 1950.

35. On the Council of Basel see H. Ameri, *Doctrina theologorum de Immaculata B.V. Conceptione tempore concilii Basileensis,* Rome, Academia Mariana, 1945.

36. The Pope did not go to the root of the debate. He defended the "Immaculate Conception" against the attacks of Bandelli and his support-

that time the phase of calm expansion of this doctrine had ended and the "immaculist" debate entered a sharply polemic phase from which it was not to emerge until almost the nineteenth century.

Apart from these rare positive traits that have just been touched upon, the fifteenth century offers a drab and mediocre picture.

On the level of doctrine there is simple repetition rather than original thought. Now that it had systematized itself, theology cut itself off progressively from its own sources and from human life. It fell victim to complexity and conceptual sclerosis. Nominalism raged uncontrollably.

On the level of devotion the liturgy progressively becomes foreign to the people since it no longer speaks their language. It is neglected in favor of private devotions that increase in number and grow corrupt.

More and more disconcerted by the abstraction of both theology and the liturgy, the people look for life elsewhere. Their fervor turns to the sentimental and the superficial, if not the superstitious. Too often it is nourished by unhealthy elements: trumped up miracles, double-meaning slogans, inconsistent babble — all as ersatz for doctrine and liturgy now and become things quite distant.

The evolution of art exhibits this sliding from mystery to naturalism and from naturalism to artifice. For the Romanesque Virgin, unperturbed throne of Incarnate Wisdom,[37] the

---

ers, who were sowing discord in declaring this opinion heretical. But he also forbade the immaculists (whose opinion he shared, as he imperceptibly hinted) to declare heretical or sinful the maculist opinion. The two opposing theses had therefore the same juridical status, which consisted for each in the prohibition of condemning the opposite view. This discretion may surprise some. But in the emotional state of confusion and immaturity in which the debate unfurled, it would not have been prudent to intervene more deeply. Full light came only with peace on the subject. Then the Church would be able to proceed to a dogmatic definition. But three centuries would be required for the Holy See to reach this result.

37. Articles by E. Male, E. Bréhier, M. Gromaire, and photo by G. Cany

twelfth century substitutes a new kind of Virgin, gracious and smiling — presenting her smile more than her Son. The infant Jesus loses his place in the center and passes to one side. For the sober and hieratic costume artists substitute feminine finery with ever more complicated folds of clothing. Little by little mannerisms and quackery replace genuine art. By the fifteenth century the Virgin on Calvary is swooning in a faint of grief. Sermons play up her tears, her sobbing, her weakness; all too often do they forget to mention her strength and her cooperation in the work of salvation.

This miserable state of affairs was just about reaching its depths when the Protestant crisis broke out. The Marian author of the hour was Bernardine de Busti whose *Mariale*, published for the first time in 1496, went through very many editions.[38] An idea of the decadence of the period can be formed from the fact that it should have esteemed so highly a work like this where traditional doctrine is drowned in a welter of outlandish and inconsistent opinions.

The time to clear the air and especially to put essential things back in place was long overdue. But the Fifth Council of the Lateran (1512–1517) had no such concern. The position of the Virgin seemed incontestable enough not to be compromised by these pious shortcomings.

In fact, on this point the position of the first reformers was a moderate one. Luther may well have written, "I should like to suppress the Virgin on account of the abuses." But he was very reserved in his criticism. He held to all that Catholic dogma had defined in her regard: Mary, Mother of God, holy, virgin before and after childbirth. One of his texts even seems to point in the direction of the Immaculate Conception. Throughout his life he celebrated the feast of the Visita-

---

in the issue #25 entitled "Vierges romanes d'Auvergne," *Le Point* 5 (1943).

38. F. Cucchi, *La mediazione universale negli scritti di Bernardino de Busti*, Milan, Ancora, 1943, loyally tried to extricate what is best from this author.

tion with particular fervor, and he consecrated a book to the *Magnificat*.[39] By comparison Calvin is in second rank, but he too keeps all the essentials.[40] It is little by little, in the aftermath of criticism of devotion to the saints, that devotion to the virgin will be eliminated. This elimination assuredly was something demanded by the radical application of the principles of the Reform: *Scripture alone, grace alone, God alone.* Protestants of succeeding generations will thus soon return to the situation as it was before Ephesus. Difficulties long since surmounted, difficulties that had been a stumbling-block to thinkers like Tertullian, Chrysostom, or Cyril are with time restored to favor in Protestantism, where sometimes even a kind of hostility toward the Virgin Mary will be found. Battle-lines are thus drawn up that condition the development of doctrine for centuries to come: disparaged by

---

39. *Note on the Virgin Mary in Luther's thought:* Any scientific study on this subject should refer to the Weimar edition of Luther's works. The principal texts have been conveniently assembled by W. Tappolet, *Das Marienlob der Reformatoren,* Tübingen, 1962, pp. 17–162. (The original text has been transcribed in modern spelling, and the Latin insertions in the sermons translated into German.) Luther's *Tractatus super Magnificat* was published in Latin in 1526 under the title *Martini Lutheri in divae* (sic) *Virginis Mariae Zachariaeque odas: Magnificat puta et Benedictus commentarii.* In recent years this work has gone through several new editions and translations.

Among the works on Luther's Marian thought the following may be noted: on the Protestant side, W. Delius, *Geschichte der Marienverehrung,* Munich-Basel, 1963, pp. 195–229; on the Catholic side, E. Stakemeir, "De Beata M. Virgine ejusque cultu juxta reformatores," *De Mariologia et Oecumenismo,* Rome, Academia Mariana, 1962, pp. 423–449, and T. O'Meara, *Mary in Protestant and Catholic Theology,* New York, Sheed and Ward, 1966, pp. 109–125.

These three studies also present the positions of Zwingli and Calvin. On Mary in Protestantism as a whole see R. Schimmelpfennig, *Die Geschichte der Marienverehrung im deutschen Protestantismus,* Paderborn, 1952 (excellent bibliography, pp. 150–160).

40. On Calvin's Mariology see, in addition to the above studies, B. D. Dupuy's article in *Istina* 1958, # 4, 479–490.

Eleventh Century to Trent 125

Protestantism, the Virgin Mary is going to be systematically exalted in Catholicism, under the force of an impulse without precedent.[41]

But the drama had not yet reached this point when the Council of Trent finished its work. In 1563 the Council came to a close without ever having treated the Marian question, which thus remained in a notably deficient state.[42]

---

41. On Protestants and Mariology cf. *infra*, Bibliography, p. 363.

42. The Council of Trent touched the Marian question only briefly and occasionally, in relation to original sin (Denz. 792 (1515)) and to the saints' images and relics (Denz. 986 (1823)). B. Korošak, *Doctrina de Immaculatae B.V. Mariae Conceptione apud auctores ordinis minorum qui concilio Tridentino interfuerunt*, Rome, Academia Mariana, 1958, gives an excellent bibliography of studies on the problem of the Immaculate Conception at the Council of Trent. It is to be noted that the behind-the-scenes activities of the "maculists" succeeded in eliminating the clause relative to the Immaculate Conception from most of the older editions of the Council's acts (Paris 1546 and 1550; Antwerp 1546 and 1556).

FIFTH PERIOD

THE POST-TRIDENTINE MARIAN MOVEMENT (1563–1958)

In the last years of the sixteenth century a Marian revival got under way, beginning in the countries untouched by the Reformation: Italy and Spain. Spain in particular was then at the height of her glory and was setting the tone in every field of activity, from theology to literature, from mysticism to fashion in dress. The leaders of the movement were the first great theologians of the Society of Jesus. In Spain they numbered Salmeron (d. 1585),[1] Suarez[2] who in 1590 was to put together the first systematic mariology, and Salazar[3] from whose pen came the first great work on the Immaculate Conception in 1618 and the first treatise precisely on the subject of Mary's part in the Redemption. Their number was

---

1. M. Andrés, "La compasión . . . segun Salmerón," EstM 5 (1946), pp. 358–388.

2. J. A. Aldama, "Piété et système dans la mariologie du Docteur Eximius," *Maria* 2 (1952), pp. 975–990, (bibliography on Suarez' Mariology, p. 990), and "Un resumen de la primera mariología del P. Francisco Suarez," *Archivo Teológico Granadino* 15 (1952), 292–337.

3. On this author's considerable influence cf. Laurentin, *Marie, l'Eglise* . . . vol. 1, pp. 232–304, and O. Casado, *Mariologia clásica española*, Madrid, 1958.

completed by St. Peter Canisius[4] in Germany and St. Robert Bellarmine[5] in Italy.

The Marian Movement of the 17th and 18th Centuries

To designate the extraordinary revival that took place beginning with the first years of the seventeenth century and extending in several waves into very recent years it is accurate to use the term "Marian movement." Taken in this sense, movement signifies a collective impulse, organic and spontaneous, tending toward the renewal or promotion of ideas, opinions, and organizations.[6] In this sense one speaks of the romantic movement or the surrealist movement in the field of literature, the labor movement or the feminine liberation movement in the sociological field, etc.

A discussion of the Marian movement brings to mind, as an image, the way a wave rolls up onto the seashore. There is no doubt a negative impulse: the concern to react against the challenges raised by Protestantism, to avenge the honor of the Virgin Mary. But the reaction to this negative element

---

4. His *De Maria Virgine incomparabili* underwent five editions: four from 1577 to 1584, the fifth in J. Bourassé, *Summa Aurea,* Tours, 1862, 8:613 to 9:408.

5. Bellarmine's Louvain sermons were published at Cologne, Henningium, 1626 during his lifetime; his Roman sermons were published by S. Tromp, *Sancti Roberti... opera oratoria posthuma,* Rome, Gregorian, 1942, t. 1, 2, 6, and 7. Monographs on his mariology are noted by G. Besutti, *Bibliografia mariana 1949–1950,* Rome, Marianum, 1951, # 146 and 147.

6. The concept of a movement, as defined above, is of recent usage. It is unknown in Littré's dictionary and could not be found in any of the dictionaries consulted at the time (1963) of the composition of chapter 2 on this subject in R. Laurentin, *La question mariale,* Paris, Seuil, 1963 (ET: *The Question of Mary,* New York, Holt-Rinehart-Winston, 1965). The notion has since been defined, on the basis of numerous examples, in Robert's dictionary which appeared in 1963. This definition is substantially adopted here, but with modifications of considerable importance.

goes far beyond sheer polemic. A constructive concern prevails, a desire to know Mary better and to glorify her in all kinds of ways.[7]

Suddenly publications dealing with her are multiplied. The number of works published each year climbs rapidly up to 1630 and attains a maximum between 1630 and 1650.

---

7. What is the place occupied by what is usually called the French School in this ensemble? The considerable interest given this sector of religious thought has in fact often exaggerated or at least badly assessed its importance. For many, the representatives of the French School are the outstanding Mariologists of the seventeenth century and the forerunners of the Marian movement. This is not the genuine picture suggested by history, as appears from the following considerations.

a. The Bérullian school is only a discreet and limited current of thought. It plays no pilot role in the spread of the Marian movement. Bérulle was dependent on the research of Chirino de Salazar, the theologian who dominated the entire problematic of seventeenth century Mariology.

b. The Bérullian school is characterized above all by a concern for fidelity to the tradition of Christocentrism and interiority, a concern that was to be a regulatory factor when the movement attained its full expansion.

c. There are few sectors where the name "French School" given to authors of this group reveals its artificial stamp more than in Mariology. The difference between Bérulle's sobriety and Olier's ebullient mysticism is enormous; with the latter the norms of reason and tradition are paired off in a rather original manner with outbursts of a lively affectivity (where psychoanalysts would want to fish, as it were, in troubled waters). Another paradox is the harmony of thought between the Abbé de Saint-Cyran and Bérulle. In their correspondence several times they expressed their community of view on Marian matters. It is even curious to observe that of the two authors, Bérulle is the more sober, the more reserved regarding mediation: nowhere does he speak of it explicitly, perhaps out of a theocentric concern not to weaken the import of the "unus mediator" (1 Tim. 2:5).

d. The Bérullian current of Marian thought, which in the seventeenth century does not occupy any first-rank position, has kept its importance because it survived: its classicism has preserved it from aging. Its spirituality passed into living institutions, while many another school or effort of the day has since fallen into the domain of archeology.

Then slowly the curve flattens out, as if the initial impulse had exhausted itself.[8]

For more than a century the movement is reanimated by several controversies into which Marian zeal throws itself headlong. There is the controversy over the *Avis salutaires de la Vierge à ses dévots indiscrets* from 1673 to 1678.[9] Another controversy is stirred up by those who attack Mary of Agreda at the end of the seventeenth century and beginning of the eighteenth.[10] Still another centers around the "vow of blood" between 1714 and 1764.[11] Throughout these years the movement is till studded with great names: St. John Eudes (d. 1680),[12] St. Grignion de

---

8. On this curve see R. Laurentin, *Le titre de Corédemptrice,* Paris, Lethielleux, 1951, especially pp. 17-22, and *Marie, l'Eglise* . . . vol. 1, pp. 258-304. The very rich collection of the Dreux library has since permitted a statistical verification of the general picture presented of this curve.

9. On the considerable controversy stirred up by the brochure of A. Widenfeld, *Avis salutaires de la Bienheureuse Vierge Marie à ses dévots indiscrets,* cf. the excellent study of P. Hoffer, *La dévotion à Marie au déclin du XVIIe siècle. Autour du jansénisme et des 'Avis salutaires',* Paris, Cerf, 1938.

10. *La mística ciudad* of Mary of Agreda (d. 1665) appeared in 1670. The controversy raged from 1696 to 1750. Cf. Laurentin, *Le titre* . . . pp. 58-59 and J.B. Carol, *De Corredemptione,* Rome, 1950, pp. 346-347, 354, 374.

11. The object of the controversy was the vow that certain proponents of the Immaculate Conception made to defend this doctrine with their lives. Muratori, under the pseudonym of Lamindus Printanius, declared this vow blameworthy: for the faith alone must one sacrifice his life, he argued in substance, and to sacrifice it for opinions would be suicide.

Julien Stricher, *Le voeu du sang en faveur de l'Immaculée Conception,* Rome, Academia Mariana, 1959, has given the fruit of twenty years' labor in compiling a complete bibliography on the subject (printed works and manuscripts) and in unraveling the almost inextricable tangle of pseudonyms. Light was thus brought into one of the most impenetrable wildernesses of Mariology.

12. A month before his death he completed his life's work, *Le Coeur admirable de la Mère de Dieu,* edited the year after (1681). A bibliography

Montfort (d. 1716),[13] whose acclaim will come only a century later, and finally St. Alphonsus Liguori, who in 1750 published his *Glories of Mary*,[14] the work that remains the most frequently reprinted Marian work of all time.[15]

After the middle of the eighteenth century, however, the movement relapsed irresistibly into silence for more than a half-century (1780–1830).

The beginning of the period now being considered is marked by a change of inspiration and an outburst of enthusiasm. The contrast is striking between the first three quarters of the sixteenth century and the beginning of the seventeenth. On the one hand there are a few short and anemic works, absorbed with polemic issues; on the other there is an abundant literature, so entirely constructive as ordinarily to be oblivious even of the existence of Protestants. The sixteenth century had limited itself to the negative task of defending a heritage. The seventeenth was concerned, sometimes excessively, with promoting unrecognized glories of Mary and stirring up new forms of devotion:[16] new feasts, sodalities and associations consecrated to

---

on this Mariology is found in Laurentin, *Marie, l'Eglise* . . . vol. 1, p. 290, n. 9.

13. His *Traité de la vraie dévotion à la Sainte Vierge,* discovered in 1842 after having lain buried in a box of his papers for a century, met with its well-known success and has become the object, each year, of numerous specialized works. Cf. for example G. Besutti, *Bibliografia mariana* 1 (1950), # 149–152, 244, 245, 729, 730, 745, 752, 762; 2 (1951), # 1103; 3 (1959), # 1008–1020, 3808–3840.

14. The fundamental work on this author remains C. Dillenschneider, *La Mariologio de saint Alphonse,* 2 vols., Paris, Vrin, 1931 and 1934. For the more recent works cf. Besutti, *Bibliografia* . . . 3 (1959), # 1028–1037.

15. About a thousand editions since 1750.

16. Among the devotions that spread abroad, the "vow of slavery" had a particularly tormented existence at the end of the sixteenth century. Confraternities of slaves of the Virgin Mary grew up in Spain. Proscribed by the Inquisition at the beginning of the seventeenth century, this devotion

Mary, monuments of every kind, vows and consecrations in the first rank of which must be placed the "vow of Louis XIII."[17]

If all these activities are to be traced to their theological root there is hardly any room for hesitation: it was the Immaculate Conception. This belief, hampered as it had been by serious theological difficulties and by the opposition of authorities as weighty as St. Bernard and St. Thomas Aquinas, was at that time also suspect in the eyes of the Roman Inquisition. Discreet action was taken by this organ against the immaculists. The Inquisition finished by secretly issuing a decree prohibiting the title "Immaculate Conception." Very precisely it was forbidden to attach the adjective "immaculate" to the "conception" of Mary; it was to be used only of her "person." To speak of "the conception of the immaculate Virgin" was permitted, but not "the immaculate conception of the Virgin." After 1627 the decree directed the inquisitors to take several actions against books still bearing the prohibited title. In 1644 this decree was made public. It put the champions of the Immaculate Conception in a difficult situation. Nevertheless, hundreds of works continued to be consecrated to this question. The authors learned how to be all the more prudent about the titles of their works, the nearer to Rome they published them. This enormous output, printed and in manuscript, has so far defied all inventory. The authors piled up witnesses, editions, reeditions, arguments, etc. — a staggering amount of work, uneven in merit, often misshapen by polemic concern. It is hardly possible

---

sprang up anew in 1842 with the discovery of the *Traité de la vraie dévotion à la Sainte Vierge*. At this period the Holy Office made no difficulty over its publication. At the canonization of Grignion de Montfort, however, the official documents, including Pius XII's discourse, contained no praise of the Marian doctrine of the saint, no doubt for the above reason. The complexity of historical problems in this domain can be imagined.

17. M. Vloberg, "Le voeu de Louis XIII," *Maria* 5 (1958), pp. 519–533.

today to get an idea of the violence of feeling that was stirred up for and against this doctrine.

This violence explains the reserve shown by the Holy See as it concerned itself above all with reestablishing peace, the condition of enlightened progress. Nothing was more difficult. On the one hand, the maculists were strongly entrenched in the Inquisition. They acted under cover. On the other, the immaculists were supported by the Christian sovereigns, with the kings of Spain in first rank. The latter sent out three solemn ambassadorial delegations, especially to Rome, instructed to obtain at any price a definition of what was then called "the pious belief." No sooner were decisions taken to put an end to the discord than they were used by the maculists as a weapon of persecution,[18] and by the immaculists as a triumphal confirmation of their own point of view. Pulled in every which way, the Holy See could have been expected twenty times and more to have lapsed into incoherence. Under the guidance of the Holy Spirit the contrary happened. Despite the succession of popes whose personal opinions were quite different, the decisions of the papal magisterium traced a firm and coherent line. These decisions are of disciplinary character, but they slowly and steadily sketch a doctrinal orientation. They accomplish a triple task:

---

18. On the elaboration of the "Decree of 1644," which was never confirmed by the Pope, cf. R. Laurentin, "Le Magistère et le développement du dogme de l'Immaculée Conception," *Virgo Immaculata* 2 (1956), pp. 29–46. The pontifical decrees that brought about the predominance of the immaculist thesis are the object of the note following this one. They were often used as a redoubtable weapon by the masters of the Sacred Palace in encounters with those who held the "pious belief." On the one hand, it was difficult for the latter to expound their opinion without becoming vulnerable to the reproach of thereby attacking the contrary opinion. The maculists, on the other hand, pretended that the decree of 1622, which forbade use of the word "conception" to designate the feast of December 8, was directed less against the noun "sanctification" than against adding the qualification "immaculate" to the noun "conception." This interpretation took shape in the famous decree of 1627–1644.

they reestablish peace, steadily reduce the opponents of the Immaculate Conception to silence,[19] and prepare the way for the definition of 1854.

In this respect the most important milestone was the Bull *Sollicitudo* promulgated on December 8, 1661 by Alexander VII. In it the pope declared positively the favor the Holy See had for the Immaculate Conception, gave some precisions in theological terms for expressing the belief, and forbade any attack on it in whatever way.[20] He did not however condemn

---

19. *Note on the progress of pontifical decisions on the Immaculate Conception in the seventeenth century:* Since Sixtus IV (cf. *supra,* p. 121, n. 36) the two opinions had the same juridical status: they were each allowed to be expressed, but it was forbidden to each to declare the other heretical or even erroneous. Pius V had renewed Sixtus IV's decision without taking any further step. In the seventeenth century the balance was gradually tipped in favor of the "pious belief" (that is, conception without stain). Each decision in the development of the matter was obtained through the strenuous efforts of a special delegation from the King of Spain; these delegations had moreover received the mission to obtain something much more, a dogmatic definition. The decisions referred to are as follows:

a) Paul V, Constitution *Regis Pacifici* July 6, 1616, simply renews the decisions of his predecessors, Sixtus IV and Pius V. But with the Bull *Sanctissimus* September 12, 1617, (*Bullarium romanum,* ed. Coquelines, vol. 5, part 4, pp. 234–235; Bourassé, *op. cit.,* 7:209), he discreetly breaks the equilibrium between the two opinions. He forbids hereafter expressing the maculist thesis in *public* acts. He nonetheless specifies that it is not his intention to cast prejudice on this opinion, and he forbids that it be attacked in any way.

b) Gregory XV, Bull *Sanctissimus* May 24, 1622, (*Bullarium romanum* . . . part 5, pp. 45–46; Bourassé, 7:220–222), extends the prohibition of his predecessor to *private* acts, but with the same qualifying clause. Deprived of every means of expression, the maculist thesis is thus condemned to a slow agony. Only the Dominicans remain authorized (by indult of July 28, 1622) to expound this opinion "among themselves and not with others." It is this Bull of May 24, 1622 that imposed the use of the word "conception" to designate the feast of December 8. On all this cf. Laurentin, "Le Magistère . . . " pp. 65–78.

20. Alexander VII, Bull *Sollicitudo* December 8, 1661, (Denz. 1100 (2015)). The action of the Spanish delegation that obtained this brief, and

the contrary opinion (which it also remained forbidden to attack). For still another fifty years the increasingly secret activity of the "maculists" would keep the partisans of the "pious belief" in suspense. But maculists were now becoming only a small coterie and kept losing ground year by year. The Thomists, who before had waged war in the name of St. Thomas Aquinas against the partisans of the Immaculate Conception, now turned all their ingenuity into making of him an immaculist that had till then escaped recognition. In the middle of the eighteenth century after the last skirmishes and last controversies, all parties were exhausted. The field was strewn with such a pile of works,[21] of authorities both genuine and invented, of useful distinctions and outlandish ones, of divergent explanations of the mystery, that no one could find his way. The gigantic effort had not been useless. But time was needed now to pour off gently what had been distilled in all the heat.[22] As after days of unrewarding research and knotty reflection the scholar sometimes during his sleep finds the solution that escaped him all along, so at the end of this barren period (1751–1851) the Church will definitively disentangle the solution in which so many of these difficulties and complications melt away.

---

the preparatory stages of the text, are remarkably presented by C. Gutierrez *España por el dogma de la Immaculada. La ambajada a Roma de 1659 y a Bula "Sollicitudo" de Alejandro VII (Miscellanea Comilas 24)*, Madrid, 1955.

21. The Jesuits alone wrote more than 300 works on the Immaculate Conception between 1600 and 1800 (C. Sommervogel, *Bibliotheca mariana de la Compagnie de Jésus,* Paris, Picard, 1885, pp. 47–49).

22. For their praiseworthy efforts to bring order into the discussion two authors should be mentioned: M. A. Gravois, *De ortu et progressu cultus ac festi Immaculati conceptus,* Lucca, Riccome, 1742; 2nd edition *(emendatior)* 1762; ed. Bourassé, *op. cit.*, 8:289–458; and B. Plazza, *Causa Immaculatae Conceptionis,* Palermo, Valenza, 1747. But both of these authors, particularly the first, have to be read discriminatingly.

The 19th Century

The first thirty years of the nineteenth century are perhaps the most barren in the history of Marian literature. Books are rare and mediocre. And yet the impulse springs up again suddenly in new and surprising forms.

First there is an apparition in 1830, the first in a long series that will characterize the nineteenth century.[23] The Virgin Mary gave the image of the Miraculous Medal to Catherine Labouré. The fact remained hidden but it led to a vast movement of devotion and conversion. Under the sign of the Miraculous Medal the Virgin appeared to Alphonse Ratisbonne. This medal — the Virgin "conceived without sin," with arms outstretched downward — seemed to set forth the program that was to guide the Marian movement for a whole century: Mary's Immaculate Conception and her Mediation.

Inaugurated by an apparition, the period was prolonged in a definition. In 1854 the Immaculate Conception was declared a dogma of the faith.[24] The infallible pronouncement came upon a theology that had not yet shown any sign of renewal. The effort of the seventeenth and eighteenth centuries seemed to have been forgotten for the while, and that of the nineteenth century was still negligible. Before defining the dogma Pius IX consulted the bishops as to the sentiment prevailing in the Church. But the theological work of preparation had not proceeded very far. There was hardly more than one general work of theology that represented if not a strict method, at least an effort of considerable scope; and its author, Carlo Passaglia,[25] who introduced Scheeben

---

23. Earlier apparitions of the 16th–17th century are known: Guadalupe (Mexico), Le Laus, Garaison (France), etc. But these apparitions had not begun any extensive movement, except perhaps in the case of Guadalupe.

24. The acts preparing for the definition were published by V. Sardi, *La solenne definizione del dogma dell' Immaculato concepimento di Maria Santissima. Atti e documenti . . .*, Rome, Vaticana, 1904–1905, 2 vols.

25. Cf. "Passaglia," DTC 11:2207–2210. More lucid perhaps, but less

to Mariology, eventually broke off relations with the Holy See over the Roman question.

In short, throughout this disconcerting period, when the Church was weakened and threatened and in so many respects was without the intellectual resources she needed, all initiative came from on top, and the quality of inspiration was often recognizable in the negligible achievements of the time. A charismatic outburst preceded the doctrinal and literary revival. As has been mentioned, the beginning of the century was markedly lacking in works on Our Lady. Then suddenly there was a shift about 1840 to an even more distressing proliferation. About this literature, the overabundance of which was only "its least serious fault," Louis Veuillot had the following to say:

> "In the mass of volumes turned out each year there are hardly more than a few that do not leave everything to be desired: awkward and sterile declamation, ill-chosen texts, readings that are without doctrine, without love, and too often without grammar. It is astonishing that the zeal of those who read these wretched things is such a poor inspiration to those who write them."[26]

The whole religious drama of the nineteenth century lies exposed there. It is a time when deep and fervent piety is nourished with a tastelessly diluted literature and a deplorable art.

---

documented, than the work of Passaglia is that of J. Perrone, *De Immaculato conceptu. An dogmatico decreto definiri possit?* Avignon, 1848 (numerous reeditions in different places), and especially the small book of Dom P. Guéranger, *Mémoire sur la question de l'Immaculée Conception*, Paris, Lecoffre, 1850. Guéranger was the author of one of the eight projects of dogmatic definition (March 1852): cf. G. Frenaud, "Dom Guéranger at le projet de bulle 'Quemadmodum Ecclesia' pour la définition de l'Immaculée Conception," *Virgo Immaculata* 2 (1956), pp. 337–386.

26. L. Veuillot, *Mélanges, 2ᵉ série*, Paris, Gaume, 1860, t. 5, pp. 605–606.

Throughout the nineteenth century theology remained enfeebled, with the exception of trailblazers unrecognized in their day: Newman[27] in England (1866) and Scheeben[28] in Germany. It is disappointing to read today the Mariologists who were then in vogue. Even the widely read Msgr. Malou[29] startles one when, for example, he calls Mary "a divine person," or "the fourth person of the Holy Trinity," — all that "according to the Fathers," without any reference being given. And one readily understands why not!

From 1900 to 1958

In spite of these weaknesses the Marian movement held its own. Theology even ended up by making some advance in Marian questions. At the beginning of the twentieth century

---

27. Cf. the bibliography on this author in Laurentin, *Marie, l'Eglise* ... vol. 1, p. 397, n. 31, and Besutti, *Bibliografia mariana* 2 (1952), # 1068, 1113, 1223, 1224, 1628; 3 (1959), # 1071–1077, 1427, 1428, 1727, 2631, 5309, 5468, 5522.

28. Scheeben's Mariology is an integral part of the third volume of his dogmatic synthesis, *Handbuch der katholischen Dogmatik*, Freiburg/Breisgau, Herder, 1882, # 274–282; cf. also # 229–231, 240. (In the new edition by Carl Feckes, *Katholische Dogmatik*, Freiburg/Breisgau, Herder, 1955, vol. 1, pp. 243–266, 335–359, and especially vol. 2, pp. 306–499.) Noteworthy also is the English translation of Scheeben's chapters on Mariology by T. Geukers, *Mariology*, London, Herder, 1948, and two volumes of an abbreviated adaptation of Feckes' edition of Scheeben's works, translated by A. Kerkvoorde, under the title, *M. J. Scheeben, la Mère virginale du Sauveur*, Paris, Desclée, 1954.

For studies on Scheeben cf. C. Feckes, "M. J. Scheeben, théologien de la mariologie moderne," *Maria* 3 (1954), pp. 553–571 (with bibliography), and J. Galot, "La nouvelle Eve d'après Scheeben," EM 14 (1956), pp. 49–66. Further bibliography in G. Besutti, *Bibliografia mariana* 3 (1959), # 1059–1068. Earlier bibliographies contained no monograph on this author; the current of interest in his Mariology began toward 1935 with C. Feckes, *Scientia sacra. Theologische Festgabe*, Düsseldorf, 1935, pp. 252–276; E. Druwé, article in EM 2 (1936), pp. 9, 12, 16, etc.

29. J. Malou, *L'Immaculée Conception*, Brussels, 1857, pp. 175–176.

the works of Terrien[30] and Renaudin[31] are representative of the progress. With 1900 there begins the era of the international Marian congresses: fervent and enthusiastic gatherings concerned with multiplying dogmas and manifestations of devotion.[32] The first congress, held at Lyons in 1900 from September 5–8, launches a movement that will eventually succeed, an appeal for the definition of the Assumption.[33] This movement will have its apostles, its magazines, its associations. It will gather 8,036,393 signatures and arouse a considerable quantity of petitions addressed to the pope. In reading this material assembled in two enormous volumes,[34] one cannot escape the impression that in all this zeal there is a streak of artifice. In contrast to the immaculist movement of the seventeenth century, the assumptionist movement is polarized less by its doctrinal object than by the desire to

---

30. J. B. Terrien, *La Mère de Dieu et la mère des hommes d'après les Pères et la théologie,* Paris, Lethielleux, 1900–1902, 4 vols. (several reeditions).

31. P. Renaudin, *De la définition dogmatique de l'Assomption . . . dissertation théologique,* Angers, 1900. A bibliography of the later works of this author is in C. Balic, *Testimonia de Assumptione,* Rome, Academia Mariana, 1950, p. 373, n. 2, comprising especially a long series of articles in the *Revue Thomiste* (1900–1902, 1904–1906) and works entitled *L'Assomption,* Paris, 1908, *La doctrine de l'Assomption,* Paris, 1912, and *Assumptio,* Turin-Rome, 1933.

32. *Enciclopedia Mariana Theotócos,* 2nd edition, Genoa-Milan, 1958, # 584, pp. 646–647. A national Marian congress held at Livorno in Italy had opened the way for the international congresses of Lyons 1900, Fribourg 1902, Rome 1904, Einsiedeln 1906, and so on to Triers 1912. Numerous national congresses were also held. From 1947 to 1958 there were 89 Marian congresses of varying size, regional, national, international. The statistics are available in Laurentin, *La question mariale,* p. 17 (ET: *The Question of Mary,* pp. 10–11). It is to be noted that the congress of Lyons 1900 was declared "international" only after the event.

33. *Congrès marial tenu à Lyon les 5–8 septembre 1900,* Lyon, 1900. On the action of this congress for the definition of the Assumption, cf. G. Hentrich, *Petitiones de Assumptione,* Rome, 1942, vol. 2, pp. 417, 936–937.

34. G. Hentrich, *Petitiones de Assumptione,* 2 vols., Rome, 1942.

promote a new glorification of Our Lady in the eyes of the whole world. The movement takes on the form of a pressure group trying by every means possible to act on the Holy See. External measures rather than theological investigations are its main result. In the final analysis it runs out of breath and dies.

In 1920 its place is taken by the mediationist movement, whose object is the definition of Mary's universal mediation. Cardinal Mercier is the promoter of this new movement.[35] He had it in mind already in 1913 but was unable to launch it successfully until 1921, after the war. At that moment the cardinal was at the peak of his prestige: it is said that he received more than ten votes at the conclave in 1922. It is to his credit above all to have set in motion a continuing interest in doctrinal studies of the question. Thus, far from wasting away and deteriorating as had the assumptionist movement, the mediationist movement develops with an unprecedented strength. And as is the case when serious work is put forth, the level rose: books, magazine articles, commissioned studies are multiplied. However, the formula that the cardinal had chosen spontaneously and without preliminary study met with difficulties from influential quarters. In particular the Holy Office took up the question: how can Mary's mediation be reconciled with the "one only Mediator" of Saint Paul? And especially, in what sense can a *universal* mediation be spoken of? Did all the graces of the Old Testament come "through Mary"? Is it through her that habitual grace comes to be? And if so, how would this be compatible with the fact that grace is an *immediate* activity of God on the soul? Is it through her that sacramental graces *ex opere operato* are conferred? If so, how would this be compatible

---

35. R. Laurentin, "Intuitions du cardinal Mercier," *Vie Spirituelle* 84 (1951), pp. 518–522. Cardinal Mercier's principal Marian writings have been gathered by A. Demoulin, *Cardinal Mercier. La Vierge Marie. Pages choisies,* Liège, 1947.

with the fact that there is question here of saving acts performed by Christ himself wherever his minister confers the sacramental sign? Several official experts remained perplexed or noncommittal regarding these questions.

Thus Pius XII returned to the Assumption, which was defined in 1950, after several years of study and a consultation of the episcopacy.[36] The pageantry surrounding this solemn act was prolonged first by the proclamation of Mary's queenship in the course of the Marian Year of 1954,[37] commemorating the centenary of the definition of the Immaculate Conception, and then by the celebration of the centenary of the Lourdes apparitions in 1958. Thus the reign of Pius XII (d. 1958) marked the official zenith of the Marian movement. Certain addresses and works at that time envisaged a crescendo of new heights and conquests.[38]

But it is rather an ebb tide that seems to be taking place. What actually is happening? The answer to this question will

---

36. The definition was prepared for by the work of M. Jugie, *La mort et l'Assomption,* Rome, 1944, which very insistently distinguished between the bodily Assumption (presence of Mary in heaven today) and the fact of her death, which the author held doubtful. This work determined the reserve of the definition on the death of Mary and gave rise to the immortalist current of thought. The Bull *Munificentissimus Deus* November 1, 1950 defining the Assumption appeared in the AAS 42 (1950), p. 767ff (cf. Denz. 2331–2333 (3900–3904)).

37. *L'anno mariano 1954,* Rome, Vaticana, 1958.

38. Indicative of this sentiment is the discourse of J. Pizzardo at the international Mariological congress of Rome 1950, published in *Alma socia Christi,* Rome, Academia Mariana, 1951, vol. 1, pp. 101–106, especially 102–104. During the antepreparatory consultation for Vatican II (May 17, 1959 to November 14, 1960) almost four hundred bishops were still asking for new dogmatic definitions. They hesitated, however, over the object of them: about 300 chose the mediation, about 50 the spiritual motherhood, another 50 the coredemption, and about 20 the queenship. The total is not exactly 400, since several hesitated between different themes. After the antepreparatory phase there was no further question of dogmatic definitions.

have to be taken up in another chapter, since the disconcerting turning-point of these last years corresponds to the transition from the post-Tridentine to the modern era, an era that can be named after Vatican II. In bringing this historical part of the study to a close, it will be important to understand the meaning of this new stage.[39]

---

39. *Note on the assessment of the post-Tridentine period:* A judgment on this period is necessary, for as it closes and yields to other impulses one runs the risk of being unjust in assessing it. This glorious and triumphalist period has its merits, to which some day justice will be rendered. Today its artificial elements, exaggerations, mythical proliferations, narrowness, and polemic harshness are much noticed. But this must not lead to a misapprehension of what is essential. In nature some flowers form inside a sort of hard protective covering that later opens up and falls away, permitting the flower to blossom out. Post-Tridentine Mariology, with its harshness toward the Reformers' excesses, reminds one of such a flower. Its exterior, both in concept and devotion, was hard, thick, and often anything but beautiful. But inside there was life. It was an error to thicken and harden the outer covering, but it would be a still more serious error to throw away the flower along with the covering. The flower must be rediscovered for what it is, beginning with its sources in revelation, where it appears as the flower stemming from the root of Jesse. Such a task has become much more urgent than the elimination of certain harsh and artificial elements.

SIXTH PERIOD

THE NEW ERA OF VATICAN II AND ITS PREPARATION

At the Second Vatican Council the text devoted to the Virgin Mary became the object of special difficulties. This turn of affairs could already be felt at the end of the first session, when a suggestion was made quickly to promulgate the schema *On the Blessed Virgin Mary, Mother of God and Mother of Men* in December 1962. This premature suggestion was immediately put aside without ado, and time did not permit any conflict to break out over the issue.[1]

The next year unrelenting requests made orally and in writing since December 1962 succeeded in bringing before the council the question, "Should the schema *On the Blessed Virgin* be integrated into the schema *On the Church?*" At that point the opposing points of view did come clearly out into the open.

One group wanted integration. It was their intention to treat of the Blessed Virgin in her place both within the communion of saints and within salvation history. They hoped thereby to bring remedy to a Mariology that too easily closed in on itself and to reduce the separation between theology and Marian devotion.

---

1. R. Laurentin, *La Vierge au Concile,* Paris, Lethielleux, 1965, pp. 10–11.

The other group held that this kind of integration was a minimizing enterprise reducing the Virgin Mary to the level of other Christians.

The propaganda put out by both sides was intense in the days that preceded the vote of October 29, 1963: individual initiatives, conferences, etc. Campaign papers were distributed in the mailboxes, at the entrance of St. Peter's, even at the bishops' places inside on the morning of the vote. One of these papers described the fears of those who opposed integration:

> "1. The traditional doctrine on the Madonna is in great danger, because she is thus considered the equal of us all.
> 2. Those who conceive of Mary as 'the type of the Church' are presenting an altogether new idea not conformable to tradition and invented only in recent years.
> 3. Such a position thus minimizes the Madonna's privileges and weakens devotion toward her."[2]

Assuredly this kind of argument went too far, since "type of the Church" is a formula of St. Ambrose, found widely among the Fathers of the Church. But such arguments made an impression. On the morning of the vote a number of bishops were perplexed. To vote for an integration of the Marian schema into that on the Church seemed to be voting against Our Lady. The results very close: 1114 votes for integration, 1074 against. Ordinarily the Council voted with a unanimity higher than 90%, sometimes even than 95%. Now for the first time it found itself divided into two almost equal parts. A shifting of 20 votes out of more than 2000 would have changed the result.

And the result was all the more paradoxical in that the schema called Mary "the artisan of unity" *(fautrix unitatis)*. There was general consternation. As he left St. Peter's that

---

2. Italian text in *Civiltà Cattolica* 4 (1963), 53.

day, the author of this study saw some in tears.[3]

What was happening? What was the meaning of this crisis that the Council immediately set about to resolve?[4]

The Ebb of the Marian Movement

The change that was setting in had already been in preparation for some time. It stemmed from a certain historical necessity, from the nature of the "Marian movement" which had characterized the life of the Catholic Church for the three centuries preceding.

1. Every historical movement disappears as it attains its goal. This is a normal and honorable end for it. Thus the "liturgical movement" is losing its existence as a movement in proportion as it is bringing about within the Church a liturgical life at last adapted to our time. With John XXIII, the distinction must indeed be made between *movements* which come and go and *doctrine* which does not pass away. A movement is not the Church herself but a particular current that runs through the Church. Just as rapids or a cascade mark a stage in the life of a river, so these "movements" occurring in history are destined to be reabsorbed sooner or later into the life of the Church. The Virgin Mary will keep forever her place in Catholic doctrine and devotion, but the post-Tridentine Marian movement could not be a phenomenon enduring eternally.

This movement had attained its major objective with the definition of 1854. From that event it received a new impetus, a second wind, so to say, that prolonged it for still another century — an exceptionally long lifetime for a movement. This survival, however, was not without an element of artifice. It became more and more evident that the movement

---

3. On this whole question cf. Laurentin, *La Vierge* . . . pp. 12–21.
4. Laurentin, *La question* . . . pp. 38–66 (ET: *The Question of Mary*, pp. 53–81) and *La Vierge* . . . pp. 51–76.

was running out of breath. Programs of conquest and innovation aroused less and less enthusiasm, as did likewise the victories won in debate. An attitude of reserve was more frequently met with. The often artificial concern to innovate yielded irresistibly to the need to situate the Virgin Mary anew in her authentic place in the plan of salvation.

2. The Marian movement had had its excesses and its extravagances. It had exalted whatever was "Marian" and had rigorously bridled criticism. But for some time now it had been causing weariness, or reserve, or other quiet reactions. Even before the opening of the Council several bishops could be heard repeating discreetly: "There must not be any exaggeration! Beware of sentimentality, of what is artificial, etc." In pushing on so far, the rising wave of the Marian movement had prepared its own ebb; it was a normal ebb.

Repercussions of the Movements of Aggiornamento

There was also a more positive factor: in every domain the Council was bringing about a renewal of perspective. No sector could escape revision, the field of Marian doctrine included. This revision was tied in with the appearance of movements of a new style: the return to sources, in the biblical and patristic movements; in the doctrinal sphere, movements such as those centering on ecclesiology or on the history of salvation; the liturgical and the missionary movements in the pastoral order; finally, the ecumenical movement. These movements all proceeded from an irresistible yearning for experiences that the Church had not had in depth for some centuries now. They sprang from a need to make what had become stiff supple again, to lay aside certain artificial elements, to complete what was partial, to enlarge what had become too narrow and tight. These movements became first-rank centers of interest in the life of the Church. And with that, the Marian movement receded into the background. Furthermore, the new movements seemed to call for a revision of it, and even to question whether it should continue. Thence arose the anxiety that reigned at the time of the vote of October 29, 1963.

What forces lay behind this uneasiness?

1. The biblical movement was recommending the primacy of Scripture and more precisely of its literal sense. This was an invitation to return to what was disparagingly but unjustly called a "primitive, archaic, underdeveloped Mariology," on the earlier side of the post-Tridentine conquests. It meant taking again into serious consideration what certain Mariologists called the "anti-mariological verses" of Scripture:

> "They did not understand what he meant" (Lk. 2:49).
> "Still happier those who hear the word of God and keep it" (Lk. 11:28).
> "Who are my mother and my brothers . . ." (Mk. 3:33–35).
> "Woman, why turn to me" (Jn. 2:4; cf. Jn. 7:2–6).

2. The patristic movement was raising the same problem still more sharply: many of the Fathers of the Church had been hesitant concerning Mary's holiness or her virginity at childbirth and after childbirth, had known little of her Assumption or Immaculate Conception, and had expressed themselves frequently on the universal extent of sin, except in Christ.

3. The ecclesiological movement seemed to suggest putting the Virgin Mary back into a more modest place, even a minimal place according to the mind of those whose fears were cited above. For them it seemed to reduce the queen of heaven to the status of a lowly Palestinian woman, a lowly member of the faithful in the primitive community, just one saint among others in the communion of saints.

4. In theology the movement centering on the history of salvation *(Heilsgeschichte)* seemed to entail a similar absorption of Mary into a broader whole. In determining her place

relative to salvation the movement seemed to put her in the background; in determining her place in history, it seemed to emphasize the meaning of the whole at the expense of her "privileges."

5. The liturgical movement was crowding private devotions into the background, devotions that post-Tridentine Mariology had seemed to identify purely and simply with "Marian devotion." Under this title, in fact, publications specializing in things Marian used to parade for review all sorts of devotional exercises but often forgot the official prayer of the Church. What is more, at a time when the Marian movement was bringing about the introduction of new feasts, vigils, and octaves into the liturgy, the liturgical movement, on the contrary, was concerned about proportion and coherence and preferred to stress the temporal cycle of feasts over the sanctoral cycle and even to suppress certain Marian feasts or reduce them in rank.

6. The missionary movement was characterized by the concern to reawaken the masses of the dechristianized world to Christ from within, to lead them to recognize and enkindle "the true light that enlightens all men" (Jn. 1:9). Thus disowning whatever smacks of artifice, this movement frowned on the "multitude of words" and the forms of religiosity closed in on itself that a certain kind of Marian zeal had fostered.

7. Finally, the ecumenical movement presaged the advance from controversy to dialogue. Dialogue presupposes in the first place that one listens to and understands the difficulties of the other person, in this instance, the Protestant. In some quarters this was viewed as giving a civic reception to the enemy against whom the Marian movement had "waged the good fight."

Thus the reaction went in each of the above cases as, more or less clearly, the progress of these movements was resented within the circle of the Marian movement, at a time when the latter had attained unprecedented recognition in official quarters and was somewhat anxiously trying to keep its place there in face of growing disenchantment and reticence.

As a matter of fact, however, the friction was superficial. It existed *to the degree* that the Marian movement was a product of the Counter-Reformation on the one hand, while on the other the movements of aggiornamento were efforts compensating those of the Counter-Reformation. To that degree the two were in opposition and at loggerheads. But to the degree that both sets of movements represented an effort to revalue a living revelation, they were in agreement more than appeared.

The new movements flowed from the very life of the Church and were geared to a renewed appreciation of aspects of tradition that had remained underdeveloped. Seen from within, these movements were not at all directed against Our Lady. On the contrary, the remarkable fact is that *each* of them in different degrees implied a positive rediscovery of the Virgin Mary in a new light. The proper task of the Second Vatican Council was to sum up this positive contribution, a large and lively one, in chapter eight of the *Constitution on the Church*.

1. The biblical movement has restored some essential features to the spiritual portrait of Mary: her faith, her charity, her humility, her "poverty" that had been too much forgotten in a too exclusive emphasis on her glory. It recognized in her life the "Daughter of Zion," the "eschatological Ark of the Covenant," the personification of the Church, and the mother of Christ's disciples.[5] This list of acquisitions, or rather of recent restorations, needs no emphasis at this point since they have all been treated in the first period of the present historical survey.

2. Likewise, the patristic movement has brought back into the foreground the importance and meaning of the Annunciation: the faith of the Virgin who "conceived in her heart

---

5. *Lumen Gentium* art. 55–59; cf. 60 and 66.

before she conceived in her body." The meaning the new Eve has in a theological anthropology was rediscovered. These items have been studied earlier where the second period of historical development was treated.[6]

3. The ecclesiological movement has thrown light again on the meaning that Mary in her exemplary role has for the Church. It has remedied the closed character and separateness that were the major weakness of post-Tridentine Mariology. It has not destroyed Our Lady's privileges, but rather has given back to them their functional meaning.[7]

4. The theology built around the history of salvation has likewise helped restore the historical, ecclesial, and anthropological meaning that the Virgin Mary has as new Eve.[8]

5. Similarly the liturgical movement has restored the essential that was being neglected in favor of the accessory. A sometimes mediocre proliferation has been brought back to unity and sobriety. New value has been discovered especially in what is the ancient traditional root and center of true Marian devotion, the place the Virgin has in the Advent and Christmas mystery — in a word, in the mystery of salvation itself. The liturgical movement has neither condemned nor destroyed popular devotions: the conciliar texts say that very explicitly.[9] It has reinstated then and classified them anew

---

6. *Ibid.* art 56, 63, 64. Paul VI positively encouraged this double orientation. He personally wanted the first two post-conciliar Marian congresses to be consecrated, the one to the study of biblical sources (Santo Domingo, March 1965), the other to the study of sources in the Fathers of the first six centuries (Lisbon, 1967).

7. *Ibid.* art. 52–53, 60–65.

8. *Ibid.* art. 55–60.

9. "Popular devotions of the Christian people are warmly commended, provided they accord with the laws and norms of the Church. Such is especially the case with devotions called for by the Apostolic See. . . . Nevertheless these devotions should be so drawn up that they harmonize with the liturgical seasons, accord with the sacred liturgy, are in some fashion derived from it *(quodammodo deriventur),* and lead the people to

according to a proper gradation, purifying them also in function of the essential. Where anarchy threatened it has introduced coherence.

6. The missionary movement made its own contribution in similarly leading Marian devotion back to what is most important and most authentic, namely, the Annunciation and Visitation mystery seen as exemplifying the Christian life. The Virgin appears there as the type of the Church's apostolate, an apostolate inspired by the Holy Spirit and founded not on powerful means of influence but on the radiation of Christ who is received and carried in faith. As soon as she receives the Spirit, Mary leaves her own home and hastens across the mountains to carry Christ to the home of the Precursor. This is what the missionary movement has so readily brought to light again, and the Council made the insight its own.[10]

7. Finally, the ecumenical movement may entail calling things into question and undergoing a kind of trial as it summons persons to divest themselves of the artificial trappings that has proliferated in the hothouse atmosphere of the post-Tridentine era. But for all that, it has its positive side also. It not only invites everyone to a renewed appreciation of the essential, but also leads to a deeper perception and

---

it, since the liturgy by its very nature far surpasses any of them" (*Sacrosanctum Concilium,* Constitution on the Liturgy, art. 13).

"(The Council) invites all the sons of the Church to foster generously the cult, especially the liturgical cult, of the Blessed Virgin. It charges that practices and exercises of devotion toward her be treasured as recommended by the teaching authority of the Church in the course of centuries. . . ." (*Lumen Gentium* art. 67).

10. "The Virgin Mary in her own life lived an example of that maternal love by which all should be fittingly animated who cooperate in the apostolic mission of the Church on behalf of the rebirth of men" (*Lumen Gentium* art. 65). Karl Rahner spontaneously gave an important place to Mary in chapter 3 of his *Sendung und Gnade,* Innsbruck, Tyrolia, 1961 (ET: *Christian Commitment,* New York, Sheed and Ward, 1963; *Mission and Grace,* vol. 1, London, 1963).

integration of values that had in some way been neglected: the gratuitous character of God's grace toward Mary, in whom everything owes its origin to "grace alone"; her exemplary faith and her poverty, praised so highly by Luther, whom the most Marian-minded Polish bishop cited in flattering terms at the Council itself. In the direction of the Orthodox an immense field of work has been opened: the task of exploring together the tradition of Fathers and Byzantine authors that is held in common, with a view to moving beyond the narrowness that Latin Mariology, which developed during the period of separation, took on as a result of insufficient contact with Eastern tradition. The fruits of this return to sources lie ahead, full of promise. The Council pointedly turned toward both the task and the promise.[11]

Thus, all these movements converge in reemphasizing a central truth: Mary's place is at the point of departure and the very center of the mystery of salvation. It is she who had as mission to enable Christ to enter the human race, to enter human history. And this primordial role of hers serves as an exemplar: it is a type in relation to the Church itself. In this perspective Mary does not shine any longer with a brightness that is borrowed from some glory apart, but with the very light of the God-Savior and of salvation in which he has given her the place of choice.

There is no need then to be uneasy about the future of the Virgin Mary in the Church. The trial that post-Tridentine forms have undergone reveals how unreplaceable she is. For, in spite of their apparently minimizing tendencies, the move-

---

11. The conciliar text of *Lumen Gentium* was drawn up with ecumenical concern as a guiding principle, according to the explicit wish of the Fathers. But the situation was still not sufficiently developed for them formally to size up the ecumenical problem in so far as it concerns the Virgin Mary. In this regard the text advanced especially by suppressing ill-adapted developments of the first schema, such as its conclusion where Protestants were invited to pray to Mary to help them to submit to the Pope.

ments of aggiornamento have richly contributed to knowledge about Our Lady in unexpected ways and on the essential level: not in the direction of spectacular innovation or external display, but in the direction of a deepening perception, a readjustment of focus, a more evident authenticity. Seen in this light the Virgin Mary, object of too many quarrels, tends to become again in the eyes of all what she actually is: one who brings people together in unity, since she was called upon to actualize in her flesh and by her faith the unity between God and the human race.[12]

---

12. The conciliar text was a milestone in the development of Marian thought. It purposed to maintain against a destructive iconoclasm what was essential in the past, and at the same time to renew and restore both doctrine and piety in function of their sources and of the most pressing needs of the day. The Council could not spell out in detail the guidelines it gave, but the direction is recognizable in which "Mariology" and the "cult of the Virgin Mary" will now move, to use the somewhat closed and dissociated terms of the post-Tridentine Marian movement. The task is simply one of reappraising knowledge of Mary within the doctrine of salvation, where it is a lived and prayerful knowledge beyond any separation between doctrine and life.

EPILOGUE

1. A Glance Backward

At the end of this historical survey it should be stressed that the development which has been followed throughout these pages is indeed a development and not an evolution; that is, unlike an evolution, it does not lead to a being specifically different from the being that was at its origin. With the end of the apostolic generation revelation came to a close. That at least is the common opinion among theologians.[1] God has not since delivered any new objective data of revelation. Mary's place in salvation history has simply been better grasped, thanks to intellectual effort and the understanding that is born of love and imitation. As the infant learns to recognize its mother by her smile, so the Church from within has learned to recognize her own type and original realization in the Virgin Mary. The Church little by little learned to distinguish herself from the Blessed Virgin, having begun with an identification witnessed to by Scripture and more explicitly by the Fathers:

---

1. This thesis has been subjected to some doubt after the Council, since the text of the Constitution on Revelation did not confirm it. The question centers about the bases of the accepted formula, "Revelation was closed with the death of the last apostle."

"There is only one virgin mother, whom I am happy to call the Church" (Clement of Alexandria, *The Pedagogue* I, 6; PG 8:300).

"The Virgin, that is to say, holy Church. . . ." (*Fourth Homily* at Ephesus, 431; PG 77:996).

"We call the Church by Mary's name" (Ephrem, in T. J. Lamy, *Hymni et Sermones,* 1:531–533).

As her consciousness of this mystery deepened, the Church more and more fully laid hold of the meaning of Mary's original purity and her eschatology. The Immaculate Conception and the Assumption are not the result of some new message God gave. They became known as the data of salvation history were integrated with Mary's destiny, under the light of the Spirit who clarifies the message of Christ in its fulness (Jn 14:26 and 16:13).

This attainment of fuller consciousness has been a laborious task, intermingled with misapprehensions, errors, and artificial display — dross that has been drained off in periods of silence and discretion, to recall the terms used above in this study. The alternation of advance and arrest that has been noted time and again in history was matched by corresponding stages in dogmatic development. But underneath these alterations the essential faith of the Church remained without change. Whether this faith expressed itself readily or was silent, whether it was inventive or more discreet, it was a faith alive and stable in its wholesomeness. And in the liturgy it continued imperturbably to extol the Virgin Mary.

To put it briefly, in Mary's case as elsewhere, revelation is a hidden treasure from which the theologian versed in God's kingdom draws out things old and new. In matters of dogma, these new things are only the unalterable freshness of God's word.

2. A Glance Forward

Should an effort be made to envisage what the future holds? The preceding editions of this *Short Treatise* risked doing so a few years before the Council, and the phases of development forecast at that time have actually come about. What may have been said with an element of venture in 1954 when the last edition appeared is somewhat trite today. What is even more, the first rays of renewal discerned in the first edition of this *Short Treatise* appear today as the dawn of a new period in history, one that can rightly be termed the era of Vatican II. And thus there is less hesitation in scrutinizing the future according to the orientations offered by the centuries-old march of history, the directives of the recent Council, and the present impulses of the Holy Spirit.

The Message of the Council

Where the Council's directives are clear there is no need to insist further: Mariology will show itself attentive to its sources and will be nourished increasingly by a knowledge of the Bible and of the Fathers. It will be more strongly Christocentric, more evidently tied in with ecclesiology. Marian prayer will be more liturgical, more actively involved in missionary preoccupation. At the same time possibilities of ecumenical reconciliation will be opened up, without either disavowal or narrowness. As a result of all this, what was said and done piecemeal will give way to a deeper appreciation not only of the internal unity of Mariology but of the unity of salvation itself in Christ, who is the Way, the Truth, and the Life.

But other lines of future development not formally taken up by the Council are nonetheless worth examining also, since they are intimately related to present-day problems and tendencies.

To begin from the outside, as it studies the Virgin Mary

theology is confronted with many a criticism originating in currents of modern thought, with both its risks and its possible contributions. It is preferable to face these risks and difficulties rather than to ignore the threat they bear.

Faith and Myth

In the first place, our era has become conscious of a mode of knowing that, whether we like it or not, has an enormous influence on knowledge in general and on religious knowledge in particular. It is the myth. The myth is a kind of knowing that is not purely abstract but stems from the resources of imagination and more profoundly yet from the innermost reaches of man. This manner of knowing symbolically seems governed by *a priori* forms of knowledge, archetypes that are the outgrowth of man's most radically primitive contacts with the world. Among these archetypes, in particular, are femininity and maternity. Whether we are aware of it or not, they are part of our inner world, they orient our manner of thinking, our speech, our poetry, and our theology when we speak of the Blessed Virgin. These archetypes cannot simply be ignored. One who would do so would risk undergoing their influence without rectifying it. He would thus without control project onto the Virgin Mary, revealed in the Bible, the archetype of the eternal feminine or the maternal archetype with its warmth if not possessiveness, as among the mother-goddesses, etc. It is because they underwent the illusion of such myths that the authors of the seventeenth century opposed Christ's avenging justice to his Mother's mercy: "Jesus wants to condemn, but his Mother wants to save," wrote an author of that time, E. Binet.[2] One

---

2. E. Binet, *Le grand chef-d'oeuvre de Dieu ou les perfections de la Sainte Vierge,* Paris, 1634, p. 673. More recently A. D. Sertillanges, *La Vie Catholique, 2ᵉ série,* Paris, Gabalda, 1922, p. 29, wrote in a similar vein: "Mary protects us against evil, and she protects us, if one dare say it,

who thought like this was only projecting onto the perfect union of Christ and his Mother the myth of virile brutality and feminine tenderness. In order not to fall the victim of myth one must undertake an analysis of these archetypes or matrices of symbolic knowledge that are part of our inner self; then one can critically appraise them in both their assimilable and unassimilable elements.

In the second place modern thought is less inclined than was Scholasticism to objective knowledge. It shies clear of any pseudo-ontological materialization of Mary's privileges, for example, or any reification of her grace. It tends, on the other hand, to esteem the elements of relationship found in her: above all, the relationship of Mary's person to the divine person of her Son. Hence Mariology, like the rest of theology, will tend to become less an ontologizing effort; it will be more existential, more personalist in terms of the personal relationship to God who is love, and thus is the source, center, object, and principle of all love. Already a transition in this regard is under way. It can be detected on comparing certain pontifical encyclicals with the conciliar texts. This evolution has to be brought to its term without losing what was essential in the reflection on being that characterized the earlier *theologia,* while at the same time surmounting whatever was artificial in a certain proneness to objectify and ontologize to excess.

More penetratingly and more positively, theology about the Blessed Virgin Mary is now being beckoned to explore the anthropological and the pneumatological — in other words, to draw on the resources knowledge about man *(anthropos)* and about the Holy Spirit *(pneuma).*

---

against her Son, as the mother in the family intervenes in the hour of virile anger."

The Anthropological Approach

The Council chose after a fashion to see things from an anthropological viewpoint. The Eve-Mary theme taken up by the Council fathers envisages Mary in terms of the divine plan for woman. There is one single divine archetype of the woman in that plan: Eve, the women good and bad of the Old Testament, the corporate personalities represented by the people of Israel (Daughter of Zion) and the Church, and finally Mary, who is the personification of the Church, are all realizations of the same divine archetype. For the archetype is realized fully or incompletely, brightly or dimly, according to the mysterious pattern wherein triumphs of grace alternate with defeats of human liberty. The best source for this kind of anthropological approach is St. John's gospel. There "the mother of Jesus" is intentionally singled out along with other women — the Samaritan woman, the sisters of Lazarus, another Mary, the Magdalen. Far from having a purely passive role, the woman, as St. John portrays her, serves as a kind of forerunner of Christ's mystery. She invites and attracts it, she goes before it and gracefully introduces it. In a way she engenders it (Jn. 16:21; 19:25-27). Thus the Samaritan woman brings the message of salvation to her entire village (3:29). Lazarus' sisters are instrumental in the resurrection of their brother — which, because it is the only resurrection reported in St. John's gospel, serves as the prototype of Christ's own Resurrection (11:4, 21-29). The Mary who anoints Jesus at Bethany (12:7) anticipates his death and burial. Magdalen announces "the Resurrection" to the unbelieving disciples, introducing them to the good news of the faith. Similarly, Mary introduces the first miracle of Jesus, the one that becomes the foundation of the faith of his disciples (2:21). Thus it is that on Calvary she becomes the type of the Church, according to a mystery of motherhood (19:25-27; cf. 16:21), a mystery bound to the gift of the Holy Spirit (19:30). This skein of reflections corresponds to one of the essential lines of thought of Orthodox theology. It would have great ecumenical value. It throws light on the meaning of woman in the gospel and in the world, a meaning so much neglected.

The Pneumatological Approach

To adopt the pneumatological viewpoint is to scrutinize the relationship of the Virgin Mary to the Holy Spirit, with the concern of giving him the central place that is his. Such a study must needs be undertaken and developed with both Mary and the Church inseparably and correlatively in view. Preliminary to this enterprise is a transitional stage. It involves passing on to a perspective decidedly Christocentric — in ecclesiology a transition from a perspective hitherto centered on the hierarchy (or on the pope), and in Mariology a transition from the simply Mariocentric perspective. The Council reached the end of this transition to Christocentrism.[3]

But it is a fair question to ask whether the Council at the same time accorded the Holy Spirit the fundamental position that is his. It is indeed an important question.

In ecclesiology, in fact, as Heribert Mühlen has shown,[4] a Christocentrism without pneumatology — in other words, an ecclesiology of Christ without the Holy Spirit — tends

---

3. Certainly Vatican II did not ignore the pneumatological problem. Msgr. Philips, the principal author of the schema of *Lumen Gentium,* was one of the promoters of the pneumatological renewal in ecclesiology through his courses at Louvain from 1957–1959, and the articles he published during the Council showed his deep concern over this problem. Some of this passed into *Lumen Gentium.* But for all that the question was not yet ripe, and particularly not ripe enough for Msgr. Philips to introduce into the conciliar text some of his deeper insights rich in promise.

4. H. Mühlen, *Una mystica persona. Die Kirche als das Mysterium der Identität des heiligen Geistes in Christus und den Christen,* Munich, Schöningh, 1964; 2nd ed., 1967.

toward a kind of ecclesial monophysitism. This is to say, it leads to a theology of the Mystical Body in which the face-to-face relationship of Christ with the Church of the redeemed is forgotten, and the personality of each member disappears, because he is considered only as an impersonal member or cell of the Body of Christ.

Now according to the Fathers of the Church, the Holy Spirit is precisely the one who realizes the unity of the many persons in the unique mystical person of Christ, and realizes it perfectly, from within the very self of the persons, without annihilating them but rather respecting and developing the personality proper to each. Even more, he respects the differences proper to each individual and to each community, for the Spirit is the deep root of liberty, initiative, and differentiated expansion, and thus of that decentralization asked for by Vatican II. Its request here and in related matters has not yet *fully* found its justification for want of a sufficiently developed pneumatology. These reflections about the place of Holy Spirit in ecclesiology today bear repetition as contemporary Mariology is examined. What was excessive and embarrassing in the developments of post-Tridentine Mariology was due to the fact that they occurred during a time when the theology of the Holy Spirit was at a standstill. These developments took place in the void left by a neglected pneumatology. This diagnosis had been suggested now for several years, not only among non-Catholics but from within Catholicism as well.[5] Certainly exaggeration and unilateral interpretation ought to be avoided here, but the very problem at issue is raised by many an adage current in Marian circles, such as the following:

> "Mary forms Christ in us." — But "to form Christ in us" is first and foremost the role of the Holy Spirit.

---

5. R. Laurentin, "Esprit-Saint et théologie mariale," NRT 99 (1967), 26-42 (Orthodox, Protestant, and Catholic insights, 26–27), and "Mary and the Holy Spirit," in *The Present Crisis* . . . pp. 295–312.

"To Jesus through Mary." — But does one not go to Jesus first and foremost by the Holy Spirit? (Jn. 14:26; 15:13–14).

"Mary, the bond between Christ and us." — But this is essentially the function of the Holy Spirit.

It should not be said that these expressions are false, for the Blessed Virgin is closely linked to the Holy Spirit. But it is important here to establish the divine role properly belonging to the Spirit and to situate in its proper place the subordinate role that Mary has in the communion of saints. This altogether positive revision would especially affect the problem of Mary's part in the Redemption: the title of Coredeemer, with the pattern of association if not of equality implied by the prefix "co-", would above all fit the Holy Spirit. It seems paradoxical that thought has never been given to applying it to him, whereas it is standard to apply it to Mary.

The same goes for the theology of mediation. Billot, who was a critically minded and even rigorous theologian in matters of coredemption, wrote that "Mary was set up by Jesus Christ . . . as source and principle of all supernatural life for us."[6] Would not these expressions be fitting rather for the Holy Spirit whom Christ called the "source of life" in the depths of the believer's soul (Jn. 7:38–39)? Mary is connected with this source, the Holy Spirit, for she gave birth to Christ who is source of salvation; but she cannot be given the name "source" except in dependence on the Holy Spirit.

Evidently there is no question of suppressing the Blessed Virgin, but of restoring her in her vital connection with the Holy Spirit. She is, in fact, the first in the history of salvation to have received salvation according to the economy of the New Testament, in order to establish the fundamental link

---

6. Introduction to J. Bainvel, *Marie Mère de grâce,* Paris, 1921.

between Christ and man. Hers it was to serve for the first insertion of Christ into the human race, and the insertion of the human race into Christ for redemption. Only advance and gain await the person who follows the light of this thought to the end. St. Louis-Marie Grignion de Montfort did so, and the result was that for him the "last days" were not to be only a Marian era but the time of the Spirit. Grignion de Montfort said that Mary is entirely relative to Christ.[7] To that it should be added that she is altogether relative to the Spirit: as witness, as sign and place of the Spirit, as icon and temple of the Spirit.[8]

---

7. L. M. Grignion de Montfort, *Traité de la vraie dévotion* . . . # 225, ed. de Pontchâteau, 1943, p. 207. Paul VI took up this expression anew in the *original* Italian text of his address of November 21, 1964 in closing the third session of the Council (*Osservatore Romano,* Nov. 22, 1964). The *official* Latin text paraphrases "Mariam . . . ad Christum . . . totam spectare." (*Documentation catholique,* 6 déc. 1964, # 1437, col. 1545, translates "entirely ordered toward God".)

8. The French Mariological Society devoted its meetings of 1968 and 1969 to the theme "Pneumatology and Mariology." Cf. EM 25 (1968) *Le Saint-Esprit et Marie I: L'Evangile et les Pères;* 26 (1969) . . . *II: Bible et Spiritualité.*

SECOND PART:

DEVELOPMENT IN THE DESTINY OF MARY

INTRODUCTION TO THE SECOND PART

The object of the second part of this study is no longer to present the history of doctrinal development but doctrine itself, no longer the conceptual developments of which Mary was the object but the Virgin Mary herself according to God's plan. Two approaches to this task are possible.

Excellence and Shortcomings of the Deductive Method

The classical method would be to adopt a logical plan. The eternal predestination of the *Theotokos* would be the starting point. From the very beginning a standpoint would be taken up within God's thought as he grasps things in their unity, and from the idea he has of Mary from all eternity the study would begin. An effort would be made to discern the fundamental trait that on this level defines the "creature blessed among all women." From it the rest would flow as from a first principle.[1]

---

1. The problem of the first principle of Mariology begins for all purposes to be taken up in the Marian syntheses the first of which is the Pseudo-Albert of the mid-13th century (cf. *supra*, p. 119); then with Gerson (d. 1420), *Opera*, Paris, 1606, t. 1, col. 451; then with Suarez (d. 1617) and Lawrence of Brindisi (d. 1619) at the dawn of the seventeenth century, etc.

Such a method has its excellence and attraction. It answers a praiseworthy demand for unity and simplicity, as well as the desire to communicate with God's designs in the loftiest manner possible. But this method runs up against difficulties on account of its immoderate ambition.

It begins with the divine intention. That is possible, since God has revealed his intention to us. Nevertheless, he disclosed this plan to us not in itself and as a whole, but in fragmentary statements, in a way that is enigmatic and not obvious. We grasp it from below through its consequences, and not from above through its inexpressible principle which is identified with God's simplicity. Certainly theology strives for such unity as its proper task, but it will always remain short of its goal. It is wiser to recognize this situation humbly, according to the counsel of the gospel, "Whoever among you intends to build a tower should first sit down and examine . . ." (Lk. 14:28).

Difficulties present themselves on two levels: the *choice of a principle of synthesis* and the *development of its consequences.*

A. Difficulties in the Choice of a Principle

Only since 1935 has the problem of the first principle of Mariology become the object of specific study. Since that time theories have proliferated, to the point that about thirty of them can be enumerated. No attempt will be made to enter this labyrinth. The variety of theories can be presented in two

---

But reflexively and *ex professo* the problem of the first principle becomes the object of study beginning in 1936 with J. Bittremieux, "De principio supremo mariologiae," ETL 12 (1935), pp. 607-609. Articles proliferate thereafter. For a good study recapitulating the question cf. C. Dillenschneider, *Le premier principe d'un théologie mariale organique. Orientations,* Paris, Alsatia, 1955. This book occasioned a penetrating review, productive of progress in the question, by A. Patfoort, "Le principe premier de la mariologie," RSPT 41 (1957), 445-454.

groups: for one group the *principle of analogy* serves as point of orientation; for the others, a *relation,* and specifically the relation implied by the divine maternity, serves this purpose.

1. Principle of Analogy as Starting Point

The theories of the first group present two rather different aspects:

a. Some of them are essentially "Christotypical," to use H. M. Köster's expression:[2] they describe Mary's privileges in the likeness of Christ's. Christ's being is characterized by the hypostatic union, Mary's by an intrinsic belonging to the hypostatic order. Christ is redeemer, she is coredemptrix. He is mediator, she is mediatrix, etc. Mariologists of this tendency construct their Mariology along these lines on the model of Christology.
b. Other theories are termed "ecclesiotypical." They consider the mystery of Mary on the analogy of the mystery of the Church. Like Holy Church, Mary is holy from her origin, according to a holiness received by grace and redemption. Like the Church, she cooperated in Christ's work and has a mediatorial role toward men, etc.

In the Christotypical approach the first principle is that Mary is the associate of Christ,[3] or the new Eve in the pres-

---

2. H. M. Köster, ". . . B.M. Virgini in cooperatione eius ad opus Redemptionis," *Maria et Ecclesia* 2 (1959), pp. 20–49; the author apologizes for his neologisms, p. 22, n. 2.

3. J. Thomas, "Quelle est la meilleure structure interne d'un traité de mariologie?" *Journées sacerdotales mariales* I (1951), pp. 113–116. The author proposes "replacing . . . the principle ordinarily given (the divine maternity, the fact of Mary's being Mother of the Redeemer as such) with another that is more essential (that of her necessary union with Christ-Mediator)." The author had already expounded his thesis, inspired by J.

ence of the new Adam — a theme that has patristic roots.[4] In the ecclesiotypical approach Mary is the prototype of the Church,[5] or again, the perfection of God's bounty toward the creature; she is the noblest fruit of the Redemption, the one most perfectly redeemed by grace, the one most perfectly engaged in cooperating in the work of Christ.[6] In her who by her faith and charity begot Christ grace reaches its zenith.[7] She is the personal summit of humanity in its covenant with God,[8] etc.

The two principles that give rise to these two extreme tendencies in Mariology, Christotypical and ecclesiotypical, are in reality less opposed than would appear. In fact, it must be said that they really amount to one. For the Incarnate Word formed Mary and the Church in his own likeness, by

---

Lebon's ideas, in *Revue diocesaine de Tournai* 1 (1946), 272: "The divine maternity is in the final analysis only an element of this association...."

4. S. Alameda, "El primer principio mariológico según los Padres," EstM 3 (1944), pp. 163–186. This principle had been adopted by L. Billot, *De Verbo Incarnato*, Rome, 1927, t. 7, p. 386: "De Virgine matre generaliter tenendum est quod in ordine reparationis eum locum tenet quem tenuit Eva in ordine perditionis — Concerning the Virgin Mother generally it is to be held that in the order of reparation she holds the place that Eve had in the order of the fall."

5. O. Semmelroth, *Urbild der Kirche*, Würzburg, Echter, 1949 (ET: *Mary, Archetype of the Church*, New York, Sheed and Ward, 1963).

6. K. Rahner, "Le principe fondamental dans la théologie mariale," RSR 42 (1954), 527.

7. A. Müller, "Um die Grundlagen der Mariologie," *Divus Thomas* (Freiburg) 29 (1951), 385–401. The author sets up fulness of grace as the principle of synthesis in the light of the patristic idea that Mary conceived the Word in her heart by faith before conceiving him in her body. To conceive God not only in spirit by the act of faith but in one's flesh would correspond to the supreme degree of faith informed by charity. This interesting view, which has meaning within the framework of the symbolic thought of the Fathers, becomes strange when understood on the level of scholastic terminology.

8. H. M. Köster, *Die Magd des Herrn*, 2nd ed., Freiburg/Breisgau, 1954, p. 140.

his redeeming grace. According to patristic theology the Church was born from his opened side,[9] and, as St. Augustine says, Mary was spiritually born of Christ "according to grace."[10] In other words, there is a triple analogy between Christ, Mary, and the Church — an analogy that proceeds entirely from the work of the Redeemer. Mary and the Church are relative to Christ and correlative to each other. This is what lies behind their resemblances. This analogy can be considered from the viewpoint of Christ who is its true principle, and then Mary appears as a feeble image of him who is by essence the image of the invisible God (Col. 1:15; 2 Cor. 4:4; Heb. 1:3). The analogy can be taken up also from the viewpoint of the Church and the possible accomplishments of God's grace in the creature, and then Mary appears as the preeminent realization of the Church. In short, there are two movements here, one descending, the other ascending. Each of the two directions has consequences in the way in which Marian doctrine is treated. As it descends, the first movement is afraid of debasing Mary, and thus is tempted to install itself on the level of Christ himself. The second movement reacts precisely against this temptation; it wishes to avoid anything like an apotheosis of Mary and intends instead to place her in her position as a creature in the presence of her creator.[11] If the two theories come into oppo-

---

9. S. Tromp, "De nativitate Ecclesiae ex Corde Jesu in cruce," *Gregorianum* 13 (1932), 489, and G. de Broglie, "L'Eglise, nouvelle Eve née du Sacré-Coeur," NRT 88 (1956), 3–25.

10. St. Augustine, *De Virginitate* V,5–VI,6, CSEL 41, pp. 239–240; PL 40:399.

11. H. M. Köster had brought out this idea into exaggerated relief in his books *Die Magd des Herrn*, 1st ed., Limburg, Lahn, 1947, and *Unus Mediator*, Limburg, Lahn, 1950. The "monophysite tendency" of these works was criticized by three authors: A. Adam, "Neomonophysitismus," *Theologische Quartalschrift* 129 (1949), 254-255; C. Dillenschneider, *Le mystère de la corédemption*, Paris, Vrin, 1951, pp. 27–61; Y.Congar, *Le Christ, Marie, et l'Eglise*, Paris, Desclée, 1952 (ET: *Christ, Our Lady and*

sition, it is not because of their objective principles but by reason of the direction in which they move and particularly the hardening of positions that sets in.

The most committed advocates of the Christotypical tendency would set up as principle an ontology of association. In it Christ and Mary would stand alone in face of the rest of mankind. The Redemption would proceed from Christ and Mary "as from a single principle" *(tamquam ab uno principio)* according to a formula borrowed from Trinitarian theology. Those of the ecclesiotypical tendency envisage this association within the communion of saints, as something common to all Christians.

There is truth in both perspectives. The first is correct in considering everything from the standpoint of the true principle that Christ is the source of all grace and beauty. The second is correct in situating Mary within the communion of saints, where she is the first both in the order of time and according to perfection in grace — and especially, in situating her face to face with Christ her Redeemer.

2. Relationship as Starting Point

But apart from these two theories, most authors look for the first principle of Mariology along another way, a way that relies not on analogy but on relationship. In this line of thought the first principle is Mary's motherhood in regard to Christ. In that perspective resemblances and association pass into the background. They are considered in function of that personal relationship which essentially implies differences, such as the infinite distance between the transcendent God

---

the Church, Westminster, Newman, 1957). All three held that, carried away by his intuition, Köster tended to minimize Christ's human fulness in order to bring into relief Mary's complementary role as a human person and representative of mankind on Calvary. In the last edition of his *Die Magd...* Köster fully corrected what could be exaggerated in his insights and is no longer vulnerable to this criticism.

and the creature chosen to give birth to him, the differentiation between man and woman, the complementarity of Son and Mother, etc. This way of looking at things goes to the heart of the matter. At the same time that it is classical, it is adapted to the modern mentality in that it is relational, existential, and personal, bringing everything down to a living relationship of person to person.[12]

But this approach, for its part also, gives rise to a variety of formulas that tend in divers ways and with more or less rigidity to pass from the divine motherhood to resemblance in grace and association in the Redemption in quest of a fundamental principle of Mariology.

Here again two sides shape up: one moves along avenues more metaphysical and ontological, the other along avenues more in harmony with living reality.

---

12. These ideas were well brought out in C. Dillenschneider, *Le principe d'une théologie mariale organique,* Paris, Alsatia, 1955, pp. 35–52. By way of example, according to M. J. Nicolas in *Revue Thomiste* 51 (1951), 221, the divine motherhood implies as a fitting element "a total union, a community of destiny between the Mother and the Son," and thus the divine motherhood is an integral motherhood. C. Journet follows an analogous way, unifying the fitting elements of divine motherhood according to the principle that the Mother of God cannot be anything but a *worthy* Mother of God. Other authors embrace under the same title "Mother" the two aspects of Mary's motherhood with regard to Christ and with regard to mankind; "Mother of the whole Christ" is the title N. García Garcés gives her in *Mater coredemptrix,* Rome, 1940; "Universal Mother of Christ and of men" says G. Roschini, *Mariologia,* Rome, 1947. The effort of all these syntheses is to lead to unity the two essential elements, namely, Mary's role as Mother and her association in Christ's work; or again, her bodily motherhood with regard to Christ and her spiritual motherhood with regard to the rest of mankind. It is in quest of this synthesis that Scheeben had forged the principle of "sponsal motherhood," a rather strange expression but a deep insight as he explains it. The divine motherhood, he shows, differs from any other motherhood in being concerned with a preexisting Son. It is this eternal Son who chose his Mother. He proposed this motherhood, proposed himself to her consent. Thus the matter is one of a free association, a bond between two persons who freely commit themselves to each other, whence the expression "sponsal motherhood."

Carried to the extreme, there would be on the first side an ontology of the divine motherhood, viewed as a formally sanctifying relationship. On the other side the divine motherhood would be situated within the context of grace proper to it, according to the gospel, but with a lively awareness of the gratuitous character evident in the different aspects of this gift: Mary became the *Theotokos* according to the free gift of God, and it is freely that she entered on her destiny. Thus her divine motherhood is seen to be the supreme and integral accomplishment both of motherhood according to grace and of relationship to God.

Once they are divested of any element of exaggeration and optical illusion, each of these points of view has its light to throw on the subject. They are like the different angles and lightings one would use to photograph a masterpiece. Some angles give a more central view, others a peripheral one; different lightings will bring out or subdue the contrasts. There is no single perspective or lighting that is absolute. In this matter we are moving around a mystery whose inexhaustible and ineffable character the East has very well extolled. This is one of the reasons for hesitating to select any one principle in preference to the rest.

B. Difficulties in Developing Consequences from the First Principle Chosen

But assuming that our choice has been made, a second and more difficult problem arises: once the fundamental principle has been chosen, in what order are the elements flowing from it to be arranged? Already in a purely human enterprise of any proportion we find it hard to untangle the web of logic; how much more ill-put are we not in the presence of a divine work! Assuredly there is logic in the divine plan. But it is a logic surpassing our own, and its choices surprise us: among all the sons of Jesse (1 Sam. 16:1–13), Yahweh prefers the youngest, the boy David who was not in anyone's mind.

When Jesus chooses the apostles, what does he see in these fishermen (Mk. 1:19-20), or even in this tax-collector (Mk. 2:13)? Why does he choose Paul the persecutor (1 Cor. 15:9-10). Why did he choose as mother that poor woman from a despised village like Nazareth (Jn. 1:46)? Finally, why is his first apparition given to Magdalen the sinner, rather than to Peter, or to his Mother herself?[13] To questions such as these one can of course find answers that suggest themselves *after* the event. Better said, one can discern something of a divine logic that outclasses our shabby human logic. But nothing permitted us to *foresee* what God would decide, and it remains impossible to *deduce* it strictly. In these matters we are often victims of hindsighted illusion that all too readily gives the character of necessity to the most unforeseeable happenings. The luckiest stroke of fortune, whether in war or at an examination, tends with hindsight to look like merited success and evidence of incontrovertible worth.

On a deeper level, in deducing Mary's privileges in too rigorous a fashion one runs the risk of infringing upon the truth in two ways. First, the gratuitous character of the divine plan, which sometimes seems to delight in disconcerting our human logic, would be obscured. And secondly, the marvelous liberty with which Mary answered divine grace at each instant of her life would be blurred. In the long run the

---

13. The theme of the Risen Christ's appearance to his Mother has been the object of a considerable output of literature and controversy. Among the most recent works are: Y. Congar, "Incidence ecclésiologique d'un thème de dévotion mariale," *Mélanges de sciences religieuses* 7 (1950), 291-292; C. Giannelli, "Témoignage patristique grec en faveur d'une apparition du Christ ressuscité à la Vierge Marie," *Revue d'études byzantines* 11 (1953), 106-119; P. Bellet, "Testimonios coptos de la aparición de Cristo resuscitado a la Virgen," *Estudios Biblicos* 13 (1954), 199-205; C. Vona, "L'apparizione di Christi risorto alla Madre negli antichi scrittori cristiani," *Divinitas* 1 (1957), 479-527; J. B. Breckenridge, "The Iconography of the Appearance of Christ to His Mother," *The Art Bulletin* 39 (1957), 9-32, etc. The most resounding controversy on the subject will be found summarized in *Marianum* 2 (1940), 410-424.

personalist perspective, so important in treating of Mary, would be dissolved, and Mary's personality would be absorbed into an abstract personification:[14] motherhood in itself, or "association with Christ the Redeemer,"[15] or "the essence of the mystery of the Church,"[15a] or the transcendent feminine, or "the eternal feminine" in the noblest sense of the expression. This would be reducing the living spontaneity of a supremely concrete personal existence to the logical deduction of an essence.[16]

But there is yet another objection to such a choice. It will rightly be asked whether actually the best perspective is one centering in a restricted way on Mary considered alone and in herself. Would it not be better to situate her within the

---

14. This danger of abstraction is very well expressed by I. F. Görres, *Nocturnen, Tagebuch und Aufzeichnungen*, Frankfurt/Main, 1949, pp. 132–133.

15. "Consortium Christi Redemptoris."

15a. "Das Wesengeheimnis der Kirche."

16. M. J. Nicolas, "Essai de synthèse mariale," *Maria* 1 (1949), p. 709, cautions: The moral appreciation of values that are tied in with one another in Marian theology is too great to allow the final criterion to appear simply as an intellectual evidence rather than as a manner of feeling and evaluating the whole." Cf. *ibid.*, p. 740: "It is true that in Marian theology nothing is implied by metaphysical necessity within the laws of nature or the essential dogmas of the Incarnation and Redemption. Or rather, if there is a necessity, it is hypothetical. It supposes a certain position taken on the part of God. . . ." These nuances, correct as they are, do not demand giving up the task of synthesis. Nicolas himself gave an excellent synthesis in *Theotokos,* Paris, Desclée, 1964. In a strictly intellectual vein also Th. Philippe, *La théologie mariale* (mimeographed), Québec, University of Laval, n.d., p. 18, declares: "In Mary *everything is gratuitous.* She is the masterpiece of the divine good pleasure. The theologian must therefore respect the discretion of the Holy Spirit and conform himself scrupulously to what Scripture and Tradition affirm. *Logic comes into play here less than in other treatises,* such as for example, in that on Christ. Most often *there is no necessary bond* between the divine prerogatives given Mary." These remarks are taken up by F. M. Braun, "La Mère de Jésus," *Revue Thomiste* 51 (1951), 39, n. 1.

Church and the history of salvation, where her place really is, in her living correlation with the whole of the mystery? One could, of course, imagine reconstructing the chateau of Chenonceaux in a downtown square of an American city. It would still be the chateau of Chenonceaux, but it would lose all its charm and the whole harmony it has with the river and valley of the Loire. More precisely, the unity of the divine plan that must be sought in the effort of understanding is not that unity which is realized on the level of "Mariology," but a unity that is realized on the larger scale of theology itself, whole and entire. Mary finds her place and value in function of the mystery of Christ and the Church. That is why a Mariologist as committed and on occasion as bold as Bonnefoy would not hear of a "first principle of Mariology" and time and again in his writing struck out against such a theory:

> "These attempts (to find a first principle) are doomed to failure from the very beginning. They proceed from an initial grave error. Mariology is neither an autonomous science, nor a science subalternate to theology or to revelation, but an integral part of theology, which, says St. Thomas, is a single science. Mariology neither has nor can have principles other than those of theology itself."[16a]
>
> "Mariology is not an autonomous science but a branch artificially detached from Christian theology. Whether one wills it or not, to treat Mariology as an autonomous science is to fragment the unity of theology."[17]

16a. J. Bonnefoy, "La primauté de la Très Sainte Vierge," EM 4 (1938), pp. 88–89.

17. *Idem*, "Le mérite social de Marie," *Alma Socia Christi* 2 (1952), p. 22. Similar ideas were more discreetly expressed by C. Zimara in an article in *Divus Thomas* (Freiburg) 15 (1937), 114–115.

Recently the same sentiment has led certain theologians to look for a principle that would situate the Virgin Mary with respect to the ensemble of salvation:

> "The Incarnation of the Savior implies a motherhood inside of the humanity that God wishes to save."[18]

Beginning with such a principle, everything would tie together according to a logic founded on salvation as a whole, not according to any internal logic of privileges.

This loyal examination of difficulties is enough to put one on guard against the danger, not an illusory one, of a Mariology closed in on itself and theological rationalism that the Church sometimes has had to tone down. For all that, there is no question of depreciating theological reasoning, for which the Church herself has such esteem. To renounce bringing to light the admirable reasons of fittingness in the divine plan, whether as a whole or on the level of Mary's destiny, would be simply to renounce theology itself. These reasons of fittingness are so harmoniously interrelated that at times they give the impression of necessity — an impression that is in part correct, for the most beautiful of God's works assuredly bears, more than does any other, the mark of unity and simplicity. Moreover, among all simple creatures, Mary is the one most faithful to God's plan: she did not cause any rifts in it, any distortions or outgrowths that deform the destiny of other men. Yet this destiny of hers falls short of the strict cohesion that Christ's exhibits. Mariology cannot match the logical precision of Christology.

---

18. G. Gironés, "Ensayo sobre el problema fundamental de la mariología," *Anales del seminario de Valencia* 4 (1964), # 8, 31–73.

The Method to be Chosen

After all the factors have been weighed, our choice in this study does not fall on the deductive approach, not on principle but out of a fear that to do so would be to overestimate our science and falsify the mystery of Mary by a premature option, or to impoverish it by reducing it to too narrow a principle. We shall approach this mystery by the most objective way, the one least open to contest. We shall follow the order in which the life of Mary unfolded. Her destiny will be studied as it developed progressively, not just from her Conception to her Assumption — too narrow a perspective that would not take account enough of Mary's integration into the history of salvation — but from its preparations in the Old Testament up to the parousia where the Church will rejoin the *Theotokos* in her integral glorification.[19]

In making this choice we do not thereby give up the search for the two elements so esteemed by the deductive method: the foundation on which the destiny of Mary rests, and the reasons of fittingness that manifest its organic unity.

The foundation of her destiny must be sought in the gospel itself, at the Annunciation. Mary is chosen by God from among all creatures to introduce Christ into human history, into the human race which he comes to save. Thus she is the Mother of God-become-Man, the Mother of the God Savior. This root "principle" is given in revelation itself. It attaches Mary to the plan of salvation and runs no risk of giving rise to a closed Mariology, at least so long as we do not ourselves close it in. Moreover, this principle leads us directly to our task, which is to consider Mary within the framework of

---

19. Mary's predestination assuredly is the governing element, but it cannot constitute a "chapter" in this plan founded on the history of salvation, for predestination is only a *moment* in this temporal development; it is a reality not only before the beginning of Mary's destiny, but before and *during* each of the instants of time whose free unfolding it gives rise to transcendentally from outside the bounds of time.

time, for, according to the principle itself, Mary's function is to introduce God into time and the history of salvation in a fitting way.

As to the reasons of fittingness that sometimes go so far as to give us the impression of necessity, we shall try to appreciate them at their just value. At any rate, they do not exhibit any geometrical necessity in strict linear deduction, but the kind of necessity we see in art or love. In a great work of art, in the depths of some meeting between two human lives, all appears to be necessary, yet all is in fact quite free and gratuitous. The necessities involved in either case are not reducible to a formula; they consist of an inexhaustible total of harmonious relations. They cannot be deduced from a single principle, but only vaguely discerned within an ensemble that admits of no change in its component parts — as in certain lines of Racine, or with the *Pietà* of Avignon, or in the way a loving couple looks back on its whole past history. So it is, in the highest degree, with the destiny of Mary, God's own masterpiece, fruit of the most lavish love he has ever directed on a created person. So it is, in a still broader perspective, with the ensemble of God's design, outside of which the intimate tête-à-tête of God with his Mother would have no more sense than the abrupt mystery of the death of God on the cross, if this latter mystery were isolated from the rest of the mystery of salvation.

The Virgin and Time

The approach we have adopted — which some may perhaps think overcautious — has a very positive advantage. To follow the chronological order of Mary's destiny is to bring to light a significant factor therein, the factor of time. Its importance will emerge from a double comparison made with the destiny of Christ and with that of the saints.

1. St. Luke said of the child Jesus that "he increased in

wisdom, in stature, and in grace."[20] Christ grew, therefore, not only physically, but spiritually. This however was a wholly accidental growth. Essentially Christ is God from his very first moment, eternal in his person, and in the divine order there was no growth possible, contrary to what was imagined by certain heretics of the "adoptionist" way of thought. From his very origin, he *is* fully God, and according to common theological opinion he *knew himself as God* in a perfect vision on the very level of his intelligence. Unlike us, he is not a pilgrim in obscure faith, traveling on the way toward the light that from all eternity has remained unknown. Whatever the hypothesis in this matter, he essentially possesses the completion of his personal destiny.[21] Though he is in time, his *personality,* and therefore his intimate destiny and undoubtedly his very knowledge transcend the order of time. For him there was no possibility of growth except on the surface, in the secondary and accidental aspects of his life.

Mary, on the contrary, lived entirely in the wayfaring state,[22] which is that of all other human beings. The law of growth is essential to her being and her knowledge: she became the Mother of God, and, before finding the beatific vision at the end of her earthly destiny, she lived in faith. Christ's career is the descent of an eternal person into time; Mary's is like ours, a gradual ascent from time into eternity: she passes from gratuitous gifts to merits, and from merits to new gifts that remain the work of grace.

---

20. Lk. 2:52; cf. 2:40.
21. During his life on earth Christ was at once a wayfarer with regard to his glorification (e.g., Phil. 2:7–11) and one who had reached his end with regard to his vision, according to the classical thesis of St. Thomas, ST III, q. 7, a. 8: "Non solum erat comprehensor, sed etiam viator."
22. "The Blessed Virgin advanced in her pilgrimage of faith. . . ." *Lumen Gentium* art. 58.

2. If now we compare Mary with the other saints, her destiny again appears more marked by time than is theirs. In the first place, better than any other saint she knew how to "make the best use of time," to redeem time, as Saint Paul puts it (Col. 4:5; Eph. 5:16). Not only did she profit more from time subjectively, but she was objectively more capable of greater progress. St. Thomas, in fact, remarks[23] that growth in grace follows a law of acceleration which in the spiritual order is analogous to the rate of acceleration of a falling body: the nearer a soul approaches God, the more swiftly it is drawn to him; the higher it is raised in grace, the swifter the ascent. Thus Mary's growth, starting at the outset with a holiness that surpassed that of all other saints, came to be the most staggering there ever was. She knew nothing of that negative progress which consists in the elimination of sin, a progress so little in harmony with the rhythm of time since it implies advance by fits and starts and the redeeming of time lost by falling behind. Hers was the very type of positive progress of the highest order, an approach toward God and a deepening in love. Whereas the destiny of every other being oscillates between the nostalgia of memory and impatience for the future, Mary knew how to live abreast of time, to "cling" to duration, to enlist the whole of time past in the service of the future, in a hope that never faltered. More than any other, she knew how to live according to the precept of the gospel without being preoccupied for the morrow (Mt. 6:34).

Finally, she had the privilege of belonging to each of the three phases of the time of grace: before Christ, during Christ's lifetime on earth, and after Christ. She was born and grew up in the Old Testament. The days of her life embraced the whole duration of the life of her Son and continued

---

23. *In Ep. ad Hebr.* 10, 28, ed. Vivès 21, p. 67b. This idea is one of the leitmotifs of R. Garrigou-Lagrange's books. On its application to Mary see his *Mariologie,* Paris, Cerf, 1948, 2nd ed., pp. 84–88.

during the earliest days of the Church. Not only did she participate in each of these three phases — Old Testament, Christ, Church — but she seems to have had a privileged role in the transition from one to the next, a factor that brings her mission into harmony with the essence itself of time. It was through her that on the day of the Incarnation Israel gave birth to Christ. We see her playing a similar connecting role between the death of Christ and the birth of the Church. Finally, by her Assumption she anticipates the parousia and thus is the connecting link between the present earthly condition of the Church and that future, heavenly, risen condition toward which it is making its way.

Our approach will therefore be to follow the development of Mary's destiny. We shall see how her life, her mission, her being all unfold in the way a flower, whose growth forces are at first hidden, gradually blossoms out. In the light of what has just been said, it is possible to distinguish the following stages in this development:

1. Before the Annunciation: Mary as Israel's choice fruit.
2. Mary at the beginning of Christ's life: her role in the Incarnation and her quality of Mother of God.
3. Mary at the end of Christ's life: her presence on Calvary and her cooperation in the Redemption.
4. From the death of Christ to the Dormition: Mary as the link between the time of Christ and the time of the Church.
5. The Assumption: Mary, "the eschatological image of the Church."[24]
6. The Parousia: the Church rejoined to Mary in the integral glory of the risen Christ.

---

24. This expression ("icône eschatologique de l'Eglise") is borrowed from L. Bouyer, *Le culte de la Mère de Dieu*, Chevetogne, 1950, p. 33. It inspired the title of part 5 of chapter 8 of *Lumen Gentium*, "Mary, a Sign of Sure Hope and of Solace for God's People in Pilgrimage."

FIRST STAGE

BEFORE THE ANNUNCIATION — MARY, CHOICE FRUIT OF ISRAEL

The first task is to situate the point of departure of Mary's destiny.

The history of the world before Christ is the closed field of two opposite movements. On the one hand, mankind is being dragged along in the dialectical struggle of sin. On the other, God's gratuitous interventions are leading it toward the victory which is to be Christ. The downward movement of degradation held sway up to Abraham (Gen. 3–11). Then God's interventions became increasingly efficacious, but within a scope that was more and more *restricted,* and on a level that was more and more *spiritual.* God chose Abraham's family, and then, among his descendants, Jacob in preference to Esau. Then, as Israel's dreams of political greatness and prosperity came to nothing, grace progressively concentrated upon an elite, obscure from a worldly point of view — the "poor," the "humble," who are the spiritual "remnant" of the chosen people — and finally upon the flower of Israel, the Virgin Mary.

The two aspects of this ascent of mankind towards its Savior can be summed up as *reparation* and *preparation.* They are two aspects closely connected, the one negative, the other positive. Little by little God purifies a chosen lineage so that Christ can be born without being touched by sin. Among them he stirs up a faith increasingly refined, increasingly explicit, so that Christ's divine coming may be the answer to a desire on man's part, something that was waited for and hoped for, a work of liberty and love, rather than a kind of intrusion marked by surprise or violence.

So it was that between Abraham and Mary a double progress was accomplished, in the order of *moral purity* and in the order of *faith*.

1. In the *moral order* it is a far cry from Israel's first ancestor, Abraham, to the Flower of Israel. The behavior of the father of believers was still crude and at times shocking.[1] The Virgin Mary's very first acts exhibit the most perfect purity. With Abraham, the "rock" in whom God began to "carve" the image of his people (Is. 51:1-2), there begins what might be called the stone age of salvation. Vigor and brute strength characterize it. With Mary comes the golden age, the achievement of perfection.

2. From the viewpoint of *belief and fidelity* a deep resemblance, rather than any further contrast, seems to emerge between Abraham and Mary. All begins with faith and ends with faith. At the outset it is the unconditional faith of the chosen people in the promise; at the conclusion it is the unconditional faith of the Mother of God in the realization of the promise (Lk. 1:38). Yet here too the evolution that had taken place is considerable. At the beginning it was an elementary faith that remained bound up in a promise of material prosperity; at the conclusion it is a faith spiritualized and enriched by the long development of revelation, of which the message of the Annunciation marked the definitive stage.

And so a double mystery invites investigation here:

---

1. Polygamy, subterfuge, disconcerting compromises for obtaining the benefits that the relations of his wife would secure from the Pharaoh (Gen. 12:16; cf. 16:6, etc.). Obviously there are impressive compensating qualities.

Mary's *original purity,* which is the transcendent completion of the long moral reparation that God effected in Israel, and Mary's *faith,* which, while remaining in the same order, is the completion of the long preparation for the coming of the Messiah.

1. The Immaculate Conception: Mary's Original Purity

Mary's original purity appears at the conclusion of the Old Testament as the key to an indecipherable and apparently contradictory enigma which arises from the very Bible itself. In fact, it consists in the most baffling element of the mystery of salvation, the love God has for man the sinner. The people that came forth from the faith of Abraham did not escape the dialectic struggle of sin. This people whom God had chosen as a "well beloved spouse,"[2] according to the teaching of the prophets, proved unfaithful. It "prostituted" itself before false gods. And yet God's love did not give up in despair. It endured even stronger. Hence, beginning with the second chapter of Hosea a mysterious promise begins to take shape: in the last days God will take up his adulterous spouse anew as an unsullied bride. At the end of this line of development, in the Song of Songs, all the past with all its reproaches is blotted out. As bridegroom, Yahweh addresses Israel, his bride, "You are wholly beautiful, my love, and without a blemish" (Song 4:7).[3] The paradox is disconcerting. How is

---

2. Hosea 2; Jer. 31:17–22; Is. 51:17, 21, 22; 52:1–2, 7–8, 12; 54:4–8; 61:10–11; 62:4–5.

3. The old argument drawn from Song 4:7 in favor of the Immaculate Conception, and the liturgical use of this verse, reveal their worth if, with A. Robert, *Le Cantique des Cantiques,* Paris, Gabalda, 1963, the Song is taken as the culmination of the Old Testament theology of the relationships of Yahweh and Israel. Where is this prophecy of the adulterous spouse become fiancée realized if not in Mary, in the main line of the unfolding plan of salvation?

This is stated in awareness of the objection that Robert himself makes

all this possible? Its possibility lies not along human ways, but along the ways God chose, ways that involved the passing of Israel into the Church, which is the new creation of the chosen people in Jesus Christ. But at the point of departure for this new creation and recapitulation there was need of a pure and unspoiled seed of growth, a bud of grace from which the Flower of Jesse might blossom forth without disgrace (Is. 11:1), a renewal of purity within which the people might give birth to God its Savior as he came into its midst for the eschatological wedding. Such is the mystery of Mary, "object of all God's favor" according to the name of grace

---

against applying the Song to Mary: "It chants the praise of merciful love . . . that *we have offended.* The expressions of the Song cannot apply to the Blessed Virgin either in the literal sense — even the fuller sense — or in the typical sense, but only as accommodations which are isolated from the central idea that animates them" (A. Robert, article in *Maria* 1 (1949), p. 33). This argument would carry weight if the Song spoke expressly of Israel's sin and the mercy shown toward it. But, as Robert himself insists in very forthright terms, Israel's faults precisely "are so completely pardoned that *no explicit mention of them is made" (ibid).* No doubt the inspired writer did not grasp *how* God would realize this return to original purity. But the apparently hyperbolic declaration that Yahweh-King makes to Israel — "There is no stain in you" — was literally realized only in the new creation that began with Mary's Immaculate Conception. Since this sense is objectively verified, since it was recognized (though manners of expression often were deficient) by an abundant tradition, the theologian is authorized to see there a "fuller sense" or further sense that corresponds to the plan of God, principal author of Scripture.

The same can be said of the text of Jer. 31:22, likewise put aside by Robert (*Maria* 1 (1949), pp. 24–26). Here again he seems to disregard the theological import of the excellent exegesis he proposes. This woman who "danced round" false gods and is going to turn around to Yahweh, in other words, to convert, is Israel. But in whom is this total and uncompromising conversion fully realized, if not in Mary and the Church? In short, these prophecies concern Mary at the same time as Israel and the Church. Likewise, according to Luke, Mary is the eschatological Daughter of Zion in whom the people of Israel become the new creation, without ceaaing to be the people of the promises. There is here a mystery of continuity of race within discontinuity of grace.

given her from on high (Lk. 1:28). It is in her that Holy Church begins, and thus it is that from the beginning God can say, not simply in poetic figure but in very truth, "You are wholly beautiful, my love, and without a blemish."

To this mystery of renewal within the continuity of the race to be saved, a mystery of re-creation by grace and of rejuvenation for a world grown old in sin, the Church has given a precise formula. On December 8, 1854 Pius IX defined the initial point of the mystery in these terms:

> "At the first instant of her conception, by the grace and privilege of Almighty God and in consideration of the merits of Jesus Christ, the Savior of the human race, the Virgin Mary was preserved and exempted from all stain of original fault."

This dogmatic formula, the terms of which were intentionally borrowed from the Bull *Sollicitudo* of Alexander VII,[4]

---

4. The two texts (as found in *Bullarium Taurinense* 16, 789, and *Acta Pii IX* 1, 616; Denz. 1100 (2015) and 1641 (2803)) read in parallel as follows:

Alexander VII Bull *Sollicitudo* Dec. 8, 1661	Pius IX Bull *Ineffabilis* Dec. 8, 1854
VETUS EST Christi fidelium erga . . . *beatissimam* Matrem	DEFINIMUS
PIETAS SENTIENTIUM ejus ANIMAM	doctrinam quae tenet *beatissimam* Virginem MARIAM
in primo instanti creationis et infusionis in corpus	*in primo instanti* suae conceptionis

joins together and sanctions the two great traditional requirements which in their apparent opposition had given rise to so many conflicts in the past:

1. From the beginning Mary was *absolutely exempt from original sin.*
2. Yet this daughter of Adam was *saved by Jesus Christ.*

The difficulty of combining these two requirements arose from the order of time: how could Mary, conceived according to the ordinary laws of nature, not have incurred, were it only for an *instant,* the sin of the *race* to which she belonged? How could she have been saved *before* Christ had redeemed the world? These two difficulties are resolved in the two words *"pre*servation" and *"pre*vision." Mary was *preserved* from original sin, in *prevision* of the merits of Jesus

fuisse speciali *Dei*	*fuisse* singulari omnipotentis *Dei*
gratia et privilegio	*gratia et privilegio*
intuitu meritorum Jesu Christi	*intuitu meritorum Jesu Christi*
ejus Filii	
humani generis Redemptoris	Salvatoris *humani generis*
a macula peccati *originalis*	ab OMNI *originalis* culpae labe
praeservatam immunem.	*praeservatam immunem* esse a Deo REVELATAM.

The identical terms have been *italicized,* and three important differences have been CAPITALIZED:

1. Alexander VII *approves* the doctrine of original preservation as a pious belief; Pius XI *defines* that it is *revealed doctrine.*
2. Pius IX suppresses the distinctions relative to *soul* and *body,* and relates the privilege to the *person of Mary.*
3. Pius IX more radically excludes all stain of sin.

Christ. Thus she was "redeemed more perfectly" than any other — *sublimiori modo redempta* — in the words of the Bull of 1854.[5]

In this admirably precise and concise definition the Pope held fast to the surest doctrine. He deliberately phrased it in terms that avoid the particular questions and controversies raised by theological schools. One of these questions, however, he seems virtually to have answered: was Mary exempt from every inclination to sin *(concupiscentia)*? The affirmative answer seems implied by the formula of the definition, which excludes "all *stain* of original fault," for the inclination to evil has indeed the character of a stain left by sin. It is, however, a fact that this formula was adopted without any positive intention of deciding the debate.[6] Another question, one of the most heatedly debated, was deliberately left aside: did Mary incur any "debt of sin" *(debitum peccati)*?[7] It would seem that the question so phrased labors under an unfortunate terminology and gives rise to a false problem, since essentially the answer is a simple one. On the one hand it is evident that Mary, as a daughter of Adam, does have a debt — a debt of thanks toward God who by his gracious kindness withdrew her from the universal sin of the race from which she issued. On the other hand, this debt does not in any way constitute a stain or a shadow on her luminous purity.[8] If I prevent a child from falling into a mud puddle,

---

5. Bull *Ineffabilis, loc. cit.,* p. 605.

6. It must even be said that the formula is accompanied by the express purpose not to settle this point, as shown by J. Alfaro, "La formula definitoria de la Immaculada Concepción," *Virgo Immaculata* 2 (1956), pp. 264–266.

7. *Ibid.,* pp. 243–245. Bianchini's proposition, which affirmed that Mary was exempt from the debitum (V. Sardi, *La solenne definizione...*, Rome, Vaticana, 1904, t. 1, pp. 528, 532), found no echo.

8. One must deem unfortunate such expressions as the following, which strangely objectify and materialize the *debitum:* "Mary sinned in Adam" (X. Le Bachelet, DTC 7:1157); "A certain flaw *(aliquid maculae)* was

will it be said that the child is stained from the fact that, but for my intervention, he *should have* fallen into it?

At this beginning of Mary's destiny everything is gratuitous on God's part. It is in her first instant that she is the object of his love, before she has been able to perform any meritorious act. But the gratuitous nature of this intervention, that by anticipation stems entirely from the merits of the God-Man, should not blind us to the way this mystery is connected with all the preparation that had gone before. In the first place, God refrains from interfering here with the biological continuity essential to the unity of the human race, or even with the ordinary process of human generation. Corresponding to this perfect continuity in the order of nature, there is a discontinuity in the order of grace — a discontinuity, however, prepared for in a certain sense. By devoting two solemn and universal liturgical feasts to the parents of the Blessed Virgin — the only Old Testament saints honored by feasts common to both East and West — the Church intends to show that in them the long moral purification begun with Abraham had reached its peak. All that was lacking was liberation from the bonds of original sin. This is the ultimate stage that God completed "in the first instant of Mary's conception."

Every word in the abstract formula of the dogmatic definition has been weighed to answer or to avoid answering this or that complex question clustering about the mystery. But what is important is to grasp the heart of the mystery. It is a mystery of love, of divine love that, unlike ours, does not depend on its object but creates it and unfolds itself therein boundlessly. In the very midst of a world grown old, divine

---

present in Mary's flesh, capable of instrumentally causing a stain in her soul itself. . . . Total preservation from original sin seems contrary to the Catholic faith. . . . The Blessed Virgin in some manner contracted it. . . ." (N. del Prado, *Divus Thomas et Bulla Ineffabilis,* Fribourg, 1919, pp. ix, 119, 229.

love takes up creation anew at its source. In his love God makes Mary the most lovable, the most attractive of creatures. She is the one in whom God can, without compromise with sin, establish his dwelling. The Immaculate Conception is indeed the triumph of God's grace alone: *sola gratia*.

2. Israel's Climax in the Advance toward Salvation: Mary's Faith

The momentum of this grace, unhampered by any interior hindrance, bore Mary toward God in a soaring impulse of faith and love. According to that law whereby the creatures most favored by God are also those that thirst after him most, Mary's strong thirst for the Most High exceeds in intensity any other desire there ever was or ever will be. Having thus reached its climax, Israel's waiting was to receive its response. That would be the message of the Annunciation, a subject to be taken up in the next chapter of this study. Before attention is turned to it, however, another aspect of the mystery of Mary Immaculate deserves to be noted. So far this mystery has been envisaged in relation to God. Now the place it conferred on Mary within mankind should be considered.

3. Mary's Position in the Human Family

By her total sanctity, which renews the regal sanctity of our first parents, Mary is raised above the rest of mankind. Alone perfectly pleasing to God in all her being as well as in all her actions, she is the first of all creatures, the queen of creation. But does this regal position alienate her from the rest of mankind? To suppose it did would be a serious error. In fact, the very opposite is true. This queen lives humbly in the world of the poor. Royal as she is in the spiritual order, exempt from sin which divides men and turns them in on themselves, endowed lavishly with grace that opens outward and unites, she is at once the humblest servant and the most majestic queen — the humblest servant *because* she is the most majestic queen.[9]

Here we touch upon an important facet of God's plan. To a degree that we shall never sufficiently comprehend, he created man according to a law of unity (cf. Acts 17:26; Col. 3:15, etc.) and solidarity. To each creature was confided a measure of responsibility proportionate to the gifts received from God. The higher he raises men, the more he calls upon them to serve, so that the greatest among them will be the "servant," and the "first . . . the slave of all" (Mk. 10:43–45). Thus Christ the Head, "the First" (Apoc. 1:17), is also the "Servant" par excellence (Is. 53), who came "not to be served but to serve" (Mk. 10:45 and Mt. 20:28; cf. Jn. 13:12–18 and Lk. 12:37). He is the one in whom supreme responsibility for mankind rests, the universal Savior who in his own person takes up the responsibility betrayed by Adam, the first head. Mary, first among those who are simply creatures, is after Christ the servant par excellence and the most responsible among human beings. This responsibility will progressively take the form of a universal spiritual motherhood, whose spirit very early she already had.

Abraham was the first to benefit from God's gifts at the origin of the plan of restoration, and he quickly understands his responsibility toward men. Standing before Sodom and Gomorrha, those foreign cities, he already feels himself "the father of nations" (cf. Gen. 17:4–5); he launches into a rather bold intercession (Gen. 18:17–33). Mary could not be inferior to him. Before Christ's coming she is already the high point of intercession on earth. In a world in crying need of

---

9. These expressions are borrowed from C. Péguy, *Porche du mystère de la deuxième vertu,* Paris, NRF, 1918, t. 5, pp. 311–317. Paul VI echoed the same thought in his address of December 4, 1963, the terms of which were taken up in *Lumen Gentium* art. 53: "In the Church Mary occupies, after Christ, *the highest place and the one nearest us.*"

its Redeemer, this first of the redeemed, this one supremely redeemed, was beginning her vocation as advocate for mankind. Her prayer is the summit of mankind's desire. By the very wealth of the grace given her, the Virgin Mary is the representative who in the name of all takes possession of the salvation destined for all — the servant of mankind in the very impulse that made her "the servant of the Lord" (Lk. 1:38).

The Church has thought fit to single out various moments in the Blessed Virgin's life before the Annunciation: her birthday, the first visible appearance of the one in whom salvation was to be given; her presentation in the Temple, the first visible expression of her yearning after God. But all these moments are only manifestations of a single mystery in which three different aspects may be distinguished: the divine gift, Mary's response to God, and her intercession for the world. This mystery made of her, in a certain sense, the summit of humanity. The true summit and only head of humanity, of course, is Christ, whom she was destined to welcome to earth. On the other hand, if she is in some sense the summit of Israel, it is only in the spiritual and interior order. She does not have any place in the priestly hierarchy or in public teaching or worship, functions reserved to men. It is not she but John the Baptist who officially prepares the coming of the Messiah. Her mission, superior to that of the Precursor, is appropriate to the condition of woman: she welcomes divine grace, and enables it to bear fruit in her, and from her to radiate life.

SECOND STAGE

MARY, MOTHER OF THE SAVIOR GOD

The crucial moment of Mary's destiny, the climax of all that went before and the foundation of all that followed, was the moment of the Annunciation. But this mystery overflows beyond the person of Mary. It is, first of all, the initial and fundamental mystery of the saving work of Jesus Christ. The Virgin Mary is an integral part of this mystery. She welcomes the Savior and introduces him into the race of mankind, along with the salvation he brings.

Although the object of this *Short Treatise* is the Virgin Mary, she must not be wrenched from the ensemble of the mystery. However great the title of *Theotokos,* Mother of God, it would be disastrous to isolate it from the whole of the mystery that it is intended to express and manifest.

This mystery defies all deductive explanation. It is irreducible to a single approach. Its logic, if it has one, is that of a work of art, not of a deduction. The only way to describe the mystery is to have recourse to successive approaches, the combination of which enables us to glimpse, beyond anything we could possibly imagine, both the logic of the mystery and its wealth of meaning. Our study, then, centers successively on Mary's *motherhood* envisaged as conscious, holy, and divine, on the *relationship* involved in this motherhood, and on the *principal elements appropriate* to it as a virginal, social, and soteriological motherhood.

A. Mary's Motherhood
1. Conscious and Free Motherhood

To understand the meaning of what Mariology calls "the divine motherhood" it is necessary first of all to go beyond the person of Mary and to grasp her place in the mystery of salvation. Some authors would have it that the Incarnation is an act whose purpose was to overwhelm the most beloved of creatures with divine favor. The Creed, of course, presents the Incarnation in an entirely different perspective. It is "for us men and for our salvation" that the Word was made flesh. The divine motherhood appears as the means whereby God realized the plan of salvation thus defined. This is the approach, then, that first must be taken up.[1]

Why did God will such a means? Why, instead of descending from heaven with an adult body, formed by the hand of God (Gen. 2:7) — a mode which apparently would have better satisfied the mentality of his contemporaries — did the Word prefer to be born of a woman (Gal. 4:4)? It is because he wanted to be the genuine stock (Is. 11:1) of the race that he was going to save. It is because he wanted to save it from within, not by some help thrown down from above but by a salvation drawn from within itself. He wanted to help mankind not as a stranger but as a brother, as perfectly man and of the race of men to be redeemed, as he was perfectly God and of the race of the offended God — in a word, a perfect mediator reuniting in his own person the two parties to be reconciled.

---

1. Salvation is *at one and the same time* the good of mankind saved (proximate end) and the glory of God (ultimate end). This glory is understood in the *propter nos homines,* which should not be taken as a negation of theocentrism.

Mary's fundamental mission, therefore, was that of connecting the Savior with the human race. This consideration puts to flight any illusion that would make of her the center of the mystery.

Does this mean that Mary was an unimportant means, or a mere means and nothing else, like the bread used at Mass to be changed into the body of Christ, or like the water used at Baptism? Such is the opinion of many Protestants, and certain Catholic theologians say that God *could have* brought things to pass in such a way.

That, however, would be another illusion. First of all, Mary is part of that mankind whose salvation God willed; indeed she is in every respect first among them. It would be thus false to set up any opposition between Mary who would be the "means" of the Incarnation, and men who would be its end. If she entered into the humility of her role as means, or better as servant (Lk. 1:38 and 48), it is according to the spirit and teaching of Christ who did not come "to call the just, but sinners" (Mt. 2:17), who left the ninety-nine faithful sheep to seek the sheep that had strayed (Mt. 18:12), and who invites those who occupy any hierarchical position to behave as humble servants, according to the model he himself set. According to this model he established his Mother in the status of humble service, a service bound up also with that friendship that he expressed in these terms: "I shall not call you servants any more . . . but friends" (Jn. 15:15). The servant of the Lord does not lie beyond the scope of this principle.

As to the hypothesis according to which God could have become incarnate without love for his Mother, it has the drawback of envisaging God's power in isolation from his wisdom and love. Would the God that we know from revelation be recognizable in a God that would have become incarnate by surprise, a God that would have treated as a mere means, a mere object, his closest "neighbor" according to relationships of human life, that is, the person of his Mother?

Would this be the God that incomprehensibly and invincibly loves men, even sinners, the God so respectful of the freedom he created in men, the God who wants to reign by the light of truth (Jn. 18:37) and not simply by his power? Would this be the God, finally, that invites every man to love his neighbor as himself, and more especially to honor his father and mother?

That theologians have been able to imagine the possibility of such a plan is only a reflection of human weakness, for such a hypothesis involves not just another plan but "another God," in so far as the hypothesis can be formulated with any meaning at all.

2. Holy Motherhood

Whatever the case of this hypothesis, the evidence of revelation is clear: the inaugural event of Redemption is integrally pure, integrally religious, and the Mother of the Savior is holy.

Mary's holiness is inscribed at the very beginning of the account of the Annunciation, before everything else, even before the announcement of her motherhood.

Her *person* is holy. She is greeted as object-of-divine-favor, in the strong sense that has already been studied: she is the object of God's creative "favor," that all-powerful favor that gives her a fulness of sanctity. She has "won God's favor" (Lk. 1:30). The Lord "is with" her (1:28) and "the Holy Spirit will come" upon her (1:35). She is "blessed among all women" (1:42) and prophetically declared "blessed" for ever (1:48). Her holiness is from God, who is its gratuitous principle; it comes also from the way the "servant of the Lord" (1:38 and 48) and the one "blessed for having believed" (1:44) corresponded with his grace.

Her *condition* is holy: she is a virgin (Mt. 1:23; Lk. 1:27), she has deliberately chosen to be a virgin (Lk. 1:34). Such a virginity precisely expresses the concept of holiness, since it is *separation* in view of total *belonging,* body and soul, to God.

Finally, the *act* by which Mary opens herself to divine action is holy. It is an act of faith, obedience, and humility (Lk. 1:38; cf. 1:45).

Considering the event of the Annunciation from this angle, one might be tempted to see Mary's motherhood as the normal fruit of her perfect holiness. In fact, between the perfection of the immaculate one before this day and that which she acquired on this day itself, there can be detected a kind of continuity which the Fathers sometimes expressed in disconcerting ways, such as: "Mary conceived in her mind before she conceived in her body,"[2] or again, "She conceived the flesh of Christ by faith."[3] What do such formulas mean? First, that the divine motherhood was prepared for by Mary's faith, that it was proposed to her faith, and that it was accomplished by virtue of a consent that was itself an act of faith. Secondly, this act of perfect faith, completed by charity and the gift of self (Lk. 1:38), was meritorious. According to the common opinion of theologians, Mary merited her motherhood,[4] assuredly not with any merit due in justice *(de*

---
2. "Fide plena et Christum prius mente quam ventre concipiens — Full of faith and conceiving Christ in her mind before she does so in her womb" St. Augustine, *Sermo 215,* 4, PL 38:1074. Cf. St. Leo, *Sermo 1 in Nativitatem,* 1 PL 54:191b: "prius mente quam corpore . . ." etc. This neglected theme has been restored by the efforts of a Mariology most attentive to its sources (A. Müller, *Ecclesia-Maria,* Freiburg/Schweiz, Universitätsverlag, 1951; H. Rahner, *Maria und die Kirche,* Innsbruck, 1951, ET: *Our Lady and the Church,* Chicago, Regnery, 1965). It was placed in the foreground in chapter eight of *Lumen Gentium,* particularly in art. 53, "Verbum Dei corde et corpore suscepit — she received the word of God in her heart and her body," and in art. 64, "Per verbum Dei fideliter susceptum . . . ipsa (sc. Ecclesia) fit mater — (The Church) becomes herself a mother by receiving God's word in faith."

3. "Christi carnem fide concipit — She conceived Christ's flesh by faith" St. Augustine, *Contra Faustum* 29, 4, PL 42:490.

4. The thesis according to which Mary "merited" the divine motherhood

condigno) or founded on any equality between the work accomplished and the recompense, but with a merit of fittingness *(de congruo)* founded on consideration and affection. God's manner of acting can be recognized here, since he delights not only in making himself desired by men, but also in enabling them to merit what he gives them out of his gratuitous purpose.

But the Fathers of the Church meant something more by their expressions. Not only is Mary's motherhood rooted in a living faith; it seems to be the reflection and perfect sign of faith. In fact, there are close resemblances and correlations between the spiritual act by which Mary accepted to become mother of the "Son of God" and the physical act by which she begot him. Both acts have the same object: the Incarnate Word. Both deserve to be called "conception," since the word "conceive" applies as well to the act of the intelligence as to the act of generation. And this is more than wordplay; it is something that belongs to the nature of faith. Like the

---

in a certain sense was favored by a shift in terminology and by a mistranslation. An enormous number of patristic and medieval texts proclaim that Mary "merited" to bear the Son of God — "quem meruisti portare — whom you merited to bear," for example, says the *Salve Regina*. But far from expressing a right or title on which Mary could base herself, these ancient expressions signified the gratuitousness of the gift received from God. Thus, according to an antiphon of the January 1 feast, we have all "merited" that the Word become incarnate for us: "meruimus auctorem vitae suscipere — we merited to receive the author of life." The *Exultet* sings in the same tone: "O felix culpa quae talem ac tantum meruit habere redemptorem — O happy fault that merited such a great Redeemer." In all these cases it is a mistake to use "merit" as a translation. The idea is that of good fortune, of grace, and it would be better to translate "She received the favor," or "the honor which fell to her," etc. These patristic expressions furnish no serious argument in favor of the thesis, which is a legitimate one moreover, according to which Mary "merited" her motherhood in the sense specified above in the text. Cf. J. M. Bakhujzen van den Brink, "Mereo(r) and Meritum in Some Latin Fathers," *Studia patristica* 3 (1959), pp. 333–340, and the article in *Bulletin de théologie ancienne et médiévale* 9, 639.

conceiving of a child, faith is, on the spiritual level, the fruitful welcome given to the seed of life. By receiving the word, say the Fathers, every Christian "conceives God in his heart."[5] From this viewpoint faith implies a kind of spiritual motherhood, and Mary's physical divine motherhood appears as the radiation of her faith in her body of flesh. Put at its strongest, certain interpreters have gone so far as to say that the supreme and, by definition, the unique degree of faith called for the Incarnation of the Word of God as for its connatural object.

This would certainly be saying too much and transposing into Scholastic terminology the formulations of symbolic theology. One would be falling into an error which is the inverse of the one indicated earlier. It was then pointed out that the idea of an Incarnation realized by surprise in a mother left on the margin of the world of grace was a false idea. False too would be the idea of a holiness such that the divine maternity would be owed to it connaturally and in justice, for no holiness could measure up to this gift of the hypostatic order.

Between Mary's holiness and her maternity, then, is there a continuity or a discontinuity? Here, as in so many fields, there is no point in trying to resolve the question by eliminating one of the terms. They are correlative terms. The comments of the Fathers call attention to a relative continuity between Mary's faith in the Incarnation and the accomplishment of this mystery in her. But from another viewpoint there is a discontinuity. The Incarnation had been prepared for, but at heights of mystery before which the mind reels. It did not come about as a break with everything that had

---

5. "Quod miramini carne Mariae, agite in penetralibus animae. Qui corde credit and justitiam concepit Christum; qui ore confitetur ad salutem parit Christum — Bring about in the depths of your soul what you see in Mary's flesh. She who believed unto justice conceived Christ; she who confessed unto salvation brought forth Christ," St. Augustine, *Sermo 191*, 4, PL 38: 1011; cf. *Sermo 189*, 3, PL 38:1006, etc.

preceded, but the proposal and accomplishment of this mystery lie beyond what could result from even a supreme degree of faith and holiness. Here as elsewhere God brings salvation closer in giving grace upon grace, but the logic is a logic of grace, and the continuity is something lived and not conceptual.

The Annunciation was, on the level of the Spirit as well as on the level of the flesh, a gratuitous gift, unforeseeable to the most penetrating gaze of any created mind. The manner in which the generation in time of the Son of God was accomplished is a sign of that gratuitousness and a sign of holiness. For it is by the power of the Most High that this generation is realized, not by ordinary biological laws, and we know from the Bible that God's action, the action of the Spirit, has holiness as its object.

That is why the words of the angel in Luke 1:35 set up an analogy between what is then being wrought in Mary and what was accomplished at the time of Moses in the Ark of the Covenant, patiently constructed by human hands, when it became the dwelling-place of the God of holiness:

> "The cloud covered the tent with its shadow and the glory of God filled the dwelling-place" (Ex. 40:35).

According to this figure from the Old Testament, the power of God comes down on a chosen place and fills it with the presence of his glory, as at the Annunciation. But in Mary, the new Ark of the Covenant, it is a new mode of presence, a presence of another order — no longer figure but ontological reality. In person God assumes the physical and substantial reality of the human being conceived by the Holy Spirit. Hereafter the "fulness of God" dwells "corporally" in this world (Col. 2:9; cf. Jn. 1:14). The figure of the Holy of Holies from the Old Testament finds in Mary a fulness of reality, a fulness of sanctity. In a word, according to Scripture itself, the Annunciation is the mystery of a holy generation by a holy virgin.

3. Divine Motherhood[6]

The adjective "holy" is however not sufficient to characterize this mystery and motherhood. For this purpose theology speaks of "divine motherhood," "divine maternity." As a matter of fact, this expression is a recent one.[7] It must also be recognized as having the disadvantage of being an abstract expression. It tends to transform the mystery into an abstract property that belongs to Mary and that can be treated by itself. In reality the mystery being dealt with is essentially personal: motherhood is essentially a person-to-person relationship. We rightly say that Mary is the Mother of God, rather than that she is endowed with a motherhood that is divine. Here too is the trap implied in this abstract manner of speaking. In all strictness and exactness of terms Mary is called "Mother of God," since her Son is God in person, whereas abstract "motherhood" is divine only relatively and by participation. To speak of "motherhood" abstractly, therefore, is to approach the mystery from an angle that diminishes its clarity and the sharpness of its relief. It involves falling at one and the same time into the temptation either of minimizing this motherhood, or of exaggerating its relief by making of it a divine hypostasis, a capacity for engendering God in his very divinity. Certain authors have not successfully evaded this trap.

It should be investigated, therefore, in what sense this motherhood can be characterized as divine, relatively and by participation. The adjective "divine" can be understood in

---

6. Cf. bibliography on the divine motherhood, *infra*, p. 356.

7. The abstract term "motherhood" is not in use among Eastern authors, nor with St. Thomas. It becomes widespread in the decadent Scholasticism of the seventeenth century. Earlier uses of it have not come to the author's attention.

On the other hand, the abstract terms "fecunditas" and "virginitas" are found in St. Augustine (Barré, *Prières anciennes* . . . p. 23, citing *Sermo 369*, 1; *Sermo 192*, 2, PL 38:1012, has "pia virginitas peperit"). But the abstract character does not pose similar problems for these two words.

three senses: according to exemplary, efficient, and final causality. In other words, this motherhood has God for its model, its beginning, and its end. The third sense is the fundamental one, since it alone permits us to say that Mary is *Mother of God*. Therefore a study of the three meanings would do well to ascend progressively from the first to the third.

1. Mary's motherhood can first be called divine because it is conformed to the *model* of the divine fatherhood. God made the human sonship of the Word an image of his divine sonship. Thus it was that he gave Mary a holiness without blemish, in the image of the Father's, and he willed that the temporal generation of the Word should be virginal, according to the model of his eternal generation. What the Fathers say about the role of Mary's faith in the Incarnation should be recalled here: her motherhood resembles the heavenly fatherhood in that it is the fruit of a *spiritual* act, a *holy* act, specifically the act of faith. The harmony here is far-reaching. We grasp something of the mystery of the first Trinitarian procession under two notions, the *conception of a Word* (by analogy with an act of human intelligence) and the *generation of a Son*. So too the action of Mary at the Incarnation is a *spiritual conception* by faith at the same time that it is a *physical generation* in body. Care must be taken not to push the resemblance so far as to confuse the two generations. The analogy remains a distant one. When we are speaking of the Trinity, our conceptual dualism (intellectual act — generative act) is wholly relative to our manner of conceiving the mystery; but when we speak of Mary, it is real. That is, in speaking of the Trinity we comprise under two complementary modalities the one single act of the Father who engenders or conceives the Son, whereas in the Incarnation Mary accomplishes two acts, each of a different order although both are vitally connected and unified — one in her mind and the other in her body. The most striking point of the analogy is therefore not in the generative act, but in what

results from it. The eternal generation and the temporal generation both concern the same Son; the Son of the Father and the Son of Mary are not two Sons, but one and the same Son, the Second Person of the Holy Trinity. It is this fundamental resemblance which dominates all the others; it draws the divine motherhood into the orbit of the divine fatherhood like some mysterious satellite.

2. Divine in its resemblance to the Trinitarian archetype, Mary's motherhood is divine also in its *cause:* she conceives "of the Holy Spirit" (Mt. 1:18, 20; Lk. 1:35). In the Virgin who had renounced "knowing man" (Lk. 1:34) in order to belong to God alone, God supplied, in a fashion evidently entirely spiritual and transcendent, for the role that belongs to man in every other human generation. This spiritual and transcendent characteristic is what gives point to the very rich expression the Fathers use in saying, "Mary conceived the Word by faith." Just as the person baptized is born again "not from the flesh nor from the will of man," but "by faith and the Holy Spirit," so Christ, the exemplar of our adoption, was born of Mary (Jn. 1:13; 3:5).

The role of the Holy Spirit, a much neglected role, must be underlined here. It has often been said that Mary is entirely relative to Christ. It has not often enough been said that she is entirely relative to the Holy Spirit. What comes about at the Annunciation can be understood only in the light of this relationship. Only in this light can a double trap be avoided — that of considering Christ's generation in a purely biological or material perspective, and that of tending to make the divine motherhood a sort of divine hypostasis.

What the Holy Spirit accomplishes at the Annunciation appears at one and the same time as a harmonious prolonging of what he realizes in the Trinity and as the pattern and principle of what he realizes in the Church by the mission that he began at Pentecost. Several texts from Vatican II's documents insisted moreover on this profound analogy between the Annunciation and Pentecost.[8] What the Holy Spirit accomplishes at the Annunciation, therefore, is more clearly seen in the light of his Trinitarian function and his ecclesial function. These two functions will now be examined simultaneously.

On the level of divine transcendence, the Spirit is, according to the Fathers, the *bond* of the Trinity. On the level of the Church, he is the one who establishes the bond between Christians and Christ, who makes of Christians dispersed everywhere one single mystical person in Christ. At the point of departure of this mystery of the Church, at the moment of the Annunciation, the fundamental bond is established between the Word and the one who in the name of the whole human race engenders him, and it is the Holy Spirit who is the transcendent agent of this initial, fundamental, and exemplary bond.

The Spirit is also the one who realizes *unity without mixture or confusion.* He accomplishes the unity of the Trinity in the distinction of persons within the identity of being; this he does because he is love, and love implies a face-to-face relationship of distinct persons without either confusion or mixture of personalities. On the level of the Church, tradition presents the Holy Spirit as the one who assures the union of many persons in a single body in the person of Christ the Head, without any confusion or assimilation of those who make up this unity of love. At the point of departure, this mystery is realized in an exemplary way between Christ and Mary: there is a unity of love in the reciprocity of motherhood and sonship. To that is added the mysterious role that

---

8. *Lumen Gentium* art. 59: "Before the day of Pentecost 'continuing with one mind in prayer together' (Acts 1:14) . . . Mary . . . prayerfully implored the gift of the Spirit, who had already overshadowed her in the Annunciation." Cf. especially *Ad Gentes* (Decree on Missionary Activity) art. 4: "It was from Pentecost that the 'Acts of the Apostles' took their origin. In a similar way Christ was conceived when the Holy Spirit came upon the Virgin Mary. . . . Throughout the ages the Holy Spirit gives the entire Church unity in fellowship. . . ."

tradition attributes to the Holy Spirit in the very realization of the mystery (cf. Lk. 1:35), that is, in the establishing of the personal bond that the Incarnation effects between the Son of God and human nature. Here again, unity is "without confusion or mixture," according to the formula of the Council of Chalcedon.[9]

The Holy Spirit is the bond of unity without confusion because he *acts from within,* respecting the distinctions and differences that are essential to love. He unifies the Church, beginning with the very diversity of the races, peoples, languages, and cultures. The sign of Pentecost is striking. The Holy Spirit abolishes the separation stemming from different languages, without doing violence to a single one of them. Each of the witnesses of Pentecost hears proclaimed "in his own language the marvels of God" (Acts 2:12). Hence it can better be understood why the Holy Spirit does not exercise the role of spouse, a virile role, with regard to Mary, on the pattern of mythology. Rather, he acts here as elsewhere from within, *ex intimo,* stirring up the life-giving potentialities of this woman who has opened herself entirely to grace, so that she becomes the Mother of the Son of God. He does not act as a kind of second cause along with the maternal causality of Mary; rather, he activates her from within. ("He reduced her to act," according to the expression of Grignion de Montfort, in his *Treatise on True Devotion,* # 20.) This is his proper manner of acting. Thus, when according to St. Paul he makes us say "Abba, Father" (Rom. 8:15; Gal. 4:6), it is not he who says the word, for he is not the Son of the Father; we alone are moved by him to say it, from the depths of our being. In a like way, he enables Mary to be Mother of a Son, of whom he is in no sense the Father. It is not unrelated to the matter to observe that in Hebrew, the first language of revelation, the word "Spirit" is of feminine gender *(ruah).*

How then can the relationship and action of the Holy

---

9. Symbol of Chalcedon, Denz. 148 (302).

Spirit with regard to Mary be aptly characterized?

First, it can be called an *anointing,* according to the vocabulary of the Bible. Anointing is an entirely spiritual action, involving the image of oil and unguent that penetrate deeply, quickening, strengthening, and perfuming. Of course, the anointing by the Spirit at the Incarnation is principally the anointing of the humanity of Christ, who is the Anointed of God. For the Hebrew word "Messiah" *(Mašîah)* and the Greek word *"Christos"* both mean "the anointed one." This is not the place to take up the double anointing of Christ — the anointing that constitutes the hypostatic union, and the messianic anointing formally attributed to the Spirit in the passage of Isaiah that Christ applied to himself at the beginning of his ministry, "The Spirit of the Lord has been given to me, for he has anointed me; he has sent me, etc." (Is. 61:1–2; Lk. 4:21). But the anointing by the Spirit refers also to the person of Mary: "The Holy Spirit will come upon you" (Lk. 1:35). She benefits from an anointing in order to be the bond, the original human link between the Word and the human race. It is therefore in and by the Spirit that Mary says in the name of humanity, "Behold the handmaid of the Lord" (1:38). And it is not surprising that immediately thereafter, led by the same Spirit, she departs on the mission of the Visitation, a mystery of communion and sanctification. Nor is it surprising that Elizabeth should be filled with the Holy Spirit and should prophetically speak, and that Mary, for her part, should reply also according to the spirit of prophecy that proceeds from the same anointing. The anointing of Mary by the Spirit, therefore, has its place as function and privilege between two other anointings: on the one hand, the anointing par excellence, which is the double anointing of Christ, hypostatic and messianic, and on the other hand, the anointing of Christians who participate in Christ's anointing through the sacrament of Christian initiation.

Hence the relationship of Mary to the Holy Spirit in the mystery of the Incarnation comes to light: she is the *place* of choice for the Spirit. She will be present also (Acts 1:14) when he comes at Pentecost. Thus in her communion with Christ she is the type of the Church. She is the living *temple* of the Spirit, the temple in which he accomplishes the implanting and first growth of the Word in the human race. She is the privileged *witness* of the Spirit, not by official testimony and preaching, as are the apostles, but as living witness of his work of sanctification. Since the Virgin Mother intrinsically belongs to the whole portrait and icon of the Incarnation, one might add that she is the image and *icon* of the Spirit, that is, the humble feminine image of the *bond* of *love* that the transcendent Spirit establishes *from within* between Christ and humanity.

3. Finally, Mary's Motherhood is divine in its *end,* the Son of God in person. The Blessed Virgin is not only Mother in the image of God and Mother because of God; she is also and especially *Mother of* God. The other divine modalities of her motherhood are subordinate to this one. If the *Holy Spirit* intervenes and makes Mary's motherhood comformable in pattern to the generation of the *Father,* it is in order to render it worthy of the *Son of God.* It was with deep insight that the Fathers perceived this connection, as in different ways of expressing it they said that a virginal generation, a generation that had for its principle the intervention of God himself, could have no other object than God, and inversely, the divine motherhood could be nothing else than virginal.[10] Here again is to be seen one of those profound reasons of fittingness, the necessary features of which, as has been observed above, are equally deserving of being called gratuitous.

Mary, therefore, is Mother of God in a sense made explicit by Saint Cyril: not mother of the divinity, but by human

---

10. This patristic viewpoint was brought to light by J. B. Terrien, *La Mère de Dieu*... I, VI, c. 3, # 3, t. 2, pp. 153–164 and by J. M. Bover in EstM 8 (1949), pp. 185–231.

generation truly mother of a Son who is God; not mother of a man who might be united with God, but mother of a man who from the very instant of his conception is God in person.

Nevertheless, the expression "Mother of God" still leaves a good number of persons today with the impression of a subterfuge. The maternal action of Mary, they observe, takes place only in the order of flesh and blood; she does not engender the divinity, and moreover, it is not from her that Christ receives his divine personality which is eternal and preexisting. To them this seems to bring into question not just the divine character of Mary's motherhood, but the very authenticity of this motherhood which is thus not like any other.

But this objection rests on a faulty understanding of the essence of motherhood. For it is a fact that neither does any other mother confer on her son the soul created by God, or the personality that presupposes this creation. Nevertheless one who has conceived and brought into the world a son is truly a mother, not only of the body of flesh and blood she has formed, but of the man whole and entire, body and soul, and thus of the person who subsists in this human composite. Similarly, Mary is not just the mother of the flesh of Jesus, she too is mother of her son, this Son named Jesus whom she conceived and brought into the world. Although the person of Jesus is divine, she is mother of this person who subsists bodily in flesh and blood. She is not the mother only of the body of Jesus, she is, no less than any other mother, the Mother of her Son — Mother of Jesus who is God.[11]

---

11. On the philosophical principle that motherhood refers to the person, cf. *infra*, Appendix # 9.

B. The Relationship Involved in Mary's Motherhood
1. Unique Relationship

It is this relationship to God which is the essential element in the divine motherhood. It sets Mary above all other created beings. In fact, this relationship is the profoundest that can exist between a *person* and God. It is still, of course, at an *infinite* distance from the relationships within the Trinity which are substantially divine. Certainly too it is less profound than the relationship of the humanity of Jesus to the Word that assumes it, that is, the relationship that makes Jesus subsist in the divine person of the Son of God.[12] But it is the most exalted relationship compatible with a created personality, the closest that binds a human person to a divine person.

2. Transforming Relationship

An effort should be made to grasp what this unique relationship entails *in Mary*. As a matter of fact, there is question here not of a merely extrinsic relationship, but of a relationship that involves her entire being.

Scripture hints at something of this transformation. The angel says to Mary, "The Holy Spirit will come upon *you* and the power of the Most High will cover *you* with its

---

12. It is not possible to develop here another comparison which appealed to several Spanish authors of the seventeenth century by its subtlety, the relationship had to the person of Christ by Mary on the one hand, and by the Eucharistic species on the other. It might be noted simply that, like the hypostatic union, the Eucharistic relationship excludes any created suppositum entirely on the side of the natural element: after the consecration there remain only the *species* or appearances of bread. No longer a created substance but a pure sign of the presence of the body of the Word Incarnate, these species are a *quo* and not a *quod,* as the metaphysicians would say. There is thus, in a complementary way, transubstantiation according to the language of traditional theology, and transignification according to the expression coined by recent theologians.

shadow" (Lk. 1:35). This is a surprising manner of expression. One would expect the action of the Spirit to be referred to the essential, that is, to the person of the Son of God, the holy being who is going to be conceived. But it is a fact that the phrase is grammatically referred to Mary.

The analogy implied in Lk. 1:35 and elsewhere according to which Mary is typologically identified with the Ark of the Covenant suggests that the action of the Spirit brings about a consecration within her. At the same time, the differences are great between the consecration of an object of cult and the consecration of a person. The consecration of the Ark was entirely relative to the people whom this sign was intended to unite to God. But the consecration of a person concerns a life. It has as object to make someone resemble God. Luke 1:35 suggests that the one who already was preeminently the object of his favor (Lk. 1:28) was made yet more profoundly connatural to the "Holy One" who was becoming her son. Luke 1:42 suggests that she was the object of a corresponding blessing: "Of all women you are the most blessed, and blessed is the fruit of your womb."

It is a deeply traditional doctrine within the Church that at the time of the Annunciation, in her very encounter with the Word of God, Mary received a new transformation in grace. More widespread in the East than in the West, this theme is ordinarily passed over in silence, because it seems to conflict with the dogma of the Immaculate Conception. Most often, in fact, the Eastern authors call this transformation a *katharsis,* that is, a purification. Certainly if one understands thereby a liberation from original sin, this doctrine would be unacceptable. But if the expression is understood to mean a new degree of purity and of assimilation to God, something like the last passing of an already pure metal through the crucible in order to bring out its temper and brilliance, then this doctrine is perfectly acceptable. Thus understood, the ancient tradition on the *katharsis* ought to be accepted.[13] It is in this sense that a good number of representative Eastern authors understood it, even after the schism of 1054. Nicholas Cabasilas (d. before 1391) is, for example, the first to be fully explicit on this subject: "If some of the holy doctors have said that the Virgin was previously purified *(prokekatharthai)* by the Spirit, they must be understood as meaning this purification in the sense of an increase in grace *(di' hagiasmou prosthēkēs hypsēloteras)*. These doctors, in fact, speak of the angels in the same way; they say that they were purified, although there was nothing bad in them."[14]

Gregory Palamas (d. 1359) is hardly less clear:

> " 'You are already holy and full of grace, O Virgin,' says the angel to Mary. 'But the Holy Spirit will again come upon you, preparing you by an addition of holiness, for the divine mystery (which is going to be accomplished in you).' "[15]

3. Analysis of the Divine Motherhood as Relationship

In trying to express more precisely the scope of this transformation it will be necessary to advance along metaphysical lines and in a more personal effort of interpretation. For both of these reasons the remainder of this section may seem somewhat more involved than what has preceded.

Two successive approaches to the grace of the divine motherhood will be made; they will however be seen to cut across each other. First, from above and beginning with what is most formal, the real *relationship* of Mary to her Son will

---

13. On the *Katharsis* cf. *infra*, Appendix # 10.
14. *Homily on the Presentation*, ed. Sophoclis, Athens, 1861, p. 123. Jugie, *L'Immaculée* . . . p. 255.
15. *Homily on the Annunciation*, PG 151:178. Cf. C. Stiernon, article in *Maria* 7 (1964), p. 296.

be studied; then, from below and beginning with what is most material, the *natural structure* of motherhood will be taken up as we try to discern what befits a Mother whose Son is God, in virtue of the principle that God does not destroy nature when he elevates it, but rather transfigures it without altering it. In other words, we shall take up the following two questions in succession: What exceptional graces are implied by this exceptional *relationship* to God? What gifts are fitting to a *Mother* whose Son is God in person?

a. Implications of the Mother of God Relationship

That Mary is truly the Mother of God, in the sense above explained, implies a real relationship to God. Now, every real relationship implies a *real foundation.*

(1) Real Foundation

First this foundation must be situated. We must be careful not to conceive of it in a way that would diminish the divine transcendence. We are not to imagine that this real relationship introduces into the Trinity anything in the nature of a revolution or intrinsic complement. Scripture is there to suggest, and metaphysics to render more precise, that God transcends every change. Any new relationship, where he is concerned, is therefore new only *on the part of the creature,* not on his. Thus the hypostatic union does not introduce any change in the person of the eternal Word. The real relationship of the human nature to the Second Person of the Trinity who assumes it has its real foundation in this *humanity,* and only in this humanity. Thus the Incarnation accomplishes the ontological elevation of human nature without degrading or altering in the least God's immutable being. In what concerns motherhood the same must be said: nothing is changed in God as such from having a Mother, but in order for her to be really his Mother something must be changed in her. Everything in her is elevated. Our question, then, comes down to the following: Since the newness of every real relation of the creature to God affects the creature alone and not God, what change takes place in Mary when she contracts this real relationship of Mother of God? In yet other terms, since whenever God takes *hold* of a being there is an *imprint* left in the latter, what imprint in Mary corresponds to God's hold as he takes her for Mother?

Carried away by the grandeur of the mystery, certain theologians give a rather bold answer to this question. From the fact alone of this metaphysical relationship they think it is possible to deduce strictly and necessarily all of Mary's privileges as privileges of the one who is pure-relationship-to-God. They push the analogy between the divine motherhood and the hypostatic union to the point of saying that the divine motherhood formally sanctifies Mary, abstracting from sanctifying grace.[16] At the other extreme will be found Tertullian, as well as certain Protestants, and the nominalists in general, for all of whom this real relationship founded on corporal realities of flesh and blood would not imply anything in the order of grace.

A proper appreciation of things calls for more refinement.

(2) Permanent and Special Foundation

Essentially, the divine motherhood is a real relationship, permanent and special. If however these two traits are to be

---

16. E. Andres, *Es la maternidad divina formalmente santificante?* (Typewritten dissertation), Washington D.C., Catholic University, 1964, gives an attentive and penetrating exposition of these theories. He concludes in favor of the divine motherhood as formally sanctifying, but with nuances assuredly more acceptable than those of the seventeenth century authors.

verified, the relationship must have, in addition to the passing foundation that generation constitutes, a real foundation that is *permanent* and *special*. This foundation is inalienable, as is motherhood itself: after having given birth to the Son of God, Mary could not cease to be his Mother. Thus this foundation is evidently distinct from sanctifying grace, which by its nature can be lost. It is therefore analogous to the *sacramental character,* and more specially to the baptismal character.

Such an analogy *sheds light* on the subject. First of all, it permits us to go beyond a false problem that has long been classical in Mariology: Is the divine motherhood more than grace? The textbooks usually give an affirmative reply, a reply which has the disadvantage of *materially* contradicting the sense and the word of Christ in Luke 11:28: "Still happier those who hear the word of God and keep it." For here Christ puts faith and charity above motherhood, understood in a material sense. If this word of Christ brings the whole matter out of the plane of flesh and blood onto a theological plane, it does not intend to put the question in the terms in which the textbooks of theology put it. In their terms, it would seem, the question is a false one, for two reasons: first, because it confronts elements that are too diverse to admit of any fruitful comparison, but in the second place, more especially because it opposes terms that are correlative. In biology, for example, it would be absurd to ask whether it is better to possess a function without the organ, or the organ without any function, since an organ exists for its function, and the function is impossible without the organ. That is why, if one wishes to set up any fruitful comparison in what might be called the order of spiritual anatomy and physiology, the terms in parallel comparison must be analogous: divine motherhood compared with the sacramental character, Mary's grace compared with the grace of the baptized. The schema of comparison would be the following:

Fulness of grace   *Sanctifying grace*
Divine Motherhood   Baptismal character

(a) Similarities between Divine Motherhood and Sacramental Character

The wisdom of such a comparison appears from the *several points of contact* between the two elements of each horizontal pair in the above schema. The sacramental character is the most radical foundation of our relationship with Christ. It is indelible: no sin can destroy it. It establishes an organic belonging to Christ. It makes us enter the ecclesial family, and thereby the family of God. As its normal vital complement it entails sanctifying grace, which permits us worthily to live out the family relationship thus established. Now the divine motherhood exhibits these very same traits: it is the most radical foundation by which Mary is put into relationship with Christ. It is indelible: if by hypothesis Mary were thought of as having fallen away in the moral order, she would still have remained Mother of God, for neither her quality of Mother nor the divinity of her Son would have been abolished. By the divine motherhood Mary is consecrated to God, belongs organically to Christ, and is established in a family bond of relationship with God. Finally, the divine motherhood calls for a complement of grace that permits her to live her life of Mother of God worthily. In a word, the divine motherhood, like the sacramental character, is not simply a relationship directed toward God *(esse ad);* it involves an ontological reality *(esse in);* it fundamentally structures the supernatural condition of Mary and calls for a blossoming out in the order of life.

Undoubtedly like any analogy this one has its *limits,* and they should be underlined to avoid all confusion: the divine motherhood proceeds from a work in the order of natures, the baptismal character from a work in the order of rites. The divine motherhood is by its very essence a family relationship with regard to God; the baptismal character involves such a relationship, but does not suffice to constitute it formally.[17]

(b) Differences between Divine Motherhood and Sacramental Character

The principal benefit of this comparison is that it enables us to grasp in sharp contrast the *differences* that arise on the basis of the analogies:

a. Sacramental character and divine motherhood involve two relationships in *inverse direction:* the relationship involved in the sacramental character has for its type the rela-

---

17. More precisely, the generative act of Mary suffices (on her side) for founding her title of Mother of God. This title is justified, abstracting from the gifts of grace that make of her a "worthy mother of God," by the fact alone that the Son whom she begets is God. On the contrary, the impress of the character, to which is limited the unfailing result of the baptismal rite, does not suffice by itself to confer the title of son of God. This title is formally conferred only if the character is completed by the grace which normally accompanies it. In fact, generation implies *similitude* of nature; now, it is grace that makes us "participants of the divine nature" (1 Pt. 1:4).

The character is only the radical principle of our divine sonship. It does not confer it, but calls for it in integrating us and configuring us to the Son of God made man. It remains in the order of sign *(res et sacramentum).* Filiation becomes real only by grace *(res).* In short: 1) We are not truly sons of God by the simple consecration of the character, but Mary is truly Mother of God by the fact alone of having begotten a Son who is God. 2) The character does not make us sons of God as properly as Mary's virginal motherhood makes her Mother of God. All this leads to qualifying the comparison above and making precise the point of its application: the character *specifies our vocation and orients our grace,* as the vocation and grace of sons of God. Similarly, Mary's motherhood specifies her vocation and orients her grace as Mother of God. The word "specify" is used in the wide sense, for sanctifying grace is formally the same for Christ and for all Christians, including the Virgin Mary. To disregard this would be serious, for then Mary would appear as a creature alien both to Christians and to Christ himself.

tionship of Son to Father, since the baptized person is established Son of God; the relationship involved in the divine motherhood imitates that of Father to Son, since Mary is Mother of God. In this connection the second relationship bears the mark of staggering paradox.[18]

b. The two relationships are *not on the same plane:* the baptized person becomes a son of God in dependence on the mystery of the Incarnation, whereas the divine motherhood is involved in the very realization of this mystery. In terms of sharper contrast, the sacramental character configures the baptized person to the Son of God according to grace, in view of divinization, whereas Mary's motherhood configures Christ to our humanity; the sacramental character integrates us in God's race, whereas the divine motherhood integrated God in the human race. And this humanization of God is the condition for the divinization of man.

c. Passing on to a consideration of the *foundation* of the two relationships, the divine motherhood is founded on a generation properly so called, although temporal and relative

---

18. Certainly *in the order of divinity* fatherhood is not superior to filiation, but *in the created order* things are not the same. In this order parents are superior to their children, and Jesus bore witness to this law in a disconcerting way, by his submission during his childhood (Lk. 2:51). One cannot conclude to a real superiority of Mary over her Son, according to the strange speculations of certain seventeenth century authors! What can be noted is simply that her quality of Mother of God is the foundation of a dignity superior to that of the baptized, who are sons of God.

It should be noted that the maternal relationship contracted by Mary on the day of the Incarnation is added to the filial relationship that was conferred on her from the beginning of her existence. Before being the Mother of the Word Incarnate, she was the daughter of the Father, for the Immaculate Conception implied with regard to God a relationship analogous to and in its effect superior to that conferred by Baptism. It must not be forgotten either that if Mary is Mother of Jesus according to generation in nature, she is entirely dependent on him according to grace: in this respect "rather is she born spiritually . . . of our head the Savior," according to St. Augustine, *De Virginitate* V, 5 and VI, 6, CSEL 41, pp. 239–240, PL 40:399.

to the flesh, whereas the baptismal character is conferred by a rite which involves a regeneration. On the one hand, generation gives birth to a new human being, Jesus, man among men; the effect is in the order of substances.[19] On the other, regeneration affects the very subject of the sacramental character, that is to say, a preexisting human subject; the effect is in the purely accidental order. In the one case, generation involves a filiation in nature; in the other there is question of an adoptive filiation.

d. The *consequences* that the divine motherhood and the baptismal character each have in the order of life can next be considered. Both these fundamental gifts involve grace, but not with the same necessity nor to the same degree. The divine motherhood calls for grace in fulness, and according to a moral necessity; the baptismal character calls for it in some measure and in a way open to failure: it is a fact that the state of the baptized person can sometimes be an obstacle to grace. It can be added that the divine maternity requires grace by anticipation, from the first instant of the life of Mary; as for the character, there is at most a restricted anticipation in the baptism of desire.

---

19. "Generationis motus in quantum terminatur ad substantiam est in genere substantiae, reductive tamen — Inasmuch as it terminates in a substance the movement of generation is in the genus of substance, but reductively," says the scholastic adage. This raises a knot of complex questions. The end product of virginal generation is the concrete human nature of the Savior. Mary is a perfecting cause of it as concerns the living body, and a disposing cause as concerns the immortal soul. The terminus *attained* (terminus of reference) is the person of the Word: this terminus is evidently extrinsic to the agent, but it is attained by the agent, from the fact that Mary's motherhood is intrinsically ordained to this extrinsic terminus. In short, the divine motherhood is correlative to the hypostatic union. It is on this basis that certain authors speak of Mary's belonging to the hypostatic order. They understand thereby that the divine motherhood intrinsically terminates in the person of the Word Incarnate. The most exact expression of this thesis is given by M. J. Nicolas, "L'appartenance de la Mère de Dieu à l'ordre hypostatique," EM 3 (1947), pp. 147–194.

e. A last trait can be enlightening, although it is only accessory. According to St. Thomas the baptismal character implies an *ecclesial status* given to faith: faith is founded *(condita)* by baptism, fortified *(roborata)* by confirmation, and endowed with communicative power by the sacrament of orders *(fides communicanda)*. In more precise terms, at baptism faith receives the fundamental status of its existence; it becomes militant and missionary at confirmation, the sacrament of witness; with the sacrament of orders it is oriented toward founding faith in others, giving it norms, and structuring it (a trait which culminates in the magisterium). Now it is clear that the faith of the Theotokos possesses a status that is not reducible to the traits of the faith marked by the sacramental characters, as described above, viz., a faith described as *founded, fortified,* and rendered *communicative.* For, as to the first mark, Mary's faith has about it rather a *founding* function, though in a much more radical way than the faith of the hierarchy has this function. Motherhood was proposed to the faith of Mary — "Blessed are you who have believed" (Lk. 1:44; cf. 1:38 and 11:28) — and she was the first to adhere to the fundamental mystery of salvation; she adhered to it "in the name of humanity," according to St. Thomas' formula. By God's gratuitous will this founding faith conditioned the realization of the mystery in some sense; by the same token it conditioned the passage from figure to reality, from promise to gift par excellence, from the Old Testament to the New. Mary's faith was the first adherence to the living Christ who in her took on his human life. As to *strength,* Mary's faith was above every falling away, so that the infallibility of the Church in believing *(in credendo)* is found realized and concentrated in her, just as the infallibility of the magisterium is concentrated in the function of the pope. As to being *communicative,* Mary's adherence to Christ in faith has an ecumenical, that is to say, a universal value. With a subjective perfection and an intensity never to be surpassed, it inaugurates the new status of the faith of the

Church. And so it remains the ideal measure of that faith, just as the magisterium is the normative measure and the beatific vision the transcendental measure. Of course, neither here nor elsewhere does Mary's faith have the mission of visible and official authority proper to the hierarchy, but it nonetheless has supreme status in the order of faith; Christ transcends this order, if along with common theological opinion we hold that he was here below established in the beatific vision. The condition of the Mother of God, therefore, seems to imply a status of faith no less marked than that of the different sacramental characters: faith that is first and inaugural, faith that is perfect and morally infallible in its assent, faith that is exemplary and of universal scope.[20]

The minute comparison that has just been completed is aimed at helping to grasp at one and the same time both the fundamental analogies of Mary's position as Theotokos with ours and the superiority of her status. But one may well feel that it is now time to take our bearings anew. Mary's state as Mother of God implies a *relationship* altogether *unique*. In contemplating it we have seen that this real and permanent relationship implies in Mary a real and permanent *foundation*, an ontological reality which is like the created inverse of this relation to the Uncreated, an imprint corresponding to the hold he takes of her. This fundamental gift seemed to be *analogous to the sacramental character*. It implies, in fact, an inalienable bond between Mary and Christ, as well as a configuration. Like the sacramental character, moreover, it normally calls for grace and life, but in a fuller and more necessary way.

---

20. In this line the following theory has been put forth: Since Christ did not have any faith, it is by participating in the personal faith of Mary that we are saved. This theory is inadmissible, because it substitutes Mary for Christ, and the subjective order of the faith of a person for the objective order of divine revelation. It has no foundation either in Scripture or in Tradition. Care must be exercised not to enter on any such avenue of thought, for it inescapably leads to deviations and heresies.

b. Qualities Befitting a Mother Whose Son is God

In order to grasp more precisely what "the grace of divine motherhood" is, we must now approach it from another angle, no longer from above and from God's perspective, but beginning with the human element, that is, with this motherhood that God takes into the work of salvation and at the same time transfigures. Here we leave the austere pathways of the metaphysics of relation and such technical comparisons as those made above, in order to begin with the simplest of realities: what it is to be a mother. We shall advance, as if by a gradual ramp, toward the grace of the Theotokos. We shall climb up the ladder of being, from animal motherhood, to human motherhood, and thus to the divine motherhood.

Two basic principles will guide our analysis:

a. Motherhood has its essential foundation in generation, which can be defined with Aristotle as the origin of one living being from another who communicates life to it in the resemblance of its own nature. Beneath the pedantic character of these terms there is more light and depth than at first sight appears.[21]

b. God's works are ordered and homogeneous. The Creator harmoniously proportions beings to the functions he gives them to exercise. He gives every mother what is fitting to her motherhood; this he does more on the level of human than of animal motherhood, and still

---

21. The Latin version does more justice to the density of this definition: "Origo viventis a vivente principio conjuncto in similitudinem naturae." The elements of the definition are the following: two living beings — proceeding immediately one from the other — the first communicating to the other the nature similar to its own by an operation tending of itself to this assimilation. This last trait, very important, enables one to understand why the Holy Spirit is not the father of Christ, although he is the principle of Christ's temporal generation: he does not communicate to Christ resemblance in his own divine nature, but intervenes in order that Christ's human nature be formed.

more on the level of a motherhood that has God for its end.

1. With the *animal,* generation sets up a temporary bond. The metaphysicians are correct in saying that once the mother or the offspring is dead, the subject or the end result of the relation disappears, and by the same token so does the real relation itself. A mother cat whose kittens are all dead *was* once a mother; she *is* no longer a mother.

The fragility of this ontological connection is transferred to the plane of life and of animal psychology: motherhood involves a transitory state, limited to the time during which elementary maternal care and affection is required for the welfare of the offspring. A year after birth, a mother cat no longer makes any difference between her offspring and any other cat.

2. Among *human* beings the whole biological picture of animal motherhood is to be found again, but at the heart of the matter there is something more. Generation establishes a bond of origin between *spiritual and immortal persons.* This relationship is contracted by bodily means, but it transcends the body. It is *spiritual* and *immortal,* as are the persons involved in the relationship of mother and son.[22] To this relationship there corresponds in the soul of the mother a permanent, real, and objective foundation, about whose nature it is very difficult to be precise.[23]

---

22. It is by a veritable abuse of terms that certain metaphysicians extend to human motherhood what is true of animal motherhood: "A mother ceases to be mother once her son is dead." If there is question of an animal who purely and simply ceases to exist, this principle is true. But if the dead son is a man, he *subsists* in what is essential to him, his personal soul, and by the very fact the relationship to his mother remains. This problem would call for an entire study, for which there is no room here.

23. Of what order is the permanent ontological foundation of motherhood? In the face of this question St. Thomas remained perplexed. In III Sent., d. 8, q. 1, a. 5, solutio, he writes on the subject of fatherhood: "Quaedam relationes non innascuntur ex actionibus secundum quod sunt in actu, sed

The psychological plane is in harmony with this ontological reality. Man, reasonable animal that he is, is not reduced to his instincts: he has been given the power to ratify and govern them by his own free will. Thus human motherhood is normally the fruit of a free act, of a permanent consent which implies a double relationship: to the *person* of the father as co-principle in generation, and to the *person* of the child as end result of generation. A woman, it is true, can engender physically without such a consent, but this is a deplorable anomaly, corresponding to a failure or an abuse of liberty. She who gives birth in such circumstances is the mother of a human being; but one could hardly call such motherhood a fully human motherhood, since there has not really been any "human act." Such motherhood is human in its end result, but animal in its mode. This disproportion is abnormal. Normally a human mother is freely involved in a double consent, both to the person of the father and to that of the child; and her consent is proportioned to this double object. Her consent is in tune with the spiritual character of these persons, her husband and her child, and with the permanence of her relationship to each. It entails a spiritual and indestructible love. Indeed, this love is not confined to biological need, but continues far beyond. It is stronger than death itself. The love of a mother for the child she has lost sometimes even has a sharper edge than her love for the children who are alive, due to the deep pain of a wound or of an absence that cannot be filled.

3. To advance now to the *divine* motherhood in Mary,

---

magis secundum quod fuerunt; sicut aliquis dicitur *pater* postquam ex actione est effectus consecutus; et tales relationes fundantur super *id quod in agente ex actione relinquitur, sive sit dispositio, sive habitus, sive aliquod jus aut potestas, vel quidquid aliud est hujusmodi* — Certain relationships do not rise out of actions according as they are in act, but rather according as they were so; just as someone is called a *father* after the effect has resulted from the action; and such relationships are founded on *what there is left in the agent from the action, whether it be a disposition, or a habit, or some right or power, or whatever else there is of this kind.*"

abstracting from the virginal mode of generation, all these human elements of motherhood are to be found. But here again there is something more. In fact, it is no longer only an immortal person that she engenders, but a divine and preexisting person. Thus there results, without alteration of either of their natures, a prodigious reversal. The Son depends on his Mother, as does every other son, in the order of flesh and blood; but in the ontological order she is dependent on him as on her Creator. This motherhood opens out into a metaphysical abyss.

This abyss, however, does not destroy the maternal psychology of Mary toward the Son born of her flesh. It does not introduce therein any violence, anything monstrous. By his grace God deepens and transforms the sentiments he has created on the level of nature, so that Mary might be a worthy Mother of God.

On the psychological level, her motherhood is by divine disposition the fruit of her consent (Lk. 1:28–30). But unlike the case of other mothers, this consent is not addressed to created persons, husband and child, but to God, for God is at once the principle and the end result of this generation. He is its principle, because it is by the spiritual transcendent operation of the Holy Spirit that Mary conceives virginally; he is its end result, because the one whom she engenders in the flesh is the very Son of God. This consent to God — to God's life-giving action, to God's coming — is a theological act. It is an act of faith and of love that has God for principle and object, as does the virginal generation that brings this motherhood about in the order of flesh and blood. Without this theological gift Mary would have been, with regard to God her Son, something like what a degenerate mother is in the order of nature — Mother of a God, but deprived of divine sentiments. The anomaly would have been as disturbing as that of a human mother deprived of human sentiments. According to a law of nature established by God, the mother who gives birth feels arising in her heart all the force of a love that makes of her not a machine for engendering but a mother. Normally her psychology rises to the level of the personal and indestructible relationship which she contracts. In that same wisdom of his God willed that his human mother should find in her heart the resources of affection adapted to her status as Mother of God.

Mary was the only woman in whom two sentiments that are in some way related coincide exactly — the love of a mother toward her Son, and the love of a creature toward her God. Motherly love sometimes borders on adoration. In Mary this adoration was well founded and could give itself free rein. Better than the theologians, poets have grasped this vital and existential point of the mystery. Basil of Seleucia (d. 459), for example, writes:

> "When she contemplated this divine child, overcome, as I would imagine, by love and fear, she must have said to herself, 'What name can I find that fits you, my child? Man? But your conception is divine. God? But you have taken the human condition. What shall I do for you? Shall I feed you with milk or extol you as a God? Shall I take care of you as your mother or adore you as your handmaid? Shall I embrace you as my Son or entreat you as a God? Shall I offer you milk or bring you incense?' "[24]

A few years back, during the last World War, at Christmas in a prison camp an atheist author was charged with the task of writing a Christmas play for his stalag. In trying to be sympathetic to the faith of his comrades he found words quite similar to those above and no less touching. In his play

---

24. Basil of Seleucia, *Homily on the Theotokos* 5, PG 85:448ab. The same theme is found in Romanos Melodus (cf. P. Regamey, *Les plus beaux textes sur la Vierge*, Paris, 1946, p. 78) and in summary in an antiphon of the first vespers of the Purification: "Ipsum quem genuit adoravit — She adored the very one whom she begot."

a blind man, operating a magic lantern show, describes how he would portray Mary:

"The Virgin is pale as she looks at her child. What must be depicted in her face is an anxious astonishment that has appeared only once on a human countenance. For Christ is her child, flesh of her flesh and the fruit of her womb. She carried him for nine months and will give him her breast, and her milk will become God's blood. For a moment the temptation is so strong that she forgets he is God. She hugs him in her arms and says, 'My little one!'

"But at other moments she remains stupefied and thinks, 'God is there,' and she is overcome with a religious horror for this speechless God, this terrifying infant. For at some moment every mother is thus brought up short before the rebellious bit of her own flesh that is her child, and she feels herself in exile before this new life that she has made with her own life, this new life where thoughts dwell that are stranger to her. But no child has ever been more cruelly and more quickly snatched away from its mother, for this child is God and in every respect he transcends whatever she can imagine. . . .

"But I think there are also other moments, rapid and fleeting moments, when she feels both that Christ is her Son, her own little one, and that he is God. She looks at him and thinks, 'This God is my child. This divine flesh is my flesh. He is made of me, he has my eyes, and the way his mouth is formed, that's the way mine is. He looks like me. He is God and he looks like me.'

"And no woman had God for herself alone, the way she did, a God who was very little and whom she could take into her arms and cover with her kisses, a very warm little God who smiled and breathed, a God who could be touched and who laughed. And it is just in that kind of a moment that I would paint Mary, if I were a painter. . . ."[25]

---

25. Jean-Paul Sartre has graciously authorized citing this excerpt from *Bariona,* an unpublished play, for which obviously all rights of reproduction are reserved.

4. The Gift of the Divine Motherhood: Summary

At the end of this double analysis we are in a position to synthesize what has been presented as the grace of the divine motherhood. This "grace" — "grace" is used here in the broad sense of a *gratuitous* gift of God — presents two aspects which, as has been explained, are related to each other as the sacramental character is to sanctifying grace. One is a gift in the order of *structure,* the other a gift in the order of *life* prolonging the first. More precisely, at the Incarnation Mary becomes a part of Christ in a way eminently analogous to the belonging brought about by the sacramental character; and she receives likewise a new deepening of her fulness of grace. These two gifts can now be summarized a final time.

a. The Gift in the Order of Structure

At the moment of Christ's incarnation Mary is the first to be mystically incorporated in him and to contract a social function in relation to him, her maternal function. She is the first to receive the imprint of the Savior. But the configuration she received was very different from others. The baptismal character configures the receiver to Christ the Son of God; the Mother of God was configured rather to the Father whose eternal Son she bore in the order of time. This configuration made her worthy to call him her Son, who till then was Son of the Father alone. The divine impression that marked her childbearing with a virginal imprint left its mark also on her person.

b. The Gift in the Order of Life

This gift analogous to the sacramental character was accompanied by a gift in the order of life, proportioning Mary, in being and activity, to her newly acquired quality. She did not, it is true, have to receive sanctifying grace, which already she had in fulness. But this grace received a new *status* and a greater *depth*.

A new status: So far this grace, like that of the baptized, had for its effect to enable her to say from the depths of her soul, "Abba, Father" (Rom. 8:16; Gal. 4:7), that is, "My God and my Father." A new grace now teaches her how to say "My God and my Son" to him whom she carried within herself. In other words, the grace she received brought her onto the level of her state of Mother of God, whatever the degrees and modes of consciousness that accompanied this grace. In her person and her supernatural organism she received a special connaturality with God, in virtue of which the one whom she bore was not a stranger to her but indeed a Son. Her creaturely adoration and her motherly love derived from a single impulse of soul. In all tenderness, as well as in total subordination, she had a mother's heart toward this God who was her Son.

A greater depth: The relationship that so deeply stamped her being opened up in her new and unprecedented possibilities in the order of grace, possibilities that God fulfilled in the act of creating them. It was not merely a matter of a new modality of her fulness of grace, which from being filial now became maternal. There was also a new enlargement of this fulness that became proportioned to her new function. One is almost tempted to speak of a re-creation of Mary's being in the sense in which Scripture speaks of baptism as a new creation (Gal. 6:15; cf. 2 Cor. 5:17). This does not mean that baptism destroys our nature or deprives it of anything positive, but that it completely transforms it in giving it a deeper dynamism and finality. Thus the re-creation which Mary underwent did not alter either her nature or her previous grace, but corresponded to the new hold that God had taken of her and to the new finality to which she found herself destined as Mother of God. It was the transfiguring of a previous grace that remained specifically what it always had been. This is what the gospel of the Annunciation hints at. There Luke suggests that the new creation announced by the prophets is about to begin: the Spirit of God who presided over the first creation (Gen. 1:2) and was to inaugurate the second (Is. 11:2) comes to rest on Mary in whom the new world begins (Lk. 1:35). This is that same notion of "new creation" that is found throughout the eastern texts on the *Katharsis* of Mary at the Annunciation. In their deepest intent these texts seem to refer to that homogeneous transmutation of Mary who is re-created in her maternal encounter with her Creator.

The reader may well have been exhausted by the heaviness of the conceptual apparatus involved in the analysis just completed. For two men to be able to reach the summit of Everest, just for a few moments, it requires tons of material. Similar demands weigh on the undertakings of the human intelligence. The theologian is well aware of the disproportion between the simplicity of the mystery and the complexity of the conceptual material that he has to take up whenever he wants to try to express the mystery in human words. Here more than at any other point the author can prepare the reader for contemplation; he cannot supply him with it. As this laborious climb reaches it end, it is hoped that the reader can glimpse the essence of this mystery, at the same time staggering to the mind and yet clearly intelligible. It is wrapped up in the dialogue between this God made man who says to the one who bore him, "My mother," and this woman who can in all truth and dignity and joy (Lk. 1:28) answer him, "My Son." It is the mystery in which the love of the most perfect of mothers for her Son coincides harmoniously with the love of the holiest of women for her God.

C. Elements Appropriate to the Divine Motherhood

Three features remain to complete our contemplation of the divine motherhood: it is virginal, social, and specifically involved in the work of salvation.

1. Virginal Motherhood[26]

The virginal aspect of the divine motherhood is undoubtedly one of the least attractive aspects it has for the modern mind, which tends to see therein an anomaly, something that is unfinished, a lack of fulfilment, and an inadmissible exception to the laws of nature.

Nevertheless, a Protestant theologian, Karl Barth, finds the essential note of Mary's virginity to lie in its being a sign and witness of God's transcendence:

> "The man Jesus Christ has no father. His conception does not stem from the law common to all. His existence begins with the free decision of God himself. It proceeds with the freedom that characterizes the unity of Father and Son bound together by love, that is, by the Holy Spirit. . . . It is the great field of God's freedom, and from that freedom proceeds the existence of the man Jesus."[27]

The Fathers of the Church attached great importance to this mystery. Mary's virginity was for them the specific sign of Christ's divinity, at the same time that it was the type of the new birth of Christians. Within this Christological mystery they appreciated at its true value the perfect and exemplary virginity of Mary, who ever afterwards remained "the Virgin" in a unique sense.

---

26. For a bibliography on virginity cf. *infra,* p. 356.
27. Karl Barth, *Esquisse d'une dogmatique,* Neuchâtel-Paris, 1950, p. 96. (ET: *Dogmatics in Outline,* New York, Harper, 1957).

She is the type of a love that gives itself to God in hope, renouncing the exclusiveness of marital love in favor of reaching a love perfectly open to all — in God, through God, at the service of men. In Mary this love found its supreme fruitfulness. It gave birth to God himself.

Understood in this sense, virginity has nothing cold about it, no incapability of giving; on the contrary, it is capable of a more demanding and more total gift of self. If today this gift goes unrecognized, it is perhaps because the attempts to realize this difficult and perilous way are often deficient and disfigured. It is also because sexual freedom and the exaltation of sex are today in a state of paroxysm. Ultimately this stems from a mentality that separates body and spirit. Our day oscillates between exalting the flesh for its own sake and giving vent to a mysticism cut off from all bodily reality. In the resulting depths of confusion the Virgin Mary remains on the horizon of dogma as a distant beacon, or as a giant but almost imperceptible star with which to keep one's bearings. The reader who wishes to go further into this mystery is referred to Appendix # 11,[28] which takes up the different aspects of Mary's virginity: before childbirth, in the act of childbearing, and after childbirth, according to the traditional formulas of the Fathers of the Church.

What they perceived could be summed up as follows: In her fulness of grace and in the movement of her total self-giving to God, a giving that prepared her for Christ, Mary discovered the meaning of her virginity. This virginity could not thereafter ever weaken or become simply a matter of the heart. God, who preserved this virginity in the very conceiving of the Son of God, did not let any blemish fall on the sign of the new birth, the living sanctuary where the God made man first dwelt.

---

28. *Infra,* 316 ff.

2. Social Motherhood

The social aspects of Mary's motherhood remain to be considered. These are fundamental aspects. In a way they integrate what we are tempted to call the "personal" aspects of motherhood. In fact, the mystery of the Annunciation has the very function of establishing the first bond between God and the human race, as has been seen. This bond is set up by an exemplary theological act, by a virginal generation. Thus the New Covenant between God and his creature is inaugurated, and with it already the communion of saints. At the same time that she incorporates Jesus in our race according to nature, Mary is incorporated in him according to grace. At that moment of time the fulness of grace, which already by anticipation proceeded from Christ's merits, made conscious contact with its source from which in ways unknown her whole life of grace was nourished.

Thus at the moment when the Virgin became Mother of the Incarnate Word, the Church takes shape in a secret and limited way, but perfectly, in its intimate essence as Mystical Body.[29] Jesus and Mary form the society not just of a son and a mother but of the Savior of God and saved humanity. This is the Church in germ, constituted in a hidden way in its two founding members, the Redeemer and the first of the redeemed. All men are called to be incorporated in this foundation, and their incorporation, which is identification with Christ, implies for them a filial relationship not only to the

---

29. One is tempted to add: In the person of its first two members the Church realizes not only its essence, but its principal notes. It is perfectly *one* and *holy*. It is virtually *catholic* (for Mary is the most universal of purely created beings); all it lacks is a catholicity in act and apostolicity. But an important restriction must be added. In her person Mary verifies the ontological reality of these notes, but secretly. They are not yet therefore real notes *(notae),* that is to say, properties that *make the Church known*. With her the Church does not yet have its visible, official, institutional, and publicly attested character, which will begin on the day of Pentecost.

heavenly Father, but to Mary, the terrestrial Mother of the Son of God. Thus the spiritual motherhood of Mary, her motherhood according to grace, reaches a new stage. In becoming Mother of Christ, head of the Mystical Body, she radically becomes Mother of the members, according to the teaching of Pius X. This motherhood will be completed when the work of salvation is accomplished.

In all of this Mary is not to be considered "in herself" or even in reference to Christ alone, but in reference also to the Holy Spirit. Her motherhood is an organic element in the communion of saints which he begins to quicken in its earliest stages. It is the Holy Spirit who establishes in her the root and prototype of the welcoming and cooperating Church, the Church he will fashion on a universal scale on the day of Pentecost and throughout the ages.

3. Motherhood Involved in the Work of Salvation[30]

The society into which Mary enters with Christ is a society of salvation. Mary joins it knowing what she is doing. She consents to become Mother of the Messiah destined to *"save his people from their sins,"* as signified by the name *"Jesus"* announced by the angel (Lk. 1:31; cf. Mt. 1:21). This complete and unconditional consent of the "handmaid of the Lord" (Lk. 1:38) is not simply consent to the Savior's birth, but to the entire work of salvation. The message of the Annunciation bears this out (Lk. 1:28–38), as does the Magnificat (Lk. 1:54–55). From that moment Mary could have had in mind the prophecy in which Chapter 53 of Isaiah announces the sorrowful sacrifice of the Messiah (Is. 53:1–5, 7, 10) and its redemptive scope (53:5, 6, 10, 12). In any case Simeon made plain to her the contradictions that her Son would undergo "for the rising of many in Israel" (Lk.

---

30. I.e., "Maternité sotériologique": "Soteriological" (from the Greek *sōtēr,* meaning "savior") signifies "having a relationship to salvation."

2:34) as well as her mysterious part in this suffering — the "sword" that was to "pierce her own soul" (2:35). She was soon to have a foretaste of this suffering, when for three days Jesus would be taken from her and she would search for him at Jerusalem. These three days of anguish (2:48) prefigured for the evangelist the three days of Jesus' death *(triduum mortis)*. Thus the next stage in Mary's destiny unfolds.[31]

---
31. R. Laurentin, *Jésus et le Temple* . . . , Paris, Gabalda, 1966.

THIRD STAGE

MARY AT THE REDEMPTIVE SACRIFICE[1]

Between the Annunciation and the death of Jesus two periods elapse that are in marked contrast, the hidden life and the public life.

In the first, Mary lives in closest intimacy with her Son. In the second she is separated from him. Jesus' words suggest that this separation was intentional. When his ministry was involved, he kept at a distance from his Mother. He already did so at the age of twelve, when he gave an indication of what his future ministry would be (Lk. 2:49); he did so a second time at Cana, at the beginning of his public life (Jn. 2:4; cf. 7:3–10). Later in the course of his preaching he acted similarly (Lk. 8:19–21 and parallels; Lk. 11:27–28): when mention was made of his Mother and his brethren, he turned his gaze toward his disciples and indicated they were his new family (Lk. 8:19–21). He invited his hearers to move higher than the level of flesh and blood relationships onto the level of faith (Lk. 11:28). In short, Jesus lived each phase of his life with those whom he called to share it, each according to his vocation. In his hidden life he associated a *woman,* Mary, his Mother. In his public life he associated *men,* and Mary was no longer at his side.

---
1. For bibliography on Mary's part in the Redemption cf. *infra,* p. 358.

But this separation was only exterior, and it was not final. On the day of his sacrifice — that hidden sacrifice whose liturgical import was veiled by the appearances of a death inflicted in condemnation — a change occurred. The disciples fled, and Mary was there at the foot of the cross. In the mystery of Redemption she again found a role analogous to the one she had had in the hidden mystery of the Incarnation. But the limits of this analogy must be noted, as well as the development of this new stage in her destiny.

Mary Associated in the Redemption by Her Consent[2]

At the foot of the cross as at the Annunciation, Mary's activity was essentially a *consent* in which her faith and love are involved. In the Incarnation it was consent to life — this human life which she gives to her Son; in the Redemption, it is consent to death — this human death that Christ had to suffer (Lk. 24:46) in order to redeem the world. But these two acts of consent were in reality only one and the same consent: the *fiat* of the Annunciation (Lk. 1:38) bore unconditionally and irrevocably on everything that was going to be accomplished.

But if Mary's consent remained the same, her *situation* and the *import of her actions* had changed. Before the Incarnation, Mary was for the while the summit of the human race, and it was "in the name of the human race," as St. Thomas explains,[3] that she gave to the Word her consent and

---

2. This is the heading used in the preceding edition of the *Short Treatise*. Today it corresponds to the theology of Vatican II in *Lumen Gentium* art. 62: "... a *consensu* quem in Annuntiatione fideliter praebuit, quemque sub Cruce incunctanter sustinuit ... — the *consent* which she gave in faith at the Annunciation and which she sustained without wavering beneath the cross." Cf. *ibid.* art. 58: "Sacrificio Ejus se materno animo sociavit ... *consentiens* — She united herself with a maternal heart to his sacrifice, lovingly *consenting*...."
3. ST III, q. 30, a. 1, c: "Exspectabatur consensus Virginis *loco totius humanae naturae* — The consent of the Virgin was awaited *in the name*

her flesh and blood. But from that moment on, her Son, God made man, was the perfect representative of the human race. The role of representative, which had been Mary's at the Annunciation, had now finished.

What then remained for her? And by what title did God associate her in the work of Redemption?

1. Associated in the Redemption in the Name of the Redeemed

First of all, her role as representative of the human race still has an object, though now in a totally dependent way.

One of the identifying traits of God's saving plan is that he wanted to save man through himself, and, what is more, to integrate redeemed men as much as possible into the realization of the work of salvation. Mary's presence on Calvary and the role she played there correspond to this exquisitely delicate divine plan.[4] At Christ's side, in total subordination, she represented those accessory aspects of humanity which he had not assumed. She is a human person; Christ is a divine preexisting person. She lived in the condition of obscure pilgrim faith; by the beatific vision Christ had the evidence of God before him on the level of his divinity and, according to the classical thesis, in his humanity itself. Mary is one of the redeemed; Christ had no need of redemp-

---

of all mankind." Cf. III Sent. d. 3, a. 2, qla. 2. The text was taken up again by Leo XIII in two of his encyclicals, *Octobri mense* September 22, 1891, ASS 24 (1890–1891), p. 195, and *Fidentem* September 20, 1896, ASS 29 (1896–1897), and by Pius XII, Encyclical *Mystici Corporis* June 29, 1943, AAS 35 (1943), p. 247. Cf. K. Schwerdt, "Die heilsgeschichtliche Stellvertretung der Menschheit durch Maria nach der päpstlichen Lehrverkündigung," *Die heilsgeschichtliche Stellvertretung der Menschheit durch Maria,* Paderborn, Schöningh, 1954, pp. 1–25 (and the other studies contained in this volume).

4. This point is treated again *infra,* pp. 256 ff.

tion. Finally, Mary is a woman, Christ a man. All the other traits are symbolically summed up in this last one. On all these grounds Mary at the foot of the cross represents the way the saved Church was associated in the sacrifice of the Savior.

Care must, of course, be taken not to exaggerate Mary's secondary contribution, by exploiting it to the detriment of Christ. It must not be thought that Christ's humanity represented the human race imperfectly and that Mary's presence at the foot of the cross would in this regard be necessary. It must not be thought either that ratification by a human *person* was necessary for the sacrifice to become the sacrifice of the human race. Christ was perfectly man, perfectly representative of the human race. If the traits described above about Mary were absent, Christ's representative quality would in no sense be lessened; its foundation would remain the same. A purely human person would not have been able to bring about a gathering together of the human race, except in a moral sense; only the God-Man could metaphysically recapitulate the human race in the very root of its re-creation. Only a man who had no need of redemption could be the redeemer.

Nonetheless, these restrictions do not render the presence of Mary on Calvary useless. Although it is not *necessary* for salvation, her role is no less real. Although it does not fill in some deficit, it is no less effective. In the human order, the presence or absence of one more delegate does not compromise the validity of a delegation. And yet each member therein plays a real and effective role. Thus the role that Mary plays is real, although it is not indispensable to the realization of the redeeming sacrifice. In a more exact analogy, on the sacramental level the priest suffices for the validity of the sacrifice of the Mass, and yet the participation of the faithful is important. In the fundamental sacrifice, Mary plays a role analogous to that of the faithful in the sacrifice of the Mass. For all its human congruity, Mary's presence at the foot of the Cross makes no necessary contribution to Christ's work, but it does bring out the rich harmony of the Redemption. On this ground God required her active participation. As the consent of the immaculate Virgin and her own flesh and blood had been incorporated into the mystery of the Incarnation, her consent and her suffering were incorporated into the mystery of the Redemption.

2. Associated in the Redemption in Virtue of Her Holiness

Mary therefore represents the cooperation of the redeemed in the redeeming sacrifice in its very accomplishment. Why was she, in preference to others, called to this high function? It was not only because she is the first of the redeemed. It was also, and even to a greater extent, because she was more radically redeemed than any other.

In the sacrifice that constitutes the source and basis of redemption, anything soiled, tarnished, or sinful even to the slightest degree would have been out of place. The new creation had to begin from an altogether pure source. For this reason, *John's* compassion — he was also present at the foot of the cross — could not be integrated into the redeeming sacrifice. Only the cooperation of the one who was exempt from all fault and immaculate from her very first moment could be incorporated into this fundamental act of salvation.

This negative side of Mary's holiness should not be separated from its positive aspects such as the perfection of her faith, hope, and love, the intensity of her suffering, the intimacy of her communion with the Savior. The purely theological role that is hers should be underlined. On Calvary Mary's sufferings are not physical sufferings. She is not crucified on a cross near her Son's. She accomplishes no work that from the outside would add to that of Christ. It is *his* own sufferings that she herself suffers. Her proper role is one of compassion, the moral piercing of her spirit foretold by Simeon. Her pain is the reflection of Christ's pain in the mirror of her motherly soul; her intentions spiritually reflect those of Christ the Redeemer himself.

3. Associated in the Redemption in Her Role as Mother

Beyond what accrues to Mary in her function representing the human race as the first of the redeemed, beyond the spotless perfection of her person and acts, she participated in the redeeming sacrifice in virtue of a third title, her divine motherhood. The one who suffered on the cross was her Son. He belonged to her in a certain sense. Benedict XV could refer to "maternal rights" which she sacrificed on Calvary.[5] The meaning of this expression must not be exaggerated. There is no question of a right in the strict sense — a right of free disposal, *jus utendi et abutendi* — but rather of those bonds of intimate love, that moral community of mother and son prolonging the original flesh-and-blood communion between them. In summoning Mary to Calvary Christ broadens this community to include the sufferings and merits of the Redemption. At the foot of the cross Mary could still say what every mother can say to her son: "He is my flesh and

---

5. Benedict XV, Letter *Inter Sodalicia* May 22, 1918, (AAS 10 (1918), p. 182): "Sic materna in filium jura pro hominum salute abdicavit placandaeque Dei justitiae, quantum ad se pertinebat, filium immolavit, ut dici merito queat, Ipsam cum Christo humanum genus redemisse — For the salvation of mankind she renounced her maternal rights and, as far as it depended on her, offered her Son to placate divine justice, so that we may well say that she with Christ redeemed mankind." H. Seiler, *Coredemptrix*, Rome, 1939, pp. 118-119 ably demonstrated the metaphorical character of the expression "maternal rights" and other expressions employed in the context. Pius XII, Encyclical *Mystici Corporis*, AAS 35 (1943), p. 247, took up the concept of "maternal right" again with many more nuances: Mary no longer *abdicates* her maternal rights but *offers them in holocaust*. In this same text the expression *"immolavit"* of Benedict XV is replaced by *"obtulit."* Vatican II ended by renouncing any use of this latter word.

blood." Thus she suffers cruelly in the presence of this torn flesh and this blood spilled out. She can add what every mother in deepest communion with her son can add: "Whatever is yours is mine, and whatever is mine is yours." By God's grace this affirmation takes on its highest meaning: "Your sufferings are my sufferings; your work is my work; the Redemption which you could accomplish alone, you have willed should be also my sacrifice."

Here the work of the Redeemer and the association of the Virgin Mother with her Son reaches the summit. Christ's transcendence is not in the least altered. Every title Mary has to this cooperation she owes entirely to him: her quality as first among the redeemed, her quality as the immaculate one full of grace, her quality as Mother. The acts by which she enters so deeply into Christ's work of salvation are, in their full extent, the work of Christ's grace. Mary therefore is not on a level with Christ, nor on our own level, but at a point between the two. Christ *alone* is redeemer of all, and thus foremost of Mary, the first of the redeemed; he alone is God, he alone died, he alone consummated the sacrifice by his resurrection and return to the father, his entry into the sanctuary of heaven, according to the theology of the Letter to the Hebrews. Mary participates in the redemption by a limited title, through her compassion and the value God attached to it: what Pius X called a merit of fittingness *(de congruo)*. In other words, by a title of singular friendship with God she merited what Christ merited in strict justice on a footing of personal equality with God. Other Christians did not participate in this fundamental accomplishment, though they cooperate, by a limited merit, in the spreading of the Redemption. When we merit our salvation, we owe our entire merit to Christ's grace. When the Virgin Mary, in Christ, merits the salvation of all, she owes this entire merit to the same grace of Christ. These merits of the redeemed do not at all subtract from the universal power of the Redemption; on the contrary, they attest, in the supreme degree, to the transforming power of that Redemption which raises men to the level of becoming "fellow workers with God" (1 Cor. 3:9). What Mary had said in the *Magnificat* is true on Calvary more than ever before: the "Almighty" has "wrought great things" in her (Lk. 1:49).[6]

Here again, therefore, Mary is seen entirely in relation to Christ. Less recognition has been given to the complementary truth that she is also entirely relative to the Holy Spirit. She acts in dependence on him. The title of "coredemptrix" which was coined for her and widely attributed to her by Mariologists, though not retained by the papal magisterium or by Vatican II, would fit the Holy Spirit in the primary and strictest sense of the term; for he is the Spirit of Christ, and by his anointing and breath the whole saving work of the

---

6. This presentation of Mary's cooperation in the Redemption is given with the impression that it meets with the important objections that have been made against this doctrine: 1) Christ alone is mediator. 2) What good is Mary's merit, since Christ's alone is fully efficacious? 3) Mary's cooperation in the Redemption presupposes that the Redemption has already been accomplished.

As a matter of fact, these are not objections to refute, but truths to integrate in the following way: 1) Mary is not a mediatrix *like* Christ, but by Christ and *in* him. Her mediation is altogether subordinated to that of Christ; it proceeds totally from his. 2) Mary's merit is not necessary for salvation; it proceeds from God's gratuitous will, full of delicate kindness toward us, according to which he decided to integrate in the Redemption as fully as possible the work of the creature thereby redeemed. 3) Men cooperate actively in the Redemption to the degree in which they have been previously redeemed by Christ. Mary, the most perfectly redeemed, is also the one who cooperated most perfectly in the Redemption. She was redeemed in a singular way, a way at once *preventive* (for she was preserved and not purified), *anticipated* (for the effect of the Redemption reached her in advance and first of all), and *integral* (for she was exempt not only from sin but "from every stain" of sin, and from the first moment was adorned with a fulness of grace). In consequence she was admitted to cooperate in the Redemption in a singular manner before all others, at the very source of Redemption, according to what had been given her by this preventive anticipation.

Redeemer is animated. The title "co-Redeemer" would aptly describe him, according to a divine equality that would give full force to the prefix "co-". Mary owes the fact that she was able to communicate in this sacrifice to the Holy Spirit, who not only cooperated in the essential work by his anointing, but also divinely stirred up the cooperation of the first of the redeemed. With him who is "co-Redeemer" she contracts this new bond at the time of the essential sacrifice. The Spirit had urged her on to Calvary so that she might stand there as the first fruits of the cooperating Church, at the very hour when the sign of the Church was to appear from the pierced side of the Savior (Jn. 19:34).

As type of the Church on Calvary, then, Mary acquires a new claim to be mother of men. While Christ effectively becomes their head in meriting the Redemption, she effectively becomes their mother in being associated in this universal merit. It is the hour when Jesus declared her motherhood: "Mother, this is your son" (Cf. Jn. 19:26).

FOURTH STAGE

FROM CHRIST'S DEATH TO THE END OF THE EARTHLY DESTINY OF MARY

Present on Calvary (Jn. 19:25–27), Mary is present also in the cenacle before Pentecost, "joined in continuous prayer" with the primitive community in expectation of the Spirit (Acts 1:14).[1] This is all that is known about her for the period that extends from Christ's death to the end of her own destiny on earth.

An idea of the importance of her presence in this period can be gathered from what went before. As she had been the bond between the chosen people and Christ when he was about to be born among them, so at this stage, though in a lesser sense, she plays a role of transition between the dead Christ and the Church about to be born. It cannot be too often pointed out how all along she is the witness and sign of the Holy Spirit.

This presence of hers takes on different meanings during the contrasting moments that make up the period after Christ's death: during the *triduum mortis,* then from the Resurrection to the Ascension, later from the Ascension to Pentecost, and finally during the beginnings of the Church.

---

1. Acts 1:14. This text is explicitly cited in *Lumen Gentium* art. 59.

1. The period now being studied begins with a tragic moment. During three days Christ was dead, and his prayer on earth was reduced to silence. At that hour when the human race carried its sinfulness to the ultimate in putting God to death, at the hour when even the best had sunk into cowardice, and the sun had darkened, and the earth was trembling as dead persons arose in frightful forewarning of the judgment (Mt. 27:51-54), at that hour when Christ's soul left earth, Mary was the only ray of light alive in this world below. She alone "found favor" with God. At a time when Christ carried his intercession into heaven in the presence of his Father, Mary continued his prayer on earth. As before the Annunciation she had been the dawn, she was now the twilight of Christ's day.

And yet daybreak is already at hand for the Church. In this desolate hour John the evangelist perceives a mysterious sign whose meaning he sums up in these terms: "There are three witnesses: the Spirit, the water, and the blood, and all three of them agree" (1 Jn. 5:7). This is the triple sign that John sees in the concrete events surrounding Christ's death. He describes Christ's last breath in these unaccustomed terms, "He gave up the *Spirit*" (Jn. 19:30).[2] In other words, this dying breath is in reality a breath of life: it is the sending of the Holy Spirit who will raise up the Church. And it is then that "the water and the blood," symbols of the essential sacraments by which the Church raises up new life, flow from the opened side of Christ. Mary has her place in this ecclesiological symbolism: standing at the foot of the cross (Jn. 19:25), she is the very type of the living Church issuing from the Redeemer's blood, empowered by the Spirit to con-

---

2. Jn. 19:30. The verb *paredōken* is in the singular here. In so using it, John wishes to show that Jesus' last breath is a prelude to the pouring forth of the Spirit according to 1:33, 3:34, 4:14, 7:37-39, 20:22. In this last verse Jesus *"breathes"* on the apostles and says to them, "Receive the Holy Spirit."

tinue to be by her prayers and charity a bond at the very origin of the communion of saints. A mystery is taking shape here: the birth of the new people from the people of old, the birth of the Church from the Daughter of Zion, the birth foretold by the prophet Isaiah.[3] Whatever the consciousness Mary then had of this mystery, it is at that moment at work in her.

2. When Christ rose, as the living sun of justice never again to set, Mary's role takes on new meaning. There is no longer question of continuing the cosmic prayer of Christ, but of preparing the foundation of the Church, and then of being associated therein. Here she is not so much Mother of the Church as principle and type of the Church, inasmuch as the Church is defined by communion with Christ and his holiness. She is the first seed of the Church's prayer and faith.

3. At Pentecost there takes place an action similar to that of the Annunciation:[4] the Spirit, who had manifested himself in secret to form the physical body of Christ, now manifests himself in a startling way to form his mystical body. His action centers now not on the birth of Christ, but on the birth of the Church. Under the shadow of the Spirit, as earlier at the Annunciation, Mary is present in the cenacle. And the episode that follows is not the departure of Mary for the home of Elizabeth (Lk. 1:39), but the departure of the apostles toward the peoples of all the earth. It is for the Church a Visitation on a world scale.

4. Mary is present at the first expansion of the Church, as she had been present at its manifestation, for she, above every

---

3. Is. 66:7–13. Verse 8 reads, "Is a country born in one day? Is a nation brought forth all at once, that Zion only just in labor should bring forth sons?" Both this text and Apoc. 12, which is inspired by it, are at one in not separating the Messiah's birth and the birth of the new people. Most often it is impossible to decide whether there is question of one or the other. Cf. also Mich. 4:9–10.

4. Compare Lk. 1:35, "The Holy Spirit will come upon you" and "the power of the Most High will cover you," with Acts 1:7, "You will receive power when the Holy Spirit comes on you."

other, had been a living member of the Savior. But she does not have any official role in this public diffusion of the Church. Her role here again is the hidden life. Lost amid the group of the faithful along with the other women, she is not charged with accomplishing any of the acts that found the new people of God. It is not she who speaks, but Peter. It is not she who baptizes, but the apostles. She has no part in the hierarchy of ministers, but her prayer, which had prepared for the birth of the Church, continues to be the highest point that the prayer of the Church reaches. And this seems to have given her so great a claim in the marvelous success of the first preaching of the gospel.[5]

Had she taken part in the supper on the evening of Holy Thursday? There are no grounds for an affirmative answer.[6] But it seems certain that she took part in the breaking of the bread in the community of Jerusalem (Acts 2:42, 46; cf. 1:14). There she appears as the model and high point of the Church on earth in its communion with the risen Savior. With the Christian community she "proclaims the death of the Lord until he comes" (1 Cor. 11:26). The eschatological yearning of the Church in the hour of its birth reaches the most intense degree in Mary. For her the consummation is near.

---

5. "As the Church was being born she stirred it by the power of her contemplation and love. She was more useful to it than the apostles, who acted exteriorly. She was for it the hidden root where the strength was prepared that burst forth in flower and fruit," C. Journet, *L'Eglise du Verbe incarné,* Paris, Desclée, 1941, c. 3, # 4, 1, p. 120, note.

6. Mary was at Jerusalem on Good Friday (Jn. 19:25-27). It is to be presumed she was there Thursday. If she took part in the supper with those to whom Christ said, "Take and eat," she was not, in any hypothesis, among those to whom were addressed the words of institution, "Do this in memory of me." The theme of Mary's presence at the Last Supper, dear to certain Mariologists but uncertain, can be advantageously replaced by that of her presence at the breaking of the bread in the primitive community.

Concerning Christ's appearance to the Virgin Mary on Easter morn, another recurring theme in Mariology, cf. *supra,* p. 173, n. 13.

FIFTH STAGE

MARY'S ASSUMPTION — THE VIRGIN, ESCHATOLOGICAL IMAGE OF THE CHURCH

The Assumption

How did Mary's life end? History has left no trace of an answer.

It is by other ways, not historical but dogmatic,[1] that Pius XII made this end of her life, or rather this completion of her life, the object of a dogma. The definition of faith is reduced to these concise terms:

> "The immaculate Mother of God, Mary ever Virgin, when the course of her earthly life was finished, was taken body and soul into the glory of heaven."[2]

---

1. The Assumption is not the object of a *historical* tradition of *apostolic origin*, but of a dogmatic explicitation rooted in reflection on the whole of revelation. This statement is a conclusion firmly established by the considerable works undertaken between 1944 and 1950. The ignorance professed at the end of the fourth century by St. Epiphanius, one of the best informed witnesses in his day, is a most significant indication in this matter (cf. *supra,* p. 67).
2. Constitution *Munificentissimus* November 1, 1950, AAS 42 (1950), p. 770, Denz. 2333 (3903).

Pius XII formally defined *Mary's presence now* with the risen Christ, in the communion of glory. He defined nothing more.

Where? When? How? The definition purposely avoids answering any of these questions. It does not even specify whether Mary died, as is ordinarily said, or whether she did not. The question raised by Epiphanius in 377 remains unanswered. Pius XII judged that this probable fact is not found with certainty in revelation. The reasons for this reserve will be treated in Appendix #12.[3]

The definition despoiled the apocryphals and Marian iconography of their imagery. It gave no heed to either myth or anecdote.

What is important and yet unrecognized is that it intentionally avoided suggesting "up there" and "down here," as well as any image of a transfer. It is inexactly and out of sheer accommodation to accustomed style that translations ordinarily say that Mary was *"raised up"* to heaven. This verb introduces a special imagery that was intentionally avoided. *"Assumpta"* means "to assume," or in other words, "to take." To the verb *"sumere"* the prefix *"ad-"* adds the notion of adjoining, aggregating, reuniting. *"Assumere"* is therefore the biblical equivalent of the Hebrew verb *LKH* (to take) which the Bible uses to signify the mysterious end of Enoch (Gen. 5:24; Sirach 44:16 and 49:16) and that of Elijah (2 Kgs. 2:3, 5, 9, 10; Sirach 48:9): God "took" them to himself. And it is on the basis of this word that the psalmists discovered the mystery of retribution in the afterlife for all the just that God "will take" at the end of their destiny (Ps. 49:16; 73:24). "You will take me into glory," says the psalmist. This is exactly the expression that Pius XII used, but he specified, "body and soul." It is integrally and not just in soul that the "immaculate Mother of God" rejoins the risen Christ.

The definition does not even specify whether there is ques-

---

3. Cf. *infra*, Appendix #12.

tion here of a unique privilege. It thus left the way open to an opinion according to which immediate bodily glorification would be the common lot of all. This new opinion has no other weight than that of the few arguments proposed in its favor, and it meets with counter arguments and objections.[4] The birth of this theory on the morrow of the definition of the Assumption, as also the expansion of the immortalist theory, attest to the reserve and extreme restraint of the dogmatic formula whose boldness has rather more often been underlined.

The only exception to the terseness that characterizes this definition is the manner in which Mary is designated: "the immaculate Mother of God," "Mary ever Virgin." These titles were not added out of a simple motive of piety or generosity characteristic of Italian style. They have dogmatic value here. The body of the immaculate one, preserved from all sin, the body of the Theotokos who engendered the Word of God, this body whose virginity the Holy Spirit integrally preserved, even in conception and childbirth, did not remain prisoner of the bonds of death.[5] In the totality of her being, the immaculate Mother of God, ever a Virgin, rejoined Christ in the communion of glory.

There remains the task of seizing the scope of this last transition.

---

4. K. Rahner, *On the Theology of Death,* New York, Herder and Herder, 1961. Among the foundations on which Rahner builds his argument is the case of the resurrected persons of Mt. 27:52, and the principle that Christ's entry into eternal glory does not open up an empty space but rather establishes a corporal community of the redeemed. In this hypothesis, the Assumption is no longer either an anticipation or a privilege. Schillebeeckx has vigorously taken a position against this thesis, but without discussing the reasons alleged. Cf. also K. Rahner, "The Interpretation of the Dogma of the Assumption," *Theological Investigations,* Baltimore, Helicon, 1961, vol. 1, p. 226.

5. Such are the terms of the prayer *Veneranda,* the most ancient Assumption prayer in the West. It was cited by Pius XII in his Constitution *Munificentissimus.* Cf. M. Jugie, *L'Assomption,* Rome, 1944, p. 263.

Mary at the End of Pilgrimage

The first thing to note appears almost paradoxical: in entering into glory Mary seems to lose something. By leaving her earthly and wayfaring condition, she loses the ability of meriting. But privation here is only apparent. If the Mother of God loses this ability, it is because her merits were at their height and her destiny had been reached.

What remains to be said beyond this first consideration is manifestly positive.

"With the Lord Forever" (1 Thes. 4:17)

First she finds her Son once again after a long separation, that of the public life and the time following his death on the cross. Henceforward their union is *definitive*. It is *without shadow*. Mary knows her Son no longer by dint of earthly signs, in a way obscure and limited, but face-to-face with his divinity. Earlier she knew him as God through his humanity. Now she knows his humanity through his very divinity.

Maternal Knowledge

In this last stage Mary's spiritual motherhood attains its consummation. Even before the Annunciation the Blessed Virgin, as has been said, had the soul of a mother with regard to mankind. Her grace of motherhood received new foundations at the Incarnation, and later on Calvary, in a way parallel to and dependent on Christ's grace of headship. While Christ, by taking on flesh, became fundamentally the head of the human race, Mary became *fundamentally* its mother. While formally he became its head by meriting Redemption on its behalf, Mary became *formally* its mother by meriting along with him: and Christ had chosen this "hour" to proclaim her maternal mission (Jn. 19:25–27). This motherhood of hers became *effective* at Pentecost, as the era of grace began. In heaven it became *conscious.* Prior to that Mary was plunged in the obscurity of faith and did not know the power and effect of her intercession. She did not know each sheep of the flock, as Christ did (Jn. 10:12). Now in God she knows each one of her children. She had loved them in her Son, with a love universal but undistinguishing; in the beatific vision she knows them individually and personally, with a motherly knowledge more intimate than that of the other saints.

One last feature reveals the warmth and intimacy of this knowledge: through her body, risen like Christ's, Mary retains a physical connaturality with us and an effective sympathy toward us, of which the other saints, according to common opinion, are presently deprived.

Maternal Activity

Mary's heavenly motherhood therefore implies a very perfect knowledge of her children, perfect in its principle since it proceeds from the vision of God, and perfect in its completeness because human knowledge finds in her its full resonance. But to be mother is more than simply to know; it involves acting also. In what does Mary's action toward her children consist? This is a difficult and much debated question.

One point is strongly attested to by tradition. The Mother of Jesus exercises a universal intercession, a living intercession that proceeds from her love. A mother does not know her children in the manner of a scientist coldly tabulating phenomena. Hers is a knowledge full of intentions and desires, like that of an artist with regard to his works, with the difference that the works in question here are persons. But Mary's desires with regard to her children are the desires of God himself. It is an absurd anthropomorphism to portray God's justice in opposition to the maternal mercy of Mary. The merciful prayer of the Virgin is efficacious because it is the very expression of the love of the God of mercy.

Does this mean that her intercessory prayer is useless? Certainly not. God is in need of no human agency, and yet it was his all-gracious design to make the Redemption the work of mankind, so that salvation might be wholly, and at each of its stages, on the heavenly as on the earthly plane, a human work at the same time as it is a divine work. He became man to save mankind; he associated a woman in his saving mission; he entrusted the Church to the hands of mere men, the apostles and their successors, and he was pleased to have them accomplish works "even greater" than his own (Jn. 14:12; cf. 4:38): he causes each man to merit his own salvation, etc. The role accorded the intercession of Mary and the saints manifests the same all-gracious design with regard to men. In this order, Mary surpasses the saints, for in her heart, as in that of her Son, divine love finds a perfect resonance — a resonance that is pure, because Mary is sinless; full, because she is full of grace; warm and sensitive, because she is already glorified entirely, soul *and body*. Finally, Mary is a woman, and that gives her intercession a note that nothing else can replace. As the heart of Christ gives an echo of manliness to divine love, the heart of Mary gives it a feminine and maternal echo. God welcomes hearing from within human freedom this double echo of his own divine intentions. That is why he values so highly the intercession of Christ's holy humanity and of the person of the Virgin Mary who is so closely and harmoniously joined to Christ.

Therefore, like the heavenly prayer of Christ and within this very prayer, Mary's prayer has, by God's free disposition, a true and universal effectiveness. What is the mode of this effectiveness? Without going into the discussions that this question raises,[6] one can offer a few positive guidelines.

---

6. On the mode of causality which is Mary's in heaven, a statement of the question will be found in G. Roschini, *Mariologia,* 1947, t. 2, part 1, pp.

Mary's love for her children is, as has been seen, full of desires and intentions that reflect, in her woman's heart filled with grace, the very desires of God. To God she repeats what she wishes along with him, somewhat as a woman likes to tell her husband — and as he likes to hear from her — a cherished thought or a secret wish in her heart. To what extent do these desires affect mankind? *By their own virtue,* they affect mankind intentionally, that is to say in thought, but not really, that is to say not in action. For human wishes, however ardent, do not carry within themselves the principle of their own realization. God alone can accomplish the supernatural wishes Mary has for her children. Does it help any to envisage her intercession in terms of an action in two phases? Just as, for example, Bethsabee is portrayed in the Bible as confiding her request to David and then letting him act (1 Kgs. 1), so Mary would be thought first to pray, then to assist as a spectator at the unfolding of divine power in response to her prayer. But this material and earthly way of thinking ignores the spiritual and heavenly communion implied by the beatific vision. Imagination can hardly be trusted here. It has been shown that Mary's intentions cannot be separated from God's; neither should God's activity and that of Mary be separated. Heaven, in fact, is for Mary what it is for all the elect, but in the highest possible degree: it is a perfect communion, a total interiority with God. So between her and him no kind of dialogue with *successive* replies is to be imagined, as if a ball were being tossed back and forth from one to the other. Just as God's intention inspires and penetrates Mary's intercession from within, so God's power is similarly interior to her. The divine power fulfills all that

---

408–421, and in E. Druwé, "La médiation universelle," *Maria* 1 (1949), pp. 558–559. The two theses proposed center on physical and on moral causality; but there are many different nuances: the causality may be intentional, or dispositive, or instrumental, etc. Helpful remarks are found in M. J. Nicolas, "Essai de synthèse mariale," *Maria* 1 (1949), pp. 739–740, as also in J. Bur, *Médiation mariale,* Paris, Desclée, 1955.

is lacking in the impotence and sterility of human wishes. In this total and reciprocal intimacy Mary's wishes attain their effect not only intentionally but really, for God's power inspires and penetrates her prayer and makes it possible for her desires — which, like all desires, are inchoative actions taking shape — to attain their end. Further precision of the way this interpenetration of divine and human activity occurs is hard to make; evidently it is an interpenetration quite different from what exists in the sacraments. But it seems fitting that a mother should thus affect her children, not only in intention but really, and it would be difficult to explain otherwise the experience of the "presence of Mary" so frequently attested in the lives of Christians.[7]

---

7. On the *"presence" of Mary,* cf. E. Neubert, "L'Union mystique à la Sainte Vierge," *Vie Spirituelle* 50 (1937), 15–29; Gregorio de Jesus Crucificado, "La acción de María en las almas," EstM 11 (1951), pp. 255–278; S. Matellan, *Presencia de María en la experiencia mística,* Madrid, Coculsa, 1962; S. Ragazzini, *Maria vita del anima,* Rome, Desclée, 1960.

The first expressions of this presence are found in the Byzantine homilists: "Just as you dwelt bodily with those of ages past, so you live with us in spirit; the powerful protection with which you cover us is a sign of your presence among us" (St. Germanus of Constantinople, *Sermo 1 in Dormitione* 3, PG 98:344d; cf. *ibid.,* 345a, 345c). "What is there sweeter than the Mother of God? She captivates my mind, she delights my tongue, I picture her to myself day and night" (St. John Damascene, *Sermo 3 in Dormitione* 19, PG 97:752bc).

"Cujus felix memoria sed felicior est praesentia — Sweet is her memory but sweeter her presence" writes an author sometime before the end of the twelfth century, perhaps St. Peter Damian in his *Liber salutatorius,* MS in the Bibliothèque Nationale, new Latin acquisitions # 186, ed. J. Leclercq in *Ephemerides Liturgicae* 72 (1958), 303.

This spiritual phenomenon is frequently met with from St. Bernard's day onward. In the seventeenth century it is found even at Port-Royal in Marie-Claude Arnauld, who calls Mary "the only way by which I am able to hope for God's mercy," immediately adding, "Most of the time I am taken up entirely with her, living only under her shadow" (*Letter to Monsieur Singlin* in *Mémoires pour servir à l'histoire de Port-Royal,* Utrecht, 1942, t. 3, p. 471). The ways of expressing this presence vary greatly: "Mary does not leave me. Although she is not visible, I feel her

"Mediation"[8]

Some astonishment may well be felt that in all this matter no mention has yet been made of "Marian mediation." The fact is that, if the question had not assumed such importance, there would be little need even at this point to speak explicitly of mediation. For the term has a wealth of meanings in tradition and, often equivocally, expresses divers aspects of Mary's mission that have already been treated under other names.

Her mediation was, first of all, the very pure intercession of her prayer before the Annunciation, an already maternal intercession, since, more than Deborah, Mary deserved to be called "mother in Israel" (Jg. 5:7). Indeed, the mediation that Israel had exercised since Abraham in favor of a sinful world (Gen. 18: 17–23) attained its highest efficacy in Mary.

---

presence and protection" (Marie-Colette du Sacré-Coeur (1857–1907), cited by J. J. Navatel, *Soeur Marie-Colette du Sacré-Coeur, religieuse clarisse du monastère de Besançon,* Paris, Gigord, n.d., p. 208). "I do not see her, but I feel her as the horse feels the hand of the rider who leads him" (Venerable Cestac, cited by Bordarrampé, *Le Vénérable L.-E. Cestac,* Paris, Gigord, 1925, p. 458). Essentially what is meant is not a sensible presence, but a presence of the order of faith and charity, a recognition of the role of Mary in the communion of saints.

This presence must be carefully distinguished from the creative presence of God. God makes us exist, he actuates us according to grace. Without his action we should cease to be. Mary's presence works nothing as radical as that. It is in the order of her communion of intention and activity with God in heavenly glory.

8. Vatican II was very discreet on the question of mediation. It insisted on the fact that Christ is the "only Mediator" (*Lumen Gentium* art. 60 and 63), and with respect to Mary it limited itself to justifying the application of the title of "mediatrix" to her, and, at that, justifying it briefly and among other titles: "Therefore the Blessed Virgin is invoked by the Church under the titles of Advocate, Auxiliatrix, Helper, and Mediatrix. These however are to be understood in such a way that they neither take away from nor add anything to the dignity and efficacy of Christ the one Mediator" (*Lumen Gentium* art 62). On the question of mediation in the conciliar text, cf. Laurentin, *La Vierge . . . ,* pp. 115–129.

Next in time, her mediation was the role she fulfilled at the Incarnation. Her holiness was a bridge between the holy God and sinful humanity. Through her the Word was able to enter unsullied into a sullied race. It was then that Mary was mediatrix in the most meaningful sense of the word, a mediatrix between human corruption and divine transcendence, for the Incarnation of the Son of God.

When the Word became man, he became the "one only Mediator" (1 Tim. 2:5). Thereafter Mary's mediation assumes quite another meaning. She no longer prepares Christ's mediation but accompanies it and participates in it from within. And this is so, even when her mediation seems to take on a kind of character all its own, as when she plays the role of bond between Christ and the Church. Undoubtedly during Christ's lifetime the material conditions of earthly existence give her a role that can in a sense be described as mediatorial: it is she who carries Jesus incarnate within her to her cousin Elizabeth and John the Baptist; it is she who hands him over into Simeon's arms. She intercedes at Cana to call Christ's attention to the material fact that the wine has run out. Now, undoubtedly the role that Mary had in all these events still keeps something of the perennial quality proper to the mysteries of Christ's life. But her mediating intervention at these moments was called for by the factual limitations under which Christ lived as a child or as a man, and in the glory of heaven these limitations are all surpassed. Henceforward she is mediatrix less *with respect to* the Mediator than *in* him and *by* him. All the resources she brings to her mediation are first and entirely a gift of the "one only Mediator." And not only that, but her whole situation as an intermediary has now given way to a state of total communion of interiority with regard to Christ. The word "mediation," then, retains only a relative meaning.

In the last analysis, the "universal mediation" of Mary, in the sense prevailing today, is only another name for her universal motherhood with regard to men. And this latter expression has several advantages over the former. It is more concrete and more biblical (Jn. 19:25-27). It is more formally taught by Vatican II.[9] It more clearly expresses the foundation of Mary's role toward men. It avoids collision with the Pauline text on Christ the one Mediator.[10] Perhaps too it says something more to the heart of man. It does seem simple. And yet it too has its complexity. Mary's motherhood with regard to men does not have the same foundation as her motherhood with regard to Christ. For Mary brought Jesus into the world corporally; it is spiritually and by adoption that she became mother of her other children. If, as St. Augustine puts it, she is spiritually "mother of us who are members . . . she is not spiritually the mother of our Head the Savior; spiritually she is born of him." The undeniable unity that exists between these two motherhoods results from the unity of Mary's mission, from the manner in which grace develops in her, from the maternal resources of her feminine heart given over to her double task toward Christ and mankind, and finally from the unity of mankind in Christ.

Queenship

Mary's queenship calls for several remarks in the same direction. Her queenship is only another way of signifying her place in glory near to Christ. In no sense does this queenship make Mary a distant sovereign. Her fulfillment in the life beyond earth does not destroy her humility or poverty, the very fabric of her glory. There is something more:

---

9. *Ibid.*, pp. 151-168. Chapter 8 of *Lumen Gentium* speaks fourteen times of the role of Mary toward men.

10. It is because of this text of 1 Tim. 2:5-6 on the "one Mediator" that Pius XII abstained more and more from using the title "Mediatrix," which does not figure in his most solemn acts and gradually ceases to appear in his addresses. John XXIII and Paul VI constantly avoided use of the term.

Christ's royalty too is woven of poverty and humility. At the time of his triumphal entry on the day of palms, he chooses a donkey for his mount. His reign he established by descending to the depths of human suffering. About his royalty there is nothing in common with the kings of the earth, who are the more conscious of their kingship the more they are raised above their subjects. Christ is the king who *serves* his servants, as he taught in the parable (Lk. 12:37), and as he expressed in act in the washing of feet (Jn. 13:4–16). He calls his subjects to *reign with him,* as St. Paul testifies (2 Tim. 2:12). Certainly it is possible for us to consider Christ our king, since he is our God in his humanity. And we can consider Mary our queen, from the fact of her first place in the kingdom, near the king whose mother and most intimate associate she is. But we are not simply slaves and subjects in face of this king and queen. We are sharers in the same royalty. "I shall not call you servants any more, but friends," Jesus said (Jn. 15:15).

In short, all these titles given to Mary — Mother, mediatrix, queen, etc. — are summed up in the fact of the communion of saints where Mary is nearest to Christ.

Eschatological Image within the Risen Church[11]

A last aspect of Mary's role refers to the future. It has to do with the exemplary and final causality she exercises with regard to the Church taken in its entirety. In the Virgin risen with Christ, the Church advancing toward the parousia already has realized the consummation of its mystery. In this first member, whose precedence still endures, the Church has attained her goal, her rest, and her fulfillment — bodily presence with Christ forever. In defining the dogma of the Assumption, Pius XII wanted to propose to the Church a renewed pledge of hope.

---

11. On this expression cf. *supra,* p. 181, n. 24.

SIXTH STAGE

THE PAROUSIA

At this point the present study could be brought to an end. But it is of the essence of the Christian message to look to the future, toward that fulfillment and consummation of everything which will be brought about by the return of the Lord.

At that hour (already present to the eternal God) the frontiers between the earthly and heavenly worlds will be abolished. The bodily world will be transfigured and God will be all in all. Time too will be at an end for the Church. This fragmentary duration, bound up with the journeying of men toward their salvation, will yield to the utterly simple rhythm of eternity, the rhythm of God summing up all duration and fulfilling every hope. Here Mary's maternal task will come to an end, but her love will remain.

Fundamentally nothing will change for her. It is the Church that will change, and because of this, Mary's situation will be modified.

From the beginning she had preceded the Church at every stage of her life; now the Church will have caught up with her. Between them there will no longer be any differences in the order of place or time. The straining of earth after heaven, of time after eternity, will have been abolished. At the conclusion of the journey they will have been perfectly reunited in that place and time whose measure is God.

Mary, as has been said, was the eschatological image of the

Church. She will no longer have that function, for the end will have been attained and there will no longer be need for any image where all share intrinsically in Christ's resurrection.

Mary, it was also said, was the first personal realization of the lot awaiting all the redeemed. That she will remain, but the distance will have been abolished.

The Church will continue to see Mary in Christ, but in a different way — no longer as its own future and a pledge of its hope, but only as the high point of its communion with Christ. The Church looked on Mary somewhat in the way a storm-tossed fleet sees its lead vessel cross the bar and make port. Now the Church will have rejoined her at the end of the journey. There no longer will be any separation or distance between the two, but rather the shared joy of reunion with Christ and that dialogue which is the overflow of their thanksgiving.

In this communion, of which Christ is both beginning and end, things are as they were at Pentecost: Mary is in the Church as are the others, but beyond this world. In the city where all is light, Mary's grandeur is no longer veiled by any shadow. The hierarchy, which was the visible summit of the Church here below, no longer has any object. The world of *signs* and *means* of grace, for the administration of which the hierarchy was responsible, will have been surpassed; reality alone will remain. The prestige of hierarchy will have given way; the prestige of holiness, at last unveiled, will have burst forth in all its radiance. In the ranks of the faithful, ordered henceforth according to their union with Christ and not their function, the Mother of Christ will have first place, a position incommensurate with the others. She will appear in the pure truth of the situation in which God placed her, at a level of grace and glory higher than that of all others. Between the Redeemer who rules over her from the infinity of his godhead, and the rest of the redeemed whom she envelops with the love of a mother, she will exult in the joy of reunion. Here her *Magnificat* will reach its fulfillment.

CONCLUSION

In the two parts of this study an effort has been made to show how the law of time and progress affects the Church's knowledge of Mary through the centuries and the very destiny of Mary herself. It remains now to grasp the connection between these two developments. In her own personal destiny, Mary goes on in advance of the Church; in its knowledge of Mary, the Church learns how to distinguish itself from her. These two points will now be considered in greater detail.

1. Throughout her destiny the Blessed Virgin has gone on in advance of the Church at each of its stages. Before the Church appeared, she was already holy and immaculate. Before the Church, she was united with Christ, forming a single body with him, a single life and love. Before the Church, she shared Christ's sufferings and cooperated in the Redemption. Finally, before the Church, she was raised to heaven, body and soul, to be with the risen Christ. In harmony with Vatican II, it must be understood that none of these anticipations is foreign to the Church, for in all of them *Mary is already the Church.* It can therefore be said as well that *in Mary* the Church begins to be holy and immaculate, to be incorporated in Christ, to be in communion with his mysteries, and to rise with him. From this point of view Mary appears as the first member of the Church. In her, in

the most perfect way and by anticipation, is realized the deepest and most inalienable essence of the Church, which is communion with Christ.

2. Thus identified with Mary at the start, the Church was gradually to learn to distinguish itself from Mary, somewhat as an infant learns to distinguish its own body from its mother's body, its smile from hers. At the beginning and for several centuries, the figure of Mary and that of the Church remained somewhat indistinct. In many a text and artistic representation of the earliest centuries, it is difficult to decide whether the one or the other is intended, or perhaps both at the same time. Little by little the Church learns, in one and the same process, to know itself more distinctly and to know Mary more distinctly. Then Mary gradually appears as the point where the Church reaches its supreme perfection, its golden age at both the beginning and the end. A golden age at the beginning, when Mary Immaculate was by herself the Church, welcoming Christ on earth; a golden age at the end, in that glorification of body and soul toward which the Church Militant moves, and which the Virgin has already attained. The farther the Church advances from its first golden age and the nearer it draws to the final golden age which will be the parousia, the more it discovers the mystery of Mary — a mystery that at the Church's origin appears as perfection in holiness, and in the Church's future as perfection in glory. The more the Church experiences its own limitations and imperfections, its own distressful condition, the more it recognizes in Mary its ideal and model, honoring her as the image and pattern of its own fulfillment and discovering the value of her daily assistance.

Mary and the Church are paradoxically related: fundamentally they are identified with each other, and yet each one includes the other. At the beginning the Church is in Mary as a plant is in the seed; at that time Mary's faith and union with Christ contain all the perfection that will come to be in the Church. But later Mary is found included within the structures of the visible Church and in humble dependence on the hierarchy.

Thus Vatican II was able to say of Mary that she is both member and at the same time type and mother with regard to the Church. The key to this complex relationship and dialectic is the role of Mary at the Incarnation and her mission as Mother of God. It is in the accomplishment of this primordial mission that Mary goes on ahead of the Church — in the presence of Christ the child, in the presence of the dying Christ, in the presence of Christ in glory.

APPENDIX # 1

THE VIRGIN MARY IN THE OLD TESTAMENT

The question of Mary in the Old Testament is in a state of total revision. The demands of scientific exegesis have brought about a break with the extreme ease with which this domain was previously handled.

Two extreme positions may serve as a starting-point. On the one hand is the pseudo-Bernard, a mystical author of the twelfth century who writes, "All Scripture concerns Mary."[1] On the other is the science of literal exegesis which more or less embraces the contrary opinion that the Old Testament says nothing about Mary.[2]

This confrontation leads to the key of the whole problem. A solution will depend on the philosophical and theological presuppositions adopted.

For an exegete lacking faith, the question would not even have any sense. If by chance his mind lingered over it, he could at most admit that Mary of Nazareth came from the people of Israel. To belong to this race and cultural environment, he might consider, would "prepare" her, though the

---
1. *Sermon 3 on the Salve Regina,* PL 184:1069.
2. In works of scientific exegesis, Catholic or not, most often there is hardly any question of Mary, except with reference to Gen. 3:15, Is. 7:17, and Mich. 5:102.

word would not be meant to signify any intended preparation.

The question takes on meaning in function of the following two principles, which are of the domain of faith:

1. God is the author of the religious history of Israel, guiding it toward a goal and giving it a meaning.
2. God is more precisely the author of the inspired Scriptures, oriented in their diversity toward the same goal, namely Christ the Savior and the salvation he brings to mankind.

In this perspective, the historical events of salvation *morally* and *typically* prepare the Virgin, Mother of the Messiah. They are sketches of her, or, if preferred, figures of her. Within this ensemble of meaning the explicit *prophecies* take on sense.

The difficulty of applying these principles consists in this: these *moral, typical,* and *prophetic* preparations do not generally unlock their meaning before the accomplishment of the event. They are too vague, too fragmentary, too indecisive. A prophecy of the Old Testament becomes clear only after the event, in the light of the New Testament. Vatican II explicitly recognized this, and precisely in its chapter on the Virgin Mary. If the texts of the Old Testament throw some light on Mary, they do so retrospectively, "as they are read in the Church and are understood in the light of a further and full revelation" (*Lumen Gentium,* 55). The prophecies are only sketches, as if in a darkened theatre — at least so might one paraphrase that other expression in the same article of *Lumen Gentium:* "She is prophetically foreshadowed" *(prophetice adumbratur).*

Here we are dealing with the mystery of time and movement, which takes its meaning only from its term. An unfinished sentence remains an enigma; it delivers its meaning only once the last word, which is its key, has been reached. Thus the Old Testament delivers its meaning in function of Christ the Savior who fulfills it.

What is true of Christ must be extended secondarily and correlatively to Mary and to the Church, for they intimately form part of the salvation realized by Christ. In this perspective Mary is seen to be envisaged in three ways by the Old Testament.

1. Moral Preparation

From among mankind disgraced by sin, God untangles a line of faith and holiness at the end of which his Son will be able to be born into the human race without the contamination of sin. The last stage of this progress is found in the privileged circle of the "poor of Israel." Mary explicitly places herself in this group in the Magnificat (Lk. 1:48, 52). This theme, already studied above, was taken up by the Council: "Mary stands out among the poor and humble of the Lord, who confidently await and receive salvation from Him" (*Lumen Gentium,* 55).

2. Typological Preparation

God's plan for the world works toward accomplishment according to the slow cadence of human duration, slowed down the more by the inertia of sin. God does not bring perfection to be all at once, but gradually. At each stage of the plan of salvation — Israel, the Church, heaven — one can discern the sketch and prefiguration of the perfect forms that will be reached at the end. At each stage in the development of an embryo the imperfect forms of the organs on their way to full formation can be detected. There is no more delicate task than to appreciate these developmental relationships. In the final analysis, only Scripture and Tradition can authentically discern typological equivalents.

In what concerns Mary, the types are found principally in three lines:

1. First there are the women of the Old Testament, notably those who were favored with miraculous births, those who were ancestors of the Messiah, those who contributed to the triumph and salvation of Israel. By taking up in connection with Mary the words that concerned Sarah, "Nothing is impossible with God," (Gen. 18:14 and Lk. 1:37), or Judith (Jud. 13:18–19 and Lk. 1:42), Luke gave the first guidelines for this typology.

2. But Luke compares Mary especially to Israel in its ensemble. He identifies her with the Daughter of Zion according to Zeph. 3:14–17, an identification that is found again in substance in John 19:25-27 and in the twelfth chapter of the Apocalypse. This theme has been studied above. Vatican II took it up thus: "With her, the Daughter of Zion par excellence, after a long expectation of the promise, the times were at length fulfilled and the new dispensation established" (*Lumen Gentium,* 55).

3. Finally, the Daughter of Zion was the place where Yahweh rested. Thus Luke glimpsed in Mary the new Ark of the Covenant, the eschatological resting-place of Yahweh Savior. In this comparison he opened the way to a typology involving sacred objects. Later this typology will be exploited more and more, until in Byzantine usage it reaches such excess as no longer to command adherence. "Ark of the Covenant" and "Temple" are the fundamental figures in this line.[3]

3. Prophetic Preparation

Mary was prefigured not only by *realities* corresponding to her in nature or function, but also by *words that announced her* in advance. This brings us to the most delicate of issues, and here, while awaiting the further progress of

---

3. Cf. *supra,* pp. 24 ff and Laurentin, *Luc 1–2,* pp. 151, 159–161.

exegesis, prudence is the indicated course. The difficulty is that allusions are involved which contemporaries understood from the merest hints given, while these meanings in between the lines escape us today. If, as is fitting, one forbids himself recourse to accommodated senses or misinterpretations, often the only other course may be to reinterpret a text, or to consider it an example of moral or typological allusion, or even, in the case of texts of which Mariology has made abusive use, to eliminate them.

At any rate, the texts are few in number that fit the description of "direct prophecy" or "oracle" formally designating Mary. Even for those, the oracle seems to remain involved with a typology from which it emerges only in a confused light, very difficult to determine.

In the light of these reservations, then, and of the progress still awaited on several of these questions, two series of texts merit attention: (a) Eschatological texts whose meaning applies to Mary and at the same time to the Church; (b) Texts that apply to the Mother of the Messiah.

a. Eschatological Texts Applying Both to Mary and to the Church

It has been shown earlier in what sense texts like the Song of Songs, 4:7 and Jeremiah 31:22 (duly purged of the classical mistranslation) should be retained (pp. 94–95): The Virgin Mary brings to realization personally and perfectly what is realized collectively and not without admixture in the ensemble of the Church.

Thus it is in Mary that the perfect "conversion" of Israel to God announced in Jeremiah 31:22 is realized.

It is in her also, the immaculate Daughter of Zion, that the word of Yahweh-King to his people is realized, "You are wholly beautiful, my love, and without a blemish" (Song 4:7).

As to oracular words whose scope is intentionally eschatological, there is prophecy in the sense that these words find in Mary's person their most precise fulfillment. But this aim remains tied up with typology, since the texts pass from Israel (the object of the most obvious sense of oracles) to Mary, and finally to the Church, where the prophecy is realized collectively in the light of Mary's presence in the Church.

Zephaniah 3:14 is to be listed in the same typological-prophetical category. Here a whole domain opens up for explanation. Vatican II encouraged entering it and carefully refrained from tracing frontiers out in advance.

b. Texts Relative to the Mother of the Messiah

Finally, three texts from Genesis, Isaiah, and Micah seem more or less formally to concern the Mother of the Messiah.

(1) Genesis 3:15 — The Posterity of the Woman, Enemy of the Serpent

After the original fall, God cursed the serpent in these terms: "I will make you enemies of each other: you and the woman, your offspring and her offspring. It will attack your head and you will attack its heel." This text is full of meaning. It signifies on the whole, without referring to the outcome, the struggle which will go on until the end of time between mankind and the devil. The Vulgate interprets the text in the light of further revelation, and in a twofold way goes beyond the inspired text in translating. "*She* (the woman) *will crush* your head." In the Hebrew, it is the *offspring* of the woman that will be struggling with the offspring of the serpent. Moreover, the *same* Hebrew verb *(shuph)* is used to indicate the attack made by each of the parties on the other. The precise meaning of this rare verb (used only in Ps. 139:11 and Job 9:17) remains hard to establish. At any rate, it is not said explicitly that either one of the two will crush the other. This outcome cannot strictly be deduced either from the respective positions of "head" and "heel," even though the position of head under heel is inferior and humiliating. Genesis 49:17 forbids drawing any argument based on relative position. In fact, this later verse of Genesis, which belongs to the same "J" (Yahwist) document, exalts the insidious position of the serpent as a title of glory and triumph. Jacob eulogizes the serpent in speaking of the seventh tribe of Israel: "Dan is a *serpent*... that bites the horse's *heels,* so that his rider falls backward." (The Oxford Bible translates "heels," the Jerusalem Bible "hock," the New American Bible "heel.")

Thus the serpent's bite is a dangerous thing, and the Fathers rightly understood it in this sense. (R. Laurentin, *L'interprétation de Gen. 3:15 dans la tradition,* EM 12, (1954), pp. 79–156).

But Genesis 3:15 has also a positive sense. In the entire passage God is giving mankind the advantage. He leaves man standing, but puts the serpent on the ground (3:14); he punishes man but does not curse him; he even remains in dialogue with him (3:8–18) and shows him a fatherly solicitude, giving the two guilty persons skin tunics with which he clothes them himself (3:21). On the contrary, he curses the serpent without giving him a hearing (3:14), and it is within this whole context that the curse of Genesis 3:15 is pronounced against the tempter.

And there is something more. In the perspective of the inspired author, in the very perspective of the "J" (Yahwist) document that he uses, Genesis 3:15 seems to imply a first sketch of the messianic hints given in Genesis 49:10 ("To him the peoples shall render obedience") and Numbers 24:17 ("A star from Jacob takes the leadership"). The messianic intention was perceptible before the coming of Christ, since the Septuagint translation understood the offspring of the woman in the sense of *one single mysterious descendant:* "He shall watch your head." Later the Pauline interpretation will also understand "offspring" in the sense of "one descendant" who is the Messiah (Gal. 3:16).[4]

The following conclusions, then, seem warranted: Exegetical probity demands that we renounce making interpretations that theologically are very appealing. The inspired text does not contain any explicit affirmation of a *complete* victory without combat, a victory whose description would be realized only in the Immaculate Conception. There is only an opening out onto a hope of victory, and an obscure hint of this distant victory. Nor would it be correct to deduce from the expression *semen mulieris* ("seed of the woman") that there is formal question of a virginal motherhood, since this expression is also used with regard to women who are not virgins (Gen. 16:10; 24:60).

In what sense does Genesis 3:15 concern Mary? First she is objectively included in the offspring of Eve, among the participants in this struggle with the serpent. Then, the emphasis placed on the woman and her motherhood and the messianic hints in the text give reason to think that the author was more especially envisaging in this universal struggle the messianic descendant and the woman who was to be his mother. Finally, it is in Mary that in the full sense this "enmity" between the woman and the serpent is realized. These different observations receive additional strength from being implied also in the Eve-Mary typology.

---

4. The original text offered a positive opening in the direction of this interpretation. Grammatically it would have been more regular to put into the plural the pronoun that represented the posterity (Gen. 15:13; 17:8–9). The use of the singular could thus set the stage for understanding posterity in the sense of one single person. But this opening must not be exaggerated, for the use of the singular is not exceptional (Gen. 16:10; 17:17; 24:60).

(2) Isaiah 7:14 — The Maiden, Mother of Emmanuel

Briefly the circumstances of the oracle of Isaiah 7:14 are the following. Syrian troops were marching on Jerusalem. King Ahaz was under the threat of being replaced by the "sons of Tabeel" (Is. 7:6). The Davidic dynasty was in danger. In this critical situation the people consulted necromancers, and King Ahaz immolated his son, "the heir of David," to false gods and put his hope in political alliances that were compromising for the purity of Yahwism (2 Kgs. 16). Isaiah the prophet reminded him that in Yahweh lay salvation, "If you do not believe, you will not stand at all" (Is. 7:9b). In Yahweh's name he proposed a sign to Ahaz, leaving him free to select it. Ahaz refused any sign — it would have obliged him to change his plans — under the hypocritical pretext that he did not wish to "tempt God." Isaiah reproached him in energetic terms, adding, "The Lord himself, therefore, will give you a sign. It is this: the maiden is with child and will soon give birth to a son, whom she will call Emmanuel."

This is not an easy text to interpret. According to the views of Mowinckel, Hammershaimb, and Ringgren, taken up again and retouched in a Catholic perspective by Cazelles,[5] there seems to be question of a dynastic sign, the birth of an heir in the line promised to David according to 2 Samuel 7:14. But is the reference to a son of Ahaz, who would be Hezekiah, or to the last one of David's line, the Messiah? Both answers are given, each depending on a different series of indications.

Certain indications of the later context suggest that the

---

5. H. Cazelles, "La Mère du Roi-Messie dans l'Ancien Testament," *Maria et Ecclesia* 5 (1959), pp. 39–56. A bibliography appears on p. 51, n. 46. Also noteworthy: A. Hammershaimb, "The Immanuel Sign," *Studia theologica* III, 2 (1949), 124–142, and J. Coppens, "La prophétie de l'Almah," ETL 28 (1953), 648–673, who is of the opinion that this is a direct prophecy that has no other object than the eschatological Messiah.

sign is very near in time: "Before this child knows how to refuse evil and choose good" — that is, before he has attained the age of reason — "the land whose two kings terrify you will be deserted" (7:16).

On the other hand, the solemnity of the oracle, its very marked eschatological coloring, the transcendent relief into which Emmanuel is brought in Isaiah 9:1–5 and 11:1–9 forbid holding simply to the immediate future.

Taking account of the prophetic mentality and of the eastern mind, which hardly cares about the univocal meaning so dear to the western mind and delights, on the contrary, in toying with a certain polyvalence of meanings, there simply is no room to choose one or the other of the two solutions cited above. The text, like many another prophetic text or like passages of Paul Claudel in our own day, intentionally has a double aim.

In its proximate aim, the one most evident to contemporaries, the sign seems to be the birth of Hezekiah. This birth was a pledge of the future for the dynasty that was threatened by enemy plots as well as by the sacrifice offered to false gods by the preceding heir.

But this immediate realization was far from exhausting the content of the oracle. The sequel of events clearly showed this. In many a regard Hezekiah's career was a disappointment. He failed in his reform. Exile followed. Hence the readers of Isaiah 7:14 found themselves ready to look for the realization of the promise in a more distant future.

Is the Septuagint version (second century B.C.) a witness of the revaluation of the text in an eschatological and messianic sense? This has been maintained on the basis of the following two indications:

1. In the Septuagint the Hebrew *almah* (maiden) is translated by the Greek *parthenos* (virgin), which thus specifies a virginal conception.
2. The present participle becomes a future verb: "The virgin *will* conceive and *will* give birth."

Again, exegetical probity will not permit one to build a case on these indications, for two reasons:

1. The word *parthenos* in the Septuagint has a very wide meaning: in Genesis 34:3 it is used to designate Dinah, who had just been raped.
2. According to the best attested Hebrew text, it is the maiden that gives a name to the child: "She will give him the name Emmanuel." And this is an indication in the direction of virginity, since this function normally fell to the father. But in the Septuagint it is Ahaz himself who accomplishes this task: "*You* will give him the name Emmanuel." Thus this interpretation moves away from both the idea of a virginal conception and the eschatological sense.

Finally, the messianic sense invoked by Matthew 1:23 in citing Isaiah does not seem to have any precedent in Jewish tradition. This is a disappointing observation as far as the literal prophetic sense of Isaiah 7:14 is concerned. But it has a positive interest as far as the historicity of the virginal conception is concerned. Matthew affirms the virginal conception because it is a fact, not because any preexisting tradition obliged him to demonstrate that the Messiah had been conceived virginally.

For all these reasons Vatican II mentioned the prophecy of Isaiah 7:14 only with the cautious indication "cf." and with the implication that it is read in the light of Mt. 1:22–23, given in the same set of references (*Lumen Gentium,* 55). Like Genesis 3:15, this text is only a sketch still obscure *(prophetice adumbratur).*

(3) Micah 5:1–4 — "She Who Is to Give Birth"

"But you, (Bethlehem) Ephrathah, the least of the clans of Judah, out of *you* will be *born for me the one who is to rule over Israel; his origin goes back to the distant past, to the days of old.* Yahweh is therefore going to abandon them *till the time when she who is to give birth gives birth.* Then the remnant of his brothers will come back to the sons of Israel. He will stand and feed his flock with the power of Yahweh. . . . He will himself be peace."

This text is patently of the same time as the preceding. It is related thereto: "She who is to give birth" is the "maiden" of Isaiah 7:14. There is no hint in Micah of a virginal birth. But the dynamic scope of the oracle is more sharply brought out. A shepherd-king, descended from David's clan, is in the forefront. His birth is clearly foretold for the future, and yet "his origin goes back to the distant past, to the days of old. . . . He will feed his flock with the power of Yahweh, with the majesty of the name of his God. . . . He himself will be peace."

4. The Background of These Three Prophecies

A study of the background of these three texts will bring significant enlightenment.

Queen mothers had an important position in eastern courts and especially in Israel. Their names have been preserved with care in the Books of Kings (1 Kgs. 14:21; 15:2, 10: 22:42; cf. 53; 2 Kgs. 9:6; 12:2; 14:2; 15:2, 33; 18:2; 22:1; 23:31, 36; 24:18). They bore the title *gebirah* and were found closely associated in the honor and position of the monarch (Jer. 13:18; 22:6). It is important to note that it was not the position of the *wife* of the king that counted, but that of the king's *mother.* Very significant in this regard is the comparison between 1 Kings 1:16, 31 and 2:19, where Bethsabee prostrates herself before King David, her husband, whereas Solomon, her son, after he has become king, prostrates himself before her and makes her sit at his right hand.

The prophetic texts studied above therefore glimpse Mary essentially as the queen mother of the eschatological king, involved as such in the honor paid his reign. Thus the Old Testament brings the positive contribution of a source to the doctrine of Mary's queenship.

In this framework two other observations emerge from the Old Testament:

1. Oriental civilizations gave their kings divine honors. It was thus a temptation for the kings of Israel to claim such a prerogative. This was forbidden in the religion of Yahweh, but the Holy Spirit left a way open on one point. The last descendant promised to David, to the exclusion of all the rest, would in reality accede to this transcendence that other kings claimed only in empty pretense. Ever since Nathan's oracle the promised heir appeared as a son of God, and this vague filiation gradually assumes transcendental dimensions in the Bible (Ps. 2:7 and 110:3). Certain authors go so far as to give to this son of David (Is. 9:5; Ps. 45:7) the title of "God." In the framework of the ideas developed above, one can glimpse the grandeur that accrued to the mother of such a king.

2. Perhaps there is something more. The three texts studied are in different degrees rather negligent regarding the role of the father, but they bring into relief the mother and her relationship with Yahweh. In Genesis 3:15 God speaks of the offspring of the woman; the man is not even taken into consideration, and if he plays a role in Genesis 4:1 and 25, Eve nonetheless attributes the generation to God: "I have acquired a man with the help of *Yahweh*" and "God has granted me other offspring." Ahaz is similarly left in the background in Isaiah 7:14.

In this connection should the group of texts be considered again in the light of the extra-biblical milieu? The question surely arises. There is, materially speaking, a remarkable similarity between Isaiah 7:14 and this text of Ras Shamra, ten centuries older: "Behold, a maiden has given birth to a son" (*Poem of Nikkal,* line 7, in G.R. Driver, *Canaanite Myths,* Edinburgh, 1956). The maiden seems to be a mother goddess. She is described as a virgin. In Egypt certain pharaohs were thought to have been born of the union of their mothers with a god.[6] It should not be ruled out that suggestions of this kind may have served as ferment to thought and as a point of departure from which to rise to the revelation of a virginal birth that was to take place by the power of the Most High. If such a tendency actually occurred, it would not be an isolated case. The comparison between the Babylonian account of a deluge and the corresponding account in Genesis 6-8, and much more precisely, between the psalm to the sun and Psalm 104 would suggest that the Bible owes something to the surrounding cultural milieu. The progress of revelation in the Old Testament took place in part thanks to reflection on data absorbed from the extra-biblical environment.

Yet it is not, for all that, simply a matter of syncretism. Quite the contrary, the inspired authors borrowed nothing without first giving it close consideration and transforming it. Between the trappings that surround the Babylonian deluge and those of the Biblical deluge, there is nothing in common. In the former, the "gods" unleash the deluge for sordid motives. It then escapes their control, as if they were amateur sorcerers. Yahweh, on the contrary, for motives of a moral order decides on a deluge of which he remains the master. In the Egyptian hymn to the sun, the sun is God; in the corresponding Biblical psalm, the sun is a star like any other, created by God (104:19, referring to Gen. 1:16). In short, where there is a borrowing, the biblical author profoundly transforms the data he uses in the objective light of Yahwism and in the inner light that the Spirit grants him. Suggestions borrowed from an extra-biblical environment are purified, refocused, reshaped, enriched by the transforming contact with revelation already received. Like a clay to be given a new shape, the Spirit takes up the cultural heritage

---

6. These biblical data have been gathered in Cazelles, *loc. cit.*

of the author he inspires. Thus the original material of reflection is less important than the work spent on it. And the end result reveals more about the Holy Spirit than it does about the cultural element used, just as a statue reveals more about the way the sculptor works than about the material he has used.

In the case at point here, the extra-biblical milieu has contributed impressive suggestions. They included the idea of a God-King; the Holy Spirit, it has been seen, caused this idea to be laid aside for the while, but made of it the valid object of an eschatological hope, hope for the Incarnation. The related idea of a royal birth too was included, in which God would substitute for the father. Yahweh's transcendence definitely excluded any of the carnal compromise characteristic of Egyptian gods; only a virginal birth could be envisaged in this direction. On this point the Holy Spirit permitted rays of light to play discreetly.

Whatever the hypothesis, Genesis 3:15, Isaiah 7:14 and Micah 5:1–2 all in varying degrees bring into striking relief a "maiden," a "queen," "one who was to give birth" in eschatological times to this "son of David," who mysteriously would be Son of God (2 Sam. 7:14; Ps. 2 and 110).[7]

---

7. The present version of Appendix # 1 is, apart from a few updatings, conformable to that of the previous edition. It had already taken a position in harmony with the orientations given by Vatican II in *Lumen Gentium* art. 55:

"... The books of the Old Testament recount the period of salvation history during which the coming of Christ into the world was slowly prepared for. These earliest documents, as they are read in the Church and understood in the light of a further and full revelation, bring the figure of the woman, Mother of the Redeemer, into a gradually sharper focus. When looked at in this way, she is already prophetically foreshadowed in that victory over the serpent which was promised to our first parents after their fall into sin (cf. Gen. 3:15). Likewise she is the Virgin who is to conceive and bear a son, whose name will be called Emmanuel (cf. Is. 7:14; Mich. 5:2–3; Mt.

* * *

5. A Note on Mary and Wisdom

Where should the classical comparison of Mary to Wisdom be situated? Apparently it is neither prophecy nor typology. Wisdom is, in truth, a hypostasis of God — the Word, the second Person of the Trinity. Its application to Mary seems therefore to be an accommodation. It cannot so be used without restriction. Mary is a creature and not a divine hypostasis; she has no real preexistence.

The liturgy has popularized the comparison of Mary to Wisdom. It is enlightening to learn how this came about.

Sirach 24:3–21, *"In omnibus requiem quaesivi,"* was first used as a supplementary epistle reading for the feast of Ss. Agnes and Agatha, virgins and martyrs. Its use is attested from the beginning of the seventh century, in the Würzburg *Comes* (edited by G. Morin in *Rev. Bén.* 25, 1910, pp. 41–74). When the feast of the Assumption was established at Rome in the middle of the seventh century this same reading was assigned to it.

Proverbs 8:22–35, *"Dominus possedit me,"* became the epistle reading for the feast of the Nativity of Mary in the tenth century. Thus in this case there is no extension to the Virgin Mary of a text already in use for virgins. The idea, it seems, was to recall how the one whose birthday was being celebrated had her origins in God's own thought.

1:22–23). She stands out among the poor and humble of the Lord, who confidently await and receive salvation from him. With her, the exalted Daughter of Zion, after a long expectation of the promise, the times were at length fulfilled and the new dispensation established. All this occurred when the Son of God took a human nature from her, that he might in the mysteries of his flesh free man from sin."

The developments of this theme in Bulgakov's works are well known. Louis Bouyer in *Seat of Wisdom* (Paris, Cerf, 1957; ET: New York, Pantheon, 1962) judiciously takes up the best in this direction. E. Catta has a very well documented study on the theme entitled *"Sedes Sapientiae"* in *Maria,* volume 7, pp. 688–866.

APPENDIX # 2

MARY'S DECISION OF VIRGINITY

In a way that is all the more striking because it is oblique, many Protestant and rationalist authors bear witness to the opinion that Luke 1:34 expresses a decision of virginity on Mary's part: they *eliminate* verse 34 as foreign to the primitive text, precisely because this decision of virginity appears to them incompatible with 1:26 where Mary is presented as engaged or married. Cf., for example, A. Harnack in an article in *Zeitschrift für neutestamentliche Wissenschaft* 2 (1901), pp. 53–57, and H. Sahlin, *Das Messias,* Uppsala, 1945. These rationalists therefore confirm the traditional opinion.

Some authors — "even Catholics," as might be said — have tried to sidestep this traditional interpretation in three ways:

1. For some of them, Mary understands that conception is imminent and answers, "How is that to be, since *at this precise moment* when you are speaking to me, I do not know man in the biblical sense of the word, in other words, I am not accomplishing the act necessary for procreation?" This explanation enjoys the patronage of Cajetan. (It is supported by D. Haugg, cited at the end of this appendix, and H. Féret, "Messianisme et Annonciation," *Prêtre et apôtre* 29 (1947), 37–38.) But it is much more plausible to recognize the pre-

sent tense "I do not know" as having to do with a condition rather than an instant of time. To give an example, if someone to whom a cigarette is offered replies, "I don't smoke," he is understood to mean "I never smoke" and not "I am not smoking right now."

2. For others, Mary would understand that, according to the message of the angel, the conception has already taken place, as in the announcement made to Hagar according to Gen. 16:11, "Now you have conceived" (Haugg, *op. cit.*, 56–59; Sahlin, *op. cit.*, pp. 104–113). But in Lk. 1:31 the angel clearly says "You will conceive" in the *future* tense.

3. According to J. P. Audet, "L'Annonce faite à Marie," RB 63 (1956), 365–372, the text would be announcing not a decision of virginity but, on the contrary, a decision of marriage. Knowing from Is. 7:14 that the Mother of the Messiah was to be a virgin, Mary would be asking the angel, "How will that be, *since then* (i.e., in order to be mother of the Messiah) I *ought not to know man,* whereas in fact I am promised to Joseph?" D'Audet's demonstration is brilliant and ingenious: he translates *epei* (normally "since") as "since then," invoking the connotation of the word in 1 Cor. 5:10, 7:14, 15:29, Heb. 9:26, 10:2; and *ou gignōskō* (normally "I do not know") he translates "I ought not to know." But this interpretation runs up against a double difficulty: (a) It stretches the limits of grammar too much; (b) It introduces outside presuppositions into the data of the text.

In all three approaches, the motive of the authors is that a decision of virginity would be an anachronism. But the practice of virginity had found favor among the Essenes, who were contemporaries of Mary, and we find it spread abroad very much from the first Christian generation on. Finally, Mary was spiritually well placed to be in the avant-garde of this discovery. Cf. Laurentin, *Luc 1–2,* pp. 175–189.

Bibliograpy: D. Haugg, *Das erste biblische Marienwort,* Stuttgart, 1938, (where the second interpretation given above is adopted). F. Ceuppens, *De mariologia biblica,* Rome,

1948, pp. 73–78. R. Laurentin, *Structure et théologie de Luc 1–2*, Paris, Gabalda, 1957, pp. 175–178. Recent well-documented studies on Mary's *vow* of virginity include D. Brodman, "Mariens Jungfraülichkeit nach Lk 1:34 in der Auseinandersetzung von heute," *Antonianum* 30 (1955), 27–44 (exegetical viewpoint), B. Leurent, "Critiques et mystiques devant le voeu de virginité," *Revue d'ascétique et mystique* 31 (1955), 225–248 (overall study with an investigation of traditional data), and J. F. Craghan, *Mary, the Virginal Wife and the Married Virgin: The Problematic of Mary's Vow of Virginity*, Rome, Gregorian, 1967.

APPENDIX #3

PARALLELS OF THE MAGNIFICAT WITH THE OLD TESTAMENT

Magnificat (Lk. 1:46–55)	*Old Testament* (according to the Greek version of the Septuagint)
46. *My soul* proclaims the greatness of the Lord,	*My soul* glories in the *Lord.* Ps. 34 (33):3
47. and my spirit *exults* in *God my savior;*	I *exult* in *God my savior.* Hab. 3:18 Cf. Canticle of Anna, Sam. 2:1
48. because he has *taken notice of the lowliness of his handmaid.* Yes, henceforth all generations *will call* me *blessed.*	*Take notice of the lowliness of your servant.* 1 Sam. 1:11 All the nations *will call* you *blessed,* land of Israel. Mal 3:12; cf. Gn. 30:13

Magnificat (Lk. 1:46–55)	*Old Testament* (according to the Greek version of the Septuagint)
49. For the Almighty *has done great things* for me. *Holy is his name.*	He *has done* great things for you (=Israel). Dt. 10:21 *Holy is his name.* Ps. 111 (112):9; cf. 1 Sam. 2:2
50. And his *mercy* reaches *from age to age for those who fear him.*	The *mercy* of the Lord (reaches) *from age to age for those who fear him.* Ps. 102 (103):17
51. He has shown the *power* of his *arm,* he has *routed* the *proud* of heart.	You will crush ... the *proud* man and with your *powerful arm* you will *put to rout* your enemies. Ps. 88 (89):11
52. He has *pulled down* the *princes* from their *thrones* and exalted the *lowly.*	The Lord *pulls down* the *thrones* of *princes* ... and establishes the *lowly* in their place. Eccles. 10:14–15; cf. 1 Sam. 2:6–8.
53. The *hungry* he has *filled* with *good things,* the *rich* sent empty away.	The *hungry* soul he has *filled* with *good things.* Ps. 106 (107):9 The *rich* are hungry and beg. Ps. 33 (34):11; cf. 1 Sam. 2:5.

	Magnificat (Lk. 1:46–55)	*Old Testament* (according to the Greek version of the Septuagint)
54.	He has *come to the help* of *Israel* his *servant*, *mindful* of his *mercy*—	You, *Israel*, my *servant* whom I have *helped*. Is 41:8, 10 He *remembered* his *mercy*. Ps. 97 (98):3
55.	according to the *promise* he made to our *ancestors*— of his mercy to *Abraham* and to his *descendants forever*.	as you *promised* our *fathers*, you will give mercy to *Abraham*, Mi. 7:20 to the *descendants* of *Abraham forever*. 2 Ch. 20; cf. 1 Sam. 2:10

The general motif of the Magnificat is inspired by that of the canticle of Anna for the birth of Samuel (1 Sam. 2:1–10): same occasion, same theological theme (reversal of the lot of rich and poor), many common terms. Nevertheless for most of the verses closer literal parallels can be found elsewhere in the Bible. The passages parallel to Lk. 2:48 and 49 are in the line of the identification of Mary with Israel suggested by other passages in Chapters 1 and 2 of Luke.

APPENDIX # 4

THE ORIGINS OF THE TITLE *THEOTOKOS*

From a study presently being made on the origins of the title *Theotokos* it is possible to draw the following conclusions:

1. The numerous witnesses of the title *Theotokos* given as prior to the second half of the fourth century are all unauthentic or suspect. Such are Hippolytus and Origen, in particular.

Hippolytus of Rome (d. 235) is cited for two texts: *Blessings of Jacob,* (according to the Greek text published in TUU 38a, p. 13, line 7): "Joseph . . . , engaged to Mary, becomes the witness of the Mother of God"; and *In Canticum* 4, 16, (according to the Syriac version published by G. Bonwetsch, GCS 1 (Hippolytus 1a), p. 359, line 9). H. Rahner, "Hippolyt von Rom als Zeuge für den Ausdruck *Theotokos,*" ZKT 59 (1935), 73–81, tried to uphold the authenticity of these texts. The publication of the Armenian version of the *Blessings* by L. Mariés, Paris, 1935, confirmed that the word *Theotokos* was an interpolation. Cf. B. Reynders in *Bulletin de théologie ancienne et médiévale* 2 (1933/1936), 601–602; J. Lebreton in RSR 26 (1936), 204; G. Jouassard in *Maria* 1 (1949), p. 86, n. 2.

Origen (d. 253/255) is cited for three texts: (a) The lost commentary *In Ep. ad Rom.*, tome 1, according to the witness of Socrates, *Church History* 7, 32, PG 67:812ab. (b) *In Lucam:* The word *Theotokos* is found in numerous fragments transmitted by the Greek catenae, but none is confirmed by St. Jerome's Latin translation of this work. Thus *Homily 6,* GCS 35 (origen 9), p. 44, fragment 10, is in fact a fragment of a text of Eusebius, PG 23:1341d–1344a; *Homily 7, loc. cit.,* p. 279, fragment 101, is suspect; fifteen other variants attested to by different catenae on Luke give evidence of the ease with which the title *Theotokos,* once it had become popular, was introduced into older texts. (c) *Selecta in Deuteron.,* PG 12:813c, is inauthentic according to R. Devreesse, "Anciens commentaires grecs de l'Octateuque," RB 44 (1935), 178, n. 10.

Likewise unauthentic, interpolated, or suspect are the witnesses of *Theotokos* attributed to Dionysius of Alexandria (d. 264) in *Ep. ad Paulum Samosat.,* which is actually a work of the fourth century, to Pierius of Alexandria (d. 290), to Peter of Alexandria (d. 311), to the emperor Constantine, to John Chrysostom, etc. The multitude of texts that exhibit such unreliability is explained by the fervor of copyists and the heat of polemic.

2. The first rigorously certain witness of the title is Alexander of Alexandria in 325, *Ep. ad Alexandrum Constantinopolitum* 12, transmitted by Theodoret, *Church History* 1, 3, PG 82:908a, published in part in PG 18:568c and in H. G. Opitz, *Athanasius Werke* III, 1, p. 28, 14–19: ". . . Our Lord Jesus Christ bore truly, and not just in appearance, a body (taken) from Mary the *Theotokos.* . . . "

It still remains possible, despite the objection of O. Stegmüller, "Sub tuum praesidium," ZKT 74 (1952), 76–82, that the *Sub tuum* is earlier than Alexander. (Its text is attested by Papyrus 470 of the John Rylands Library: "Under your protection we fly to you, O *Theotokos* . . ."). It is not excluded that the prayer may date from the end of the third century (cf. "Sub tuum," *Enciclopedia Cattolica* 11:1468–1469, where a photographic reproduction of the papyrus appears, on which it can be seen that the word *Theotokos* subsists, marvelously preserved, on a fragment shredded on all sides).

It is not excluded either that one or the other of the witnesses mentioned above as inauthentic or suspect might actually turn out to be earlier than Alexander. It is plausible that he did not coin the expression but rather was echoing a usage already received in his day.

At any rate, the title has no revolutionary ring about it. Scripture had hinted at it meaningfully. St. Luke in particular calls Mary "the Mother of the Lord" (1:43) — in the transcendent sense of "Lord," it seems (Lk. 2:12) — and the Fathers from the second century on had explicitly said that the Son of Mary was God.

3. From the second quarter of the fourth century on, witnesses suddenly multiply, so that by the end of this century the title is universally spread abroad. It is found especially among the Alexandrians: Athanasius (d. 373) and diverse pseudo-Athanasian writings, Serapion of Thmuis (before 359), Didymus the Blind (d. c398), and several monuments. Witnesses from elsewhere should also be noted: in Arabia, Titus of Bostra (2nd half of the 4th century); in Palestine, Eusebius of Caesarea (d. 340) and Cyril of Jerusalem (d. 396); in Cappadocia, Basil (d. 379), Gregory of Nazianzus (d. 389) and Gregory of Nyssa (d. 394); and even in the region around Antioch, Eustathius (d. before 377), a probable witness, along with Apollinaris of Laodicea (d. c390), Diodore of Tarsus (d. before 394), who while not daring to refuse the title tries to explain it in a restricted sense, and Severian of Gabala (d. shortly after 408). Finally, the title *Theotokos* is professed even by the Arians, as witness Asterius the Sophist (d. after 341) and the *Vita Constantini.*

4. Among the Latin writers, the earliest use of *Theotokos* appears as *Mater Dei* in Ambrose, *De Virginibus* 11, 65, PL 16:282c. This Latin title implies a different nuance. *Mater Dei* (Mother of God) signifies the personal relationship of

Mary to God; *Theotokos* (the one who begets God) signifies the foundation of this relationship. The Greek suggests even "the one who is brought to childbed with God" according to the medical realism of the term. The Greek suffix *-tokos* is the exact equivalent of the English suffix *-parous*, used in words like "oviparous," "viviparous," etc. The word "primipara" used today by doctors to designate a woman that has given birth for the first time is the exact transfer into Latin of the term *prōtotókos* (not to be confused with *prōtótokos*, meaning "first born") used by Greek doctors in antiquity. Thus the literal English translation of *Theotokos* would be "Deiparous."

Bibliography: V. Schweitzer, "Alter des Titels *Theotokos*," *Der Katholik* Series 3, 28 (1903), 97–113; R. P. Clement (= Dillenschneider), *Le sens chrétien et la maternité divine de Marie aux IVe et Ve siècles,* Bruges, Beyaert, 1929; G. Jouassard, "Marie à travers la Patristique: Maternité divine, virginité, sainteté," *Maria* 1 (1949), pp. 85–86, 112–136.

APPENDIX # 5

MARY IN THE INFANCY APOCRYPHALS

The first edition of this *Short Treatise* (1953) already spoke of "apocryphals of Mary's death," known also as Assumptionist apocryphals, but contained not a word about a more ancient group, the infancy apocryphals. At that time the dating of these works and the very condition of their original texts raised so many problems that one hardly knew where or how to begin speaking of them. The problem has since made considerable advance, and can be treated under three headings.

1. Antiquity of the *Protevangelium of James*

In 1958 a previously unknown text of the *Protevangelium of James* was published by G. Testuz, *Papyrus Bodmer V. Nativité de Marie,* Geneva, 1958. The papyrus in question dates from the third century, and to the astonishment of specialists offers for the *Protevangelium* a text of unhoped for antiquity. What is more, this text is close enough to what is known as the "long text" of the *Protevangelium;* it contains the conclusion called "The Apocryphal of Zachary," which criticism (Harnack, C. Michel, P. Peeters) had been in agreement in assigning to the sixth century.

The Testuz edition confined itself to giving the text of the papyrus. Shortly afterward the critical edition of the *Protevangelium* was realized by E. de Strycker, *La forme la plus ancienne du Protévangile de Jacques. Recherches sur le papyrus Bodmer V. (Collection Subsidia hagiographica)*, Brussels, Bollandists, 1961. This edition was made from three papyri, numerous manuscripts (one a palimpsest of the 9th century), and the oriental versions (Syriac, Armenian, Sahidic) including especially the Georgian version derived from the Armenian and beautifully published by G. Garritte in *Muséon* 70 (1957), 233–265.

Thus it is now established that the *entire work* existed already at the end, and perhaps even by the middle, of the second century.

From this solid basis it is henceforth possible to give the *Protevangelium of James* its proper place in the development of dogma, in an epoch clearly contemporary with St. Irenaeus. The certainty of this early dating gives the work renewed importance.

2. Implications of the *Protevangelium*

In the work is found the oldest expression that has come down to us of Mary's holiness, of her virginity *post partum,* of her virginity *in partu,* and perhaps even of the Immaculate Conception, *but under a mythical form.*

As to Mary's holiness, the *Protevangelium* has materialized it by a series of ritual proceedings that totally *separate* the daughter of Anna from the secular world. At her birth she is placed by her mother in a "sanctuary" that is immediately set up "within her room." Thence she passes (without ever having "walked on the ground") to the Temple, where she receives "her food from the hand of an angel," thus ruling out any alimentary waste.

As to her virginity *post partum,* the author already sets up the picture in making Joseph an old man and suggesting that the "brothers of Jesus" are sons of Joseph, born of an earlier marriage.

Witness to Mary's virginity *in partu* takes the form of an observation of Salome, the midwife: " 'If I do not put my finger to explore . . . , I will not believe. . . .' And Salome verified etc. . . ."

As to the Immaculate Conception, it seems to come through in rough outline in the affirmation that Mary was conceived virginally, without the intervention of her father Joachim. He retired to the desert where he was fasting "forty days" (I, 4, ed. Testuz, p. 2), when the angel said to his wife Anna, "Behold you will conceive" — in the *future* tense, which supposes that the conception has not yet taken place (IV, 1, *loc. cit.,* p. 7). Then shortly afterwards Joachim receives the same message in the form, "Behold your wife has conceived" — in the *past* tense. He receives this message in the desert where he has been all the time. According to the *Protevangelium,* therefore, the conception took place without his intervention. The textual reading involved here was, until now, considered suspect and ordinarily eliminated. Attested to by the *Bodmer V Papyrus,* it is henceforth certain.

3. Weight of the Apocryphals

These observations lead one to generalize in the direction indicated in Appendix # 6 on the Assumptionist apocryphals. Like the latter, the infancy apocryphals appear as a crude anticipation of truths that later, and in entirely different terms, will be recognized by the Church.

Should these crude anticipations be taken as the fruit of

an explicit historical tradition of apostolic origin that had become corrupted? Assuredly not.

The apocryphals represent something entirely different: a first cognizance of non-explicit revelation on the level of the imagination. Capable of genius when under the impulse of some thought, imagination seems sometimes to run ahead of dogmatic explicitation, which the intelligence of faith will reach later (cf. *supra,* pp. 153 ff.)

But the other side of this judgment cannot be too much stressed: (1) Only to the degree that imagination purloined some spark of true light was it able to run ahead of intelligence. (2) This fleeting and pre-intellectual cognizance is always defective; it is approximative, gross, tainted, inextricably mixed with sheer fable. Of itself it is unacceptable. The legitimate reaction that these tales stirred up often blocked the authentic development of dogma for centuries, as was the case in the West from the eighth to the twelfth centuries for the Assumption. Dogmatic explicitation could take place only after a break with these mythical approximations that had preceded it, or at least, in the most favorable cases, only after purifying them and seeking other sources for their basic content. The apocryphal accounts furnished only the material for reflection. The weight of suggestions that stemmed from them could be wholesomely appreciated only after long critical work stemming from entirely different domains.

As to the domain of the apocryphals, and more widely that of symbolic thought, so strongly represented in Christian antiquity, precisions would be in order. Involved is the whole problem of myths, archetypes, their value and limitations. But this enormous problem, on which almost everything remains yet to be said, far surpasses the framework of the present study.[1] This appendix is intended simply to show

---

1. Cf. R. Laurentin, "Foi et mythe en théologie mariale," NRT 89 (1967), 281–307; "Faith and Myth in Marian Theology," *The Present Crisis . . . ,* pp. 175–202.

the interest of the problem and to fix in true perspective the grandeur and the *misery* of the apocryphals. And, so that the point not be missed, perhaps the stress should be laid on the word *misery.*

APPENDIX # 6

THE WEIGHT OF THE ASSUMPTIONIST APOCRYPHALS

Much debate has been spent on the value of the apocryphals. It has been well established that they are not the vehicle of any explicit apostolic tradition. Are they idle tales, or do they represent a cognizance, by intuitive approach and under mythical form, of postulates implicit in revelation?

The answer depends on the value one accords to the imaginative faculty. For a long time it was under-estimated as a result of the rationalist approach in vogue since Descartes. Today, in a justified though at times excessive reaction, heed is being paid to the fact that this faculty (whose exercise is linked to that of the intelligence) is capable of attaining the real, even what underlies the real: in the "myths" which this faculty elaborates, a profound truth is sometimes contained within the moralizing framework of the fable. The apocryphals of the Dormition are to theological thought on the Assumption what the myths of Greek tragedy are to ancient philosophical thought: the expression of a valid intuition underneath the exterior of a fable. This impulsive expression is confused and expansively abundant, mixed with groundless and errant elements. At the very least it calls for a critical purification.

It would be dangerous to propose this analogy with the

myths of tragedy if two very important precisions were not added:

1. The imaginative faculty in question here is not imagination in its pure state, but imagination acting *under the impulse of intelligence.* The animal, deprived as he is of intelligence, is capable of images, but incapable of "myths," and more generally of all creative imagination.

2. The point of application of human faculties in the development of Greek thought and in that of Assumptionist theology is *something entirely different.* Greek tragedians and philosophers expressed human data essentially under a human light. The concept of destiny expressed in imaginative approach in the myth of Oedipus, and in rational approach in the thought of the Stoics, corresponds to an underlying presupposition of Hellenism. The authors of the apocryphals and theologians attempt to give explicitness to a *higher object* under a *higher light.* On the one hand, the hidden and reshaped object with which they are concerned is not a human thought but the divine thought enclosed in revelation. On the other hand, the exercise of their imagination is enlightened not only by intelligence but by the sense of the faith which the Holy Spirit illuminates in fleeting presentiment. This exercise remains a very uneven thing. If at some moments the apocryphals rise high enough to reach realities hidden in the implicitness of the data of faith, at other times they degenerate into sterile yarn-spinning, if not into tales in bad taste. The fruit of passing touches of the Spirit is thus found mingled in with the pranks of the imagination, that Lady Fancy capable also of genius. There is no question, then, in what is being said here of rehabilitating imagination to the point of ranking its exercise as equal to that of intelligence, and still less of placing it higher, in the line of surrealism.

But neither should it be on principle disdained. Imagination witnesses to the humble condition of human thought. Man, this reasonable animal, attains the most genial of his possibilities, not when he struggles to think in the pattern of the angels, as if he were pure spirit, but rather when he thinks as the reasonable animal that he is, that is, within the very heart of the image, which is indispensable to his mode of understanding. One can thus gauge the importance of works that attempt to measure the weight of symbolic thought, which has gone more and more unrecognized since the end of the Middle Ages.

Bibliography: R. Laurentin, "Foi et mythe en théologie mariale," NRT 89 (1967), 281–307, and "Mythe et foi dans le développement dogmatique concernant la Vierge," presented at the Fifth International Mariological Congress held at Lisbon, August 2–7, 1967. The first of these articles appears in English translation in R. Laurentin, *The Present Crisis in Mariology: Rise or Fall of Mariology?* (Mimeographed notes of summer school lectures), Dayton, University of Dayton, 1968, pp. 175–202.

APPENDIX # 7

JOHN 19:25–27 AND THE SPIRITUAL MOTHERHOOD AMONG EASTERN WRITERS

Christ's word to the disciple, "Behold your Mother," is generally interpreted by the Fathers in the sense of a material task confided to St. John. This text furnishes them with an argument to prove that Mary had no other child than Jesus, whose word in this instance was only an act of filial piety.

A double exception to this trend of interpretation has been noted (cf. *supra*, pp. 72 ff.): Origen and, following his lead, Nilus both place the accent on spiritual motherhood, and not on material assistance. But there is no question with them yet of a maternal function exercised by Mary. Nor is there much more in the apocryphals of the Dormition, where the idea makes its way and begins to develop. In the most ancient, *Apocryphal R* (end of 5th or early 6th century), edited by A. Wenger, *L'Assomption* . . . , John calls Mary "my sister who became mother of the twelve branches," i.e., twelve apostles (# 16, *loc. cit.*, p. 220); "my mother and sister" (# 21, p. 222); "Mary, our Mother" (# 27, p. 227). Further on, the apostles approach her saying, "Mary, our sister, *mother of all those who are saved*" (# 28, p. 227). These expressions are repeated in divers forms by later apocryphals. Here again the meaning is that the disciples of Christ, *inasmuch as they are identified with the Savior,* are sons of Mary. Therefore, certain apocryphals, taking up anew the ancient texts on Mary, mother of the disciples, return to the formula "Mother of the Lord" (*Ibid.,* p. 42). Theoteknos (end of 6th century) broadens the perspective and explains, "Mother of all, since the only Son called his own disciples 'brothers' " (*Encomium in Assumptione* 9, 7b, *loc. cit.,* p. 276, 9). The Pseudo-Peter of Sicily (probably 11th century), *Historia Manichaeorum* 29, PG 104: 1283, is a simple echo of these expressions. In short, the apocryphals saw in Mary, still alive on earth, the mother of the disciples, and with greater insistence, the mother of John. Did they think of John 19:25–27? Indications are lacking to assure this.

George of Nicomedia therefore marks a step in advance in explicitly commenting in this sense on Jesus' word in Jn. 19:26, "Behold your son," as if Jesus were saying, "You have with you the friend who rested on my breast . . . , so take my place, remaining with him and with those around him. To you I confide also, through him, the rest of my disciples. . . . Become for them everything that a mother is by nature" (*Sermo in S. Mariam assistentem Cruci,* PG 100:1476cd). A bit farther on Jesus is portrayed saying to John, "Now I establish her as mother (and) guide *(hōs tekousan, kathēgoumenēn),* not only for you but for the rest of my disciples *(tōn loipōn . . . mathētōn;* cf. Apoc. 12:17), and I sovereignly desire that she be honored with the dignity of mother. . . . Though I have forbidden you to give anyone on earth the name of father, I want you to give her the name of mother" (*Ibid.,* 1477b).

It is difficult to assess the weight of this text. Through John Mary's motherhood extends *to the other disciples.* Who is meant here? The disciples reunited in the cenacle and the role Mary exercises in their regard during their earthly life after Christ's departure, according to the perspective of the Assumptionist apocryphals? Or all the disciples of Christ throughout the ages, and the universal mission Mary exercises in their regard as mother of mankind? It is hard to decide, for the text, open and suggestive as it is, spells nothing out.

APPENDIX # 8

THE FIRST MARIAN FEAST IN THE WEST

It is an extraordinary spectacle for the historian to see Mary take her explicit place in the liturgy in the shadow of the mystery of Christmas. This all occurs sporadically; the liturgical form and the date of the celebration differ according to countries, and the dates of the adoption of the feast are spread out from one to two centuries apart. Such convergence amid diversity shows that what is in question is no arbitrary creation, but a necessary flowering, as that of leaf and blossom in springtime when the time has come. Scripture, dogma, the spirit of the liturgy all bore the necessity of this first Marian flowering.

But it is important here to be precise. The data are at once complex and scarce, and nowhere have they been completely gathered.

They will be given below, reduced to their essentials, according to the chronological order of the institution of these feasts, *inasmuch as evidence of it has reached us.* Almost never, in fact, is any record of the institution of a feast available; instead it is seen emerging almost imperceptibly in the life of the Church.

1. Last Sunday of Advent: Northern Italy, mid-5th Century

The Marian character of this last Sunday before Christmas is attested from the mid-fifth century onward by *Letter 61* (PL 54:697) of St. Leo (d. 361) and especially by four *Sermons on the Annunciation* (# 140, PL 52:575–577; # 142–144, *ibid.*, 579–588) of St. Peter Chrysologus (d. c450) destined for this Sunday. Cf. M. Jugie's study in PO 19:311–314. This Marian character is further present in the liturgy of Aquila: "Quinta dom[inica] Luc. 1, Mense sexto messus est angelus Gabriel" (*Codex Evangeliorum Rehdigeronus,* 7th century, cited by G. Morin, "L'année liturgique à Aquilée antérieurement à l'époque carolingienne," *Rev. Bén.* 19 (1902), 1–12). In the Ambrosian liturgy likewise the last Sunday of Advent bears the mention: "Dom. VI Adventus item ad sanctam Mariam" (Lejay, "Ambrosien," *Dictionnaire d'archéologie chrétienne et de liturgie* 1:1393).

2. January 18: Gaul, 6th Century

In Gaul at the end of the sixth century the Auxerre version of Jerome's martyrology for January 18 bears the mention: "Depositio sanctae Mariae" (G. Morin, "Notes liturgiques sur l'Assomption," *Rev. Bén.* 5 (1888), 342–346). This celebration, coming "mediante mense undecimo," would be the one referred to by Gregory of Tours (d. 593/594) in *Historia Francorum* X, 31, PL 71:566, and by an ancient homily that Dom Morin attributes to Caesar of Arles (*Loc. cit.,* 344). If this last hypothesis is founded, the celebration would thus date from the first half of the sixth century. Traces of the feast survive into the 10th–11th centuries (H. Barré, article in *Rev. Bén.* 68 (1958), 225, n. 4).

3. January 1 (Octave of Christmas): Rome, between 550 and 595

At Rome, between 550 and 595, the first Marian Mass is instituted, destined to celebrate the virginal motherhood (B. Botte, "La première fête mariale de la liturgie romaine," *Ephemerides Liturgicae* 47 (1933), 425–430, with precisions from A. Chavasse, *Le sacramentaire Gélasien,* Paris, Desclée, 1958, pp. 381–383, 651–657). This feast disappears in the second half of the seventh century, when Marian feasts coming from the East take up its elements.

4. Wednesday and Friday of the Tenth Month Fast (later, Advent Ember Days): Rome, Beginning of the 7th Century

From the beginning of the seventh century the readings of what today are known as Ember Wednesday and Friday of Advent (then known as the "tenth month fast") were fixed. On Wednesday, when the station was at St. Mary Major, the epistle read was the prophecy of Emmanuel (Is. 7:10–14), and the gospel that of the Annunciation (Lk. 1:26). On Friday the epistle was the *Egredietur virga de radice Iesse* (Is. 11:1–5) and the gospel that of the Visitation. The *Comes of Würzburg* (beginning of 7th century) bears mention of the epistles (cf. the edition of G. Morin, "Le plus ancien *comes* ou lectionnaire de l'Eglise romaine," *Rev. Bén.* 27 (1910), 63–64, # 161–164). As for the gospels, the evangeliary of Würzburg dates from fifty years after the lectionary, but it witnesses to a usage contemporary with that of the epistles, that is to say, the beginning of the seventh century at the latest.

It is important to note that these readings, which show Mary's place in the Advent mystery, do not in any way have the character of Marian "feast" exhibited in varying degrees by the other celebrations mentioned here, and this remains true no matter how integrated these readings are in the "temporal cycle." The Marian character of Ember Wednesday of Advent will be accentuated later on, until it gives rise to the devotion of the "Golden Mass" (cf. U. Berlière, article in *Questions liturgiques et paroissiales* 5 (1920), 210–216).

5. December 18 (Octave before Christmas): Spain, 656

In 656 the Council of Toledo assigned to December 18, "ante octavam diem quo natus est Dominus," the celebration of the "day of his Mother": "Genetricis dies habeatur celeberrimus et praeclarus" (Mansi, t. 2, col. 33–34).

This decision, effective for Spain, was recommended by the custom of *distant churches:* "In multis namque ecclesiis a nobis et spatio remotis et terris, hic mos agnoscitur retinere" *(Loc. cit.).* According to M. Jugie (PO 19:311), the churches in question are those of the *East.* No ancient text confirms this hypothesis. All that is found in this direction is a series of *late* attestations of a feast of the angel Gabriel for December 18:

a. Arabian Coptic Menology (PO 10, appendix 3, p. 226);
b. Calendar of Abou'l Barakât ("day of the angel Gabriel," PO 10:261);
c. Ethiopian synaxary (PO 26:30–38) which specifies: "On this day also is the commemoration of the feast of the Annunciation by the glorious Gabriel." There is a reference to an apparition of the Virgin Mary to the bishop Daqseyos "of the region of Rome" (no doubt Constantinople, the new Rome), in which she prescribes that the Annunciation should be celebrated on December 18 and not March 25, which occurs during Lent.

These three witnesses seem to be of Coptic origin. But nothing proves that the feast in question therein is the one known to the Spanish churches.

Bibliography: A. Wilmart, "Expectatio partus," *Dictionnaire d'archéologie chrétienne et de liturgie* 5 (1922), 1027–1029; H. Barré, "La fête mariale du 18 décembre à Bénévent au VIIIe siècle," EphM 6 (1956), 451–461.

APPENDIX # 9

THE PHILOSOPHIC PRINCIPLE THAT MOTHERHOOD RELATES TO A PERSON

The philosophic principle involved in the dogma of the divine motherhood is that, in the case of the human species, *motherhood relates to the person* of the child. The psychological and "personalist" sense of this principle is evident. To disengage its objective basis will not be without interest.

The fundamental principle is that every relation founded on an action terminates (as does the action itself) in the concrete being, the existing subject, that is affected or modified by the action. If one heals or transports another, it is properly the person of the other that is healed or transported, and there would be no sense in imagining that the action can take place without affecting the person on whom it confers some determination.

This truth, that every action concerning a person relates to that person, is realized in the fullest sense of the words whenever there is question of an action whose *very terminus* is in the order of substance. This is the case in generation. What is generated is therefore fully and always a substantial subject of existence, and, if this subject subsists in a rational nature, subject of a person.

It will be objected that the proper causality of parents is in the material order: they dispose living matter, whereas God alone creates the soul. Thus they are the efficient causes of the disposition of this matter, but God alone is the cause of the form wherein resides the principle of substance. This is not a valid enough objection to bring back into question the principles enunciated above. In the terms of this objection, however, one would be tempted to say that parents are simple biological agents in the formation of a body into which God infuses a soul over and above. The dignity of fatherhood and motherhood would thus be entirely extrinsic. Minds today are not too much drawn to this kind of dualist perspective.

It should thus be observed in reply that the material cause and the formal cause are reciprocal. In acting in the realm of dispositive causality, parents exercise a causality with regard to the form, by means of the disposition which they effect. The *proper* effect of their action is *living matter,* which, as such, is not exempt of form. Much more, their action strictly demands, according to the order established by God, the infusion of a form which will not be limited to the strict accomplishment of biological functions but will be a spiritual and immortal soul resembling that of the parents. If, for the sake of hypothesis, it were supposed that God would not create a soul for the bodily matter thus disposed, there would not be any generation properly so called, but rather generation in an equivocal sense, and a monstrosity in the strict sense. (There is generation only where there is *resemblance of nature* between the one engendering and the engendered; cf. *supra,* p. 221, n. 21.)

A more extensive study would develop the following two precisions: (1) The terminus *reached* by the action of parents (the whole person of the child) extends beyond the terminus *produced* (living matter). (2) The efficient causality that parents exercise in the line of matter, and that of God who creates the form due this matter, are joined in the *ultimate disposition,* which is at the same time both the culmination of the ascending process of dispositive causality and the first effect of the infusion of the form. It is there that the gradual action of the parents and the instantaneous action of God reach, under two different relationships, the entire human composite, this new personal human individual who comes into existence.

The fact that the Word of God preexisted before the human nature which he assumed changes nothing in these general principles. The terminus of Mary's generation is the concrete subject to which belongs the human nature that has come into existence through this act of hers. Mary's motherhood, therefore, rightly and correctly refers to the divine person of the Incarnate Word.

The above reasoning, pursued here within the convenient and tested framework of scholastic philosophy, would be easy to transpose into an existential vocabulary.

APPENDIX # 10

THE *KATHARSIS* OF MARY AT THE ANNUNCIATION

The doctrine of the *katharsis* (purification) has been studied by M. Jugie, *L'Immaculée Conception,* Rome, 1952, passim. The author leans toward explaining the texts in reference to the *debitum peccati,* a somewhat artificial position in a question that concerns the East. D. Stiernon, "Théologie mariale dans l'Orthodoxie russe," *Maria* 7 (1964), pp. 283-298, gives a well documented study on the subject. The theme was specifically taken up by M. Candal, "La Virgen santisima 'prepurificada' en su Annunciación," *Orientalia Christiana periodica* 31 (1965), 241-276. At Vatican II Dom Butler's project for the Marian chapter of *Lumen Gentium* proposed assuming the doctrine of *katharsis* in a positive sense; cf. Laurentin, *La Vierge . . .* p. 184, n. 16.

The dossier of texts is considerable and demands delicate interpretation, for they are or appear ambiguous to the modern reader. One of the principal causes of ambiguity is the Platonic idea that the flesh as such is tainted. Origen's opinion concerning Christ himself should not be forgotten: "You ought to know that Jesus was tainted, by his own free will, because he took on a human body for our salvation" (*In Lucam* 14, 3, PG 13:1834b; ed. *Sources chrétiennes* 87, pp. 218-219 and the notes); cf. 2 Cor. 5:21.

Candal's attentive study, cited above, proposes the following conclusions:

1. The long series of texts on the *katharsis* depends on Gregory of Nazianzus, according to whom Christ was conceived of the Virgin who in body and soul was "prepurified" *(prokathartheisēs)* by the Holy Spirit (*Oratio 38,* 13, PG 36: 325b = *Oratio 45,* 9, PG 36:633c). For Gregory, to "prepurify" means to remove an obstacle which can arise from diverse causes; nothing, says Candal, ever indicates that Gregory thereby understood sin or moral taint.

2. Later on the Fathers give this word a double signification: a) sanctification (Sophronius, PG 87:3:3048); b) an action which elevates Mary to the divine sphere and brings about the virginal conception (John Damascene, PG 96:221d–224a and 704a).

3. Thence arises the very developed explanation given by theologians of the fourteenth century of an *increase of grace.* Certain authors add other nuances: they see in this "prepurification" an illumination by the Spirit, a special action on Mary's body. They compare this purification to that of the angelic spirits.

4. The interpretation according to which Mary would have been purified of sin is a late one. It is traceable to Nicephorus Callistus (d. c.1335) and remains isolated until the fourteenth century. At that time the theme of the prepurification begins to be used more and more massively as an argument against the Latin thesis of the Immaculate Conception. But that this purification should have had original sin for its object is foreign to the ancient eastern tradition.

These conclusions from Candal's study call for certain reservations. In reality, the theme of prepurification is very ambiguous with St. Gregory of Nazianzus, for whom certain implications of his vocabulary do refer to sin. What is true is that what at first was ambiguous was brought out explicitly at a later date, in two directions: the erasing of sin, on the one hand, and an altogether positive consecration on the other.

The paradoxical fact is that it was with the Latins that the theme of prepurification became widespread, taking on a "maculist" sense, as, for example, in St. Thomas (ST III, q. 27, a. 3).

That the idea is expressed in a dogmatic context now obsolete should not lead one to disregard the traditional element that inspired these texts. For if one disregards this element, it becomes impossible to understand the authors of the thirteenth century, and one ends up making of the dogmatic development of the Immaculate Conception a staggered development. The homogeneity of the development does not appear unless one knows how to recognize and retain the traditional elements that were the spark of truth of these otherwise deficient doctrines.

APPENDIX # 11

THE THREE DOGMATIC ASPECTS OF MARY'S VIRGINITY

As has been seen, the councils of the fourth and fifth centuries defended three aspects of Mary's virginity: before the birth of Christ, during childbirth, and after birth. Some precisions are necessary on these questions, which involve a number of problems.

1. Virginity before Birth (ante partum)

By the virginity before birth is understood the fact that Mary conceived "without knowing man" (cf. Lk. 1:34), according to the biblical sense of the word "know" (Gen. 4:1, 17, 25).

The virginal conception is firmly attested by the evangelists. Mt. 1:18–25 and Lk. 1:34–35 teach it formally. Allusions to this mystery have been detected also in the other two evangelists. Whatever the reading of Jn. 1:13 — *"those whom* (or *him whom*) neither blood, nor the will of the flesh, nor the will of man, but God has engendered" — there is an allusion to the virginal birth of Christ as prototype of the spiritual birth in baptism (Laurentin, *Luc 1–2,* pp. 137-138). As to Mk. 6:3, he calls Jesus "son of Mary" where the parallel text of Mt. 12:46 has "the son of Joseph." It would seem that Mark wished to clear up something equivocal that did not exist with Matthew on account of the latter's prologue. However, Paul's epistles have not a word of the "virginal conception." A Catholic author has even maintained that Paul did not know of it (A. Legault, "Saint Paul a-t-il parlé de la maternité virginale?" *Sciences ecclésiastiques* 16 (1954), 480–495).

In recent years within Catholicism a question has arisen on the subject. Does the affirmation of Mary's virginity stem from a historical tradition or from an intimate revelation by the Holy Spirit? In other words, is it a reminiscence handed on by Mary or Joseph, the only witnesses, that reached the evangelists? Or did it come about that in meditating on the virgin of Isaiah the evangelists concluded that Mary had conceived virginally? In the latter case the process of cognizance would be analogous to that of the dogma of the Assumption. (The problem is phrased here as it arises within the Catholic faith, without entering into those viewpoints outside Catholicism that refuse the dogma and fact of virginity.)

In answer to the question thus phrased, the historical origin of the tradition is to be held, for two reasons:

1. The study of Mt. 1–2 and Lk. 1–2 reveals two traditions altogether independent. The episodes that the two evangelists narrate do not coincide. Matthew *(and Matthew alone)* recounts Joseph's doubt, the episode of the Magi and the star, the flight into Egypt, etc. Luke *(and Luke alone)* recounts the Annunciation, the Visitation, the visit of the shepherds, the purification and the finding of the Child. There are no common formulas between the two, no indication of harmonization at points where the difference of their viewpoints poses problems. The two infancy gospels, therefore, proceed from two traditions: Matthew's represents the viewpoint of Joseph and was probably transmitted by the "brothers of Jesus" who were integrated into the primitive community

(Acts 1:14; 1 Cor. 9:5; Gal. 1:19); of them there will be question shortly; Luke's proceeds from the Virgin Mary and was transmitted in the Johannine milieu, which is likewise Judaeo-Christian. It is all the more striking, then, that these two accounts are in agreement on the essential points: Mary is engaged (or married) to Joseph, son of David, but she is a virgin (Mt. 1:16, 18, 20, 24–25; Lk. 1:27; 2:4–5); the name of Jesus is given from on high (Mt. 2:21; Lk. 1:31); Christ is born at Bethlehem (Mt. 2:1, 5–6; Lk. 2:4–5, 11), in Herod's day (Mt. 2:1; Lk. 1:5); he passes his childhood at Nazareth (Mt. 2:23; Lk. 2:39, 51). Among the common points recorded in such different contexts is the virginal conception. This *concordantia discordantium* shows the fundamental authenticity of the two traditions.

2. The Jewish theology of their environment did not push the evangelists to an affirmation of virginal conception. In the rabbinic tradition Is. 7:14 was not interpreted in that sense. Thus the teaching of Luke and even of Matthew had no apologetic motive. Its motive and origin were historical.

2. Virginity after Birth (post partum)

Mary's virginity after Christ's birth is not taught by the New Testament. It is essentially the result of a cognizance based on certain biblical indications, and especially of an overall view of the implications of the plan of salvation. The ancient conviction of the Church is that the virginal consecration of Mary was sealed and animated in her heart by the Holy Spirit. From within she understood what St. Paul had understood in Jesus Christ (1 Cor. 7:8), what he counseled and "prescribed" even with insistence (7:18) to Christians of the mid-first century, for the perfection of their "undivided attention to the Lord" (7:35) and their freedom in God, that is, "that each one should continue as he was when God's call reached him" (7:17 — an aphorism repeated in vv. 19 and

24; cf. also v. 39). Mary remained "such as she was when God's call reached her," that is, in the state of virginity of the Annunciation (Lk. 1:27, 34). She is for always the type or icon of virginity, that is, of the eschatological life (1 Cor. 7:29–31) lived already here below, or, in other words, of the total and direct gift of self to God. This ideal does not imply any disdain or disparagement of marriage, for marriage normally involves for each of the spouses the reciprocal gift of self to the other and the gift of both to their children. One would have to be blind indeed not to be led to admire the treasures of generosity, delicateness, and disinterestedness that this way of nature, consecrated by a sacrament, unfolds in the heart of men, making egoism and hardness melt like snow under the sun. This way can lead to a total gift of self to God. Not passing by way of these natural mediations, consecrated virginity is an access more abrupt, that is more direct, but also perilous. It is like the vertical ascension of the face of a mountain, compared to the road that leads to the same spot by longer and gentler curves. If it be permitted to pursue the metaphor, Mary should be said to be the best prepared person ever for accomplishing, by God's grace, this first "ascent" by a woman, this way of consecrated virginity. This was already the opinion of certain contemporaries of Origen, and of Origen himself who records their reflections: "It is right to recognize the first fruits of virginity in Jesus for men, and in Mary for women" (*Comment. in Mt.* 10, 17, GCS 40 (Origen 10), p. 21; PG 13: 877a).

Two problems arising from the subject should now be examined.

a. Is Mary's Virginity after Birth (post partum) Not the Fruit of a Tradition Properly Called Historical?

The question arises in the light of the antiquity of the texts where this belief is attested.

According to the second-century *Protevangelium of James*

(9:2; 17:1ff; 18:1; ed. Strycker pp. 106, 140–142, 146), the *Gospel of Peter* (cited by Origen, GCS 40 (Origen 10), p. 21), a doubtful fragment of Justin, Clement of Alexandria (*Adumbrationes in Ep. Judae,* PG 9:922), Origen (*In Lucam* 7, GCS 35 (Origen 9), p. 44; PG 13:1818; *In Joannem,* fragment 31, GCS 10 (Origen 4), p. 506), etc., the "brothers of Jesus" would be children of a first marriage of St. Joseph. Is that a reminiscence handed down from contemporary witnesses? Or is it the fruit of a deduction made to resolve the first objections against Mary's virginity? The second hypothesis seems probable. Eusebius (*Church History* 3, 11, 1), writing about Pope Eleutherius (174–189), takes Simeon and Jude, the "brothers of Jesus," to be "sons of Clopas" and Clopas to be "brother of Joseph." The apocryphals seem thus to have sought a hasty explanation to reconcile the existence of "brothers of Jesus" with the virginity of Mary. Whatever the case, these texts manifest the antiquity of the belief in Mary's virginity *post partum*. This belief is more ancient and more firm than the tradition on Mary's holiness. Only Tertullian and Helvidius departed from the belief. And the opinion of the latter stirred up an immediate dogmatic reaction, as has been seen (cf. *supra,* p. 61 ff).

b. Do Certain Texts of Scripture Not Attest that Mary Had Other Children than Jesus?

Certain critics have affirmed this. The texts they invoke should be examined.

1. Jesus is called the *"first-born"* of Mary *(prōtótokos)* in Lk. 2:7. (Cf. Mt. 1:25 according to the Vulgate where *primogenitum* is added.) The word "first-born" designates the first child of a woman, the one who "opens the womb" (Lk. 2:23), without any reference to the existence of a second child. This is very clear in the Greek epitaph of Tel el Yaoudieh, published by J. B. Frey in *Biblica* 11 (1930), 369–390, where there is question of a young mother who died in

bringing her first child into the world. She says: "In the pain of delivering my first-born child, destiny brought me to the end of life." Obviously this woman had no other child than this "first-born." (Cf. also G. Jouassard, "Le premier-né de la Vierge chez saint Irénée et Hippolyte," RSR 12 (1932), 509-533; 13 (1933), 23-37.)

2. Mt. 1:25 says that "(Joseph) did not know her *until* she had borne a son . . . Jesus." "To know" evidently has here the biblical sense of intercourse, contrary to the interpretation proposed by certain Fathers of the Church. But may one conclude therefrom that Joseph "knew" Mary afterwards? No, for this expression "until" does not in any way anticipate what came to pass afterwards. According to Semitic usage it simply marks the term and limit of the author's interest. The most striking example is 2 Sam. 6:23, "Michal the daughter of Saul had no child *until* the day of her death." Obviously she had none afterwards either. Similar uses are in Gen. 8:7, Dt. 34:6, Num. 20:17, Ps. 110:1, 1 Mac. 5:54, 1 Tim. 4:13, Is. 14:2, Mt. 16:28, 28:20, 1 Cor. 4:5. The expression "until" in no way implies a change of situation after the limit mentioned.

The same must be said of the similar expression *"before"* in Mt. 1:18, "Before they had come together, she was found with child." It must be added too that *sunelthein* (come together) signifies not intercourse but the rite of introducing the bride into the home, according to Jewish custom. It is the same sense as in Mt. 1:20 where the angel declares, "Do not fear to take Mary as your wife" (P. Bonnard, *L'Evangile selon saint Matthieu,* Neuchâtel, 1963, p. 21). Here the reference is not to intercourse but to cohabitation.

3. What is to be thought of the "brothers of Jesus" of whom there is mention in the following texts: Mk. 3:31 (= Mt. 12:46-47; Lk. 8:19-20); Mk. 6:3 (= Mt. 13:55-56); 1 Cor. 9:5; Gal. 1:19; Jn. 7:3, 5, 10, and perhaps 2:12 (although this last text and Jn. 7:3 are discussed by Boismard and Lollat, for whom the "brothers" here represent rather the

small band of disciples, as in Jn. 20:17); Acts 1:14–15, 9:30, 10:23, 11:1?

It is important to remember that the Hebrew language has no word for "cousin." It uses the word "brother" *(ah)* to designate in a broad sense all the members of the family group. Thus, for example:

"We are brothers" says Abraham to Lot his nephew (Gen. 13:8).
"His brother Lot" says Gen 14:14, 16, with Abraham in mind.
Jacob calls himself a "brother" of Laban his uncle (Gen. 29:12).
"You are my brother" says Laban in turn to Jacob his nephew (Gen. 29:15).

In Lev. 10:4 the "brothers" are cousins.

In 1 Ch. 23:21 the sons of Kish, "brothers" of the daughters of Eleazar whom they marry, are in reality their cousins.

Note also 2 Kgs. 10:13 (the "brothers" of Ahaziah) and Job 42:11 (clarified by Job 19:13, 14), as well as the 77 "brothers" in the inscription of Panamou (ERS 495f).

There are, moreover, a number of indications that the "brothers" of Jesus are actually his "cousins."

The firmer indications may be summed up as follows. The "brothers of Jesus" are a group of some numerical importance, as appears from Acts 1:14 and especially Mk. 6:3 and its parallel Mt. 13:55–56. These last two texts explicitly name four "brothers" of Jesus: "James and Joset, Jude and Simon"; they speak in addition of *"all* his sisters" (Mt. 13:-56), and, as St. Jerome already noted, "Omnes nisi de turba non dicitur — 'All' is not said except for a crowd" (*Adversus Helvidium,* PL 23:200). It must be added that the four names mentioned do not exhaust the number of "brothers" of Jesus, for three of these four were believers and important members of the primitive Christian hierarchy, and thus are to be distinguished from the numerous group of whom Jn. 7:5 said, "Not even his brothers had faith in him" (cf. Mk. 3:21). More precisely, James and Joset are sons of a Mary that cannot be identified with the Virgin Mary: while the latter is generally called "the mother of Jesus" (Jn. 2:1, 3; 19:25; Acts 1:14), the other Mary is always designated as "the mother of James and of Joset" (Mk. 15:40 and Mt. 27:56) or "the mother of Joset" (Mk. 15:47) or "the mother of James" (Mk. 16:1), precisely to avoid confusion. Moreover, she is always named *after* Mary of Magdala.

A second set of indications, of unequal value, tends to confirm the interpretation that the "brothers" are "cousins" of Jesus:

a. Jesus is designated as *the* son of Mary, with the article (Mk. 6:3; cf. M. J. Lagrange, *Evangile selon Marc,* Paris, 1929, p. 83).

b. Mary had a *sister,* we learn from Jn. 19:25. This sister seems to have had children, and nothing would be more normal than to designate them as "brothers of Jesus." This is the foundation of the solution St. Jerome gives in his *Adversus Helvidium.*

c. The two infancy gospels do not mention any other children in the household of Mary and Joseph. The episode of the finding in the Temple (Lk. 2:40–52) is of particular significance in this regard, from the fact that Jesus was twelve years old and the circumstances of the pilgrimage would normally have led to the mention of his "brothers," if he had had any.

d. Jn. 19:25–27 furnished a classical argument, one of the most current with the Fathers and ancient authors (T. Koehler, "Les principales interprétations de Jn. 19:25–27, pendant les douze premiers siècles," EM 16 (1959), pp. 119–155): If Jesus confided Mary to St. John, that presupposes that she had no other children to take care of her. But it seems to us that Jn. 19:25–27 is intended to signify above all Mary's spiritual motherhood with regard to the disciples of

Christ, a meaning unrecognized by the Fathers. Their argument is proportionately weakened. But it does not for all that lose its value entirely, in the opinion of P. Benoît, *Passion et Résurrection,* Paris, Cerf, 1966, p. 217. John's symbolism always has a material base which here could be Christ's act of filial piety in confiding his Mother to the disciple who "took her to his own."

We conclude that is is clear that several of the persons called "brothers of Jesus" are not sons of his Mother, and no text invites us to think that the case of the others is any different. Thus no difficulty from the side of history encumbers either the very ancient dogmatic tradition of the Church or the tradition which, at the time when the reminiscences of the "brothers of Jesus" were fresh, was exempt from objection in the order of history.

3. Virginity In Childbirth (in partu)

The most delicate and difficult point is undoubtedly Mary's virginity in childbirth *(virginitas in partu),* likewise affirmed by the Councils (Denz.-Schön. 291, 299, 368, 442, 503, 571, 1880). Recently Pius XII drew an argument from the virginity *in partu* in his Constitution *Munificentissimus* defining the Assumption (AAS 42 (1950), p. 761), and Vatican II's Constitution on the Church, *Lumen Gentium* art. 56, recalled that "her first-born Son ... did not diminish (his mother's) virginal integrity but sanctified it — virginalem eius integritatem non minuit sed sacravit."

Why does this doctrine stir up so much uneasiness today? What is its meaning? No matter how delicate the subject, these two questions cannot be put aside.

Contemporary Difficulties

A first obstacle comes from the fact that our culture is more or less marked by the influence of Plato or Descartes. Under this idealist influence we have trouble believing concretely in the resurrection of the body, and we remain rather unresponsive to morality though attracted by mysticism. The root of these deficiencies is a more or less deep failure to appreciate the substantial unity of body and soul. In the wake of presentations all too current and sometimes at home even in certain catechisms, the soul is portrayed as a partner doubled up with the body and beyond it, whereas in reality the soul is the body's substantial and constitutive form. Unfortunately the body is thought of as a piece of clothing, almost as the "tattered clothing" or the "prison" of the soul, whereas it is really the living and transparent organ of the soul, its connatural sign. Our contemporaries readily think that what happens to the body has no importance for the "soul." There is nothing surprising, then, in the fact that the bodily and spiritual mystery of virginity in general and specifically of Mary's virginity in childbearing should appear devoid of religious meaning, or that the Transfiguration of Christ, so treasured in Eastern spirituality, should be a stumbling-block, as are also more generally all the mysteries that imply a radiation of spiritual realities on the level of the body.

A second obstacle that presents itself, no longer to our intelligence, but to our religious sensibility, is the clumsiness and indelicacy with which many an author treats this question.

Renewed Interest in the Question, 1952–1960

Nevertheless one owes the reader a rapid survey of the question and the recent debates. These debates, in so far as Catholics are concerned, do not bring into question the validity of the expression "virginity in childbirth" *(in partu),* but only what that expression implies.

Mariologists ordinarily give the expression a double content: the absence of the pains of childbirth and the preservation of the hymen, sign of virginity. They discuss the "how" of Christ's birth — whether a *dilatatio* (that is, expansion without rupture) or a *transitus* (that is, a passing analogous to the risen Christ's passing through closed doors, as in Jn. 20:26). These theses, universally accepted from the fourth century on, were admitted in Catholic circles without debate until the mid-twentieth century. They were first questioned by A. Mitterer, *Dogma und Biologie der heiligen Familie,* Vienna, 1952, pp. 98–130, and "Marias wahre Jungfraülichkeit und Mutterschaft in der Geburt," *Theologische-praktische Quartalschrift* 108 (1960, 188–193). Mitterer did not take a position on the fundamental point of the question, but held only that the two traits affirmed by tradition did not belong to the essence of virginity, and that they implied a diminution of motherhood. He was followed by C. E. L. Henry, "A Doctor Considers the Birth of Jesus," *Homiletic and Pastoral Review* 54 (1953), 219–233. J. Galot, "La virginité de Marie et la naissance de Jésus," NRT 82 (1960), 449–469, tried to minimize the weight of the texts of tradition and argued in favor of a "painful" delivery with "rupture of the hymen."

To place the debate on the anatomical and physiological plane as was done both by Mariologists of late and by those who debated with them on this plane, is to obscure the very meaning of tradition. The only step is to non-suit both adversaries, and avoid this indiscreet and dead-end approach to the problem.

It must however be recognized that these discussions, which had both courage and frankness to their credit, have not been without profit. Mitterer's analyses posed a real question: How is virginity to be defined? What in consequence does Mary's virginity imply?

The three following conclusions seem to emerge:

a. Mary's virginity ought not to be affirmed to the detriment of her motherhood. According to tradition, in fact, she is perfectly "Mother" at the same time as perfectly "Virgin." Virginity no more diminishes motherhood as such, than Christ's divinity diminishes his humanity. It must therefore unhesitatingly be said that Mary, integrally Mother, brought Christ into the world by her natural forces, with those sentiments of gift of self, of mastery of self, and of liberty that are proper to an authentic motherhood, as in a mother who today practices the technique of "painless childbirth." In dissipating the terrifying myth of the "birth pangs" and their unwholesome inhibitory influence, this technique has revaluated motherhood, as Pius XII recognized at the first onset. In that recognition he unwrapped the shrouds of darkness from around the joyful mystery of Christ's birth.

b. The absence of pains of labor does not belong to the essence of virginity. But neither does the presence of pains of labor belong to the essence of motherhood. The absence of these pains in Mary is related, in a sense, to her virginity, as a witness that virginity is a "spiritualization of the order of flesh," according to the expression of J. H. Nicolas, *La Virginité*, Fribourg, 1962.

c. The essence of virginity is in the moral order, in the heart, in the biblical sense of this word. "If you do me violence, my virginity will only be redoubled," was the bold reply of a virgin martyr of the first centuries to her executioner. But every virgin violated has been wounded in her very virginity, and that is no empty thing, even if Christ's Redemption, in which everything is grace, is able to turn this evil into a greater good. Virginity in childbirth, if it is not an empty word, signifies full virginity in body and soul, and there is some artifice in the attempt to dissociate "biological virginity" and "spiritual virginity," denying all value to the former.

A more extensive study could stop to analyze the definition that Mitterer gives of virginity: "The will to abstain from all the impressions and emotions attached to the exercise of the sexual function." Virginity is more profoundly the will to abstain from the form of exclusive gift that sexuality implies, along with the consequences of this decision, which are renouncement of fecundity and of sensual impressions. J. H. Nicolas, *op. cit.,* pp. 27–31, has aptly drawn up this criticism.

The Decree of the Holy Office

What was the attitude of Rome in face of these new theories? In July 1960 the Holy Office drew up a decree but did not publish it officially. Instead it transmitted the document to a certain number of bishops and religious superiors as a monitum, asking their concern in preventing the spread of the ideas in question. It is apparently with the consent of the Sacred Congregation, perhaps even on its suggestion, that several journals published the document, which, though drawn up in Latin, seems to have been communicated in the vernaculars. (It appears in Italian in EphM 11 (1961), 138 and *Marianum* 23 (1961), 336, and in French in *La Vie des Communautés Religieuses* (Montreal) 18 (1960), # 8.) In translation based on the French version the document reads as follows:

> "This supreme Congregation has often observed recently, and with deep concern, that theological works are being published in which the delicate question of Mary's virginity *in partu* is treated with a deplorable crudeness of expression and, what is more serious, in flagrant contradiction to the doctrinal tradition of the Church and to the sense of respect the faithful have. Consequently in its plenary session of Wednesday, the twentieth of this month, it seemed necessary to the eminent Fathers of the Holy Office, by reason of their

serious responsibility to watch over the sacred deposit of Catholic doctrine, to see to it that for the future the publication of such dissertations on this problem be prohibited."

This decree essentially belongs to the area of discipline; it is addressed to superiors so that they prevent the publication of new theories, but it does not urge the teaching of the doctrine that is contested. The reasons adduced remain vague. It is a matter of avoiding the crudities of expression (of bad taste, it might be said) that abound in such articles, and also of avoiding the expounding of a thesis contrary to tradition and the sense of the faithful. The decree in no way specifies in what manner tradition is being thus contradicted.

The Doctrine of Vatican II

Vatican II did not ignore this problem. The first draft of a schema on the Virgin Mary (1962) bore evidence of the intention of excluding the new thesis according to which "the virginity *in partu* is univocal and, without the addition of any other element, identical with the virginity *ante partum.*" In other words, the thesis repudiated was the opinion according to which virginity in childbirth would mean nothing more than virginity in conception — except to add that Mary had no sexual relations during her pregnancy. This opinion was cited among the "errors" and "erroneous" opinions that the text rejected. But this declaration figured at the head of the notes, and not in the text, and the text itself only indirectly touched on the point at issue, in an incidental clause *(in obliquo)* that according to the ordinary norms of interpretation could not involve the Council's authority. It is interesting to compare the formula of the first schema (published in French translation by C. Falconi, *Documents secrets,* Monaco, 1965, p. 134) with the text finally adopted by the Council:

1st Schema 1962–1963 (Art. 4)

"Mary (was) mother and at the same time always virgin in spirit and in body. . . .

"It was absolutely proper that the Son, *who towards his mother bore very particular sentiments of love and who willed that his mother's bodily integrity remain intact and incorrupt during childbirth itself, so that, with the glory of virginity remaining, a light might spread over the world . . . ,* should not allow her sacred and virginal body, the august temple of the Divine Word . . . to be reduced to dust."

Lumen Gentium (Art. 57)

"In his birth . . . her first-born Son . . . did not diminish his Mother's virginal integrity but sanctified it."

(This classical expression is taken from the liturgy and in the footnotes is supported by conciliar and patristic texts: Council held at the Lateran in 649, canon 3 (Denz. 256 (503)); St. Leo, *Letter to Flavian ("Tome of Leo")*, PL 54:759; Council of Chalcedon, Mansi 7, 462; St. Ambrose, *De institutione virginum*, PL 16:320.)

*·*In order that it might be identified as being *in obliquo,* the long incidental clause between asterisks is left intact in translation, despite the resulting inelegance of the text.

The Council did not intend to condemn the new thesis, as had been envisaged, nor did it intend to approve it either. It recalled the essentials of tradition as they are expressed by the liturgy, refusing to enter any indiscreet physiological specifications.

The Council's discretion is a model and inspires the following formula: In childbirth Mary remained integrally a virgin in body and soul, and thus she remains, in her very motherhood, the Virgin par excellence, the Virgin before every other.

In what way was the power or the providence of God able to intervene to assure this integrity, which presupposes not only the essential but also the accidental perfection of virginity, integrity of the body at the same time as integrity of the spirit? The Fathers of the Church were of the opinion that there was something exceptional here, if not strictly prodigious. They expressed their mind on this subject in a religious and poetic language, not in clinical terms. Their discretion deserves to be imitated, for it holds to expressing the heart of the mystery and is aimed at nourishing faith, not curiosity. To say with them that God respected the virginal integrity suffices here, without entering into any kind of material or medical description that would be beyond what revelation has given us to know with certitude.

Meaning of this Doctrine

The religious meaning of this mystery is the essential and deserves attention.

For the Fathers it is less a privilege of Mary than an appanage of Christ's birth. They were penetrated with the symbolic and dogmatic unity that linked the three births of the Word to one another: he is born of the Father from all eternity, born of the Virgin Mary in time, and born of every Christian soul by faith and baptism. The second birth has the value of sign in relation to the other two: it is the temporal attestation and replica of the first, the pledge and exemplar of the last. Therefore God made this bodily birth participate in the supernatural and spiritual condition of the other two births, by exempting it in certain respects from the disabilities and limitations of the flesh. This exemption is manifest at the beginning in the miracle of the virginal conception *(ex fide et Spiritu Sancto),* and at the end in the virginal childbirth. The birth of Christ attests that the Son born of Mary in human nature is the Son of God from all eternity. It attests that the fallen creation is taken up again from the beginning. It announces that the triumph of the redeeming Incarnation extends into the realm of the flesh.

In this regard it is an eschatological anticipation, and such an anticipation is in harmony with two signs that the gospel describes explicitly in the account of Christ's birth: the star, "a sign in the heavens" (Mt. 2:9; cf. 24:29), and the appearance of the angels, an advance sign of the "day of Yahweh" (Lk. 2:10-14; cf. Mt. 24:31). In a humble, restrained, and fleeting way God is pleased to manifest at the beginning of his works something of the perfection and joy that they will attain in a triumphant, universal, and permanent way, when, after the time of crucifying travail and reversal, they reach their term.

In a secondary way, the sign of the virginal birth is related also to Mary. It was fitting, in fact, that God should integrally preserve virginity in her who is its exemplar. If her virginity had been altered in the corporal order, its essence no doubt would have remained untarnished, but it would no longer have been perfect in the order of sign. Mary would no longer be the Virgin par excellence, the image and icon of virginity and, according to the profound insight of the Church Fathers, the perfect image and icon of faith which is the soul of virginity. It must be remembered, in addition, that Mary is not only the ideal for consecrated virgins, but the prototype of the Church's virginity. According to a thought very frequently expressed by St. Ambrose (*In Lucam* 127, PL 15:1555b), in her faith she realizes bodily what the Church realizes spiritually, namely, virginity in fecundity, for she conceived God in her heart before she did so in her body (St. Augustine, *Sermon 215,* 4, PL 38:1074). To deny her bodily integrity would thus be to lay hands on the faith of the Church in its sign, this faith without stain or wrinkle, this *fides incorrupta* of which the *Virgo incorrupta* is the icon, the symbol revealed in the realities of the flesh.

Finally, the miracle of the virginal birth manifests the fulness of the mystery of the Immaculate Conception and is a prelude to the eschatological mystery of the Assumption. The preserving grace that exempted Mary from original sin freed her likewise from its principal personal consequences, not only in soul *(concupiscentia)* but in body as well. Mary, the New Eve, the point of departure for the new creation, incurred neither original sin nor the pains promised the sin of the first Eve (Gen. 3): the servitude of libido (3:16b), the pains of labor (3:16a), the corruption of the tomb (3:19). If she remains subjected to the exterior servitude of the world of sin wherein she is born (the crib at Bethlehem witnesses thereto), she is freed from that other kind of servitude which the after-effects of sin cause to spring up from within. The sign of the virginal birth corresponds to the design that appeared in the conception by the Holy Spirit and was to culminate in the Assumption, that is, the triumph of the Redeemer who saves and transfigures not only souls but bodies. This is what the Church Fathers understood in the notion of incorruptibility, a notion at once moral and physical.

Thus the mystery of Mary's virginity *in partu,* like that of the Assumption, recalls for us truths that are overlooked and yet are essential to the Christian mystery: the body is an integral part of man, it is saved by Christ and associated in the whole attainment of salvation, it has been promised an eternal destiny. Already here below the body is affected by the work of grace, for the new creation is at work (Rom. 8:22). God did not refuse to let signs of this appear sometimes in his own body in the form of miracles (Mk. 6:45–49), such as his walking on the waters (9:1), his Transfiguration (Lk. 4:30, Jn. 6:21, 18:6), and finally his Resurrection. The virginal integrity of the Mother of God belongs to this order of signs.

Certainly these signs are difficult to appreciate. Moreover, they are repugnant to the contemporary mind. And yet, one cannot reduce the ensemble of signs and prodigies *(sēmeia kai terata)* in the gospel or those that appear in the life of the Church to pure mythical constructions, in the pejorative sense of the word. Secularized to this degree, the mystery of salvation and its root, which is the mystery of the redeeming Incarnation, would be betrayed.

As to childbirth without pain, which tradition affirms without debate since the fourth century, it is paradoxical that it should begin to be contested in the very day when scientific progress is beginning to speak of "painless childbirth" as available to all women. It is surprising that certain theologians and preachers should begin to praise the "crucifying" sufferings of Mary at the Lord's birth, just at the time when obstetrical clinics are most concerned with denouncing the pains of labor as an alienating and dehumanizing myth.

The sign of painless childbirth witnesses in its own way to the fact that virginity is a spiritualization of the order of the flesh, and that Mary is, in certain respects, the model woman, the woman of the future — just where she might appear to be the exceptional woman.

APPENDIX # 12

WHY DID PIUS XII NOT DEFINE MARY'S DEATH?

The dogmatic definition of the Assumption abstracts from Mary's death, without at the same time making Pius XII an advocate of the immortalist thesis. The Pope wanted to abstract from this question, and where he speaks *in his own name* he avoids any expression that signifies death in her regard. He did not, however, go as far as to lay aside the traditional witnesses that speak of the Assumption in connection with her death. In no way did he censure this tradition or render it suspect. He cited witnesses who speak of her death, but he did not wish to pronounce on the dogmatic character of such an affirmation.

1. Does Tradition Teach the Death of Mary as It Teaches Her Assumption?

The answer to this question is more difficult than first appears. Certainly Mary's death has been taught far and wide since the fourth century. Numerous authors hold this affirmation to be inseparable from the Assumption and an integral part of the faith. (Cf., for example, the resume given by H. Barré, "Immaculée Conception et Assomption au XIIe siècle," *Virgo Immaculata* 5 (1955), pp. 176–180.)

But a question has been raised: Is this Tradition in the strict sense (transmission of divine revelation in the Church), or did a tradition of human origin come to be mixed into the matter? The question is all the more pressing, in that the apocryphals, which spread the theme of Mary's death, contain many another detail that has long been passed on without having the slightest dogmatic or historic value.

Another question arises: Neither at the time when silence reigned concerning Mary's death nor during the long centuries when the idea of her death was spread abroad, had it been discovered that she was exempt from original sin. If she was thus so easily subjected to the common law of death, is it not in large measure because she was held to be subject to the universal law of original sin, according to the expression of David of Benevento (ed. E. K. Rand, Munich, 1906, p. 78): "In praevaricatione primi parentis, peccatrix fuit, sicut et omne genus humanum — In the sinfulness of the first parent, she was a sinner, as also the entire human race?"

Two minor considerations must likewise be added:

a. The immortalist opinion has been expressed in the Church and has not been censured. It is found for the first time with the priest Timothy of Jerusalem or of Antioch (4th–5th century), according to M. Jugie: "The Virgin is immortal to this day, since he who made his dwelling in her transferred her to the place of his Ascension" (PG 86:1:248; critical edition in M. Jugie, *La mort et l'Assomption,* Rome, Vaticana, 1944, p. 72). In the seventeenth century an anonymous author wrote a *Tractatus de immortalitate B.V.M.* that C. Balic published in Rome in 1948. M. Jugie, who was involved in drawing up the terms of the dogmatic definition, is at the origin of the modern immoralist current, which has as its principal representatives T. Gallus and G. Roschini. Certain of these authors say they were encouraged by Pius XII himself.

b. If this immortalist current of thought is minute in comparison with the ensemble of tradition, one should nevertheless note in the tradition itself the doubts, hesitations, or reservations that are voiced concerning Mary's death. They begin with the first text that formally takes up the question, that of Epiphanius of Salamis (d. 403), cited *supra*, p. 63. Without doubting her death, Gottschalk of Limburg (d. 1095) adds this restriction: "Non est dignum tuam corporis solutionem appellare mortem, sed tantum Virginis dormitionem vel Assumptionem — It is not proper to call your bodily dissolution death, but only the dormition or Assumption of the Virgin" (*Opusc. 5, Sermo de B.V.M.* 13, ed. G. Dreves, Godescalcus Lintpurgensis . . . , Leipzig, Reiland, 1897, p. 164).

2. Is Mary's Death Implied in the Dogmatic Affirmation of the Assumption?

One fact has impressed theologians who seriously reflect on this question: whereas all sorts of reasons of fittingness and implications converge unrestrictedly on the fact of the Blessed Virgin's bodily glorification, the reasons of fittingness in favor of her death are at once less numerous and contradicted by other reasons.

a. The strongest argument in favor of Mary's death is that she should be *configured to Christ in her death* before having part in his Resurrection. This seems all the more proper in that she is the universal model of the redeemed. But one might ask in reply whether it did not suffice for her to be configured by her compassion on Calvary, when "a sword" of sorrow "pierced her soul" (Lk. 2:35), at which time she *"died in spirit"* with Christ, according to a traditional expression that goes back to Arnold of Chartres (12th century). If her configuration to the death of Christ was realized only in this way (spiritually and not materially), her relation to Christ and the Church appears only the more harmonious in many respects. In fact, from several angles, Mary resembles the Church more than she does Christ. More precisely, *where she is different from Christ, it is in order to resemble the Church.* Since she did not die on Calvary at the same time as Christ did, but was configured to his death spiritually, as is the Church by faith and the bath of regeneration, it would be fitting that she share also with the Church the privilege of immortality. For, to interpret the texts correctly, it seems that the Church, on the day of the parousia, will not die (1 Thes. 4:17, 1 Cor. 15:21, 2 Cor 5:2–4; cf. F. Prat, *Théologie de saint Paul,* 16th ed., Paris, 1927, t. 1, pp. 90–92, and L. Cerfaux, *Le Christ dans la théologie de saint Paul,* Paris, Cerf, 1951, pp. 33–46). Immortality is therefore called for by the law that has been seen verified throughout the length of this treatise: Mary anticipates in her own person whatever the Church after her realizes collectively, from her holy and spotless origin to her bodily glorification. In being clothed with immortality without being deprived of her mortal body, Mary would be more perfectly the eschatological image of the incorruptible Church. The strongest of the reasons given in favor of Mary's death is therefore neutralized in many regards.

b. Another reason given for her death goes like this: Mary never knew sin, but she at least took upon herself the penalties of sin, since this enabled her to cooperate more effectively in the redemption from sin. In this regard, is it not fitting that she assume the principal penalty, that of death? In reply one might observe that the argument is impressive, but that it too finds itself counterbalanced. In fact, according to the firm belief of the Church, Mary was exempt from the principal penalties inflicted on Eve: disorder in the instincts *(concupiscentia),* servitude to sexual libido (Gen. 3:16b), the pains of labor (Gen. 3:16a), as has been seen in Appendix # 11, *supra.* Immortality would harmoniously crown this series of exemptions.

Undoubtedly Mary was not freed from all the sufferings introduced into this world of sin. She suffered anxiety at the time of Joseph's doubt (Mt. 1:19), she suffered the trip to

Bethlehem, the futile search for lodging, the discomfort of the stable (Lk. 2:1–7), persecution from Herod, the flight into Egypt (Mt. 2:13–19), the life of poverty at Nazareth, the loss of Jesus in the Temple (Lk. 2:41–50) — first touch of the "sword" predicted by Simeon (Lk. 2:35) — compassion on Calvary (Jn. 19:25–27), and finally the persecutions against the Church (Acts 1:14, 4:1–7, 5:33–42, 12:1, 25; cf. Apoc. 12:2, 13–15).

In short, Mary bore most of the burdens common to humanity, but not all. The law that accounts for this double series of observations can be formulated thus: Mary suffered pains of external origin (persecutions, wickedness and perversity of men, trials linked to the complexity of the world as well as to its disorder), but not pains originating from within, that is, not those that for every man stem from the degradation of his own nature. In this respect the solution that would "take care of everything" would be that Mary, like Christ, should die a violent death. That is why Epiphanius and several others were impressed by the hypothesis of martyrdom. But nothing confirms such a supposition. If God had wished to give her that kind of conformity to his Passion, would he not have let something be known about it? Of what, then, did the immaculate Virgin die? It is hard to see why an excess of love should have caused the *separation* of her *soul,* rather than the *Assumption* of her virginal *body.*

c. The arguments given in proof of the Assumption have a tendency to "prove too much," as has been remarked by those who have evaluated them seriously. In other words, these arguments tend to prove her *exemption* from death, not her *death* and resurrection.

Such is the case with the argument drawn from the divine motherhood, as developed by Dom Frenaud, "Preuve théologique de l'Assomption corporelle de Marie, fondée sur le dogme de la Maternité divine," EM 6 (1948), pp. 119–147: "The divine motherhood, as relation and attitude, was at least partially not subject to loss. . . . The state of death for

Mary would stain this relation and attitude with an essential imperfection" (*Ibid.,* p. 146). In this perspective, says Dom Frenaud, "the real problem and difficulty lie . . . in finding the accidental motive strong enough to justify a death contrary to the natural exigencies of the divine motherhood" (*Ibid.,* p. 144).

The argument drawn from the virginity *in partu* involves the same difficulty. In its most characteristic form, the text of St. John Damascene (PG 96:741b), it was given by Pius XII in the Bull *Munificentissimus* (AAS 42 (1950), p. 761): "It was fitting that she who had kept her virginity intact in childbirth, should keep her own body free from all corruption. . . ." Whether one wants it or not (and this is valid for the two arguments cited here, as well as for the classical argument drawn from the Immaculate Conception), death, however brief, ineluctably implies corruption of the body of the Theotokos, of that virginal body, that body of the one who was without sin from her conception on.

In fact, taking death to be, at least according to the Thomist thesis generally received, the separation of soul and body, the body is left corrupted as soon as the soul separates from it, for the soul is not only the vital principle of the body, it is its substantial form and constitutes it intrinsically. The fundamental distinction to establish is not between *soul and body,* but between *the soul and the matter that it informs.* For the corpse, despite appearances, is no longer the body. A body is living matter informed by the soul. The corpse is the figure left on this matter by the soul that has disappeared, like the imprint left by the foot on soft ground. It is therefore no longer a body, but lifeless matter, endowed with a new and inferior form; indeed, there is no longer question of one single form, but of a multiplicity of forms, for the corpse has no more unity than the ensemble of the grains of sand in which the foot has imprinted its form in passing. This matter has ceased to belong to the *dead person* and has returned to the cycle of nature. Death, wherein the substantial form lets go in favor of inferior forms, corresponds very exactly to the philosophic definition of corruption: *corruptio est motus quo amittitur forma substantialis* — corruption is the movement in which substantial form is lost. That the corpse should be kept from falling apart by certain natural conditions or by God's miraculous intervention does not prevent this matter from being alienated; the change of the body into a corpse realizes the concept of corruption.

The problem that arises is evident. Theological argument tends to establish the incorruptibility of Mary's body. And that is what a great part of tradition confirms. There is thus some repugnance in speaking of corruption in her regard. Would God have abandoned this body, preserved in so striking a fashion in its bodily virginity, to much more serious toll of loss?

This development is not aimed at exaggerating the difficulty, but at honestly evaluating it. A distinction may help to smooth it out to some extent:

a. On the one hand there is the *philosophical notion* of corruption that has just been defined. And Christ himself underwent this, according to St. Thomas (*Quodlibet* 3, art. 4, ed. Vivès, t. 15, pp. 400–401). Certainly, *on the level of his person* his unity was not destroyed. His body remained hypostatically united to the Word. (There remained in this regard a divine mystery during the *triduum mortis.*) But *on the level of nature* this unity was destroyed. There was *vera mors, vera corruptio,* says St. Thomas following in the footsteps of St. John Damascene.

b. On the other hand there is the *empirical notion* of corruption. Here corruption is the destruction and dissolution of the elements which composed the body. Christ did not undergo this decomposition of the organism that was his. And this is the sense in which St. Thomas, again following St. John Damascene, understands the words of Ps. 15:10, "Non dabis sanctum tuum videre corruptionem — You will not allow your faithful one to see corruption." Mary did not undergo corruption in that sense either. According to the constant tradition of the Church, Christ did not permit the flesh of his Mother — the *Virgo incorrupta* — to undergo putrefaction. But there is no absolute objection to her having undergone corruption in the first sense of the word.

However, from the metaphysical point of view this somewhat rough and ready solution is not wholly satisfactory. In fact, the body of the dead Christ *keeps its identity in some way.* As St. Thomas says (ST III, q. 50, a. 5, ad 2), it remained *idem numero ratione suppositi* (the same numerically by reason of the person that assumed it), although by the fact of death it was no longer *idem numero ratione speciei* (the same numerically by reason of the species), for the corpse as such no longer belongs to the human species. The body of the dead Christ no longer had the unity that comes from being informed by a soul, but rather that which was preserved for it by its hypostatic belonging to the person of the Word. On the contrary, the corpse of the Virgin Mary, if she died, lost this identity. It became purely and simply something else, foreign to the person of Mary. It returned to pure multiplicity in the cycle of nature. Nothing connected to the Mother of God the residue of this body that had engendered the Son of God, and the foundation of the divine motherhood was for the moment altered. In the absence of any sure positive data on this point, one is left to wonder whether he who preserved the body of his Mother, as a sanctuary, from the very least taint, permitted the alienation and, even if it is only apparent, the real disintegration that is implied by *metaphysical corruption.*

The resulting perplexity is translated into a great variety of solutions. Without speaking of the old eastern theory, according to which Mary's body was placed beneath the tree of life to await the day of judgment, authors envisage a more or less slow death, or even an instantaneous one. In an extreme solution, C. de Coninck, *La piété du Fils,* Québec, 1954, upheld the following thesis: Mary was glorified instantaneously, but this glorification implied death, a death without corruption since it coincided strictly with the instant of glorification. But the knowledge and ingeniousness which the author marshals in the service of this appealing hypothesis only bring out more clearly the desperate character of the undertaking (R. Laurentin, "Du nouveau sur l'Assomption," *Vie spirituelle* 93 (1955), 185–189). Similarly, the opinions of other authors cover a wide range concerning the reason for her death, its natural cause such as martyrdom, accident, or even sickness, or again, a death brought about by consuming love, etc.

Assuredly, everything would be simplified in the revolutionary hypothesis of K. Rahner (cited *supra,* p. 250, n. 4) according to which every soul in the instant of death would find a glorified body in the new creation, by virtue of Christ's Resurrection. In this hypothesis these risen bodies would no longer owe anything to matter here below, and the empty tomb would become an embarrassing element. Is it necessary to adopt as radical a "demythologization" as that, however prone the modern mentality is to emptying the mystery of salvation of any interference whatsoever in the order of secondary causes?

A reserved position on these questions therefore suggests itself, since we know practically nothing in this realm — as little about the elements of the experience of death, or the condition of after-life, or the exact mode of the resurrection, as about the earthly end of Mary's destiny, of which history is totally ignorant. That Mary died may be the plausible opinion, and its plausibility has been rendered respectable by the flood of authors that have accepted this opinion. But one has the right, with Epiphanius, to go on thinking that the end of Mary remains a mystery, hidden in God, and that here below we must resign ourselves in this matter simply to not knowing.

BIBLIOGRAPHY

A complete bibliography on Mary would comprise about 100,000 titles. Hence a rigorous selection must be made. The selection that follows, consisting largely of works in the French language, was guided by criteria of quality, documentary value, and availability.

Bibliographical Collections

G. Besutti, "Note di Bibliografia mariana," *Marianum* 9 (1947), 115–137 (presenting the sources and method of Marian bibliography); *Bibliografia mariana* 1 (1948–1949); 2 (1950–1951); 3 (1952–1957); 4 (1958–1965), Rome, Marianum, 1950 and following years. Each of these four collections contains from 982 to 7000 titles and appeared in *Marianum* prior to being printed separately. Besutti has also a select and commented bibliography entitled "Panorama bibliografico mariano" in *Enciclopedia mariana Theotócos,* Milan, Massimo, 1954, pp. 801–834. Thanks to these resources, the following summary indications can be completed.

General Works

1. Manuals

A great number were published between 1939 and 1950. G. Roschini, *Mariologia,* Rome, Belardetti, 1947, 4 vols., is one of the most documented; but the documentation, often second-handed, always requires rechecking. Roschini adapted this work in an Italian version intended for a wider public under the title *La Madonna secondo la fede e la teologia,*

Rome, Ferrari, 1953-1954. Two other shorter systematic treatises deserve mention: J. Keuppens, *Mariologiae compendium,* 2nd ed., Louvain, Collège théologique des Missions africaines, 1947 (of manageable proportions, 224 pages, and completed by a collection of Mariological texts), and B. Merkelbach, *Mariologia,* Paris, Desclée, 1939 (Spanish translation by P. Arenillas, 1944). J. B. Alfaro, *Adnotationes ad tractatum de B.V. Maria,* Rome, Gregoriana, 1958 (mimeographed).

2. Overall Studies

M. J. Scheeben, *La mère virginale du Sauveur,* translated from German by A. Kerkvoorde, Paris, Desclée. J. B. Terrien, *La mère de Dieu,* Paris, Lethielleux, 1902, 4 vols. (solid and clear; in several later editions, the last with a long preface by H. Rondet). E. Dublanchy, "Marie," DTC 9:2339-2374. R. Bernard, *Le mystère de Marie,* Paris, Desclée, 1933; new edition 1954. R. Garrigou-Lagrange, *Mariologie,* 2nd ed., Paris, Cerf, 1948. J. Guitton, *La Vierge Marie,* 2nd ed., Paris, Aubier, 1954. J. Nicolas, "Synthèse mariale," *Maria* 1 (1949), pp. 707-744. L. Bouyer, *Le trône de la Sagesse. Essai sur la signification du culte marial,* Paris, Cerf, 1957 (ET: *Seat of Wisdom,* New York, Pantheon, 1962). M. M. Dubois, *Petite Somme mariale,* Paris, Bonne Presse, 1958. E. Schillebeeckx, *Marie, Mère de Rédemption,* Paris, Cerf, 1963 (ET: *Mary, Mother of the Redemption,* New York, Sheed and Ward, 1964). M. J. Nicolas, *Theotokos,* Paris, Desclée, 1965.

3. Encyclopedias

H. du Manoir, *Maria,* Paris, Beauchesne, 1949-1964, 7 vols. (An eighth with indices and tables is announced — a mine of documentation). P. Straeter, *Katholische Marienkunde,* Paderborn, Schöningh, 1947-1951, 3 vols.: 1. Revelation; 2. Theology; 3. Devotion (Italian translation, Turin, Marietti). J. B. Carol, *Mariology,* Milwaukee, Bruce, 1955-1961, 3 vols.: 1. History; 2. Theology; 3. Devotion.

3a. Dictionaries

Lexicon der Marienkunde, Regensburg, Pustet, 1957-, 8 fascicles (out of 25) to date. G. Roschini, *Dizionario di Mariologia,* Rome, Studium, 1961.

4. Publications of the International Marian Academy of Rome (Via Merulana 124)

Founded and presided over by C. Balič, OFM, the Pontificia Academia Mariana Internationalis has been frequently cited above, in particular for the following:

a. Acts of International Mariological Congresses

1. *Alma socia Christi* (Acts of Congress at Rome 1950), 13 vols.
2. *Virgo Immaculata* (Acts of Congress at Rome 1954), 18 vols. (21 tomes).
3. *Maria et Ecclesia* (Acts of Congress at Lourdes, 1958), 16 vols.
4. *Maria in Sacra Scriptura* (Acts of Congress at Santo Domingo 1965), 6 vols.

b. Collections

1. *Bibliotheca mariana medii aevi,* 8 vols. to date.
2. *Bibliotheca Assumptionis,* 5 vols. to date.
3. *Bibliotheca Immaculatae Conceptionis,* 9 vols. to date.
4. *Bibliotheca mediationis,* 2 vols. to date.
5. *Bibliotheca mariana moderni aevi,* 3 vols. to date.
6. *Bibliotheca mariana Biblico-Patristica,* 1 vol. to date.
7. *Studia mariana,* Acts of Franciscan Marian congresses, 9 vols. to date.

5. Mariological Societies

Those publishing annual bulletins are indicated here, as well as the German society which publishes a volume every two years or so.

Flemish Society: *Mariale Dagen,* Tongerloo, 1931–.

French Society: *Etudes Mariales,* Paris, Lethielleux, 10 rue Cassette, 1935–.

Spanish Society: *Estudios Marianos,* Madrid, Buen Suceso 22, 1941–.

American Society: *Marian Studies,* Washington, 1600 Webster St., NE, 1950–.

German Society: *Mariologische Studien,* Essen, Driewer, 1963–, 4 vols. to date, preceded by various bulletins published between 1952 and 1958.

Among the other Mariological societies (Portugal, Belgium (French-speaking), Mexico, etc.) whose existence was more or less enduring, note should be taken of three: the Canadian Society, which published regularly for about ten years after 1949; the Polish Society, which seems to be in full progress and has brought a symposium, *Gratia Plena*, Warsaw, 1965; the English Society presently (1967) being founded.

6. Periodicals

Two periodicals of theology: *Marianum*, 6 Viale XXX Aprile, Rome, founded in 1938. *Ephemerides Mariologicae*, Buen Suceso 22, Madrid, founded in 1951.

A pastoral periodical, *La nouvelle revue mariale*, founded in 1954, became *Les cahiers marials* in 1957.

History of Marian Theology

7. General History

Two complete but rapid histories appeared simultaneously in 1963–1964: Hilda Graef, *Mary. A History of Doctrine and Devotion*, London, Sheed and Ward, 1963–1965, 2 vols. (Catholic, critical spirit). W. Delius, *Geschichte der Marienverehrung*, Munich, Reinhard, 1965 (Protestant; cf. review by D. Montagna, *Marianum* 27 (1965), 241–243).

To note also, the specialized study of M. Brlek, "De B.M. Virgine in iure ab initiis usque ad constitutionem 'Lumen Gentium'," *Antonianum* 41 (1966), 546ff.

On the problem of development, C. Dillenschneider, *Le sens de la foi et le progrès dogmatique du mystère marial (Bibliotheca mariana moderni aevi 2)*, Rome, Academia Mariana, 1954, and C. Journet, *Esquisse du développement du dogme marial*, Paris, Alsatia, 1954.

Sacred Scripture
Old Testament

8. Overall Studies

F. Ceuppens, *Theologia biblica, 4. Mariologia biblica*, Rome, Marietti, 1948. M. Peiñador, *Temas de mariologia biblica*, Madrid, Coculsa. A. Feuillet, "Marie dans l'Ecriture," *Maria* 6 (1961), pp. 15–70. O. da Spinetoli, *Maria nella Bibbia*, 2nd ed., Genoa, Bibbia e Oriente, 1964. A. Robert, "La Sainte Vierge dans l'Ancien Testament," *Maria* 1 (1949), pp. 21–39. J. Coppens, "La Mère du Sauveur à la lumière de la théologie vétéro-testamentaire," ETL 31 (1955), 7–21.

8a. Gen. 3:15

Cf. the extensive bibliography in R. Laurentin, "L'Interprétation de Gen. 3:15 dans la tradition," EM 12 (1954), pp. 77–156, and, for new and interesting suggestions, H. Cazelles, "Genèse 3:15. Exégèse contemporaine," EM 14 (1956), pp. 91–99.

8b. Is. 7:14

J. Coppens, "La prophétie de l'Almah," ETL 28 (1952), 648–678; "La prophétie de l'Emmanuel," *Attente du Messie,* Paris, Desclée, 1954, pp. 39–50. H. Cazelles, "Emmanuel," *Catholicisme,* fasc. 13, p. 56, and especially "La Mère du Roi-Messie dans l'Ancien Testament," *Maria et Ecclesia* 5 (1959), pp. 39–56, with the review in *Vetus Testamentum* 12 (1962), p. 348. R. Criado, "El valor de laken (Vulgate: propter) en Is. 7:14. Contribución a lo studio del Emmanuel," *Estudios eclesiásticos* 34 (1960), 741–751.

8c. Mich. 5:1

The articles on Is. 7:14 generally examine the text of Micah which witnesses to the same tradition. Cf. also L. B. Gorgulho, "Ruth et la Fille de Sion, Mère du Messie," *Revue Thomiste,* 63 (1963), 501–574, and "A profecia de belém-efrata en Mich. 5:1–5," *Rev. Cult. Theol.* (São Paolo) 3 (1963), 20–38.

8d. Songs and Jer. 31:22

Cf. *supra,* p. 184, n. 3.

8e. Mary, Daughter of Zion

Cf. *supra,* p. 30; also R. le Déaut, "Miryam, soeur de Moïse et Marie, Mère du Messie," *Biblica* 45 (1964), 198–219.

New Testament

9. Overall Studies

P. Gächter, *Maria in Erdenleben. Neutestamentliche Marienstudien,* Innsbruck, Tyrolia, 1953; "La Bible et la Vierge," *Evangile* 35 (1954), new series, # 13; "L'Epouse et la Parole," *Bible et vie chrétienne* (1954), # 7. J. Galot, *Marie dans l'Evangile (Museum Lessianum 52)*, Paris, Desclée, 1958.

9a. Mt. 1-2

N. van Boehmen, "Gegevens over Maria in het Mattheus-evangelie. Toeglicht vanuit hun Christologische context," *De Standaard van Maria* 38 (1962), 137-146, 203-211. X. Leon-Dufour, *Etudes d'Evangiles,* Paris, Seuil, 1965, pp. 47-83. A. Pelletier, "L'Annonce à Joseph," RSR 54 (1966), 67-69.

9b. Lk. 1-2

R. Laurentin, *Structure et théologie de Lc 1-2,* Paris, Gabalda, 1957 (including an annotated bibliography of 500 titles); *Jésus au Temple. Mystère de Pâques et foi de Marie, en Lc 2:48-50,* Paris, Gabalda, 1966 (with detailed bibliography on the finding in the Temple.

9c. Lk. 2:35

A. de Groot, *Die Schmerzhafte Mutter und Gefährtin des göttlichen Erlösers, in der Weissagung Simeons (Lc. 2:35). Eine biblische theologische Studie,* Kaldenkirchen, Steyler, 1956. A. Feuillet, "L'épreuve prédite à Marie par le vieillard Siméon (Lc 2:35)," *A la rencontre de Dieu. Mémorial Geslin,* LePuy-Lyon-Paris, Mappus, 1963. F. Neirynck, "Le Messie sera un signe de contradiction (Lc 2:33-40)," *Assemblées du Seigneur* 11, pp. 29-42. P. Benoît, "Et toi-même, un glaive te transpercera l'âme," *Catholic Biblical Quarterly* 25 (1963), 251-261.

9d. Jn. 2 and 19.

From a multitude of Johannine studies the following are noted:

9d1. General Johannine Works

F. M. Braun, *La Mère des fidèles. Essai de théologie johannique,* Paris-Tournai, Casterman, 1953 (ET: *Mother of God's People,* Staten Island, Alba, 1967), a basic study summing up previous works.

9d2. On Cana

M. E. Boismard, *Du baptême à Cana*, Paris, Cerf, 1956, pp. 153-159. J. P. Charlier, *Le signe de Cana*, Brussels, Pensée catholique, 1959. A. Bresolin, *L'esegesi patristica di Giov. 2, 4*, Vicenza, 1964. J. P. Michaud, *Le signe de Cana dans le contexte johannique*, Montréal, Montfortaines, 1964. A. Feuillet, "La signification fondamentale du premier miracle de Cana," *Revue Thomiste* 65 (1965), 517-535.

9d3. On Jn. 19:25-27

M. de Groot, "Un schème de Révélation dans le quatrième Evangile," *New Testament Studies* 8 (1961-1962), 142-150; "Bases bibliques de la maternité spirituelle," EM 16 (1959), pp. 35-54. A. Kerrigan, "Jn. 19:25-27 in the Light of Johannine Theology and the Old Testament," *Antonianum* 35 (1960), 369-416. A. Feuillet, "Les adieux du Christ à sa Mère et la maternité spirituelle de Marie (Jn 19:25-27)," NRT 96 (1964), 469-489. This study was taken up anew and expanded in *Biblica* 47 (1966), 169-184, 361-380, 557-573.

9d4. Apocalypse 12

B. LeFrois, *The Woman Clothed with the Sun, Apoc. 12. Individual or Collective?*, Rome, Orbis catholicus, 1954. L. Cerfaux, "La vision de la femme et du dragon de l'Apocalypse en relation avec le Protévangile," ETL 31 (1955), 21-34. A. M. Dubarle, "La femme couronnée d'étoiles," *Mélanges bibliques . . . A. Robert*, Paris, Bloud, 1957, pp. 512-518. A. Tabucco, "La donna ravvolta di sole (Apoc. 12)," *Marianum* 19 (1957), 289-334 (on the Catholic exegesis of Apoc. 12 in the mid-19th century). S. Lyonnet, "Maria santissima nell' Apocalisse," *Tabor* (Rome) 25 (1959), 213-222. P. Prigent, *Apocalypse 12. Histoire de l'exégèse*, Tübingen, Mohr, 1959. A. Feuillet, "Le Messie et sa mère d'après le chapitre XII de l'Apocalypse," *Revue biblique* 66 (1959), 55-86 (supporting a new thesis: "The Messianic birth that Apocalypse describes is not that of Bethlehem but that of Easter; as for the pains of labor, they correspond to Calvary" p. 60).

The studies of the Marian sense of Apoc. 12 have been specially noted, but another current of interpretation remains reserved or negative (cf. R. Laurentin, "Bulletin marial," RSPT 46 (1962), 333-334, 50 (1966), 509).

Tradition

10. Patristic Age

G. Jouassard, "Marie à travers la patristique: Maternité divine, virginité, sainteté," *Maria* 1 (1949), pp. 59-157 (bibliography, pp. 154-157). This basic work does not treat the Eve-Mary-Church theme — cf. *infra,* # 26 — nor the question of Marian cult, linked to homiletic development — cf. *infra,* # 27, Montagna. H. Weiswiler, "Das frühe Marienbild der Westkirche unter dem Einfluss des Dogmas von Chalcedon," *Scholastik* 28 (1953), 321-360, 504-525. Several articles on the Immaculate Conception among Eastern and Western Fathers in *Virgo Immaculata* 4 (1958).

11. Middle Ages

H. Barré, "Marie et l'Eglise du vénérable Bède à saint Albert," EM 9 (1951), pp. 59-143 (excellent synthesis of this period). L. Scheffczyk, *Das Mariengeheimnis in Frömmigkeit und Lehre der Karolingerzeit (Erfurter theologische Studien* 5), Leipzig, St. Benno, 1959.

The centuries (1270-1600) following the Carolingian epoch are not covered by any overall study. A series of monographs moves from the origins of Benedictine monasticism to St. Francis de Sales in *Maria* 2 (1951), pp. 540-1107. Rich documentation grouped by theological themes is given by B. Korošak, *Mariologia S. Alberti Magni ejusque coaequalium (Bibliotheca mariana medii aevi 8),* Rome Academia Mariana, 1954. The first seven volumes of this *Bibliotheca* are to be noted, as well as *Virgo Immaculata* 5 (1958).

12. 17th-18th Centuries

G. Flachaire, *La dévotion à la Vierge dans la littérature catholique au commencement du XVIIe siècle,* Paris, Leroux, 1916. P. Hoffer, *La dévotion mariale au déclin du XVIIIe siècle. Autour . . . des "Avis salutaires,"* Paris, Cerf, 1938. C. Dillenschneider, *Mariologie de Saint Alphonse de Liguori,* Fribourg, 1931 (on the 18th century, in the framework of which St. Alphonse is situated in Tome 1).

Cf. also the numerous monographs in *Maria* 2 (1952) and 3 (1954), and in *Virgo Immaculata* passim.

13. 19th-20th Centuries

R. Laurentin, *Marie, L'Eglise et le Sacerdoce,* Paris, Nouvelles Editions Latines, 1952, vol. 1, pp. 346-628 and 649-670, describes the attainments and shortcomings of this period. A series of monographs appears also in *Maria* 3 (1954).

14. Pontifical Magisterium

A. Tondini, *Le Encicliche mariane,* Rome, Belardetti, 1950, new edition 1955 (text and translation of Marian documents of the Holy See, 1849-1949). J. Bourassé, *Summa aurea,* Paris, Migne, 1862, t. 7, col. 9-643 (Documents from earliest times to 1860). *Collection des Enseignements Pontificaux,* # *205 Notre Dame,* Paris, Desclée, 1957 (French translation of texts from Benedict XIV to Pius XII; ET: *Papal Teachings — Our Lady,* Boston, St. Paul, 1961). D. Bertetto, *Il Magisterio mariano di Pio XII,* Rome, Paoline, 1958; "Acta mariana Johannis Papa XXIII," *Ateneo Salesiano* 1964; "Maria . . . nel Magisterio di Papa Giovanni XXIII," *Salesianum* 25 (1963), 519-579 (synthetic study).

15. Vatican II

R. Laurentin, *La Vierge au Concile,* Paris, Lethielleux, 1965. Commentary studies by the Mariological societies: *La Vierge dans la Constitution sur l'Eglise,* EM 22 (1965); *Doctrina Mariana del Vaticano II,* 2 vols., EstM, 27-28 (1966). G. M. Besutti, *Lo schema mariano al Concilio Vaticano II,* Rome, Marianum, 1966 (with bibliography).

Doctrine

16. Methodology

R. Laurentin, "Un principe initial de méthodologie mariale," *Maria* 1 (1949), pp. 695-706. G. Roschini, *Mariologia,* Rome, 1947, vol. 1, pp. 323-337 (for the state of the question concerning basic principles). G. Philips, "Perspectives mariologiques," *Marianum* 15 (1953), 6-13. R. Laurentin, *La question mariale,* Paris, Seuil, 1963 (translated into six languages; ET: *The Question of Mary,* New York, Holt-Rinehart-Winston, 1965); "Bulletin Marian," RSPT 50 (1966), 535-541 (additional treatment of Marian question); "Foi et mythe en theologie mariale," NRT 89 (1967), 281-307; "Faith and Myth in Marian Theology," *The Present Crisis in Mariology* (Mimeographed), Dayton, University of Dayton, 1968, pp. 175-202.

17. First Principle

A. Müller, "Um die Grundlagen der Mariologie," *Divus Thomas* (Fribourg) 29 (1951), 384–401. K. Rahner, "Le principe fondamental de la théologie mariale," RSR 42 (1954), 481–522. C. Dillenschneider, *Le principe premier d'une théologie mariale organique,* Paris, Alsatia, 1955, along with the reviews by A. Patfoort, RSPT 41 (1957), 445–454, and R. Laurentin, *Supplément à la Vie Spirituelle* 1956, # 37, 227–228. Several articles in MS 10 (1959). C. Vollert, "The Fundamental Principle of Marian Theology," *A Theology of Mary,* New York, Herder and Herder, 1965. G. Gonzalo Girones, "Ensayo sobre el problema fundamental de la mariología," *Anales del Seminario de Valencia* 4 (1964), # 8, 31–72.

18. Immaculate Conception

Because the history of this dogma was entirely renewed by studies made on the occasion of the 1954 centenary, the bibliography is more extensive.

18a. Overall Studies

M. Jugie and X. LeBachelet, "Immaculée Conception," DTC 8:848–1218 (a study that remains valuable in its broad lines). Several papers in MS 5 (1954). *L'Immaculée Conception. Compte rendu . . . des travaux du VIIe Congrès marial national de Lyon,* Lyon, 5 rue du Mulet, 1954. *Virgo Immaculata* (Acts of Congressus mariologicus internationalis), Rome, Academia Mariana, 1954–1958, 18 volumes (of which vols. 7 and 8 comprise three tomes each).

It is impossible to cite all the congresses and their acts (Québec, Saragossa, etc.) or the special numbers of periodicals consecrated to the Immaculate Conception in 1954. Noteworthy are: *Analecta beatica,* Dec. 1954; *Antonianum* 29 (1954), fasc. 4; *Archivo Ibero-Americano* 15 (1955); *Ciencia Tomista* 81 (1954), # 252–253; ETL 31 (1954), fasc. 1–2; *Eidos* 1954, # 1; *Estudios eclesiásticos* 28 (1954), # 110–111; EstM 16 (1955); *Miscellanea Comillas* 1954–1955, etc. An excellent collection of studies with international collaboration was made by E. D. O'Connor, *The Dogma of the Immaculate Conception,* Notre Dame, N.D.U. Press, 1958.

18b. Sources

1. *Eastern Origins:* The oldest texts known were occasioned by the feast of the Conception and are the sermons of John of Euboea (7th–8th century; PG 96:1459–1500), George of Nicomedia (9th century; PG

100:1335–1402), Peter of Sicily (PG 104:1351–1366), Cosmas Vestitor (8th century; PG 105:1005–1012), and the canons of Andrew of Crete (d. 704; PG 97:1305–1316) and of an anonymous author (PG 106:1013–1018).

2. *Twelfth Century:* The principal writings, still very much scattered, can conveniently be grouped under four headings:

a. *Before St. Bernard:* Eadmer, *Tractatus de Conceptione* (PL 159:301c–318d; critical edition by H. Thurston and T. Slater, *Eadmeri monachi Cantuarensis, Tractatus de Conceptione sanctae Mariae,* Freiburg/Breisgau, Herder, 1904); Osbert of Clare, two letters and a *Sermon on the Conception* about 1125–1130 (*Ibid.,* pp. 53–83); anonymous writers of Heiligenkreuz, three *Sermons on the Conception* (Codex 14; the last two, fol. 73rb–76rb, are earlier than St. Bernard; the first, fol. 70ra–76rb, is later); Pseudo-Peter Comestor (published in two very rare books by P. Alva y Astorga, *Radii solis,* Louvain, 1666, pp. 614–621, and *Monumenta antiqua Immaculatae Conceptionis,* Louvain, 1644, pp. 2–12).

b. *St. Bernard:* in opposition to the doctrine, dating from about 1130–1140, *Ep. 174* (PL 182:332–336).

c. *After St. Bernard:* Controversy of Peter of Celle against Nicholas of St. Albans (PL 202:613–632); Master Nicholas, *De celebranda Conceptione contra Bernardum* (edited by C. A. Talbot, *Rev. Bén.* 64 (1954), 92–117; contrary to the editor, L. Modrič, *Virgo Immaculata* 5 (1955), p. 21, n. 31, thinks that the author is not Nicholas of St. Albans but another Nicholas); Pseudo-Anselm, *Sermo de Conceptione* (late 12th century; PL 159:319–324); unknown author toward 1200, *Sermo de decem privilegiis Mariae* (Paris, Bibliothèque Nationale, MS Lat. 13203, fol. 140^v, edited by J. Leclercq, *Revue du Moyen Age latin* 3 (1947), p. 132, n. 102 and in imperfect state in *Miscell.* V, 125, PL 177:807d); two sermons from second half of 12th century, *In Conceptione B. Mariae* (Munich, Clm 27129, edited by H. Barré, *Sciences ecclésiastiques* 10 (1958), 353–359); the anonymous Parisian author of late 13th century (Paris, Bibliothèque Nationale, MS Lat 5347, fol. 197–210^v).

d. *Of uncertain date in the course of the 12th century:* Pseudo-Peter the Cantor, *Sermo Venerandam Conceptionis,* and Pseudo-Peter Abelard, *Sermo Plerique tanto devotionis,* both edited in Alva y Astorga, *Monumenta . . .* pp. 107–138, cited above. Note that the famous

Peter of Compostella, who had been taken as the first western witness to the Immaculate Conception, is in reality an author of the 14th century (cf. L. Modrič, "De Petro Compostellano qui primus assertor Immaculatae Conceptionis dicitur," *Antonianum* 29 (1954), 563-572).

3. *13th-14th Centuries:* G. Guarrae, J. Duns Scoti, P. Aureoli, *Quaestiones selectae de Immaculata Conceptione,* Quaracchi, 1904; *Tractatus quattuor de Immaculata Conceptione, nempe Thomae de Rossi, Andreae de Novo Castro, Petri de Candia et Francisci de Ariminio (Bibliotheca franciscana scolastica medii aevi 16),* Quaracchi, 1954; C. Balič, *Joannes Duns Scotus, Doctor Immaculatae Conceptionis, I: Textus auctoris (Bibliotheca Immaculatae Conceptionis 5),* Rome, Academia Mariana, 1954, and *Joannis de Polliaco (Pouilly) et Joannis de Neapoli Quaestiones de Immaculata Conception B.V. Mariae (Bibliotheca mariana medii aevi 1),* Sibenici, Kačič, 1931.

4. *17th Century:* Documents on the important Spanish delegation of 1659 and the preparation of the Bull *Sollicitudo* of 1661 are in *Miscellanea Comillas* 24 (1955), 80-480 (with an introduction, 1-75).

5. *Definition:* The documents deposited with the Secretariat of Briefs by Msgr. Pacifici (secretary for Pius IX and the congregations preparing the definition) were edited by V. Sardi, *La solenne definizione del dogma dell'Immacolato Concepimento di Maria Santissima. Atti e documenti,* Rome, Vaticana, 1904-1905, 2 vols.

18c. Studies on the History of the Dogma of the Immaculate Conception

Overall view in *Virgo Immaculata,* vols. 1-9, Rome, Academia Mariana, 1955-1958.

East: M. Jugie, *L'Immaculée Conception dans l'Ecriture et dans la tradition orientale,* Rome, Academia Mariana, 1952. Cf. also *Virgo Immaculata* 4 (1955).

West (in chronological order according to the periods studied): L. Modrič, *Doctrina de Conceptione B.V. Mariae in controversia saeculi XII,* Rome, 1955 (pp. 1-62 reappear in *Virgo Immaculata* 5 (1955), pp. 13-73); H. Barré, "Deux sermons du XIIe siècle pour la fête de la Conception," *Sciences ecclésiastiques* 10 (1958), 341-359; A. M. Cecchin, "L'Immacolata nella Liturgia occidentale anteriore al secolo XIII," *Marianum* 5 (1943), 58-114; F. de Guimaraens, "La doctrine des théologiens sur l'Immaculée Conception de 1250–1340," *Etudes Franciscaines* 3 (1952), 181–204, 4 (1954), 23–52, 167–188; L. Rosato, *Doctrina de Immaculata B.V.M. Conceptione secundum Petrum Aureoli*, Rome, 1959; B. Hechich, *De Immaculata Conceptione secundum Thomam de Sutton, O.P. et Robertum de Cowton, O.F.M.*, Rome, 1958; C. Sericoli, *Immaculata B.M. Virginis Conceptio iuxta Xysti IV Constitutiones (Bibliotheca mariana medii aevi 5)*, Rome, Libri Catholici, 1945; H. Ameri, *Doctrina theologorum de Immaculata B.V. Mariae Conceptione tempore Concilii Basileensis*, Rome, Academia Mariana, 1954; M. Tognetti, "L'Immacolata al Concilio Tridentino," *Marianum* 15 (1953), 304–374; B. Korošak, *Doctrina de Immaculata Conceptione apud auctores O.F.M. qui concilio Tridentino interfuerunt*, Rome, 1958; J. I. Tellechea Idigoras, *La Inmaculada Concepción en la controversia del P. Maldonado, S.J., con la Sorbonna (1574–1577)*, Vitoria, 1958; anonymous author, "Preparando una ambajada concepcionista en el año 1656," *Miscellanea Comillas* 23 (1953), 25–64; L. Vasquez, *Las negociaciones inmaculistas en la Curia romana durante el reinado de Carlos II de España (1665–1700)*, Madrid, 1957; J. Stricher, *Le voeu du sang en faveur de l'Immaculée Conception*, Rome, 1959, 2 vols.

In addition, numerous historical studies will be found in the collections and periodicals mentioned above under *18a. Overall Studies*, notably in *Virgo Immaculata, Archivo Ibero-americano* (on the 17th century in Spain), *Miscellanea Comillas* (same subject).

19. Divine Motherhood

The fundamental studies are by J. Nicholas, *Le concept intégral de maternité divine*, Saint-Maximin, Revue Thomiste, 1937, and *Theotokos*, Paris, Desclée, 1965, and by H. Manteau-Bonamy, *Maternité divine et Incarnation*, Paris, Vrin, 1949. On the difference between the two authors cf. *Revue Thomiste* 51 (1951), 214–222. Also noteworthy: papers in EstM 8 (1949) and 25 (1964), and C. Wessels, *The Mother of God. Her Physical Maternity: A Reappraisal*, River Forest, Aquinas Library, 1964 (an attempt to analyze the biological implications of divine motherhood).

20. Virginity

This question is receiving fresh attention amid great confusion. An excellent overall study is that of J. H. Nicolas, *La virginité de Marie. Etude théologique*, Fribourg, Editions Universitaires, 1962. Also noteworthy:

papers in EstM 21 (1960) and MS 13 (1962) and 21 (1970); J.A. de Aldama, "La maternité virginale," *Maria* 7 (1964), pp. 117–152, and *Virgo Mater. Estudios de teología patristica (Biblioteca teologica Granadina 7),* Granada, Facultad de teología, 1963. Finally, the well documented Protestant study by T. Boslooper, *The Virgin Birth,* London, S.C.M. Press, 1962 (reviewed in EphM 16 (1966), 349–352). All these studies have additional bibliography.

On the controversy over the virginity *in partu* a bibliography was given by R. Laurentin, "Bulletin marial," RSPT 46 (1962), 357–360; cf. *supra,* Appendix # 11.

21. Spiritual Motherhood

J. B. Terrien, *La mère des hommes,* 1st ed., Paris, Lethielleux, 1902, tome 1. Papers in EstM 7 (1948). A. Baumann, *Maria, mater nostra spiritualis,* Brixen, Weger, 1948 (Magisterium of Council of Trent and Popes to 1948). T. Koehler, "La maternité spirituelle de Marie," *Maria* 1 (1949), pp. 573–601. L Marvulli, *Maria, madre del Cristo mistico. La maternità di Maria nel suo concetto integrale,* Rome, Pontificia Facolta teologica, 1948. G. Geenen, "Marie, notre mère. Esquisse historique et évolution doctrinale," *Marianum* 10 (1948), 337–352. H. Barré, "Marie et l'Eglise," EM 9 (1951), pp. 77–81 (documentation and bibliography on the historical aspect of the question). Papers in MS 3 (1952). T. M. Bartolomei, "La maternità spiritualuale di Maria," *Divus Thomas* (Placentia) 55 (1952), 289–357. R. Laurentin, "Lettre sur le problème de la maternité spirituelle à l'égard des infidèles," *Union missionaire du Clergé* 13 (1953), # 4, pp. 148–155. W. J. Cole, *The Maternity of Mary according to the Writings of Father W. J. Chaminade,* Dayton, Kaye-Schooley, 1958. Papers from Canadian Mariological Society in *La maternité spirituelle de la Bienheureuse Vierge Marie,* Ottawa, Editions de l'Université, 1958, 2 vols. Papers in EM 16–18 (1959–1961): *La maternité spirituelle de Marie,* 3 vols. Articles in acts of *Huitième Congrès marial national, Lisieux, 1961. La maternité spirituelle. Rapports doctrinaux,* Paris, Lethielleux, 1962. Articles collected by Mexican national commission for definition of Mary's spiritual motherhood, *La maternidad espiritual de María, Estudios teológicos,* Mexico, La Guadalupe, 1961. D. M. Montagna, *Rassegna bibliografica sulla maternità spirituale di Maria,* 1947–1964, Vicenza, 1964.

22. Coredemption

C. Dillenschneider, *Marie au service de la Rédemption*, Haguenau, Bureau du Perpétuel Secours, 1947; *Pour une corédemption mariale bien comprise*, Rome, Marianum, 1949; *Le mystère de la corédemption mariale*, Paris, Vrin, 1951. J. B. Carol, *De corredemptione beatae Virginis Mariae, disquisitio positiva*, Rome, Vaticana, 1950 (the most extensive inquiry on the subject). R. Laurentin, *Le titre de Corédemptrice*, Paris, Lethielleux, 1951.

23. Assumption

M. Jugie, *La mort et l'Assomption*, Rome, Vaticana, 1944. C. Balič, *Testimonia de Assumptione*, Rome, Academia Mariana, 1948–1950, 2 vols. (collection of witnesses on the Assumption). Papers in EM 6–8 (1948–1950): *Assomption de Marie*, 3 vols. B. Nieto, *La Asunción de la Virgen en el Arte*, Madrid, Aguado, 1949. A. Wenger, *L'Assomption de la Très Sainte Vierge dans la tradition byzantine du VIe au Xe siècle. Etudes et documents*, Paris, Institut d'études byzantines, 1955 (a work that completely renews the history of this dogma and the spread of the apocryphals, in the East as in the West). M. Haibach-Reinisch, *Ein neuer Transitus Mariae des Pseudo-Melito*, Rome, Academia Mariana, 1962 (in which, not aware of Wenger's work, he demonstrates that the Pseudo-Melito, studied in a new version, is much older (from the 5th–6th century) than formerly assumed).

24. Mary's Present Role of Mediation

J. Bittremieux, *De mediatione universali*, Bruges, Beyaert, 1926. W. Sebastian, *De beata Virgine Maria mediatrice. Doctrina franciscanorum ab anno 1600 ad 1730*, Rome, Academia Mariana, 1952. P. Pedrizet, *La Vierge de miséricorde*, Paris, Fontemoing, 1908 (iconography). M. Vloberg, *La Vierge, notre médiatrice*, Grenoble, Arthaud, 1938. E. Druwé, "La médiation universelle de Marie," *Maria* 1 (1949), pp. 417–571 (on both coredemption and mediation). R. Laurentin, *La Vierge au Concile*, Paris, Lethielleux, 1965, pp. 115–129.

25. Mary's Queenship

H. Barré, "La royauté de Marie pendant les neuf premiers siècles," RSR 29 (1939), 129-162; 304-334; "Marie, reine du monde," EM 3 (1937), pp. 21-90 (both basic studies). Articles in *Souveraineté de Marie. Congrès marial national, Boulogne-sur-Mer,* Paris, Desclée, 1938 (studies by P. Aubron, pp. 101-126, C. Dillenschneider, pp. 126-148, H. Barré, pp. 149-173). M. J. Nicolas, "Le Christ-Roi des nations," *Revue Thomiste* 44 (1938), 437-481; "La Vierge-Reine," *Ibid.* 45 (1939), 1-29, 207-231. A. Luis, "La realeza de María en los ultimos veinte años," EstM 11 (1951), pp. 221-252. Papers in MS 4 (1953). Pius XII, Encyclical *Ad coeli Reginam* October 24, 1954 (which occasioned a number of studies, including the remaining entries). Papers from Canadian Mariological Society in *La royauté de l'Immaculée,* Ottawa, Editions de l'Université, 1955. Papers in EstM 17 (1956). Abundant bibliography in *Maria* 5 (1958), pp. 1072-1080. Papers read by French Mariological Society at 1958 international congress at Lourdes in *Maria et Ecclesia* 5 (1959): *Mariae potestas regalis in Ecclesiam.*

26. Eve, Mary, and the Church

H. Coathalem, *Le parallélisme entre la Vierge et l'Eglise dans la Tradition latine jusqu'à la fin du XIIe siècle,* Rome, Gregoriana, 1954 (first penetrating study of the theme in the west, this thesis was defended in 1936 and later published). O. Semmelroth, *Urbild der Kirche,* Würzburg, Echter, 1950 (ET: *Mary, Archetype of the Church,* New York, Sheed and Ward, 1963). A. Müller, *Ecclesia-Maria,* Freiburg/Schweiz, Paulus, 1951. H. Rahner, *Maria und die Kirche,* Innsbruck, Marianischer Verlag, 1951 (ET: *Our Lady and the Church,* Chicago, Regnery, 1965). Papers in EM 9-11 (1951-1953): *Marie et l'Eglise,* 3 vols. (bibliography at end of first volume), and 12-15 (1954-1957): *La nouvelle Eve,* 4 vols. Papers in EstM 18 (1957). Papers in MS 9 (1958). Acts of the 1958 international Congress at Lourdes in *Maria et Ecclesia,* Rome, Academia Mariana, 1959-1962, 16 vols. L. Cignelli, *Maria nuova Eva nella Patristica graeca,* Assisi, Porziuncula, 1966 (limited to a study of four authors).

Cult, Devotion, Spirituality

27. Cult and Liturgy

Numerous articles in *Maria* 1 (1949), pp. 215–416. T. Maertens, "Le développement liturgique et biblique du culte de Marie," *Paroisse et liturgie* 36 (1954), # 4, pp. 225–251. Symposium, *La Madonna nel culto della Chiesa*, Brescia, Queriniana, 1966. C. Dillenschneider, *Le mystère de Notre-Dame et la dévotion mariale*, Paris, Alsatia, 1962. Studies of German Mariological Society in *Mariologische Studien 3. Maria im Kult*, Essen, Driewer, 1964. Cf. also the encyclopedias mentioned *supra*, (# 3), which cover the maze of manifestations of Marian devotion. The remainder of the works cited here are specialized historical studies of high quality.

27a. On the Fathers

D. M. Montagna, "La liturgia Mariana primitiva (sec. IV–VI). Introduzione ad uno studio sull' omelitica mariana graeca," *Marianum* 24 (1962), 84–128 (with an important critical report on the authenticity of Greek homilies, in 59 pages also printed separately); "La lode alla Theotokos nei Testi greci dei secoli IV–VII," *ibid.*, 453–543 (also printed separately). H. Barré, *Prières anciennes de l'Occident à la Mère du Sauveur,*" Paris, Lethielleux, 1962 (on the origin of prayer to Mary in the Middle Ages).

27b. On Marian Devotion in Germany

S. Beissel, *Geschichte der Verehrung Marias in Deutschland während des Mittelalters*, Freiburg/Breisgau, Herder, 1909; *Geschichte der Verehrung Marias in 16. und 17. Jahrhundert*, ibidem, 1910. B. Pereira, *Teología de los Santuarios marianos*, Santiago, Sociedad del Apostolado Católico, 1965.

28. Lives of Mary

E. Neubert, *Vie de Marie*, Mulhouse, Salvator, 1936. F. M. Willam, *Maria, Mutter und Gehährtin des Erlösers*, Freiburg/Breisgau, Herder, 1953. G. Roschini, *Vita di Maria*, Rome, Belardetti, 1945. M. Vloberg, *Vie de Marie*, Paris, Bloud, 1945 (illustrated). Lazaro de Aspurz, *Historia de Maria*, Madrid, 1955.

29. Spirituality

L. M. Grignion de Montfort, *Le traité de la vraie dévotion à la Sainte Vierge*, Paris, Bonne Presse, 1953 (ET: *True Devotion to Mary*, 1st ed., New York, Montfort Press, 1957). Numerous commentaries and reeditions exist. M.V. Bernadot, *Notre-Dame dans ma vie*, Paris, Cerf. (ET: *Our Lady in Our Life*, Westminster, Newman, 1949). F. Sheen, *The World's First Love*, New York, McGraw-Hill, 1952. R. Laurentin, *Notre Dame et la Messe*, Paris, Desclée, 1954 (ET: *Our Lady and the Mass*, New York, Macmillan, 1959).

K. Rahner, "Die Weihe an Maria in der marianischen Kongregationen," *Quatrième centenaire des Congrégations mariales. Documents du Congrès européen, Rome, 8–12 septembre 1963*, Rome, Matutina, 1963, pp. 57–80; *Sendung und Gnade*, Innsbruck-Vienna-Munich, Tyrolia, 1961 (ET: *Christian Commitment*, New York, Sheed and Ward, 1963; *Mission and Grace I*, London, Sheed and Ward, 1963). On the question of the presence of Mary, cf. *supra*, p. 255, n. 7.

30. Collections of Texts

P. Regamey, *Les plus beaux textes sur la Vierge Marie*, Paris, Colombe, 1941. F. J. Sheed, *The Mary Book*, Sheed and Ward, 1950.

Apparitions

31. Place of Apparitions in Theology and Life of the Church

H. Holstein, "Les apparitions mariales," *Maria* 5 (1958), pp. 757–778. K. Rahner, "Notations théologiques sur les révélations privées," *Revue d'ascétique et mystique* 25 (1949), 506–514. Papers in *Maria et Ecclesia* 12 (1962): *Apparitiones Marianae earumque momentum in Ecclesia;* cf. the review by R. Laurentin in RSPT 48 (1964), 116–119. L. Lochet, *Apparitions*, Paris, Desclée, 1957. J. Goubert and L. Cristiani, *Les apparitions de la Sainte Vierge*, Paris, Colombe, 1952 (on 19th century apparitions, usually not yet the object of scientific study). H. Maréchal, *Mémorial des apparitions de la Vierge dans l'Eglise*, Paris, Cerf, 1957 (same object as preceding work).

32. Lourdes

R. Laurentin, *Sens de Lourdes,* Paris, Lethielleux, 1955; *Lourdes. Documents authentiques,* Paris, Lethielleux, 1958, 7 vols. to date (vols. 3-6 in collaboration with Dom Bernard Billet, editor of vol. 7, to which Laurentin furnished documentation and two appendices); *Lourdes. Histoire authentique des apparitions,* Paris, Lethielleux, 1961-1964, 6 vols.; *Les apparitions de Lourdes. Recit,* Paris, Lethielleux, 1966 (the account of the apparitions, taken from the 6-volume work).

33. LaSalette

L. Bassette, *Le fait de La Salette,* Paris, Cerf, 1954. J. Jaouen, *La grâce de La Salette au regard de l'Eglise,* Paris, Cerf, 1965. Association de recherches historiques, *Pour servir à l'histoire réelle de La Salette. Documents,* Paris, Nouvelles Editions Latines, 1963-1964, 2 vols. (interesting documents but published without order or critical method).

Catechetics and Practical Questions

Special issue, "La doctrine mariale dans l'exposé de la foi," *Évangéliser* (1953), 315-317. Special number, "La Vierge Marie et la formation religieuse," *Lumen Vitae* 8 (1953), # 2, 196-312. M. J. Gerlaud, *Les ouvriers et la Vierge Marie,* Paris, Editions ouvrières, 1958. Anonymous, *Marie, l'Eglise, et le militant,* Montréal, 1958. F. Alvear, "Reflexiones sobre la pastoral mariana en Chile," *Teología y vida* 5 (1964), 159-206.

Ecumenism

34. General Works. Studies Appearing in the Following Collections:

EstM 32 (1961). EM 19-21 (1962-1964): *Mariologie et Oecuménisme,* 3 vols. C. Balič (ed.), *De Maria et Oecumenismo,* Rome, Academia Mariana, 1962.

35. Catholic Studies on Protestant Mariology

C. Crivelli, "Marie et les protestants," *Maria* 1 (1949), pp. 675–695. G. Philips, "L'opposition protestante à la mariologie," *Marianum* 11 (1949), 469–488. J. Hamer, "Les protestants devant la mariologie," *Journées mariales sacerdotales* 1 (1951), 125–149. Y. Congar, "Marie et l'Eglise chez les protestants," EM 10 (1952), pp. 87–106. J. Hamer, "Marie et le protestantisme," *Maria* 5 (1958), pp. 983–1006. T. O'Meara, *Mary in Protestant and Catholic Theology*, New York, Sheed and Ward, 1966 (the most complete overall study to date).

For authors of the 17th–19th centuries bibliography additional to what the above authors give is available in A. Roskovany, *Immaculata ex monumentis omnium saeculorum*, Budapest, 1873–1881, t. 1, pp. 298–303; t. 3, pp. 1–4, 545–554; t. 6, pp. 418–421, and is continued in G. Roschini, *Mariologia*, 1947 edition, t. 1, pp. 306–316. For the modern period, cf. G. Besutti, *supra*, in the "bibliographical collections."

36. Studies by Protestant Authors

R. Schimmelpfennig, *Die Geschichte des Marienverehrung in deutschen Protestantismus*, Paderborn, Schöningh, 1952. W. Tappolet, *Das Marienlob der Reformatoren: Luther, Calvin, Zwingli, Bullinger*, Tübingen, Katzmann, 1963 (with Luther's texts uniformly translated or transcribed into modern German). M. Thurian, *Marie, Mère du Seigneur, figure de l'Eglise*, Taizé, 1962 (ET: *Mary, Mother of All Christians*, New York, Herder and Herder, 1964). C. A. de Ridder, *Maria als Miterlöserin*, Göttingen, Vandenhoeck und Ruprecht, 1965 (translated from the Dutch, *Maria Mederverlosseres*, 1965). W. Borowsky, *Verdrängt Maria Christus*, Schwenningen/Neckar, Kronenstrasse 7, 1964.

37. On Anglicanism

S. Cwiertniak, *La Vierge Marie dans la Tradition anglicane*, Paris, Fleurus, 1957. E. L. Mascall, *The Mother of God*, London, Dacre, 1949 (with Orthodox collaboration) and *The Blessed Virgin Mary*, London, Darton, 1963.

38. On the Waldenses

G. Miegge, *La Vergine Maria,* Torre Pellice, 1950 (their reactions to contact with Italian Mariology).

39. On the Orthodox

M. Gordillo, *Mariologia Orientalis,* Rome, Pontificium Institutum Orientalium Studiorum, 1954. Studies in *Virgo Immaculata* 2 (1955), pp. 170–247. A. Wenger, "Foi et piété mariales à Byzance," *Maria* 5 (1958), pp. 932–982. D. Stiernon, "Marie dans la théologie orthodoxe gréco-russe," *Maria* 7 (1964), pp. 239–336 (excellent bibliography, pp. 315–336). B. Schultze, "Marie et l'Eglise dans la sophiologie russe...," *Maria* 6 (1961), pp. 213–240.

40. On Islam

J. M. Abd el Jalil, *Marie et l'Islam,* Paris, Beauchesne, 1950 (substantially his article in *Maria* 1 (1949), pp. 183–211).

Iconography

A bibliography on this theme is particularly difficult because there is a mass of works for either the general reader or the collector of deluxe editions, and yet only a scattering of scientific studies. Suggestions are limited to the latter. J. Lafontaine-Dosogne, *Iconographie de l'enfance de la Vierge dans l'empire byzantin et en Occident,* Brussels, Palais des Academies, 1964. M. Vloberg, *La Vierge et l'Enfant dans l'art français,* Paris, Arthaud, 1954; *La Vierge, notre médiatrice,* Paris, Arthaud, 1938 (along with his many other works of quality in the popular vein).

NAME AND SUBJECT INDEX

Abelard, P., 111
Abraham, 48, 182–183, 188, 191
　as Father of nations, 98
Acathistos Hymn, 82
Achaz (King), 13
Adam, 40, 54, 56, 108, 188, 191
Adam, A., 167–169
Adjutorum simile sibi, 118
"Adonai," 25
"Adoptionist" theology, 179
Advent, 306
　Ember Days, 307–308
　last Sunday of, feast of, 78
　liturgy of, 82
　Mary's role in, 149
Adversus Haereses, 55
Aggiornamento, Movements of, 145–152
Agreda, Mary of, 129
Akathistos, 104
Alameda, S., 168
Albert the Great (Saint), 117, 119
Alcuin, 100, 113
Aldama, J. A., 126

Alexander of Alexandria, 291
Alexander VII, 133–134, 133, 186–187
Alfaro, J., 188
'Almah (Hebrew for unmarried maiden), 12, 43
Alphonsus de Liguori (Saint), 130
Ambrose, 58, 63
Ambrose (Saint), 58, 63, 110–111, 118, 143, 330, 332–333
Andrés, M., 126, 213
Andrew of Crete, 86, 89, 101
Animal motherhood, 222–226
Anne (Saint), 81–82, 294–296
Annunciation, 17–18, 20–26, 30, 113, 203–204
　feast of, 204
　holy motherhood of Mary and, 197–200
　Israel and, 190
　katharsis of, 313–315
　missionary movement and, 150

patristic movement and, 148–149
predestination of Mary and, 177–178
as transforming relationship, 210–211
Annunciation, feast of, 82, 113
Anselm of Canturbury (Saint), 105, 114, 118
Anselm of Lucca, 39, 105, 112
Anthropological theology, Mary and, 157–159
"Antimariological verses," 10
Antioch, Church of, 58
Antipater of Bostra, 104
Apocryphal gospels, 62–63, 294–298
Apollinaris of Laodicea, 292
Apostles, Mary among, 4, 246–247
Apparitions of Mary, 135–136, 172–175
Archambault, G., 53
"Arguments of fittingness," 30, 241–242
Ark of the Covenant, 28–30, 34–35, 148, 200, 210, 270
Arnauld, Marie-Claude, 255
Arnold of Bonneval, 111, 112
Arnold of Chartres, 337
"Artisan of unity," Mary as, 143–144
Art, Mary in, 122–123
Ascending movement, 15
Ascension, 244–245
Aschendorff, 119
Assumption, xx, 46
celebration of relics and, 81
Eastern theology and, 103–104
eschatological theology and, 248–259
feast of, 94
Greek establishment of, 106–109
liturgical development and, 80–81, 83–86, 95–99
Marian congresses about, 138–139
Mary's death and, 337–343
theological issues of, 67–68
Assumptionist apochryphals, 299–301
Asterius the Sophist, 292
Athanasius, 292
Aubron, P., 106
Audet, J. P., 285
Augustine (Saint), 50, 58, 64, 69–70, 72, 97–98, 169, 197, 199, 201, 217, 332–333
Autpert, Ambrose, 95, 98, 100, 112–113
Auxerre, School of, 100
Avis salutaires, 129

Bainvel, J., 161
Bakhujzen van den Brink, J. M., 198
Balic, C., 120, 138, 336
Bandelli, 121–122
Baptismal character of motherhood, 218–220
Baptism of Jesus, 27
Barré, H., 74–75, 94–96, 100, 104–109, 111–114, 118, 201, 306, 335
Barth, Karl, 230

Basel, Council of, 121
Basil of Seleucia, 92, 225
Basil (Saint), 58, 75, 77
Belief, 183
Bellarmine, R., 127
Bellet, P., 173
Benedict XV, 240
Benoît, P., 40, 324
bequirbek, 24
Berengaudus, 115
Bernard, P., 106
Bernard (Saint, Abbey of Clairvaux), 106–107, 111, 114, 131
Bérulle, 128
Bérullian school, 128
Besutti, G., 74, 127, 130–131
Betulah (Hebrew for virgin), 12
Biblical movement, 146, 148
Billot, L., 161, 168
Binet, E., 156
Birth narratives, 22–23
Bittremieux, J., 166
Blachernae, Church of, 81–82
Bodmer V Papyrus, 294–296
Boetheia/boethos terminology, 91
Boismard, M. E., 37, 321
Bollandus, J., 97
Bonnard, P., 321
Bonnefoy, J., 175
Bonosus, 58
Bordarrampé, P., 256
Botte, B., 307
Bourassé, J., 127, 133
Bouyer, Louis, 181, 283
Bover, J. M., 207
Braña Arrese, A., 121

Braun, F. M., 43, 45–46, 37, 174
Breckenridge, J. B., 173
Brehier, E., 122
Broglie, G. de, 169
"Brothers of Jesus," 61, 317–324
Bulgakov, S., 283
Bullarium Taurinense, 186
Bull *Munificentissimus*, 46, 340
Bull of 1854, 188
Bull of May 24, 1622, 133
Bull *Sanctissimus*, 133
Bull *Sollicitudo*, 133, 186–187
Bultmann, R., 47
Bur, J., 254
Burridge, A. W., 107
Busti, Bernardine de, 123
Butler, Dom, 313
Byzantine theology, 99–100, 103–104, 151, 255
  Immaculate Conception and, 86–88

Cabasilas, Nicholas, 69, 119
Caesar of Arles, 306
Cajetan, 284
Calvary, Mary's role at, 39, 98, 110, 123, 337, 238–241
Calvin, J., 124
Camelot, T., 65
Canal, J. M., 105
Cana, wedding at, 36–39, 257
  See also Scripture index
Candal, M., 313
Cany, G., 122–123
Capelle, B., 80, 94
Cappadocia, liturgical feast at, 77–79

Carolingian era, 99–101
Carol, J. B., 119, 129
Caro, R., 89
Casado, O., 126
Cascante, J. M., 95
Catharsis. *See Katharsis*
Catholicism, Mary and, 47, 232–233, 317
Catta, E., 283
Cazelles, H., 275
Cecchetti, E., 74
Cecchin, A. M., 107
Cenacle, Mary's presence at, 4
Cerfaux, L., 43, 45, 338
Ceuppens, F., 18
Chaine, 59
Chalcedon, Council of, 205, 330
Charismatic movements, Marian theology and, 136
Charlier, Dom C., 37, 96
Chavasse, A., 93, 307
Chevalier, C., 86
Christian catechesis, 4–5
Christmas, 77, 80, 149, 225, 305–309
Christmas Ember Days, 93
Christocentrism, 21, 52, 118, 128, 155–156, 159–162
"Christotypical" theories, 167–170
Chrysolaras, Demetrius, 69
Chrysostom, 124
Church, Mary's role in, 167–170, 180–183, 232–233, 246–247, 261–265
Circumcision, 22, 29–30
Claudel, Paul, 276
Clement of Alexandria, 154, 320
Clopas, 320

Coathalem, H., 109
Collum Ecclesiae, 114
Collyrida sacrifice, 59
Communion of saints, Mary's role in, xviii, 71–75, 161, 256
Concupiscence, 333, 338
Congar, Y., 111, 169, 173
Connick, C. de, 342–343
Consent of Mary, 236–237
Constitution *Munificentissimus*, 324
Constitution on Revelation, 153
Coppens, J., 275
Coptic theology, 50, 308–309
Coredemptrix, Mary as, 242–243
Coredemptrix (Mary's title), 102
Cosmas Vestitor, 86, 104
Counter-Reformation, Marian movement and, 148
Cousins of Jesus, scriptural references to, 62
Cucchi, F., 123
Cullmann, O., 38
Cyril of Alexander, 61, 89, 124, 207
Cyril of Jerusalem (Saint), 51, 61, 207, 292

Daughter of Zion, 24–25, 30, 41, 246, 270, 271–272, 282
"Daughter of Zion," Mary as, 24–25, 30, 41, 148–149, 158–159, 246, 270–272, 282
David of Benevento, 336
Death, of Mary, 84–86, 335–343
"Debt of sin," 188
Decree of 1622, 132
Decree of 1644, 132

Deductive method, 165–166
Definition of 1854 (of immaculate conception), 133, 144
Delius, W., 124
Del Prado, N., 189
Demoulin, A., 139
de Roover, E., 10
Descartes, 325
Devreesse, R., 291
Didymus the Blind, 292
Diepen, H., 18
Dies natalis, 68, 80, 83, 94
Dillenschneider, C., 130–131, 166, 168, 171
Dinah, 13, 277
Diodore of Tarsus, 292
Dionysius of Alexandria, 291
Divine fatherhood, 202–208
Divine motherhood, 52, 57–61, 171–172, 196–208
 elements of, 230–234
 as gift of God, 227
 metaphysics of, 224–226
 order of life in, 227–229
 order of structure in, 227
 qualities of, 221–226
 as relationship, 211–212
 sacramental character and, 215–220
 as special relationship, 213–220
Divine sonship, 216
Divinity of the Messiah, 24–26
Docetism, 5, 63, 66
Doctrine, vs. movement, 144–145
Dominicans, 133
Dormition. *See* Assumption

Dreux library, 129
Dreves, G., 105
Driver, G. R., 279–280
Druwe, E., 137, 254
Dubarle, A. M., 36, 43, 45
Duclos, G., 112
Duprey, P., 59
Dupuy, B. D., 124
Duration. *See* Time

Eadmer, 108, 114
Eastern theology, 103
 liturgical development in, 76–86
 spiritual motherhood in, 302–304
Ecclesiological movement, 146, 149
"Ecclesiotypical" theories, 167–170
Ecclesium theology, 160–161
Ecumenical movement, 147–148, 150–151
Eighteenth century, Marian movement during, 127–135
Eleutherius (Pope), 320
Eleventh century, 103–125
Elizabeth, 21, 28, 206, 257
Ellero, G. M., 58, 78
Emmanuel, Mary as mother of, 275–277
Emmen, A., 113
Engelbert of Admont, 119
Ephesus, Council of, 8, 62, 65, 70–102, 124, 154
Ephrem, 89
Epiphanius of Salamis (Saint), 46, 56, 59, 67–68, 71, 74, 83, 248–249, 337

Epiphany, 77
Episkiasei, 27–28
Esau, 182
Eschatological theology, 38, 259
   Mary and Church in,
     271–272
   parousia and, 260–261
Eskenosen, 34
Etheria, pilgrimage of, 77
Ethiopian synaxary, 308
Eucharist, Mary's role in, 38,
   43, 116, 209
Eusebius of Caesarea, 292, 320
Eustathuis, 292
Eustratiades, S., 91
Euthemaiac history, 81–82, 104
Eve-Mary parallel, 9–10, 40,
     52–57, 71, 88, 90, 118, 149,
     158–159, 273–274
Exegetes, 30, 274

Falconi, C., 329
Fatherhood, order of divinity
   and, 217–220
Fathers of the Church, 53–57,
   116–117, 143,
   151, 160, 230–231, 331–334
Feasts of Mary, 305–309
Feckes, Carl, 137
Feuillet, A., 37, 41, 43, 45, 48
Fidelity, Mary and, 183
Fifteenth century, Marian
   theology in, 117–125
Flight into Egypt, 15
Follieri, E., 86
Fourteenth century, Marian
   theology in, 117–125
Franciscan National Marian
   Council, 53

Frangipane, D., 18
Free motherhood, 194–196
Frenaud, G., 75, 136, 339
French Mariological Society,
   162
French School, 128
Frey, J. B., 320–321
Fries, A., 119
Froidevaux, M. M. L., 55
Fulbert of Chartres (Saint), 101,
   105

Gabriel (Angel), 17, 20, 48,
   89–90
Gallus, T., 336
Galot, J., 137, 326
García Garcés, N., 171
Garçcon, J., 53
Garitte, G., 86
Garrigou-Lagrange, R., 180
Garritte, G., 295
Geiselmann, J. R., 96
Gelin, A., 19
Genealogy of Christ, 16
Generative act, of Mary, 216,
   221
Geoffrey of Vendôme, 111
George of Nicomedia, 39,
   91–92, 112, 303
Germanus of Constantinople,
   85–86, 90–92, 101, 104, 255
Gerson, 165
Geukers, T., 137
Giannelli, C., 173
Girones, G., 175
Gnosticism, 77
Goedt, M. de, 41
Golden mass, of Mary, 307–308
Görres, I. F., 174

Gottschalk of Limburg, 105, 337
Grace of Mary, 20–22
Gravois, M. A., 134
Greek philosophy, Assumption and, 300–301
Gregorio de Jesus Crucificado, 255
Gregory of Nazianzus, 58, 74, 88, 90, 292, 314
Gregory of Nyssa, 79, 292
Gregory of Tours, 306
Gregory the Great (Saint), 94
Gregory XI, 81
Gregory XV, 133
Grignon de Montfort, St. Louis-Marie, 129–131, 205, 162
Gromaire, M., 122
Grosjean, P., 107
Grumel, V., 86, 91
Guéranger, Dom P., 136
Guimaraens, F. de, 121
Gutierrez, C., 134

Haibach-Reinisch, 85
Hammershaimb, A., 275
Harnack, A., 284
Haugg, D., 284–285
Helvidius, 62, 320
Henry, C. E. L., 326
Herbert, A. G., 47
Hermann of Tournai, 114, 118
Hesbert, G., 86
Hesychius of Jerusalem, 78
Hezekiah, 13–14, 276
Hincmar of Rheims, 100
Hippolytus of Rome, 290–291
Historicist interpretation, 30

Hoeck, J. M., 86
Hoffer, P., 129
Holiness, of Mary, 64–65, 239–240
Holstein, H., 73
Holy motherhood. *See* Divine motherhood, of Mary
Holy Office, Decree of, 328–329
Holy of Holies (Old Testament), 200
Holy See, 132–133, 139
Holy Spirit, 20–21, 150, 157, 159–162, 242–243
  divine motherhood and, 224–226
  Marian movement and, 132
  Mary and, 203–208
  Pentecost and, 4
Hoskyns, E., 47–48
Huhn, J., 63
Human family, Mary's role in, 190–192
Hypapante, feast of, 77–79, 82, 93–94
Hypostasis, 15, 203–204, 212–213

Ildefonsus of Toleda, 94–95
Immaculate Conception, xx
  centenary of definition of, 140
  as dogma of faith, 135
  Eastern theology and, 103–104
  feast of, 86–88
  Greek establishment of, 106–109
  as katharsis, 210–211
  Marian movement and, 131–135

purity of Mary and, 184–190
theological issues in, 68–71,
  105–106, 121–125
western liturgical
  development and, 95–99
Immaculism, 121–123
Incarnation, 24–25, 31, 51
  communion of saints and, 72
  divine motherhood and,
    217–220
  liturgical development and,
    74–75, 77–78
  Mary and, 194–196, 198–200,
    212–213
  mediation and, 256–258
  virginitas in partu and, 66–67
Infancy Gospels, 11, 15–16,
  29–30, 63, 294–298,
  317–318, 323
Inquisition, 130, 132
Intercession, prayer of, 88–95,
  252–255
International Mariological
  Congress (1967), 41, 75
Irenaeus (Saint), 51, 53–56, 71,
  88, 91
Ishmael, 13
Isidore of Seville (Saint), 95
Israel, Mary and, 182–192,
  256–258

Jacob, 182, 273
Jerome (Saint), 63, 291, 323
Jerusalem, Jesus' trip to, 22
Jesuits, 134
Joachim, 81–82, 294–296
Johannine Gospel, 41
John Chrysostom (Saint), 58,
  78–79

John Damascene (Saint), 86,
  101, 255, 314, 340–341
John Eudes (Saint), 129–130
John, Gospel of, Council of
  Ephesus and, 50–75
John of Salerno, 101
John of Thessalonica, 84
John (saint), 8. *See also* Index
  to Scriptures, 33–46
John the Baptist, 25, 28, 34–35,
  81, 87–88, 192, 257
John the Geometer, 92, 100
John XXIII, 144, 258
Joseph, 16–17, 31, 321, 338–339
Jouassard, G., 53, 55, 57–58,
  62–63, 65, 67, 69–71, 74,
  85, 290, 321
Jourjon, M., 73–74, 88
Journet, C., 171, 247
Jude, 320
Jugie, M., 81, 140, 250, 308,
  313, 336
Julian, of Eclanum, 69–70
Jurgens, 55
Justin (Saint), 53–56, 320

Katharsis, 228–229, 313–315
kecharitomene, 20
"Kenosis," 9
Kervoorde, A., 137
Koehler, T., 74, 323
Kolping, A., 119
Korosak, B., 119, 125
Koster, H. M., 167–170

Laboure, Catherine, 135
Lagrange, M. J., 18, 323
Lamindus Printanius, 129
La Piana, G., 79

Last Supper, 247
Lateran, Council at, 123, 330
Latin iconography, 104
Lattey, C., 18
Laurentin, R., 18, 25, 29–30, 32, 47, 56, 72, 86, 90, 102, 105, 111, 117, 119, 120, 126–127, 129, 132, 138–139, 142, 160, 256, 285, 297–298, 313, 316–317, 342–343
Law, Mary and, 9, 22–23
Lawrence of Brindisi, 165
Lazarus, sisters of, 158
Leander of Seville (Saint), 95, 98
Le Bachelet, X., 107
Leclercq, Dom J., 106
LeFrois, 43
Legault, A., 10, 317
Leo (Saint), 197, 306, 330
Leo XIII, 237
Liber pontificalis, 93
Littre, E., 127
Liturgical cycle, temporal perspective on, 115–117
Liturgical movement, 147, 149–150
Liturgy, 74–86, 189–190
Lollat, 321
Lourdes, centenary at, 140
Lumen Gentium, 72, 148, 150–152, 159, 181, 191, 197, 204, 236, 256, 258, 268–270, 277, 281, 313, 324, 330
Luke (Saint), *See* scripture index

Luther, Martin, 123–124, 151
Lyonnet, S., 8, 43, 47

Maculism, 121–123, 132–134
Magi, 15
Magnificat, 19, 23–24, 124, 261, 269, 287–289
Mahuet, J. de, 82
Maiden, in Old Testament, 275–277
Maieul (Saint), 101
Male, E., 122
Malou, J, 135–137
Manichean theology, 61–62, 69
Mariale super missus est, 117–125
Marian congresses, 138–141
"Marian devotion," xviii, 147
Marian encyclicals, 11
Marian movement, 127–135
  ebb of, 144–145
  nineteenth century, 135–137
  Post-Tridentine era, 126–134
  twentieth century, 137–141
"Marian theology", xvii–xviii
Marian Year of 1954, xvii, 140
Maries, L., 290
Married virgin hypothesis, 18
Mary Magdalen, 32, 111, 158, 323–324
Mass of the Virgin, 100
Massoretes, 25
Matellan, S., 255
Mater Dei, *Theotokos* and, 292–293
Maternal activity, of Mary, 252–255
Maternal knowledge, 251–252
Maurice (Emperor), 80–81

Mediation, 161
  Greek establishment of, 106–109
  Mary's role in, 88–95, 139, 256–258
Mediatrix, title of, for Mary, 97, 109
Meersseman, G. G., 74, 97, 98, 102, 109
Melodos, Romanus, 90
Mercenier, Dom, 73–74
Mercier, 139
Merit of Mary, 197–198
Messiah,
  divinity of, 14–15
  human origin of, 24–25
  Mary as mother of, 272–274
Metaphysics, motherhood of Mary and, 222–226, 342–343
Michael, 42
Michaud, 37
Middle ages, 103–125
Milo of St. Amand, 98, 100, 111
Miraculous Medal, 135
Missionary movement, 147, 150
Mitchel, V. A., 86
Mitterer, A., 326
Modestos of Jerusalem, 85
Moholy, N. F., 53
Montagna, D., 77–80, 82, 85
Moral order, 183
Moral preparation, 269
Morin, G., 97, 282, 306, 307
Mosaic worship, 28
Mother-goddess imagery of Mary, 65
Motherhood of Mary, 194–208
  divine interpretation of, 201–208
  redemption and, 240–243
Mother of God, Mary as, 193–234, 202–208, 212–220
Mother of mercy, 100–102
Mother of the Church, 114–115
Movements of Aggiornamento, 145–152
Mowinckel, 275
Mühlen, Heribert, 159
Müller, A., 168, 197
Muratori, 129
Mystery, of Mary, 12–13
Mysticism, 325
Myth, faith and, 156–157

Nathan, oracle of, 279
Nativity, of Jesus, 338–339
Nativity of Mary, 81, 94
Navatel, J. J., 256
Nestorius, 51, 58, 61, 65
Neubert, E., 255
Neumann, C., 63
New Covenant, 232
Newman, 137
New Testament, Mary in, 8, 161–162, 318–324
Nicephorus Callistus, 314
Nicholas Cabasilas, 211
Nicholas of Clairvaux, 105
Nicolas, J. H., 327–328
Nicolas, M. J., 171, 174, 218, 254
Nilus a Sancto Brocardo, 65
Nineteenth century, Marian movement in, 135–137
Nominalism, 122

O'Connor, E. D., 81
Octave after Christmas, 93, 307
Octave before Christmas, 93, 307–309
Odilo of Cluny (Saint), 105
Odo of Cluny (Saint), 101
Odo of Ourscamp, 111
Old Testament, 6–7, 180–181, 267–283, 287–289
O'Meara, T., 124
Oriental theology and, 279–280
Origen, 39, 58, 72–73, 78, 112, 290–291, 313, 319
Original sin, theology of, 108
Osbert of Clare, 108
Osty, E., 8, 18

Paganism, mother-goddesses in, 59
Pain of childbirth, 44–45, 318–324
Palamas, Gregory, 211
Panarion, 59, 67
Papyrus 470, 291–292
Papyrus 479, 73
Parousia, xx, 181, 260–261
Parthenos (Greek word for virgin), 13
Paschal mystery, 32–33, 77
Passaglia, Carlo, 135
Patfoort, A., 166
Patristic theology, 146, 148–149, 168
Paul (Saint), 8, 71–72, 205
Paul the Deacon, 97, 104, 113
Paul V, 133
Paul VI, 149, 162, 191, 258
Peguy, C., 191
Pelagian theology, 66, 69

Pelster, F., 119
Pentecost, 4, 203–208, 232, 244–247
Peretto, L. M., 81
Perniola, E., 86
Perrone, J., 136
Personalist view of Mary, 310–312
Peter (Saint), 4–5, 247
Peter Canisius (Saint), 127
Peter Chrysologus (Saint), 72, 97–98, 306
Peter Damian (Saint), 101, 105, 109, 114, 255
Philippe, Th., 174
Philips, G., Msgr, 159
Pieta, of Avignon, 178
Pilgrimage, Mary at end of, 251
"Pious belief," 132, 134
Pitra, J., 111
Pius V, 133
Pius IX, 135, 186–187
Pius X, 102, 233, 241
Pius XI, 102, 187
Pius XII, 46, 82–83, 131, 140, 237, 240, 248–250, 258–259, 324, 327, 335–343
Pizzardo, J., 140
Plato, 325
Plazza, B., 134
Plumpe, J. C., 62
Pneumatological theology, 157, 159–162
Polycarp (Saint), 51, 80
Polygamy, 183
Posterity of women, 272–274
Post-Tridentine Mariology, 126–141
"Poverty" of Mary, 19, 148

Prayer of the Virgin, 252–253
Prayers, of Mary, 73–75, 247–248
Predestination, of Mary, 177–178
Presbia/presbus terminology, 91
Principle of analogy, 167–170
Principles of Mariology, 166–172, 172–178
Proclus of Constantinople, 71, 80, 104
Prokekatharthai, 211
Prologue of St. John, 34, 37
Prophecies, Marian theology and, 270–281
Prostasia/prostatis terminology, 91
Protestantism, Marian movement and, 47, 124–125, 127, 130–131, 151, 284
Protoevangelium of James, 81–82, 294–296, 319–320
Przbylski, B., 53
Pseudo-Albert, 118–120, 165
Pseudo-Augustine, 105
Pseudo-Bernard, 267
Pseudo-Caesarius of Nazianzus, 59
Pseudo-Comestor, 107
Pseudo-Dionysius, 104
Pseudo-Ephrem, 92
Pseudo-Ildefonsus, 98
Pseudo-Jerome, 96–97, 100, 108, 113
Pseudo-John, 84
Pseudo-Melito, 85
Pseudo-Origen, 97
Pseudo-Peter of Sicily, 303

Publications, of Marian theology, increase in, 128–129, 139
Puig, Ramon Roca, 75
Purification, 22, 29–30
Purity, of Mary, 184–190

Queenship, of Mary, 258–259, 279
Quievreux, F., 47

Rabanus Maurus, 100, 113
Radbertus, P. *See* Pseudo-Jerome, 96
Ragazzini, S., 255
Rahner, H., 197
Rahner, K., 150, 168, 250
Rand, E. K., 336
Ras Shamra, 279
Ratramnus, 100
Redemption, Mary's role in, 40, 70, 235–243
 western liturgical development and, 95–99
Redemptrix, Mary's title of, 101–102
Reformation, 124
Reichenau, Abbey of, 99, 104
Relationship theology, 170–171, 209–229
Renaudin, P., 138
Resurrection, Mary's role in, 72, 244–245, 333
Revelation, Mary as, 153–154
Reynders, B., 290
Richard of St. Lawrence, 114
Righetti, M., 80
Ripberger, A., 96
Robert (Dictionary), 127

Name and Subject Index

Robert, A., 184–185
Robilliard, J. A., 120
Robinson, F., 59
Romanos Melodus, 91, 225
Roschini, G., 120, 171, 253, 336
Rupert of Deutz, 39, 112

Sabbe, E., 99–100
Sacramental character of divine motherhood, 215–220
Sacred Congregation, 328–329
Sagnard, 55
Sahlin, H., 47, 284–285
Saint-Cyran, Abbe de, 128
Salazar, 126
Salmeron, 126
Salvation, Mary's role in, 146, 149, 151, 194, 233–234
Samaritan woman, 158
Samson, 13
Sarah, 23
Sardi, V., 135
Sartre, Jean-Paul, 226
Satan, 42
Scheeben, M. J., 135–137, 171
Scheffczyk, L., 100
Schimmelpfennig, 124
Schmeid, G., 62
Scholasticism, 103, 157, 199
Schwerdt, K., 237
Science, of Mary, 51–52, 267–268
Scotus, Duns, 120–121
Scripture, Mary in, 8–49
Seiler, H., 240
Semeion, 43
Semen mulieris, 274
Semmelroth, O., 168

Septuagint, 13–14, 273–274, 276–277
Serapion of Thmuis, 292
Sergius, 93
Serpent,
  Mary and, 272–274
  of Michael, 42
Sertillanges, A. D., 156
Seventeenth century, Marian movement during, 127–135
Severian of Gabala, 71, 292
Silence of Scripture, xvii, 4–7, 46–47
Silent growth, Eve–Mary antithesis, 52–57
Simeon, 15, 29–30, 64, 77–78, 239–240, 257, 320
Sixtus IV, 121–122, 133
Slaughter of the innocents, 15
Slaves of the Virgin Mary, 9–10, 130
Socia Christi, 118
Social motherhood, 232–233
Society of Jesus, 126
Son of God (title of Jesus), 27–28
Sophronius, 314
Spain, Marian movement in, 126
Spiritual maternity, of Mary, 45, 88–95, 97–99
"Sponsal motherhood", 171
Stakemeir, E., 124
Stegmuller, O., 74, 291
Stiernon, C., 211, 313
Strabo, Walafrid, 100
Stricher, Julien, 129
Strycker, E. de, 295, 320

St. Therese of the Child Jesus, 19
Suarez, Francisco, 126, 165
Sub tuum prayer, 73–75, 88, 291–292
Synoptic evangelists, 11

tapeinosis, tapeinos, 19
Tappolet, W., 124
Tel el Yaoudieh, 320
Temple, Christ's visit to, 31–32, 38, 78, 111
Tenth century, 99–102
Tenth Month Fast, 307–308
Terrien, J. B., 138, 207
Tertullian, 10, 58, 63, 124, 320
Testuz, G., 294–295
Theocentrism, 194
Theodoret, 291
Theodosius of Alexandria, 59
Theodotus of Ancyra, 71
Theoteknos of Livias, 85
Theotokos, 51
   communion of saints and, 71–75
   liturgical development and, 80–83, 83–86
   mystery of, 193–194
   origins of, 57–58, 290–293
   spiritual quality of, 91–92
   theological opposition to, 65–67
Thirteenth century, Marian theology in, 117–125
Thomas Aquinas (Saint), 119–120, 131, 134, 175, 180, 201, 219–220, 222, 236–237, 315, 341–342
Thomas, J., 167–168

Thomist movement, 134
Thurian, M., 47
Time, Mary and, xix–xx, 5, 115–117, 178–181
Timothy of Jerusalem, 336
Titus of Bostra, 292
Toledo, Council of, 308–309
Transcendence of God, 230
Transfiguration, 27, 325, 333
Transforming relationships, 209–211
Trent, Council of, 125
Triduum mortis, 111, 234, 244–247, 341–342
Trinitarian theology, 137, 170, 202–204, 212–213
Tromp, S., 127, 169
Turnhout, 86
Twentieth century, Marian movement in, 137–141
Typological preparation, 269–270

Unique relationship, of Mary, 209

Vailhe, S., 86
Vatican II, xvii–xviii, 11, 72, 141–152, 155–162, 203–204, 240, 242, 256–258, 268, 277, 281, 329–334
Vena pura hypothesis, 108
Vestitor, Cosmas, 101
Veuillot, Louis, 136
Virginal birth, 34–35
Virginal motherhood, 230–231
Virginity,
   divine motherhood and, 230–231

dogmatic aspects of, 316–334
  linguistic interpretations of,
    12–14
  Mary's decision of, 284–286
  modern discussions of,
    325–328
Virginity ante partum, 316–318,
  329
Virginity in partu, 57–64, 296,
  324, 329, 333
Virginity post partum, 57–61,
  61–67, 296, 318–324
Visitation, feast of, 20–21, 28,
  123–124, 150, 206
Vives, J., 98
Vloberg, M., 131
Vona, C., 173
"Vow of blood," 129
"Vow of Louis XIII," 130
"Vow of slavery," 130
Vulgate Bible, 20, 29, 320

Ware, 121
Warren, F. E., 101
Wayfaring state, of Mary,
  179–180
Wenger, A., 69, 84, 86, 92, 96,
  101
Western liturgical development,
  93–95
  Marian feasts and, 303–309
Widenfeld, A., 129
William of Malmesbury,
  114
Wilmart, A., 112
Wisdom, of Mary, 15, 282–283
Worship, Mary's role in, 71–75

"Yahweh," 25–26

Zechariah, 17
Zimara, C., 175
Zwingli, U., 124

INDEX TO SCRIPTURE REFERENCES

Genesis:		4, 1	18, 25, 279, 316
		4, 17	316
1,1	48	4, 25	25, 40, 279, 316
1, 2	229	5, 24	249
1–3	48	6	280
1, 16	280	7	280
2, 7	194	8	280
2, 18	56, 118–119	8, 7	321
2, 20	118	12, 16	183
2, 21	56, 118	13, 8	322
3	40, 44, 333	14, 14	322
3, 8–18	273	14, 16	322
3–11,	182	15, 13	274
3, 14	273	16	13
3, 15	6, 36–37, 40, 44, 48, 55, 267, 272–274, 277, 279, 281, 348	16, 6	183
		16, 10	274
		16, 11	13, 285
3, 16	44, 64	16, 16	25
3, 16	333, 338	17, 4	191
3, 16	333, 338	17, 5	25, 191
3, 19	48, 333	17, 8	274
3, 20	9, 36–37, 40, 48, 56	17, 9	274
		17, 15	25
3, 21	273	17, 17	274
3, 24	40	17–23	256

17, 25	18
18, 14	23, 270
18, 17–33	191
19, 5	18
19, 6	18
19, 41	40
21, 6	25
24, 43	12
24, 60	274
29, 12	322
29, 15	322
30, 13	287
34, 3	13, 277
38, 26	78
41, 55	38
49, 10	273
49, 17	273

Exodus:

2, 8	12
22, 20–24,	19
25, 8	34
26	34
40, 34–35	28, 34
40, 35	200

Leviticus:

10, 4	322
19, 10	19
19, 20	19
23, 22	19

Numbers:

20, 17	321
23, 21	15
24, 17	273

Deuteronomy:

10, 21	288
15, 11	19
24, 12	19
24, 12–17	19
32, 11	42
33, 5	15
34, 6	321

Judges:

5, 7	256
6, 37–40	114
11, 12	37
13, 24	13

Samuel I:

1, 11	287
2, 1	287
2, 1–10	289
2, 2	288
2, 5	288
2, 6–8	288
2, 10	289
8, 6–19	15
16, 1–13	172

Samuel II:

6	29, 35
6, 1	28
6, 1–14	28
6, 5	28
6, 14	28
6, 23	321
7, 1–17	28
7, 12–16	27

Index to Scripture References

7, 12–17	15	24, 18	278
7, 14	16, 275, 281	25, 21	37
12, 25	25		
16, 10	37	Chronicles I:	
19, 23	37		
		23, 21	322
Kings I:			
		Chronicles II:	
1	152		
1, 16	278	2, 20	289
1, 31	278		
2, 19	278	Judith:	
14, 21	278	13, 18–19	29, 270
15, 2	278		
15, 10	278	Maccabees:	
17, 18	37		
22, 42	278	5, 54	321
22, 53	278		
		Job:	
Kings II:			
		9, 17	272
2, 3	249	19, 13	322
3, 13	37	19, 14	322
5	249	42, 11	322
9	249		
9, 6	278	Psalms:	
9, 18	37		
10	249	2	15, 281
10, 13	322	2, 2	15
12, 2	278	2, 7	279
14, 2	278	2, 9	42–43
15, 2	278	15, 10	341
15, 16	278	33, 3	287
15, 33	278	33, 11	288
16, 5–9	275	34, 3	287
18, 2	278	34, 11	288
22, 1	278	44	15
23, 31	278	45, 7	15, 279
23, 36	278	49, 16	249

68, 26	12
72	15
72, 5–12	15
73, 24	249
88, 11	288
89, 11	288
97, 3	289
98, 3	289
102, 17	288
103, 17	288
104	280
104, 19	280
106, 9	288
107, 9	288
109	15
110	281
110, 1	15, 321
110, 2	15
110, 3	15, 279
110, 4	15
110, 5	15
111, 9	288
112, 9	288
139, 11	272

Proverbs:

8	15
8, 15–16	15
8, 22–23	282
30, 19	12

Songs:

1	12
3	12
3, 6	6
4, 7	184–185, 271
4, 16	

6	12
6, 10	6
8	12

Wisdom:

7, 15–30	15
8, 1	15

Ecclesiasticus (Sirach)

1, 1–10	15
10, 14–15	288
24	15
24, 3–21	282
44, 16	249
48, 9	249
49, 16	249

Isaiah:

6, 1–12	15
7, 6	275
7, 9	275
7, 10–14	307
7, 14	6, 12–14, 16, 18, 25 43, 275–277, 279, 281, 285, 318, 348
8, 8	14
8, 10	14
9, 1–6	13, 276
9, 5	15, 279
9, 6	15
10, 2	19
11, 1	185, 194
11, 1–5	307
11, 1–9	13, 276
11, 2	14, 21, 229
14, 2	321

26, 17	41
41, 8	289
41, 10	289
51, 1	183
51, 2	183
51, 17	184
51, 21–22	184
52, 1–2	184
52, 7–8	184
52. 12	184
53	191, 233
53, 1–5	233
53, 5	233
53, 6	233
53, 7	233
53, 10	233
53, 12	232
54, 4–8	184
61, 1	206
61, 2	206
61, 10	184
61, 11	184
62, 4	184
62, 5	184
66, 7	246
66, 8	41, 246
66, 9	41, 246
66, 10–13	246

Jeremiah:

2, 18	37
13, 18	278
22, 6	278
22, 16	19
31, 17–22	184
31, 22	184–185, 271, 348

Daniel:

7, 13–14	15
7, 25	42

Hosea:

1, 4	25
1, 7	25
14, 1	37
2	184

Joel:

2, 21–27	24

Micah:

2, 13	15
4, 9	246
4, 10	246
5, 1	43, 267, 277–278, 281, 348
5, 2	6, 16, 43, 277–278, 281
5, 3	277–278, 281
5, 4	277–278
7, 20	289

Habbakuk:

3, 18	287

Zephaniah:

1, 14	25
3, 14	24–25, 270, 272
3, 15	16, 24–25, 270

3, 16	24–25, 270	10, 17	319
3, 17	24–25, 270	11, 29	19, 22
		12, 46–50	11, 317, 321
Zachariah:		13, 52	50
		13, 55	321–322
9, 9	24	13, 56	321–322
		16, 16	27
Malachi:		16, 28	321
		18, 12	195
3, 12	287	20, 28	191
		22, 1–14	39
Matthew:		24, 29	332
		24, 31	332
1, 1–16	55	25, 1–13	39
1–2	5, 16, 74, 81, 317, 349	27, 51–54	245
1, 16	16, 318	27, 52	250
1, 18	14, 16, 203, 318, 321	27, 56	40, 323
1, 18–23	14, 16, 318	28, 20	321
1, 18–25	14, 77, 316		
1, 19	338	Mark:	
1, 20	203, 318, 321		
1, 21	14, 16, 25, 233	1, 19	173
1, 22	277, 281–282	1, 20	173
1, 23	196, 277, 281–282	1, 24	37
1, 24	277, 281–282, 318	2, 13	173
1, 25	15, 281–282, 318, 320–321	2, 17	195
		3, 20	11
2, 1	318	3, 21	11, 323
2, 1–12	77, 180	3, 31–35	11, 22, 146, 321
2, 5	17, 318	5, 7	37
2, 6	17, 318	6, 1–6	11, 321–322
2, 7	17	6, 3	317, 321–323
2, 9	332	6, 45–49	333
2, 13–19	339	9, 1	333
2, 21	318	10, 43	191
2, 23	318, 320	10, 45	191
5, 17	23	15, 40	323
6, 34	180	15, 47	323
		16, 1	323

Index to Scripture References 387

Luke:

1	29, 43, 289, 349	1, 34–46	24
1, 2	3–4, 43	1, 39	28, 48, 246
1–2	3–4, 16–18, 23, 28, 33–34, 43, 47, 72, 74, 81, 317	1, 39–45	21
		1, 39–46	35
		1, 39–56	17
		1, 41–45	35
1, 5	318	1, 42	21, 23, 29, 79, 196, 207, 270
1, 5–25	34, 87		
1, 13	34	1, 44	34, 196, 219
1, 17	34	1, 45	17, 20, 22, 196–197
1, 20	17	1, 46–55	287–289
1, 26	18, 284, 307	1, 46–56	48
1, 26–35	78	1, 48	19–22, 195–196, 269
1, 26–38	23, 87	1, 49	20, 22, 242
1, 27	196, 318–319	1, 52	19, 269
1, 28	19–20, 22, 24, 78–79, 186, 196, 207, 219, 224, 229	1, 54	17, 233
		1, 55	233
		1, 57–58	34
		1, 76–77	34
1, 28–33	25	1, 76, 78	34
1, 28–38	22, 233	1, 76–80	34
1, 28–55	25, 43	2, 1–7	339
1, 29	12, 17, 24–26, 224	2, 3	35
1, 30	20, 22, 24, 196, 224	2, 4	35, 318
1, 31	16, 18, 24, 288, 285, 318	2, 5	18, 318
		2, 6	320
1, 32	21, 33, 35	2, 7	35
1, 32–33	28	2, 8–20	23
1, 34	12, 16–18, 24, 35, 196, 203, 284, 316, 319	2, 10	332
		2, 11	318, 332
		2, 12	21, 332
1, 35	16, 20–21, 24, 26, 28, 33, 35, 53, 196, 200, 203, 205–206, 210, 229, 246, 316	2, 13	332
		2, 14	17, 22
		2, 16	21–22
		2, 19	17, 22
1, 37	23, 270	2, 20	22
1, 38	17, 48, 53, 79, 183, 192, 195–197, 206, 219, 233, 236	2, 21	22
		2, 22	23, 48
		2, 24	23

2, 22–29	22	4, 30	333
2, 22–35	22, 77	4, 34	37
2, 22–38	22–23, 78	6, 20	19
2, 26	30	8, 19–21	11, 235, 321
2, 27	21, 23	8, 28	37
2, 29	30	9, 35	27
2, 30	35	11, 27	21, 235
2, 32	22–23, 29, 35	11, 28	21–22, 146, 214, 235
2, 33	11	11, 29	22
2, 33–40	349	12, 37	39, 191, 259
2, 34	234	14, 28	166
2, 35	21, 32, 43, 64, 68, 110, 234, 337, 339, 349	16, 24	32
		16, 25	32
		18, 18	22
2, 35–52	21, 33,	22, 15–20	38
2, 39	23, 318	22, 70	27
2, 40	35, 179	23, 46	32
2, 40–51	22, 323	24, 6	32
2, 41	32	24, 46	236
2, 41–50	339	25–28	23
2, 42	23, 32	30–33	23
2, 43	32	34–36	23
2, 45	32	47	23
2, 46	32		
2, 48	11, 31–32, 234, 289	John:	
2, 48–50	30, 32, 349		
2, 49	30, 32, 35, 38, 146, 235, 289	1	34, 72
		1, 1	48
2, 50	12, 17	1, 9	147
2, 51	11, 17, 22, 32–33, 217, 318	1, 13	203, 316
		1, 14	20, 37, 200
2, 52	34, 179, 323	1, 29	41
3, 19–20	33	1, 33	245
3, 22	27	1, 36	41
3, 23	16	1, 46	176
3, 23–28	55	1, 47	41
3, 38	16	2	36–37, 48, 349
4, 21	206	2, 1	48, 323
4, 22	11	2, 1–12	5, 37

Index to Scripture References

2, 1–13	38	16, 21	41, 158
2, 2	48	18, 6	333
2, 3	38, 48, 323	18, 37	196
2, 4	38, 146	19	36, 45, 349
2, 5	38	19, 22	37
2, 11	36–37	19, 25	5, 37–411, 43, 45, 48, 73, 112, 158, 243–245, 247, 251, 257, 270, 302–304, 323, 339
2, 12	37–38, 158, 321		
3, 29	158		
3, 5	203		
3, 34	245		
4, 14	245	19, 26	4–5, 37–41, 43, 48, 73, 92, 158, 244, 247, 251, 257, 270, 302–304, 323, 339, 350
4, 32–34	30		
4, 38	253		
6	43		
6, 21	333	19, 27	4, 12, 36–41, 43, 47–48, 73, 92, 158, 244, 247, 251, 257, 302–304, 323, 339, 350
6, 42	11		
7, 2–6	146		
7, 3	321		
7, 3–10	321	19, 30	37, 48, 158, 245
7, 5	321–322	19, 34	56, 243
7, 10	321	19, 36	45
7, 37	245	19, 41	48
7, 38	161, 245	20	245
7, 39	161, 245	20, 17	322
10, 12	252	20, 26	326
11, 4	158	21	245
11, 21–29	158	22	245
12, 7	158		
13 4–16	259	Acts:	
13, 12–18	191		
14, 2	46	1, 4	48
14, 12	253	1, 7	246
14, 20	51	1, 14	3–4, 204, 207, 244, 247, 318, 322–323, 339
14, 25	51		
14, 26	154, 161		
15, 13	161	1, 15	322
15, 14	161	1, 21	4
15, 15	195, 259	1, 22	4
16, 13	154	2, 12	205

2, 14	4
2, 17	4
2, 17–36	4
2, 42	247
2, 46	247
4, 1–7	339
5, 32–42	339
9, 30	322
10, 23	322
10, 36–43	4
11, 1	322
12, 1	339
12, 25	339
17, 26	191
20, 38	32

Romans:

1, 3	9
2, 21–25	9
7	9
8, 15	205
8, 16	228
8, 22	333

Corinthians I:

3, 9	60, 242
4, 5	321
5, 10	285
7, 8	318
7, 14	285
7, 17	318
7, 18	318
7, 19	318
7, 24	319
7, 29	319
7, 30	319
7, 31	319
7, 35	318
7, 39	319
9, 5	318, 321
11, 26	247
15, 9	173
15, 10	173
15, 21	338
15, 29	285

Corinthians II:

4, 4	169
5, 2	338
5, 3	338
5, 4	338
5, 17	228

Galatians;

1, 19	318, 321
3, 15–4, 7	9
3, 16	274
4, 4	10, 23, 194
4, 5	8–10
4, 6	205
4, 7	228
6, 15	228

Ephesians:

5, 16	180

Philippians:

2, 7	9
2, 7–11	179

Index to Scripture References   391

Colossians:

1, 15	169
2, 9	200
3, 15	191
4, 5	180

Thessalonians I:

4, 17	251, 338

Timothy I:

2, 5	256–257
2, 6	257
4, 13	321

Timothy II:

2, 12	259

Hebrews:

1, 3	169
9, 26	285
10, 2	285

Peter I:

1, 4	216

John I:

5, 7	245

Apocalypse:

1, 17	191
5, 6	44
9	41
11, 19	34
12	43–46, 246, 350
12, 1	34, 43, 46
12, 2	41, 44–45, 339
12, 4	41
12, 5	41, 43
12, 6	41, 46
12, 9	44
12, 12	43
12, 13	43–44, 339
12, 13–17	42–43, 339
12, 14	44, 68, 339
12, 15	339
12, 17	36–37, 44–46, 303
21, 3	34
21, 7	37

POSTSCRIPT
Postconciliar Times and the Future of Mary in the Church

The Second Vatican Council was the greatest council of all times if one considers the number of participants and the breadth of its program. No other council had revised and rethought the whole Church, or transformed it, to this extent. It was impossibly ambitious.

The Council was impossible and yet it was admirably successful, even if it was not able to accomplish all it had set out to do. Unfortunately, the postconciliar time was one of laxities, mistrust and discreet apostasy on the left, and rigidity and schism on the right. The critical wing, buoyed by so many changes and purifications, pushed "criticism" and "contestations" to the point of disintegration, not without ruinous improvisations, against the Council itself.

The Vatican II chapter on the Virgin (Constitution *Lumen Gentium*, chapter 8) had reformulated in biblical and ecumenical terms everything the Church knows concerning Mary Mother of God as well as [teachings on Mary in] the encyclicals, including the participation of Mary in the Redemption according to Luke 2:22–35 and John 19:25–27, two remarkable and misunderstood texts.

Before the Council, the Marian movement—fervent, anti-Protestant and animated by the desire to promote the glories of Mary—had seemed to place the Virgin *outside* and *above* the Church (in a way parallel to the pope in the juridical order). It reduced the status of bishops and collegiality to better show her primacy. Vatican II reminded us that Mary and the pope are *inside and at the summit* of the Church: the pope in the order of visible government, and the Virgin in the mystical order.

The insertion of the Virgin in the *Constitution on the Church* caused the promoters of the Marian movement to fear that this recovery would reduce the Virgin to nothing: that was not in any way the case with the Council; the opposite was true. Unfortunately, subsequent events have often shown them to be right, because too many theologians and pastors turned the attempt at re-establishing equilibrium into the opposite disequilibrium.

The Council had redefined the Virgin by her *duties*, which are the foundation, the mission and the very meaning of her *privileges*. It spoke of these "duties and privileges" (LG 67) without separating them. Now we have so reduced those privileges that we have also dwarfed her primordial duties in the Church. She was indeed the only human cause of the Incarnation, which extends her compassion to the redemptive Sacrific of the Cross (John 19:25–27) and her significant presence at the feast of the Pentecost, where her maternal and feminine role belongs to the integrity of the Church, of which she was and remains the summit and prototype. But she was viewed instead as an obstacle to ecumenism.

> — *"What on earth has happened to the Virgin Mary such that hearts should no longer be as fond of her as they once were?" exclaimed Paul VI in 1974.*

[218][1] One of the first reasons for this deplorable alienation is that after three and a half centuries of the Marian movement

---

1. The page breaks in the French 6th edition are indicated with the page number in brackets.

—concerned as it was with promoting "the glories of Mary" (1600–1958) by creating new dogmas, doctrines, feasts, excesses, and innumerable devotions—her role and preeminent dignity in the Church were relativized and even contested. For, as the Fathers of the Church said, the Son of God has only one Father in heaven, and one Mother on earth (René Laurentin, *Mélanges*, Balic, 1972).

In our medieval sanctuaries, popular devotion had clothed the admirable 12th century Roman statues with beautiful silk robes, so much so that one could no longer see the statue. On these robes, so many jewels were affixed that one could no longer see the robe. After the Council, all the ornaments were removed so that one could see the "faithful wood" as the ancient sculptors had fashioned it. But the concern with authenticity sometimes got carried away, scraping the paint, thereby irretrievably damaging the old wood.

This parable illustrates postconciliar excesses. In contrast to what some once derogatorily called "Mariolatry," in postconciliar times Mary was reduced and put aside: her privileges were relativized or eliminated. This could have been, in a way, appropriate: indeed, in theology, everything is relation. God himself is love, and therefore relation. Christ's hypostatic union is the transcendent relation of his humble humanity to the person of the Word. Divine maternity is Mary's relation to the divine *Person* of the Son of God. All of creation exists in pure relation to God the creator, who alone exists of Himself.

Yet, these fundamental relations do not lead to relativism. They have direct reference to the Absolute. God is love, the principle and measure of all the rest, including Mary, Mother of the Lord. The interpenetration of these relations is not articulated. The Visitation: it does not minimize, but rather it appreciates and discerns the primordial value of these various relations to God. Mary, being the most intimate to the very Son of God, is implicated in his eternal Relation to the Father.

Illumined by the Second Vatican Council, postconciliar theology also relativized Mary's functions and privileges, but in a very different way.

1. The Immaculate Conception

In 1854, Pius IX had defined the immaculate origin of Mary, preserved from sin by God's gracious action.

Before and during the Council, some Mariologists wanted to enrich this privilege. In their view, Mary has been predestined with Christ before the Fall, independently from other human beings. As the New Eve, she is anterior to sin, and does not belong to Adam's descent. She was exempt from original sin. She did not have the "debt of sin" with respect to God—the *debitum peccati* as they say; she might even seem to have no debt of gratitude for having been redeemed by Christ, since she would have belonged to the first creation, before the Fall

In a completely different manner, the definition of Pius IX takes its point of departure from the universal Redemption by Christ: Mary, daughter of Adam, would have normally inherited original sin like all the others, but God *preserved* her from it by the anticipation of the merits of Christ—the precise formula of Pius IX. Mary was truly redeemed by Him. That is an integral part of the dogma.

Before and during the Council, I criticized the excesses of the "ultras."

[219] By contrast, after the Council, many authors—of whom I kept track in my *Bulletins sur la Vierge Marie*, in the review *Sciences Philosophiques*—elaborated on the following theme: every child at the time of conception (and until the age of reason) has not acquired responsibility, since his conscience is not yet awakened. There is no sin without responsibility. The Immaculate Conception, therefore, is not a privilege, but rather given to all men. The only difference left was doubtless the fact that all men do not have the fullness of grace (and some rightly insisted on this).

It is true that original sin is neither a formal sin nor a personal responsibility. It is a disequilibrium of instincts that follows from solidarity, as shown in the Bible. That is why theology called this sin *concupiscentia*, the disorientation of desires. Freud too saw this: the child is *polymorphously perverse*. The Virgin was preserved from this disorientation in order to be the starting point of the new Creation announced by the prophets and the first fruits of the new solidarity of humans in God the Redeemer.

May the celebration of the 150th anniversary of the dogma restore the equilibrium: Mary, like us, a descendent of Adam, was redeemed by Christ to be the point of departure of the new Creation announced by the prophets, into which we enter through faith and baptism. She is therefore not a stranger to our world, into which she introduced Christ from within.

2. Virginity

According to Christian tradition, Mary is the Virgin *par excellence*: this has indeed become her most frequent title in the West.[2] Since before the Council, critical movements sought to erode the integrity of this foundational virginity.

1. Fr. H. Feret and others went to battle against the "vow or proposal of virginity" attributed to Mary. In Lk. 1:3–34, though invited to become the mother of the Messiah, Son of God, she objects:

"How will this be since I know not man?"

To "know" in the biblical sense, for she knows well Joseph, to whom she is already married (according to the firs phase of Jewish marriage, the sacred consent, *kidusim*). The meaning of this little phrase was diverted by many exegetes, who gave it a different meaning—which included liturgical translation—i.e.:

---

2. Translator's note: the expression "Chrétienne," literally "Christian," often in French refers solely to Catholicism.

"for I am (still) a virgin." To do this is to ignore the structure of the story, which presented Mary as a *"virgin married to a man"* (Lk. 1:26), and it insists on the word virgin, picking it up again a line later. For Mary's objection to God is based on the sexual meaning of not "knowing man." This is a problem that many other maidens would have to face during Christian civilization, until the beginning of the 20th century. Many families immediately married off maidens whom God had inspired with the same object [i.e., sexual virginity]; these [maidens] solved these difficulties each in her own wa .

Like Saint Augustine, the Greek Fathers recognized Mary's discourse and called her a "voluntary Virgin"—that is to say, a virgin by a free decision—going against the familial and cultural pressures that [then] held sway. But both scripture and tradition are today largely disregarded.

2. [220] Also before the Council, in 1958–1960, A. Mitterer and J. Galot observed that the pains of childbirth and the feminine hymen are alien to [the notion of] virginity itself, as mentioned in the present work (appendix 11). There is no need to return to this. The Second Vatican Council affirmed without restriction that according to the divine plan and the Gospel, Mary was wholly virgin in her body and in her mind. Those who tried to deny her virginity *in partu* used the following arguments:

a. Tradition holds that Mary gave birth without the pains of childbirth. A. Mitterer and J. Galot, who seem ignorant of this tradition, claim that this has nothing to do with virginity.[3] It is altogether foreign to this notion. This observation is fair, especially since some Russian physicians made the possibility and technique of "painless childbirth" famous. They noted that some women could attain this [goal] by achieving an optimal coordination between their breathing and muscles.

---

3. Translator's note: In other words, virginity *in partu* contains two tenets: integrity and painlessness. Mitterer and Galot attack the meaning of the term.

It is therefore regrettable that critical theologians and the filmmaker Delannoy should portray Christmas through dramatic shrieks of Mary. Such a portrayal accords neither with tradition, nor with medicine, nor with the Gospel of Luke (2:7), the echo of Mary's memories (Lk. 2:19 and 51): *She gave birth to her firstborn son and wrapped him in swaddling clothes and laid him in a manger.*

God was able to choose for his mother the joy of a serene childbirth, which those women were also capable, whose natural techniques were judiciously observed by their Russian doctors.

b. The two theologians mentioned above describe, not without relish, a violent and bloody childbirth. It is not only indiscreet, but it also goes against the tradition based on Lk. 2:7 to describe the Christmas birth in this sordid manner. They criticize, not without derision, the Fathers of the Church who attempted to explain this mystery in their books or homilies. Yet the Fathers, respectful of Mary and discreet—in spite of the importance once accorded to this, and indeed still accorded to it today in Arabic Islam—did not enter into medical descriptions of the anatomical sign of virginity. Their language is not technical but symbolic. In order to intimate that God's power was able to conserve Mary's integral virginity in the birth of Christ, they only say that if the Risen Christ was able to enter the locked upper room where the disciples were gathered, he was able to be born of Mary without violating her virginity in this way or another, arguing for the flexibility of organic tissue. These were poetic and hypothetical analogies, not factual explanations.

We have absolutely no idea of *how*. It is vain and ridiculous to imagine it groundlessly. Every child respects his mother's anatomy, just as all avoid the thought of incest. The Fathers held that Mary gave birth to her Son, in harmony with the most joyful of mysteries. The doctrinal commission of the Council, of which I was an expert, respected this tradition of modesty. We avoided any *discussion* on the *how* of Mary's integral virginity. Msgr. Phillips, the redactor, proposed the solution that confirms the dogma without violating it, by citing the Mediaeval antiphon: *"the birth of Jesus has not diminished but rather consecrated his mother's virginity,"* and the Second Vatican Council added "all joyful" (LG 8 n. 57). Here we can quote the proud response of a Christian virgin to a persecutor who sought to defile her: [221] *"you will not change my heart, you can only redouble my virginity."* As the Scripture says, God's ways are not our ways.

The Councils and Christian tradition have defined Mary as perfectly virgin. It is useless and indelicate to attempt an anatomical reconstruction of the virgin birth, which God has kept secret.

Scripture and tradition only teach us two things: Mary actively brought forth to the world her Son Jesus, swaddled him herself, and this birth, in full harmony with the joy of Christmas, neither diminished nor disgraced her integral virginity.

3. Critical theology also attacked the virginal conception. I had followed the first tentative but discreet criticisms of some German theologians before the Council. These criticisms were given free rein after the Council, in the professional academic discourse that retained the words of tradition while emptying them of their meaning. Mary is a virgin morally but not corporally or biologically [they claimed]. Her virginity is symbolic (not physical or sexual, they insinuated). In this sense, all honest mothers of families would be virgins. They don't seek to be such in their spousal and maternal realism, but a large part of Christian opinion was swayed by this "more natural" interpretation.

In catechism classes, Mary's virginity is rarely taught to children who already know everything about sexuality. The baby Jesus' dad and mom are mentioned as if we were referring to any other family. The liturgical translations of Luke 1–2 and Matthew 1–2 weaken the biblical texts, whose novel and significant expression is rendered mediocre. [These translations] insinuate that the Holy Spirit is the inseminator, or Father, of Jesus: this would be a gross heresy.

The virginal conception is an unavoidable fact of Revelation. The great theologian Karl Barth, formed in liberal Protestantism, reacted from within this hypercritical milieu; and the majority of American Lutherans believe in this biblical doctrine, which is also taught by the Qur'an. Barth's reasoning consists in the following: sexuality, the normal sign of human birth, is not suitable to signify the coming of the Son of God:

> In every natural generation, it is man, conscious of his power, strong in his will, proud of his creative power, autonomous and sovereign, who is in the foreground; and this would not be an adequate sign for the mystery [of the Incarnation], which is the matter to indicate here. [. . .] The sign of human eros [. . .] could not be the sign of divine agape which, for its part, does not seek its own interest. Man's desire for power and domination, as it is expressed especially in the sexual act, implies something entirely other than the majesty of the divine mercy, etc. (*Dogmatics in Outline*).

Barth speaks pejoratively of sexuality: he had some difficulty resolving his problems on that score. But, without going into the particulars of his depreciation (similar to that of St. Augustine), his intuition is profound and just, and I have not ceased to deepen and draw upon it since 1971 (in *Studia Mediaevalia*, Rome, Antonianum, 1971, 515–542).

Indeed, marriage is the summit of creation according to Genesis 1:25–28. Through conjugal love, man and woman are creators, with God, of every new human person. This is a privilege that God did not give the angels, and which [222] the devil does not cease to degrade in sexuality. Yet we fin more often than we think an authentic expression of love in marriages worthy of the name: "*this is a great mystery,*" as St. Paul stated (Ephesians 5:32). The point is not to lower marriage, even though human selfishness and savagery often disfigure it. [Marriage]'s greatness is fascinating; but the birth of the Son of God into humanity is another mystery. This is not a new human person who is born, but the person of the Son of God: a divine person, not only immortal, but eternal and pre-existing. This unique event called for a specific sign. The Virgin Mary herself learned this in the reply to her objection: *I do not know man* (Lk. 1:34), to which the response was:

> *The Holy Spirit will come upon thee and the power of the Most High will overshadow thee. This is why the child to be born of thee will be called Holy, the Son of God.* (Lk. 1:35)

God could only be born in the shadow of transcendence. Freud's student, the psychoanalyst Jones, along with some critical theologians, falsified and even degraded this mystery by presenting the Father and the Spirit as male fertilizers, when in fact their transcendent creative power awakens Mary to her virginal fecundity for the purpose of conferring humanity upon the Son of God.

This message is a literal repetition of the one that described the coming of God upon the Ark of the Covenant (see pp. 28–30 above, [comparison of Luke with Exodus 40:35]), the cloud signifying this transcendence, while the radiant glory of the Ark signifies God's immanence. This figure of the Old Testament is accomplished in Mary, new Ark of the Covenant, when she conceives in her flesh the Son of God, who will say: *I am the light of the world* (Jn. 8:12; 9:5; Jn. 1:4–9).

Lk. 1:35, Mt. 1:18 or Jn. 1:13–14 signify the Incarnation in symbolic, metaphysical, and spiritually rigorous terms, not at all like a divine-human coitus in the manner of pagan mythologies or the psychoanalyst Jones; for whom the Holy Spirit, being a "dove," has its beak as a phallic symbol. Nothing could be more foreign to the Gospels and the ancient Christian rejection of pagan theogamies. The risk of turning the humble historical woman Mary into a sort of cosmic goddess held the Fathers of the Church back from the risky paths of Mariology. What they thought without making it explicit, what they received, is that the temporal and maternal birth of the Son of God is the image of the eternal birth, which is virginal. They see a necessity here: the Son of God could only be born of a virgin, and the son of a virgin could only be the Son of God. In 1900, Terrier gathered the various texts that fell under these two reciprocal propositions. They thus expressed a fittingness that imposed itself on them, as a necessity (R. Laurentin, *Mélanges*).

The human birth of the Son of God on earth, therefore, could only be virginal; from the first centuries they developed this in many ways.

The eternal Father is not Christ's temporal and earthly genitor: he is not his human father. The same is true of the Holy Spirit, through whom the Father brings about the Incarnation. The mark of the Paraclete consists in arousing the sanctification of each creature from within its own autonomous activity; not like a marionette. This is the principle of creation. The Holy Spirit awakened the supreme resources of womanhood in Mary to give birth to the person of the Son of God.

[223] We no longer teach children this unavoidable mystery of faith. They would not understand it, it seems. And yet, at this age, they might understand if we appealed to that open receptivity which is proper to youth. An intelligent woman who had replied in this way to a young girl's question got the following answer: "*I suspected this. I am glad to know it.*"

4. Mary's virginity after childbirth has been the most frequently attacked. When criticized for making Mary the mother of a large family, Duquesne's reaction was to turn to Fr. Refoulé, OP, who had influenced him in this direction. Fr. Refoulé in his turn published an exegetical book to defend this thesis that is contrary to dogma. He was subsequently named Director of the Institute of Biblical Studies in Jerusalem a few days before his death. Duquesne struck again in 2004 with

his book *Marie*, to answer his adversaries by radicalizing his critique.

To this, we replied in advance, above on pp. 317–324. The four brothers of Jesus mentioned by Matthew and Mark are sons of another woman and therefore cousins. A second century author, Hegesippus, cited by Eusebius in the fourth century, makes it clear in a discussion concerning ten among them [bishops], that Simon was chosen as second Bishop of Jerusalem because he was "another cousin (*anipsios*) of the Lord."[4] These two "brothers" of Jesus—according to the Hebrew and Biblical Greek meaning of the word—are therefore affir ed as these two persons of the Gospel whom some at all costs have wished to make sons of Mary.

3. Mother of God

At the time of the Council, I opposed the misleading formulas of the "Mariology of glories" (overstatements, excesses, and drifts) because they made even Catholic theologians such as Father Congar uneasy. Since the postconciliar excesses of the sixties, I have had to do the opposite in order to defend the very Revelation that was being thrown out. I spent the best of my time fighting quiet apostasy and debacles, including those against the Virgin Mary, the concrete sign of the Incarnation, whom the Fathers of the Church had understood more profoundly than Karl Barth.

Divine motherhood—which East and West identify as the fundamental function and privilege of Mary, Mother of the Lord—has also been the object of various reductive and divergent criticisms.

Freudian pansexualism dissociated these three essentially linked dimensions of human functions: love, sex, and the child. Sex was exalted while the child was devalued by French

---

4. Translator's note: See Eusebius, *Ecclesiastical History, Books 1–5*, IV.22. Fathers of the Church 19, translated by Roy J. Deferrari (Washington, D.C.: The Catholic University of America Press, 1953), 254.

tribunals[5] as an undesirable and disposable commodity without rights or value before birth.

Motherhood was terribly devalued. Women had been the protectors of life and of peace. The media showcased those who glorified their abortions in order to obtain a law that sanctions, normalizes, and facilitates this right of all women. In her *Mémoires*, Brigitte Bardot spoke of her only child's gestation as an annoying tumor that degraded her prestigious anatomy. . . . [224] Extremist feminism, spawned by Simone de Beauvoir—who kept herself from motherhood—influenced these devaluations [of motherhood]. In radical circles (not only *women's lib* in America) lesbians spoke with authority and mothers of families who adhered to this movement humbled themselves in order to be forgiven.

In exegesis, R. E. Brown, sensitive to the winds of modernism according to which the Bible ignored Mary's virginity, brilliantly started a movement to re-center Mariology, no longer on divine maternity, but on Mary's faith: as a believer rather than as a mother. This is not groundless, for he based himself on the words of Christ in Lk. 8:21 and 11:27–28 in his response to the cry:

> "— Blessed is the womb that bore you!
> — Blessed rather are those who hear the word of God and keep it."

This teaching of Christ must be accepted without qualific-tion. During the Council, as an expert, I fought for those verses (considered anti-Mary by some Mariologists) to be included in the chapter on the Virgin (LG, chapter 8).

Divine motherhood is not a privilege of the flesh, but of faith accomplished in the fl sh. This is no small thing: it is essential to the mystery of the Incarnation. The Church Fathers do not dissociate Mary's faith from her maternity.

---

5. After a reckless driver caused an accident that provoked a spontaneous abortion, the child was not recognized as a human person.

They repeated in various ways that *Mary conceived Christ in her heart before she did so in her body*. Her motherhood is the supreme accomplishment of faith (Aloïs Müller, *Maria-Eclesia*, Fribourg, 1951).

In another article of *Divus Thomas* (29, 1951, pp. 385–401) [Müller] adds that it is the fundamental principle of the Church Fathers' Mariology. In this, he added, Mary is our model. Through faith, following Mary, we give birth to Christ in our hearts and in the world. Salvation in Christ is the continuation of the Incarnation, the fruit of the perfect and supreme faith of Mary, who was called by God to this foundational grace.

In my last course at the University of Dayton (2003), I analyzed the converging influences (ideological, sociological, legal, theological) whose impact have devalued motherhood at all levels. Mary did not escape this devaluation. It is important to restore the harmonious order of her qualities because motherhood is the summit. The fact that our faith profoundly resembles Mary's maternal faith, in the image of the eternal Father, must not allow us to forget Mary's preeminence. Let us not say that we are on an equal footing with Mary because we too give birth to Christ through faith. For Mary alone gave human birth to Jesus. And since her motherhood concerns the person of the Son of God, Mary is in a unique personal relationship with Him and thus with the Father and the Holy Spirit, these two other persons who are one God. This unique Love further penetrates my *Traité sur la Trinité*.

It is through Mary that He took our humanity to give us his divinity, in a full sharing of supreme Love so that we might be identified with God who is all in all. Mary is the point of departure for salvation in Jesus Christ, whom she *made* man and thus priest and victim capable of offering and of suffering for us. Let us first see why Mary is at the summit of Creation.

Motherhood is an anthropological summit. The first stage is the progression from the mineral world to vegetable life, the animal and then the human. This is the summit of evolution, since God gives man an immortal soul [224], destined to survive the body, as the Greeks well understood. This makes man thus endowed with reason the king of creation as Genesis 1:26–28 and 2:18–20 demonstrate. Life gives matter an autonomous mode of existence, with a double capacity of *reparation* and *reproduction*; our industrial products are still incapable of such. The modes of reproduction progress together:

1. First, cell division: an identical doubling without genitor or engendered.
2. The next stage is sexual reproduction, in which two living beings (male and female) give birth to a new living being, their descendent, whose youth follows the aging of the genitors and makes the species immortal after their death.

At the animal level, then, the conjunction of genitors becomes a sensible and psychological attraction. Human generation marks a new stage because it is a personal act of love that gives birth to a new spiritual and immortal human person. Motherhood and fatherhood are no longer a passing function but create a definite and indestructible relation worthy of the immortal soul.

This relation requires the prohibition of incest, unfamiliar to animal species, and this is profoundly significant. It grounds the family in a normative and durable way, since the forming of a human person requires a durable setting. This is why the family has a demanding and stable character (personalized, monogamous) with a new articulation of *eros* and *agape*, of desire and gift.

Certainly, father and mother have like creative status with God, inseparable and undeniable; but within this common dignity, motherhood reveals itself to be superior to fatherhood.

From Antiquity to the Middle Ages, according to Aristotle and Hippocrates, the man alone was [considered] the principle of life. The mother (*mater*) only provided matter (*materia*): the blood was where the man sowed the seed of life. A better knowledge of the course of life (which Galen already sensed in the 2nd century B.C.[6]) inverts this hierarchy. Not only is the woman also the principle of life and provides a fundamental "seed," but this principle, and the role of the woman, are superior:

    a. The egg is more necessary to generation than the sperm which, at different levels, can be replaced by a material substitute. Parthenogenesis exists in different species in nature, at different levels. Androgenesis, however, is impossible because the sperm does not contain an autonomous programming for life.

    b. The mother's contribution is not as instantaneous as is that of the father. It takes place within a necessary time. Motherhood is indispensable, and even sufficient. The mother is necessary for physical and psychic buildup. It is within her that fertilization takes place. She shelters, protects, feeds the child. [226] The rhythms of the mother's breathing, the beating of her heart, and her voice rock the dawn of fetal consciousness in its uterine night. The firs maternal contacts—breast-feeding, kissing, care, and caresses—stimulate these wonders. Children abandoned and taken care of by animals, and later found in forests have never been able to progress to the human stage; and the American experiments of the 1930's when babies were brought up under bells by masked and gloved nurses, had disastrous results. The children died or remained mentally underdeveloped. Rightly do psychologists say that a child is completed at 3 or 4 years of age. He owes this "completion" to his mother, from the listening to the beating of her heart and then to the sound of her voice during the last three months of gestation. All this culminates in the vocal exchange and the child's first smile—not the blissful post-feeding smile, but the smile that responds to the mother's smile. The following beautiful verse by Virgil was ever ambiguous:

---

6. According to Galen, the mother furnished a complementary principle of life, but he maintained the inferiority of the woman: subordinate to the man and endowed with a colder and more humid organism (*De usu partium corporis humani*, 14, 5 in *Opera omnia*, edition of C. K. Kün, pp. 131–165 and *De semine* 2, 5, pp. 631–642).

Disce, puer, risu cognoscere matrem
Learn, child, to know your mother by the smile.

Mary realized perfectly these principles of human maternity within the sphere of human generation. In this way we are better able to see why the human birth of the Son of God had to be virginal. This does not make Mary the spouse of the Father, as some have wrongly stated, but she is the mother of the same Son according to humanity. *She is the only human cause of the Incarnation of the Word.* For the eternal Father is not the human father of Jesus through a second fatherhood. There is only one divine Fatherhood, one Son of God, one filial relation of Christ, extended to Mary in the order of humanity for the salvation of the human race. According to John 1:13, Jesus was born "*not of the will of the flesh, nor of the will of man, but of God.*" These traits are characteristic at different levels: the eternal birth of the Word, the temporal birth from Mary, and his birth by faith and baptism in the hearts [of men].

Jesus speaks of [these] births as one because the latter two are merely the temporal progression of the first. The Father thought the other two within the same divine orbit, each at its own stage and according to its own kind. As St. Thomas Aquinas perceived, Mary shares in the Son's unique relation to the Father, which she reflects and makes visibly manifest on earth. This is not a metamorphosis of the Son—unchanged through eternity—to whom Mary gives a new human and temporal existence.

If the council of Ephesus (431) confirmed, against the Patriarch Nestorius, that Mary is Theotokos (the birth giver of God), it is because motherhood is about the person [who is born]. Mary's motherhood refers to the *divine person* of the Son of God. Her motherhood, therefore, is truly divine, through the intrinsic relation to the divine person of her Son, incarnated by her.

This principle is very important and today neglected. In order to justify abortion, father and mother are now considered mere producers. Yet it would be absurd to claim that the father is the father of the sperm, or that the mother is the mother of the egg and the genetic information it carries. No, all parents know that they *together* (and irrevocably) are father and mother of their child, through one indissoluble relation that they have contracted with God, the Creator, who creates the transcendent soul at the meeting of their free human initiative: a free human initiative at the meeting of which God never disappoints. [227]. But would He give a soul to a cloned baby, if ever such unnatural monster born not of love, but technology, were to be produced? One must forget all this to uphold the principle that a gestating baby is a disposable item subject to his mother's whim.

According to the same anthropological principle, the Son of God has only one Father in heaven and one mother on earth. The eternal Father is neither the sperm donor, nor the *human* father of Jesus, nor Mary's spouse, but rather He who shares his Son with her, by the work of the Holy Spirit who awakens the virgin's feminine nature so that she can be the true mother of the Son of God according to the flesh.

If, therefore, Mary has the same grace as we do in fullness, if she is indeed one of us, redeemed too (but by preservation), she has a profoundly unique relation to God through this personal and specifically maternal relationship with the Son of God. She also has a specifi ally familial relationship with the three Persons of the Trinity (*Traité sur la Trinité*). Mary's motherhood, then, has a double perfection, and a double anthropological and theological fullness.

4. Participation in the Redemption

Mary's active participation in Christ's Redemption—about which this Treatise manifests the unrecognized richness—has also been misunderstood and devalued.

Already the future Cardinal Journet, in an attempt to make this doctrine more acceptable in his dialogue with Protestants—for the sake of the then popular but ambiguous term of co-redemptrix,—said *"we are all co-redemptors."* He said this according to the Apostle Paul: "For we are all co-workers of God" (1 Cor. 3:9).

However, this leveling of all under this same word should not make us forget that Mary, for all the reasons mentioned above, cooperated with the one Redemption at a supreme level and with a unique intimacy. I recently confirmed this in the last chapter of the book on *Marie Deluil-Martiny, Precurseur et Martyre* (Fayard, 214–250): the depth of Mary's cooperation is dizzying, on the human and on the divine level. She was indeed the closest to Christ, humanly as mother, and divinely through grace. In Christ she assumed aspects of redeemed humanity that He had not taken on insofar as she was a redeemed creature and especially as a woman, representing an eminent half of humanity. And her origin as well as her immaculate life made possible the pure integration of her compassion with the redemptive Passion of Christ.

5. The Assumption

As to [Mary]'s personal glorifi ation, Karl Rahner reduced this privilege to one that anticipates the common condition, and he sustained the doctrine in the following manner: Our resurrection does not await the final judgment. The substantial human soul joined to the body that animates it, cannot be deprived of it; death makes us depart from the successive duration that is time, to make us enter into God's simultaneous duration, i.e. eternity, where everything is synchronic (*tota simul* according to the Latin formulation). The souls of the just then immediately regenerate a glorious and spiritual body [228].

Schillebeeckx thought this opinion was a "crypto-heresy" against the Last Judgment as described by Matthew 25 and the apostle Paul. I will not go as far, but it is indeed another attempt at leveling. Not that this "privilege of Mary" should render her alien to our condition; on the contrary, she is in all domains the initiating prototype of grace, of charisms, and of salvation in

Jesus Christ. We live the same divine Love. We are called to the same Resurrection, but Mary's anticipation as eschatological icon of the Church is full of meaning, in both senses of the word. She manifests the meaning and the dynamic of the salvation that she inaugurated by giving birth to Christ the Savior. The Assumption gloriously completes the order of Mary's foundational tasks. There, as elsewhere she is at the summit, but inside the Church in her grateful union to Christ.

Backward Motivations

Why was the promotional thrust of the Marian movement, expressed by the phrase *de Maria numquam satis* (of Mary one can never get enough) replaced by a large movement whose motto seems to be *de Maria nunc est satis* (With Mary, enough for now): Enough? Enough?

Various reasons have converged to demote Mary, the most illustrious of women, to the most ordinary: ". . . bent back, tired eyes, worn out" by her work and her many pregnancies, as a recent best seller (J. Duquesne, *Marie*) would have it. The author, an eminent journalist, only proclaims loudly what famous exegetes and theologians whisper: Fathers Refoulé, Boismard, and so many others.

Why this demotion, which extends from universities to catechesis, to journalism and common opinion?

1. A first reason is ecumenism. This factor was already very present in the Council, where the slogan *"this is not ecumenical"* (unacceptable for our separated brethren) was frequently a winning argument. In spite of my initial concern with preserving the unity desired by Christ (John 17:21–29), I have always refused to use [that argument] and I regularly minimized it by saying:

> — *The problem is not whether it is ecumenical or not, but whether it is true or not. If it is false, let us abandon it. But if it is true, let us see how it could be dusted off, cleaned up, better expressed based on the common*

sources of Revelation, and in what terms it could be acceptable today in various cultures and traditions. The key is to situate accurately Mary's grace and her glory in relation to God's transcendence and the goals of salvation.

2. The reaction to the excesses and polarizations of the "Marian movement" continued along the same trajectory: theologians (not only Congar) were shocked by narrow-minded Mariology, which they perceived as a crypto-Mariolatry. Some were reacting in the name of 17th century French Theo-centrism. The truth is that the unilateral concern with glorifying Mary led not only to the concocting of worthless jewels and to the destabilization of the equilibrium of Christian doctrine through the reduction of Theo-centrism to Mario-centrism. One attributed, in principle, more or less systematically, all the titles and privileges of Christ to Mary by transposing them. He was a mediator, she was a mediatrix; He was redeemer, so she was a redemptrix or co-redemptrix, and so on. The list got longer without sufficient emphasis on the differences or the relationship of [229] dependence. They wanted to make Mary another Christ (as with the pope: *alter Christus*, when he is in truth his vicar, his visible delegate as successor of Peter).

Mary is everything through Christ and He has become savior and mediator, priest, and victim in and through the humanity of which Mary is the only human, maternal, and material cause. However, their resemblance and identification must not make us forget Christ's transcendence and Mary's specificity. These are profoundly tied yet distinguished by their relation.

—In 1950, the definition of Mary "mediatrix of all graces" had been prepared for so long that all Christians venerated her under that title but were ignorant of the fact that Christ is the only mediator. Pius XII, who had begun work on the definition, gave it up.

In the same way, Christ is the only redeemer, and John XXIII had requested the Council's commission not to use this ambiguous term [co-redemptrix] for theological and ecumenical reasons. It was important to remain focused on the divine transcendence of Christ. Grignion de Montfort insisted no less than Luther on the formula "*God alone*," which was the constant conclusion of his letters as well as his works.

What contributed the most to the devaluation of the Virgin Mary are the methodological and ideological deviations of exegesis and theology. In short, [contemporary] exegesis focuses too narrowly on the study of the historical and cultural conditions of the Bible with no thought for Revelation. This now is the essential problem: by default the Bible appears to be no different than any other book. There is nothing to prevent a phenomenological study of the Bible from being open to Revelation and Transcendence. This is the fundamental conviction of the Church and the primordial concern of my research.

The task of theology and exegesis is the "intelligence of the faith," but they often understand this in a rationalist manner:

— *Greek rationalism, from which sprouted the heresies of the early centuries;*
— *the abstract rationalism of Scholasticism, which often denuded the symbolism of the Bible;*
— *and finally Cartesian and Kantian idealist rationalism and its reductive criticism.*

As a result of this, the Virgin was reduced and marginalized. *In*telligence is *in*tuitive, as the common prefix indicates. Therefore, it is alien to rationalism, whose analytical (though complementary) functions are different.

The desire to be "scientific" persuaded many a theologian that science must abstract from faith, set it aside, which often amounts to eliminating faith. Every science has its own light, just as the arts [such as] painting and music do. All the difference between the true and the false scientist or artist lies in this. The Bible (and theology) is a message of faith, written in faith by believers for believers. To neglect the light of faith is to be like a craftsman who works in the dark to prevent his work from being hurt by the light. But intellectual light, like material light, neither interferes with nor falsifies the object, but illuminates and reveals it.

Mariological rationalism obscures our perception and understanding of Mary. Once it constructed marginal or fake privileges. Today it tears up and reduces the dogma itself. In every domain, including the scientific, one appreciates enlightened minds. Why not in theology? [230]

As for the Marxist and idealist ideologues, all of them Hegelians, who deformed theology, it would take too long to address them here.

As a reaction to the Marian recession that John Paul II tried to combat, some frustrated Christians have reacted by returning to the disparaged reflexes of the Marian movement. They sign petitions for new definitions of "Marian privileges" that are often confused, ill-placed, and badly integrated. The clashing of cymbals and the proclamation of titles will not make the knowledge of Mary and her presence in our lives grow. The royal path is that of the Second Vatican Council: it is biblical, anthropological, but also theological and ecumenical as Paul VI reminded us in *Marialis Cultus*. It is within the light of faith, lived in connaturality with the incarnate Word, and therefore with Mary, that we will grow.

In this way will true life in God with Mary, with the rigorous help of scientific means, be renewed. In this way too will we avoid artificial formulas, tiresome repetitions, and marginal renewals that do not help us penetrate the very mystery and person of Mary. Indeed, there is nothing static or calcified in the biblical tradition. It is a living tradition and a source of life. The more I study the Virgin, the more dazzled I am by her splendor, so simply human, so transcendentally divine by her intimate reference to God (Lk. 1:25–56), regretting that age should now restrict my capacity to devote more time to her study. I am tempted to say that Mary is the summit of the equation between transcendence and immanence in creation.

In God, there is not the smallest difference between transcendence and immanence. He is perfectly identical to Himself in and through the Love that makes the unity of the Three Persons.

In creation, God loses nothing of His being; he creates *ex nihilo* without losing anything. There is an infinite distance between the Creator and his creation, but He is present by the immanence of the Holy Spirit, living fount of every being, every intelligence, every freedom, every life. Being the very love of the Father and the Son, He also makes, through love, the unity in God of created persons, and through them the unity of the new creation announced by the prophets.

God calls his creatures to the reciprocity which is the expansive love of the three Persons. Mary is the summit of this adequation between the gift of God and the response of a creature that has been divinized by Love. In her there is not a single failing, not the smallest "stain" [*estingement*] as the English say.[7]

---

7. *Du nouveau sur Duns Scot, découvreur de la préservation immaculée de Marie*. The research on Duns Scotus, which continues at the Franciscan University Antonianum, brings new elements that I did not yet have access to when I wrote my article, [namely] Father Stefano Cecchin, OFM's book on the Immaculate Conception, *L'Immacolato Concezione*, and another forthcoming book.

In short, the critical edition of the work of Duns Scotus shows that he not only established the possibility and fittingness of the Immaculate Conception, but that he clearly affirmed it. If in some works, prudence kept him from the affirmation of which he became the promoter par excellence, in his teaching at Oxford and Paris as well as in several of his written works, the affirmation is clear: Mary did not contract original sin (*Ordinatio*, 2, d. 3, q.1).

In this same work, n 21, he does not only say that God "could" have preserved Mary, but he explicitly concludes: therefore God has *done* it. This, too, is what one of his Parisian students understood perfectly in his notes, edited today: "*the perfection of the Mediator requires [. . .] the preservation from all faults, even original: therefore the Virgin Mary was exempt of all original stain* (*Reportatio parisiensis*, III, d. 3, q.2).

Scotus deserves recognition and merit more for the doctrinal arguments he was the first to bring up, for creating and specifying exactly the notion of *preservation*, and for linking Mary's Immac-

As to the paths of renewal concerning the Virgin, in spite of the considerable work I have dedicated to the apparitions of the Virgin, I do not think that spiritual renewal will come from that avenue.

Apparitions are an eschatological anticipation of her presence. What counts with authentic visionaries is not so much the apparition, since the sensible aspect (visible, auditory, and even tactile) is merely the sign of a mystical and foundational union in God's light reflected by Mary. These diverse happenings in the life of the Church, often creative and foundational, are not a theological *source* according to the norms of the Church. Any renewal will come tomorrow as it did yesterday, through Scripture, for Revelation has not opened up all its secrets to us. It will come from a better evaluation of the symbolic dimension of Scripture. Yet this study remains in its infancy in spite of the first steps of semiotics in the 1960's. It will come from a diachronic study of the Bible, one focused on grasping the progression of Revelation through the great historical and cultural, but also semantic and spiritual, currents. It will be born of a new insight into Mary's relation to the Trinity, which greatly enlightened me from the last word of Revelation: *God is love.* Love is a gift. It is reciprocal; it is relation. It is the supreme Absolute, it is communicative, "*diffusivum sui*" (self-diffusive) according to the medieval formula.

Mary is first among creatures in the order of Love, in her inseparable divine-human union with Christ. She participates, with all the fibers of her feminine being, in its radiation. Her eminence does not put her "above" the others, because Love excludes domination. It leaves Mary with all her humility, her

---

ulate Conception to the merits of Christ the Redeemer *alone* than for affirming this preservation. But it is a fact that he did affirm it in several of his works and his teaching. This discovery of *the critical edition* of Duns Scotus deserved to be stressed. This is why I have insisted on clarifying this point, which completes what I said previously about the major role which Duns Scotus played in the history of this dogma.

modesty, her transparence. It is this purity, but especially the total, free, compassionate gift of her person with the dying Christ that complete her meaning and touching grandeur. Mary is indeed "*the greatest because she is the smallest; the most glorious because she is the most modest; the most joyful because she is also the most sorrowful,*" as Péguy unceasingly elaborates.[8]

---

8. Translator's note. See Charles Péguy, *Portal of the Mystery of Hope*, trans. David Louis Schinder, Jr. (Grand Rapids: Eerdmans, 1996), 39, where the text is rendered:

To she who is infinitely lofty.
Because she's infinitely lowly.

To she who is infinitely great.
Because she's infinitely small.
Infinite humble.
A young mother.
. . .

To she who is infinitely joyful.
Because she's also infinitely sorrowful.

www.ingramcontent.com/pod-product-compliance
Lightning Source LLC
Chambersburg PA
CBHW070247010526
44107CB00056B/2362